Depositions:
The Comprehensive Guide for Expert Witnesses

STEVEN BABITSKY, ESQ.
JAMES J. MANGRAVITI, JR., ESQ.

SEAK, Inc.
PO Box 729
Falmouth, MA   02541
www.seak.com
(508) 457-1111

Depositions: The Comprehensive Guide for Expert Witnesses
ISBN: 978-1-892904-32-4

Copyright ©2007 by SEAK, Inc.

CONTENTS

About the Authors

Steven Babitsky, Esq., (sbabitsky@aol.com) is the President of SEAK, Inc. He was a personal injury trial attorney for twenty years and is the former managing partner of the firm Kistin, Babitsky, Latimer & Beitman. Mr. Babitsky is the co-author of the texts *The A–Z Guide to Expert Witnessing; How to Become a Dangerous Expert Witness: Advanced Techniques and Strategies; Writing and Defending Your Expert Report: The Step-by-Step Guide with Models; How to Excel During Cross-Examination: Techniques for Experts That Work; The Comprehensive Forensic Services Manual: The Essential Resources for All Experts;* and *How to Excel During Depositions: Techniques for Experts That Work.* Attorney Babitsky is the co-developer and trainer for the "How to Be an Effective Medical Witness" seminar, the seminar leader for the Annual National Expert Witness and Litigation Seminar, and the scriptwriter for the videos, "How to Be an Effective Medical Witness" and "The Expert Medical Deposition: How to Be an Effective and Ethical Witness." Mr. Babitsky trains hundreds of experts every year.

James J. Mangraviti, Jr., Esq., (seakincjm@aol.com) has trained hundreds of expert witnesses across the United States and Canada. He is a former litigator with experience in defense and plaintiff personal injury law and insurance law. He currently serves as Vice President and General Counsel of SEAK, Inc. Mr. Mangraviti received his BA degree in mathematics *summa cum laude* from Boston College and his JD degree *cum laude* from Boston College Law School. His publications include the texts *SEAK Law School for Physicians; Law School for the Safety and Health Professional; The Independent Medical Examination Report: A Step-by-Step Guide with Models; The Successful Physician Negotiator: How to Get What You Deserve; How to Excel During Cross-Examination: Techniques for Experts That Work; How to Excel During Depositions: Techniques for Experts That Work; The Comprehensive Forensic Services Manual: The Essential Resources for All Experts; Writing and Defending Your Expert Report: The Step-by-Step Guide with Models; Cross-Examination: The Comprehensive Guide for Experts; How to Become a Dangerous Expert Witness: Advanced Techniques and Strategies; The A–Z Guide to Expert Witnessing;* and *Writing and Defending Your Independent Medical Examination Report: The Comprehensive Guide.*

Related Products by SEAK, Inc.

TEXTS
The A–Z Guide to Expert Witnessing
How to Become a Dangerous Expert Witness: Advanced Techniques and Strategies
National Guide to Expert Witness Fees and Billing Procedures
Cross-Examination: The Comprehensive Guide for Experts
Writing and Defending Your Expert Report
The Comprehensive IME System
Writing and Defending Your IME Report

SEMINARS & CUSTOMIZED TRAINING
National Expert Witness Conference
Advanced Cross-Examination Workshop
Advanced Deposition Skills Workshop
Advanced Trick and Difficult Questions Workshop
The Biggest Mistakes Experts Make and How to Avoid Them
How to Become a Dangerous Expert Witness
Persuasion Skills Workshop for Experts
How to Start and Build a Successful Expert Witness Practice
Expert Report Writing Workshop
Testifying Skills Workshop
Advanced Testifying Skills Workshop: The Master's Program
Law School for Experts
Expert Witness Practice Management Workshop
How to Be an Effective Medical Witness
IME Best Practices
Disability Consulting for Physicians

CD AUDIO PROGRAMS
Law School for Experts
Marketing Your Forensic Practice
Achieving Success As a Medical Witness
How to Be a Successful Independent Medical Examiner

DVD VIDEOS
The Expert Deposition: How to Be an Effective and Ethical Witness
Winning Over the Jury: Techniques for Experts That Work
Cross-Examination: How to Be an Effective and Ethical Expert Witness
The Most Difficult Questions for Experts: With Answers

DIRECTORIES (www.seakexperts.com)
SEAK, Inc. National Directory of Independent Medical Examiners
SEAK, Inc. National Directory of Experts

For more information, please call SEAK at (508) 457-1111. Inquiries may also be addressed to SEAK, Inc. at PO Box 729, Falmouth, MA 02541. Fax (508) 540-8304; e-mail address: mail@seak.com, internet address: www.seak.com.

Preface

The authors have trained thousands of expert witnesses from across the United States. One thing we have consistently found in our training sessions is that highly qualified, honest experts often underperform when writing reports, testifying at trial, and testifying at deposition. This underperformance is most often a direct result of a lack of training in the skills of being an effective expert witness. (The other most common cause of a highly qualified, honest expert's underperformance is the expert's failure to devote the necessary time, diligence, and energy to researching and forming the opinion, writing the report, and preparing to testify.)

The highly qualified, honest experts who consistently perform well usually end up with more lucrative work than they can handle. Those who do not often see their forensic practices falter.

This book has been written to help train experts to excel at their depositions. With the increasing number of settlements prior to trial, the depositions of expert witnesses have taken on even more importance. We have designed this book to empower experts from all fields to:

- understand the deposition rules and strategies of counsel,
- prepare for their expert depositions, and
- excel at their depositions.

For those wishing live training in depositions, SEAK has developed a one-day workshop, *Advanced Deposition Skills for Experts,* that we put on regularly or that can be brought to your organization as customized training. This seminar features numerous mock deposition demonstrations with volunteer attendees and numerous video clips of experts testifying at deposition in real cases. For more information, please visit www.seak.com or contact one of the authors directly.

As always, we welcome your feedback on this work.

Steven Babitsky, Esq. (sbabitsky@aol.com)
James J. Mangraviti, Jr., Esq. (seakincjm@aol.com)

SEAK, Inc.
PO Box 729
Falmouth, MA 02541
Telephone: (508) 548-7023
www.seak.com

Acknowledgements

The authors would like to acknowledge the invaluable assistance of the following persons in the creation of this work: Karen Babitsky, Kenneth Kolpan, Rebecca Wilson Lundin, Ryann Muir, Dee Netzel, and Danielle Tarlow.

Chapter 1 Deposition Law and Procedure

1.1 Introduction and Executive Summary

During a deposition, an expert witness will testify under oath but not in open court. Because a majority of cases settle before going to trial, experts need to excel during their depositions. The authors recommend the following for experts to succeed at giving effective testimony at depositions:

- Do not be evasive when answering counsel's questions.
  - Evasiveness will ultimately reflect poorly on the expert.
- Always assume that what you say during deposition will be "on the record."
- Determine in advance whether the deposition will be videotaped.
  - Some depositions are videotaped while others are recorded through a written transcript.
- Retaining counsel may not object to difficult and probing deposition questions if counsel previously agreed to the "usual" or "standard" stipulations.
  - Under this agreement, retaining counsel will only object to questions because of their form (for example, a question may be leading, compound, or confusing).
  - Listen very carefully to objections made by retaining counsel because counsel may be using the objection to coach or suggest answers to the expert being deposed.
- Attorneys at deposition are required to behave professionally.
  - Attorneys can be sanctioned for insulting, demeaning, sarcastic, and threatening comments.

Depositions are a component of the discovery process, which allows each party to understand the other side's case. The effective expert understands several aspects of the discovery process:

- The discovery rules governing the deposition vary from jurisdiction to jurisdiction.
- "Fishing expeditions" are generally allowed during discovery.
  - Do not get flustered when counsel goes on a fishing expedition during deposition.
- Privileged information is not discoverable and therefore cannot be addressed during the deposition.
  - Commonly asserted privileges include doctor-patient and attorney-client privileges.
- Attorney work product is usually not discoverable.

The expert is entitled to be paid a reasonable fee for deposition testimony:

- The opposing side is generally responsible for paying the expert's fees if they call the expert's deposition.
  - Experienced experts often include a clause in their fee agreements stating that retaining counsel will pay all deposition fees.
- Reasonable fees may be collected for travel time.

1.2 Deposition Basics
A deposition is defined as:

> A witness's out-of-court testimony that is reduced to writing (usually by a court reporter) for later use in court or for discovery purposes. Also termed examination before trial.[1]

Depositions in civil cases are engendered and governed by the rules of civil procedure of the court where the action is pending. These rules will vary from state to state. For example, the rules of civil procedure governing a civil action filed in a Massachusetts state court are not the same as the rules that would govern a civil action filed in a New York state court. The Federal Rules of Civil Procedure govern actions filed in federal court in all fifty states. The Federal Rules have a strong influence on many of the state rules and will be the basis for many of the discussions in this work.

Expert Witness Depositions
Depositions of expert witnesses are allowed under the Federal Rules of Civil Procedure. The applicable Rule states:

> FRCP 26(b)(4)(A): A party may depose any person who has been identified as an expert whose opinions may be presented at trial. If a report from the expert is required under subdivision (a)(2)(B), the deposition shall not be conducted until after the report is provided.

Under the Federal Rules, a person may only be deposed once. Please see Fed. R. Civ. Pro. 30(a)(2)(b), which states:

> A party must obtain leave of court, which shall be granted to the extent consistent with the principles stated, if the person to be examined already has been deposed in the case.

Practice Pointer: Some states require a special court order to take the deposition of an expert witness and some states go so far as to not permit the depositions of experts at all.

---

[1] Henry Campbell Black, *Black's Law Dictionary,* 8th edition (St. Paul, MN: West Publishing Co., 2004) p. 440.

Experts need to excel during their depositions. Because the vast majority of cases settle, depositions are a crucial part of the outcome of a case. Even if the case does not settle, it is likely that the expert's deposition will be used against him at trial. An expert who wants to excel while testifying at deposition should have a full understanding of the rules under which the deposition will be conducted.

The witness whose deposition is being taken or who is being deposed is called the *deponent.* The deponent's testimony during a deposition is made under oath under the pains and penalties of perjury. Generally, depositions may also be taken by means of written questions propounded to the deponent.[2] In practice, however, this form of deposition is utilized only very rarely because it does not allow for the all-important follow-up questions to an evasive or noncooperative deponent.

Example 1.1: Follow-up questions at an oral deposition allow a competent and persistent attorney to lock down evasive or non-cooperative deponents
Q: But specifically, Doctor, have you been asked to take an individual worker or a group of workers at Argo Motor Company who have carpal tunnel syndrome and tell Argo or the UAW what caused their carpal tunnel?
A: That would be more of a—I specifically look at the jobs. And some of those people have been diagnosed with carpal tunnel.
Q: But were you asked by Argo and the UAW to tell them what caused their carpal tunnel?
A: What caused it? Well, I think the known cause is the work, but I identified the specific aspects of the job.
Q: You went in and identified the workplace for risk factors and said here's how to correct it, correct?
A: We know that carpal tunnel is caused by the work. They don't ask that question. It's not an issue.
Q: So, you weren't asked to do that, correct?
A: No. They don't ask that 'cause they know the jobs, that type of work can cause carpal tunnel.

Practice Pointer: Experts should not be evasive at depositions. A good attorney will keep asking questions until the expert is forced to answer. Evasiveness reflects poorly on an expert.

Recording of Depositions
Depositions are recorded in one or more ways. Normally, a written transcript is prepared by a stenographer who records what is said "on the record" at the deposition. It is also common for those present to have "off the record" discussions

---

[2] See Federal Rule of Civil Procedure 31(a)(1), which states in part, "A party may take the testimony of any person, including a party, by deposition upon written questions without leave of court...."

during a deposition that are not reflected in the transcript. Deponents should *always* assume that whatever they say at a deposition is being recorded *on* the record.

Videotaped Depositions
Depositions may also be videotaped. Expert depositions are frequently videotaped. Videotaped depositions are especially useful to an attorney if the attorney plans on submitting the deposition testimony at trial in lieu of the deponent's live testimony. They can also be quite useful to show a jury the expert's demeanor or evasiveness at deposition.[3]

Presenting expert testimony at trial by way of a videotaped deposition is more economical because the parties do not have to pay for the expert's time to testify at trial. Videotaped depositions may also be used when the attorney is concerned that the witness will not be available for trial because of illness, upcoming travel plans, or other reasons. Please see Chapter 9 for a more complete discussion of videotaped depositions.

Practice Pointer: Experts should always find out in advance of the deposition whether the deposition will be videotaped. This information may be contained in the notice of deposition (see FRCP 30(b)(2)) or it may be learned from retaining counsel.

The Standard or Usual Stipulations
A *stipulation* is an agreement between counsel regarding facts or procedure. In many jurisdictions counsel will start the deposition and agree to the "usual" or "standard" stipulations. Frequently, these stipulations are spelled out by counsel for the record. For example:

> It is hereby stipulated and agreed by and between counsel for the respective parties that the witness shall read and sign the deposition transcript within 30 days of receipt of said transcript, otherwise, it shall be deemed to have been waived and the notarization of the witness's signature is waived. It is further stipulated and agreed that all objections, except as to form, and motions to strike are reserved until the time of trial.

What this stipulation means is that the lawyers are agreeing that they won't make any objections to questions except as to the form of the question. Under this agreement, counsel could object if she felt the question was compound, leading, or confusing, but she would reserve objections with other evidentiary bases such as relevancy, unfair prejudice, and hearsay until trial. A frequent complaint by experts regarding depositions is that "the attorney just sat there, silent," while the other attorney questioned the expert closely. Often, the reason why attorneys don't object

---

[3] This technique was used quite effectively in the Microsoft anti-trust case where the government showed clip after clip of Bill Gates stating, essentially, that he knew nothing.

during depositions is that under the standard stipulations, the only proper objections are to the form of the question. For more on objections, please see Section 1.7.

Example 1.2: Counsel agrees on the record to "the usual stipulations"
Counsel A: We'll have the witness read and sign. Otherwise, usual stipulations?
Counsel B: Yes.

Practice Pointer: It is important for you to understand what these usual or standard stipulations are and mean.

Reading and Signing the Deposition Transcript
State and local rules and customs may vary from jurisdiction to jurisdiction. Thus, the expert should acquaint herself with the local rules and customs or stipulations at deposition. Note that in the standard stipulation, the expert witness has 30 days within which to read and sign the deposition transcript. During this 30-day period, the expert can correct any errors in the deposition transcript. If the expert is not clear about the stipulations or does not agree with them, she must speak up immediately to preserve her rights because retaining counsel does *not* represent the expert witness. Consider the following example.

Example 1.3: Expert who wants to read and sign the transcript objects to the usual stipulations
Counsel A: Stipulations?
Counsel B: She would like to waive the reading and signing.
Expert: I would like to read and sign the deposition, sir.
Counsel B: Sorry. The witness reserves the right to read and sign the deposition transcript within 30 days of receipt of said transcript.

Practice Pointer: The witness generally has a right to read and sign her deposition. Under the Federal Rules of Civil Procedure, this right to read and sign is not self-executing. The party or deponent must *request* reading and signing prior to the completion of the deposition. The deponent will then have 30 days to read and sign the transcript after being notified that the transcript or recording is available. (See Fed. R. Civ. Pro. 30(e).)

The witness should not let counsel waive the right to read and sign unless she wants to. There are competing schools of thought on the wisdom of experts reading and signing. One school of thought is that experts should read and sign to correct any transcription mistakes or mistaken testimony. The competing school of thought is to waive reading and signing. That school of thought is motivated by the fact that if the witness reads and signs the transcript, she is reaffirming her testimony and the transcription thereof and it will be that much harder to explain away any parts of the transcript she might be impeached with later at trial.

5

Note that under the Federal Rules and many state rules, the deponent is allowed to correct not only transcription errors, but she may also make substantive changes to her testimony. The court may require, however, that the expert provide the necessary explanations for the changes. (See 1998 U.S. Dist. LEXIS 21856.) Of course, any substantive changes are likely to be the focus of intense cross-examination questioning at trial and may result in the reopening of the deposition. A sample completed errata sheet can be found in Appendix G.

1.3 Depositions Are a Component of the Discovery Process

Under the Federal Rules of Civil Procedure, a party is allowed various methods of *discovery*. These discovery methods are designed to obtain facts and information about the case from the other parties, persons, or entities. *A deposition is merely one of the procedural methods available under the Rules of Civil Procedure as part of discovery.* Other methods of discovery include written interrogatories, production of documents or things, permission to enter upon land or other property, physical and mental examination, and requests for admissions.

The Federal Rules of Civil Procedure (FRCP) permit very liberal and broad-based discovery. There are two rationales for the liberal discovery procedures that dominate today's civil lawsuits: eliminating surprise at trial and encouraging settlement. The theory is that if all parties know all there is to know about the other side's case, they will be able to evaluate the merits and weaknesses of the case rationally and settle the matter. Additionally, if the suit does go to trial, the outcome will be less dependent upon gamesmanship because the possibility of unfair surprises has been minimized through the liberal discovery process. *An understanding of these two rationales is absolutely essential for any expert who wants to understand his role in a civil litigation deposition. These two rationales are the reasons why attorneys are allowed to ask broad, ranging, and pointed questions at expert depositions and, in effect, to go on "fishing expeditions."*

To effectuate the goals stated above, the Rules provide for *very broad-based* discovery.

Fed. R. Civ. Pro. 26(b)(1) Discovery Scope and Limits

Parties may obtain discovery regarding any matter, not privileged, that is relevant to the claim or defense of any party, including the existence, description, nature, custody, condition, and location of any books, documents, or other tangible things and the identity and location of persons having knowledge of any discoverable matter. For good cause, the court may order discovery of any matter relevant to the subject matter involved in the action. Relevant information need not be admissible at the trial if the discovery appears reasonably calculated to lead to the discovery of admissible evidence.

Because information sought at deposition need not be admissible—just reasonably calculated to the discovery of admissible evidence—very few areas of inquiry are closed to inquiring counsel at a deposition.

Example 1.4: Fishing expedition
The deponent is a 75-year-old physician expert witness. He is asked to recite every place he has worked and lived since he was sixteen years old. These types of questions would generally be allowed at deposition because they could reasonably lead to information relevant to the deponent's credibility.

Practice Pointer: Sophisticated experts do not get flustered when counsel goes on a fishing expedition at deposition. There are two important reasons for this. First, in most jurisdictions, the party questioning the expert (the opposing party) pays the deponent's fee. Answering questions about where you lived in college is a pretty easy way to make hundreds of dollars an hour. Second, many jurisdictions limit the length of depositions to so many hours. For example, under the Federal Rules, depositions are limited to "one day of seven hours" (see Fed. R. Civ. Pro. 30(d)(2)) unless authorized by the court or the parties otherwise agree. In Illinois, oral examination of any witness shall not "exceed three hours regardless of the number of parties involved in the case" unless there is good cause to warrant a lengthier examination or all the parties have agreed (see Illinois Civil Procedure § 8.02). The more time opposing counsel spends on fishing expeditions, the less time he will have to inquire on areas of substance.

1.4 Privilege
Although discovery is broad-based, it is not unlimited. Privileged information is generally not discoverable.[4] For example, unless the privilege was waived or an exception applies, a privilege may protect information known to a physician about that physician's patient due to the physician-patient privilege. Other commonly asserted privileges include the spousal privilege and the attorney-client privilege. The existence and precise scope of the various privileges varies from state to state. If a valid privilege exists, then the expert deponent may refuse to answer questions that would violate that privilege.

Practice Pointer: *Fed. R. Civ. Pro. 26(b)(1) provides that privileged information is not discoverable.* Privileges include attorney-client, spousal, and doctor-patient. *In most jurisdictions, there is no attorney-client privilege between attorney and expert because the expert is not represented by the attorney.* Therefore, asking about communications between the expert and retaining counsel does not call for privileged information. In most jurisdictions, experts will be required to answer questions at deposition regarding communications with retaining counsel.

---

[4] Fed. R. Civ. Pro. 26(b)(1).

1.5 Work Product

In addition to privileged material, attorney *work product* is usually nondiscoverable. This exception to liberal discovery is designed to allow the adversary process to function properly. The work product exception to discovery as it applies to expert witnesses is governed by Federal Rule 26(b)(4). This rule, with some exceptions, protects experts *who are not to be called as witnesses* at trial from being subject to discovery. *Thus, if you are an expert who is working as a consultant and the party retaining you does not intend to call you as a witness at trial, Federal Rule 26(b)(4) will in most cases protect you from ever having to give a deposition in the case.* Experts who are identified as potential trial witnesses may, however, be deposed.

Fed. R. Civ. Pro. 26(b)(4) Trial Preparation: Experts

(A) A party may depose any person who has been identified as an expert whose opinions may be presented at trial. If a report from the expert is required under subdivision (a)(2)(B), the deposition shall not be conducted until after the report is provided.

(B) A party may, through interrogatories or by deposition, discover facts known or opinions held by an expert who has been retained or specially employed by another party in anticipation of litigation or preparation for trial and who is not expected to be called as a witness at trial, only as provided in Rule 35(b) or upon a showing of exceptional circumstances under which it is impracticable for the party seeking discovery to obtain facts or opinions on the same subject by other means.

(C) Unless manifest injustice would result, (i) the court shall require that the party seeking discovery pay the expert a reasonable fee for time spent in responding to discovery under this subdivision; and (ii) with respect to discovery obtained under subdivision (b)(4)(B) of this rule the court shall require the party seeking discovery to pay the other party a fair portion of the fees and expenses reasonably incurred by the latter party in obtaining facts and opinions from the expert.

Practice Pointer: If you are an expert who is working as a consultant and the party retaining you does not intend to call you as a witness at trial, Federal Rule 26(b)(4) will in most cases protect you from having to give a deposition in the case.

1.6 Discovery Sanctions

Expert witnesses are potentially subject to sanctions for their conduct at depositions. If an expert witness unjustifiably refuses to disclose requested information, the party seeking the information can make a *motion to compel* the party or deponent to provide the requested discovery. This motion is made to the court (the judge). If the motion to compel is granted, the party seeking the discovery may also seek sanctions against the party, deponent, and/or attorney refusing to provide the discovery.[5] The potential sanctions include the costs of bringing the motion to compel, including attorney's fees. If the motion to compel is *denied,* the party and/or attorney bringing the motion to compel may be ordered by the court to pay the attorney's fees and costs of the person or party from whom discovery is sought. For example, if you refused to answer certain questions during your expert deposition, counsel could file a motion to compel to have the court order that you answer the propounded questions. If this motion is granted, counsel can then move for sanctions against you. If counsel's motion to compel is denied, you could move for sanctions against the attorney.

Example 1.5: Uncooperative with taking of deposition, expert barred from case
Waicis v. Superior Court, 226 Cal. App. 3d 283 (Cal. App. Dist. 1, 1990)
In this medical malpractice case, the plaintiff's expert on standard of care, a D.M.D., refused to cooperate in the taking of his deposition. The expert forced a rescheduling of his deposition six times, often with little notice, and insisted that it be scheduled in the evenings and at awkward times. In the middle of a Saturday deposition, after "clear representation to the trial court that [the expert] would be available all Saturday," the expert claimed he had a personal appointment and left the deposition. The appellate court stated, "The trial court did everything it could to permit Dr. Frankel's deposition but the witness simply would not cooperate, even to the extent of directly violating the court's order that he be available for all of Saturday for his deposition." Additionally, it declared, "Not only is the evidence that [the expert] was uncooperative in permitting his deposition to be taken substantial, it is overwhelming."

   The court approved the trial court's exclusion of the expert's testimony and awarded costs to the defendant, stating: "It is an affront to the orderly and expeditious disposition of cases for any witness, especially an expert witness, to be so uncooperative…[the expert's] conduct smacks of game playing."

Practice Pointer: Experts who act in good faith should be able to arrange convenient times for their depositions. The above result is what can happen when the expert does not act in good faith.

Example 1.6: Sanctions assessed against plaintiff for expert's failure to answer questions at deposition after being instructed not to answer by retaining counsel
Cabana v. Forcier, 200 F.R.D. 9 (D. Mass. 2001)
In this case, a truck driver who worked as an independent contractor brought suit against a truck leasing business and one of its clients, seeking damages for injuries allegedly caused by exposure to hazardous waste. The defendant took the deposition of Cabana's treating physician and expert witness, Dr. Sica. On the second day of

---

[5] See, for example, *JSC Foreign Economic Ass'n v. Int'l Dev. & Trade Services, Inc.,* 2005 U.S. Dist. LEXIS 16772, and *Walker v. McCrea,* 725 N.E.2d 526 (Ind. 2000).

that deposition, defense counsel asked Dr. Sica whether she had ever been a party to any litigation, and whether she had ever been the subject of a disciplinary proceeding. Counsel for Cabana objected to those questions on the grounds that Dr. Sica's involvement in prior litigation and/or disciplinary proceedings was not relevant to the instant case and, accordingly, Dr. Sica was instructed not to answer. Defendant then moved for an order compelling Dr. Sica to answer the two questions and to recover the "reasonable expenses incurred in making the motion." Cabana responded by moving for a protective order on the grounds that the questions were asked in bad faith or unreasonably to annoy, harass, or embarrass Dr. Sica.

The court found that Dr. Sica's involvement in any prior litigation or disciplinary proceedings was clearly relevant to the instant suit and was, therefore, discoverable.

> Questions regarding such litigation or disciplinary proceedings are likely to lead to evidence relevant both to Dr. Sica's skill as a physician and her credibility, especially regarding her diagnosis of Cabana with multiple chemical sensitivity ("MCS"). Accordingly, the motion to compel Dr. Sica to answer deposition questions regarding her involvement in any prior litigation or disciplinary proceedings will be allowed. At 17.

The court then considered whether it should order the plaintiff to pay the defendant's reasonable expenses incurred in bringing the pending motion or if it should refrain from such an order because 1) the opposition to the motion to compel was "substantially justified," or 2) other circumstances make an award of expenses unjust. The court found that the plaintiff's opposition to the motion to compel was not "substantially justified" and that an award of expenses would not be unjust in this case. The court stated:

> The objections made by Cabana's attorney at Dr. Sica's deposition constitute the kind of frivolous delay of discovery that Rule 37 was designed to prevent. Cabana's attorney was not trying to preserve a privilege or enforce a limitation on evidence ordered by this Court. Furthermore, there is simply no evidence that counsel for [defendant] harassed Dr. Sica. Accordingly, the objections were inappropriate under Rule 30(d)(1), and [the defendant's] motion to compel will be allowed. At 17–18.

Practice Pointer: Note that the court found that the expert's involvement in prior litigation and disciplinary proceedings was "clearly relevant." The only guaranteed way to avoid being asked such questions is to not agree to serve as an expert witness.

1.7 Objections
Objections are generally reserved for trial unless they go to the form of the question. Please see Section 1.2 on the usual stipulations. Allowable "form" objections that can be made at a deposition include:

- ambiguous,
- unintelligible,

- complex or confusing,
- compound,
- misleading,
- calls for speculation,
- unfair characterization,
- misstates prior testimony,
- assumes facts not in evidence,
- argumentative,
- calls for a legal conclusion,
- asked and answered, and
- calls for an opinion beyond the expert's qualifications.

The reason why form objections are allowed at trial is that these objections can be cured on the spot by counsel simply rephrasing the question. For example, if a compound question is put forth and objected to, counsel can break the compound question into two simple questions.

Objections that are generally *not* allowed at deposition but are reserved for trial include:

- relevancy,
- hearsay,
- unfair prejudice,
- confusion of the issues,
- misleading the jury,
- waste of time, and
- needless presentation of cumulative evidence.

Because the above objections are not allowed at depositions, deponents may be required to answer questions that they would never have to answer had the question been asked at trial. Please see Section 1.3 dealing with fishing expeditions and the liberal rules of discovery.

Practice Pointer: Your role as an expert is not to argue evidence or procedure. You are *not* an advocate and will lose credibility if you appear to be one. With this in mind, the authors recommend that experts do the following when an objection is made:

1. Stop testifying immediately.
2. Listen carefully to the objection because it may reveal some tips or insight into the questioning.
3. Learn as much as you can about the grounds for the objection.
4. Stay above the fray and let the lawyers battle it out.
5. Resume testifying when counsel so instructs you.

Some lawyers use *speaking objections* to coach, tip off, or suggest answers to experts who are being deposed. While this practice is against the Rules[6] and can result in sharp rebukes to counsel, it is not uncommon. Experts should, therefore, listen very carefully to the objections of counsel.

Example 1.7: Listening to the objection assists the witness in answering
Q: Your testimony was, "So we have to establish exactly under what conditions it is possible." Do you recall saying that?
A: I don't recall those words, no.
   Counsel: What was the reference for…?
Q: Page 181, lines 12 through 16.
   Counsel: I have an objection. It's out of context.
A: I was just going to say it's out of context. I can't comment on it.

Q: My question is: Accepting as true that he is of the opinion or he did a study in which he showed where patients with a Glasgow Coma Scale of 15 in the emergency room, he has documented, have had long-term traumatic brain injury.
   Counsel: I object to the form of the question. I don't think it's fair to the witness to even ask a question like that without giving him the opportunity to know more about what the Reiten study is, who was studied, why they were studied, and whether there was traumatic injury or whether it was stroke, or whatever.
A: I really need to know more about the study before I answer that question accurately.

Practice Pointer: The experts in the above cases carefully listened to the objections. This may have helped them to organize their thoughts in preparation for truthful, non-objectionable answers.

1.8 Expert Witness Fees at Deposition
The opposing side is generally responsible for paying the expert's fee if they call the expert's deposition.

FRCP 26(b)(4)(C): Reasonable Fee Requirement
Unless manifest injustice would result, (i) the court shall require that the party seeking discovery pay the expert a *reasonable* fee for time spent in responding to discovery under this subdivision…. *(Emphasis added.)*

Some jurisdictions have different rules.

---

[6] The Federal Rules of Civil Procedure require that objections be stated in a "non-suggestive manner." See Fed. R. Civ. Pro. 30(d)(1).

Practice Pointer: It is usually good practice to have a clause in your fee agreement that states that retaining counsel will pay all deposition fees and that he can then seek payment from the other side. That way, you do not have to deal with the other side.

Practice Pointer: The fact that opposing counsel is paying or has paid your deposition fee can be used to the expert's advantage at trial.

Example 1.8: Expert cites fact that opposing counsel paid part of fee to parry "hired gun" cross-examination at trial
Q: You have been paid $17,000 for your work to date on this case, correct?
A: That's correct. $12,000 from attorney Mangraviti and $5,000 from you.

Reasonable Fee
Generally, the expert is entitled to be paid a "reasonable fee" for his deposition time. What is reasonable and which time (preparation, travel, etc.) needs to be paid for are matters that vary amongst jurisdictions and may depend upon the particular facts at hand. When a fee dispute takes place, it is usually resolved by the aggrieved party filing for a protective order to limit the expert's fee.

The federal courts frequently rule on what is "reasonable" in terms of expert deposition fees. Expert fees are frequently reduced as a result. In ruling on this, the federal courts often weigh six factors:

1. the witness's area of expertise;
2. the education and training required to provide the expert insight that is sought;
3. the prevailing rates for other comparably respected available experts;
4. the nature, quality and complexity of the discovery responses provided;
5. the local cost of living; and
6. any other factor likely to be of assistance in balancing the interests implicated by Rule 26.[7]

Practice Pointer: To avoid being paid less than your full fee scheduled rate, you should have a clause in your fee agreement stating that retaining counsel will pay your full fee, regardless of what is ultimately collected from the other side.

Preparation Time
The federal courts are split on whether preparation time is "reasonable." Some courts hold that it is. (See *Hose v. Chicago and North Western Transportation Co.*, 154 FRD 222 (S.D. Iowa 1994).) Some hold that it is not. (See *Rhee v. Witco Chemical Corp.*, 126 FRD 45 (N.D. Ill. 1989).) Some hold that preparation time is only compensable in complex cases where there has been a significant delay between the

---

[7] *Profile Products v. Soil Management Technologies,* 155 F.Supp2d 880 (N.D. Ill. 2001).

expert's work and the deposition. (See *S.A. Healy Co. v. Milwaukee Sewerage District,* 154 FRD 212 (E.D. Wis. 1994).)

Practice Pointer: To avoid worrying about being compensated for preparation time, an expert should consider having a clause in his fee agreement specifically stating that retaining counsel will pay for all his reasonable preparation time and that it is retaining counsel's burden to seek reimbursement from opposing counsel.

Travel Time
Reasonable fees for travel time may be collectable from the other side if the opposing party selects the location as one to which the expert must travel. (See *M.T. McBrian, Inc., v. Liebert Corp,* 173 FRD 491 (N.D. Ill. 1997).)

Practice Pointer: If you don't mind traveling and like collecting for travel time, you might not want to have a place suitable for depositions available at your office.

Reading and Signing
In terms of payment, at least one federal court has held that an expert is not entitled to compensation *from the other side* for reading and signing the deposition transcript unless the other side "strongly encouraged" this. (See *Patterson Farm, Inc. v. City of Britton,* WL 702322 (D.S.D. 1998).)

Practice Pointer: If you choose to read and sign, you may want to include a clause in your fee agreement that provides that retaining counsel will pay you to do so.

1.9 Instructions Not to Answer
You may be instructed not to answer by counsel who retained you. Under the Federal Rules, an attorney may only properly instruct a deponent not to answer under very limited circumstances:

- to preserve a privilege (see Section 1.4),
- to enforce a limitation of evidence directed by the court, or
- to present a motion that the deposition is being "conducted in bad faith or in such a manner as unreasonably to annoy, embarrass, or oppress."[8]

Ultimately, the legitimacy of any instruction not to answer may be evaluated by the court. Under the Federal Rules, the deponent or party may be forced to pay the other party's attorney's fees involved in bringing a motion to compel an answer if the instruction not to answer was not substantially justified.[9] If the motion to compel asking the court to order that the deponent answer the question fails and was not substantially justified, the expert and party may file a motion to collect their

---

[8] Fed. R. Civ. Pro. 30(d)(4).
[9] Fed. R. Civ. Pro. 37(a)(4)(A).

attorney's fees associated with the filing of the motion to compel.[10] For example, attorney's fees were awarded after improper instructions not to answer were issued in the cases *JSC Foreign Economic Ass'n v. Int'l Dev. & Trade Services, Inc.,* 2005 U.S. Dist. LEXIS 16772, *Walker v. McCrea,* 725 N.E.2d 526 (Ind. 2000), *Nationwide Mutual Fire Insurance Company v. Smith,* 174 F.R.D. 250 (D.Conn. 1997), and *Hearst/ABC-Viacom Entertainment Services v. Goodway Marketing, Inc.,* 145 F.R.D. 59 (E.D. Pa. 1992).

Example 1.9: Instructing the deponent not to answer
Q: And it's your testimony that you did not intentionally give false testimony to the jury in that trial?
A: That's correct. May I consult with counsel?
Q: No.
A: I need a break, sir. After break....
　　Counsel: I am going to object to the question as being asked in bad faith with the intention of embarrassing the witness....I am instructing the witness not to answer the question.
Q: Counsel, if you are asserting a privilege, please state it for the record. If not, the witness is to answer the question.

Practice Pointer: Instructions not to answer are only proper under limited circumstances. Misuse of the instruction not to answer may result in the deponent and/or the attorney paying the opposing side's attorney's fees associated with bringing a motion to compel. Under the grounds of bad faith and embarrassment, an instruction not to answer will only be upheld if the objecting party suspends the deposition and immediately files a motion for a protective order. Please see Fed. R. Civ. Pro. 30(d)(4) and Section 1.10 below. Note that expert witnessing is a "contact sport" and that courts will generally allow litigants substantial leeway in questioning experts. The court realizes that experts are unique among witnesses in that they are both volunteers and highly paid. Thus, the courts give counsel greater leeway to question experts than they would other witnesses.

1.10 Unprofessional Attorney Conduct
Experts should be aware that attorneys at deposition are required to behave professionally at all times. As one judge put it:

　　A deposition is an extension of a judicial proceeding. It should be attended and conducted with the same sense of solemnity and the same rules of etiquette that would be required were the parties in the courtroom itself. The lawyer conducting the examination must ask questions and obtain answers, not demean, insult or hurl epithets at the opposing witness or counsel. The lawyer

---

[10] Fed. R. Civ. Pro. 37(a)(4)(A).

representing a witness must make objections, when objections are required, succinctly and with the same brief precision required during the trial itself. If either lawyer encounters what he or she perceives to be an impenetrable roadblock, the remedy provided by the rules is clear: the deposition should be halted until a judicial resolution can be obtained....Self-help through bombast or insults is not an option.[11]

Practice Pointer: Conduct such as making insulting, demeaning, sarcastic, and threatening comments is unprofessional and may warrant sanctions. (See *Freeman v. Schointuck,* 192 FRD 187 (D. MD 2000).) If subjected to unprofessional conduct, an expert might want to remind the attorney of his ethical obligations.

Questions propounded in "bad faith" or "in such manner as unreasonably to annoy, embarrass, or oppress" are not allowed. If questioning counsel is warned and continues along this path, the deposition may be terminated. *If this happens, a motion for a protective order must be sought <u>immediately</u> by the person or party terminating the deposition.* Failure to bring the motion immediately can be interpreted as an admission of illegitimate grounds for adjournment. (See *Hearst/ABC-VIACOM v. Goodway Marketing,* 145 FRD 59 (1992).) If the motion is not granted, costs and other sanctions may be assessed against the deponent. As such, depositions should not routinely be suspended to make a motion for a protective order. For a detailed example of abusive behavior at a deposition that was sanctioned by the court, please see Appendix C.

Practice Pointer: The expert who is being embarrassed, oppressed, or abused should "make a record" of such at the deposition. At least one or two warnings on the record would be appropriate before seeking a protective order. In many cases, a warning will suffice to resolve the situation. If the warnings do not end the abusive behavior, the expert has built a record to support his motion for a protective order.

1.11 Deposition Practice and Procedure[12]
Experts who have a working knowledge of deposition practice and procedure are best positioned to excel at their depositions. Some of the more important points of deposition practice and procedure are summarized below.

- **Reserved Objections.** All objections are usually reserved until trial except for form. FRCP 32(d).
- **Review and Signing of Transcript by Deponent.** The witness and parties usually waive this. FRCP 30(e).
- **Filing Certified Transcript with the Court.** Unless ordered, transcripts are not to be filed with the court. FRCP 30(f).

---

[11] *Cholfin v. Gordon,* 3 Mass. L. Rptr. No. 17, 356 at 362 (Ma. Super. Ct. 1995).
[12] Thomas Vesper, *ATLA Deposition Notebook* (Thompson West: 2005) p. 95.

- **"One for All" Objections.** Any objection by one party is deemed to be made by all unless otherwise noted.
- **Time Schedule.** Recesses and time limits will be discussed and agreed to in advance.
- **Exhibits.** Marking, handling and preserving all deposition exhibits will be agreed upon in advance.
- **Guidelines for Deposition Conduct.** The following guidance is from *Hall v. Clifton Precision, a Div. of Litton Systems, Inc.,* 150 F.R.D. 525, 27 Fed. R. Serv. 3d (LCP) 10 (E.D. Pa. 1993):
  1. *Instructions not to answer.* Counsel shall not direct or request a witness to not answer.
  2. *Coaching a witness.* Counsel shall not object or make statements which might suggest an answer to a witness. Objections shall be succinct, verbally economical and state their basis and nothing more.
  3. *Off the record conferences.* Counsel and witness-clients shall not engage in private off-record conferences during deps/breaks/recesses, except to decide whether to assert a privilege.
  4. *Inquiry about conferences.* Any such conferences are [the] proper subject for deposition inquiry to ascertain whether and what coaching occurred.
  5. *Note the conference.* Any such conference(s) shall be noted upon the record by all participating counsel. Purpose and outcome of such conference(s) shall also be noted on the record.
  6. *Documents.* Deposing counsel shall give counsel a copy of any documents shown to a witness. Copies shall be provided before the deposition begins or contemporaneously with the showing of each [document] to the witness. Witness and counsel have no right to discuss the documents privately before the witness answers questions about them.

1.12 Conclusion

Expert witnesses are well served to understand the legal rules governing their depositions.

Chapter 2 Understanding the Strategies and Goals of Opposing Counsel

2.1 Introduction and Executive Summary

Opposing counsel generally has one or two overall objectives for deposing an expert witness. Either the deposing attorney wants the expert's deposition testimony for discovery purposes or he seeks to preserve the expert's testimony for use at trial. This book's focus is on discovery depositions.

Counsel can be expected to prepare very diligently for an expert's deposition. To excel, the expert must prepare as hard or harder.

Counsel's questioning techniques and demeanor are likely to be far different than what an expert would face at trial. At deposition, an expert is likely to face a seemingly friendly attorney who asks open-ended questions with the goal of getting the expert to talk as much as possible.

The goals of counsel when deposing an expert witness for discovery purposes will include some, if not all, of the following:

- Learning the opinions of the expert.
  - The deposing attorney wants to eliminate new or additional opinions by the expert at trial.
- Learning the expert's qualifications.
  - Juries will consider the expert's education, experience, and other qualifications when weighing the expert's opinion in the case.
- Locking down the opinions of the expert.
  - Opposing counsel can impeach the expert at trial with his prior inconsistent testimony if the expert attempts to change his opinion.
- Sizing up the expert's effectiveness as a witness.
- Determining if the expert is biased in the case.
  - Experts should refuse to get involved in cases where they are biased or where they can be reasonably perceived to be biased.
- Discover factual assumptions used by the expert.
  - An expert's credibility can be damaged if his assumptions are incorrect.
- Gather as much information as possible.
  - Counsel may also size up the witness's ability to explain complicated technical principles to the jury.
- Use the expert to help counsel's case.
  - Counsel may attempt to get the expert to make concessions or appear inflexible.
- Learn about the opponent's case to evaluate the settlement value of the case.
- Learn what the expert did.

- Set the stage for a later motion to disqualify the expert or throw out the expert's opinion.
  - The expert's qualifications and methodology will be examined closely.

2.2 Preservation of Evidence Depositions

The deposing attorney's goals in an expert deposition will vary depending upon the reason why she is taking the deposition (that is, whether the deposition is for discovery purposes or to preserve testimony to be used at trial in lieu of the expert's live appearance).

If an expert is deposed by retaining counsel, this is most likely done in an effort to preserve the expert's testimony for trial. The attorney who retained the expert is taking the deposition because: a) she is concerned that the expert will not be available to testify at trial due to death, disability, or travel, b) she does not want to pay the expert to appear live at trial and testify, or c) the trial judge has deemed that the testimony of the expert witnesses be presented by video at trial. When the retaining party notices an expert's deposition, she is most likely planning on either reading the deposition transcript to the jury at trial or showing the jury the videotape of the deposition.

In these preservation of evidence depositions, the expert will undergo a direct examination and a cross-examination much the same as he would at trial. Opposing counsel will not be saving anything for the trial and will actually cross-examine the expert because this may be her only opportunity to do so. Experts should use the testifying techniques used at trial when testifying at preservation of evidence depositions.[1]

When an expert is notified of his upcoming deposition, he should determine if it will be a videotaped deposition and if the deposition will be a preservation of evidence or discovery deposition. For additional information on videotaped depositions, please see Chapter 9.

2.3 Understanding How Opposing Counsel Will Prepare for the Expert Deposition

To understand the strategies and goals of opposing counsel, it is a good idea to understand how a good lawyer will prepare to depose an expert. She will do the following:

- Carefully study the expert's report, his answers to interrogatories, and other discovery.
- Talk to other lawyers to get the word on the expert.
- Get ideas on questions from her own expert.

---

[1] For information on testifying at trial, please see Babitsky and Mangraviti, *How to Become a Dangerous Expert Witness* (SEAK 2005) and the list of course offerings at www.seak.com.

- Obtain old transcripts.
- Obtain the expert's writings.
- Perform Internet searches.
- Conduct FOIA (Freedom of Information Act) searches, including requests to licensing and certifying agencies.
- Gain a detailed knowledge of the facts of the case.
- Talk to other lawyers who have gone up against the expert.
- Conduct Westlaw or Lexis searches on the expert's name in reported cases.
- Search news databases for the expert's name.
- Learn the expert's field of expertise.
- Map out strategy, tactics, and a plan of attack with checklists, outlines, etc.

2.4 How Counsel's Deposition and Trial Questioning Techniques Differ

Counsel will employ completely different strategies and techniques when cross-examining an expert at deposition than she would at trial. When trial lawyers were asked, "When cross-examining a witness during depositions, do you use different tactics and strategies than you would use during the trial?," the unanimous answer was "yes." When asked to describe the differences, here are some of the answers:

1. Totally different—befriend him—treat him as objective—woo him! Then rush him and be painstaking in factual development—cover all points even though they might hurt you: get his story out completely; use all documents you can. Even use filler questions.
2. Deposition is to get facts and have witness cement himself into a story to be dealt with later.
3. Usually, deposition is to develop areas to use during trial cross, not to rehearse witness to respond better next time.
4. I will never attempt to impeach a witness on deposition unless I am sure the deposition will be read into evidence. I also attempt to be very friendly during depositions.
5. As a woman, I find that witnesses usually do not give women credit for knowing a great deal. By playing dumb, I get information the witness would not volunteer to a man. A deposition is to find out all a witness knows; a cross-examination at trial is to let the jury know only such portions of the witness's knowledge as will help you or hurt the other side. I do not attack witnesses at deposition. Nothing is ever gained and a lot can be lost.
6. I want statements during a deposition that can be used against the witness later; the question and answer must be simple, understandable, and complete; it must stand alone or it is useless later.
7. Order of questioning is not significant, also, you can ask the why and how questions.

8. Depositions are intended to exhaust the witness's recollections on relevant points. To fix testimony. To provide a basis for impeachment. It is encyclopedic. Trial cross-examination is specific, focused, and intended to make valuable points, not to acquire information.

9. I ask open-ended questions to get the witness to tell all. At trial I control the length of the response with narrowly phrased questions: "Isn't it true that…"

10. Be more thorough—fish around a little—get to know personality of witness.

11. Seek discovery rather than impeachment.

12. 1. Less confrontation. 2. Open-ended questions. 3. Leave some questions unasked for a surprise at trial.

13. I'm very thorough and calm during depositions. I can be more dramatic during trial.

14. Don't always use the "clincher" in deposition. Save the kill for the courtroom.

15. In deposition I usually seek long, detailed answers and ask many more questions than I ever would at trial.

16. Don't impress anyone. Get answers. Drone on and on and on until the answer is in the record.

17. Depositions are more rambling, like direct testimony. Witness should be more at ease, willing to provide narratives.

18. At trial, you confine yourself only to questions the answers to which you feel confident will be helpful to your case. In most depositions, especially when the witness is likely to be available for trial, you can afford to get "discovery" of both the good and the bad.

19. At deposition, I try to discover information and pin a witness down to his version of the facts. My approach is therefore more open and friendly. At trial, I make more use of leveling questions and less use of "open-ended" questions to control the witness's testimony.[2]

2.5 Goals of Counsel at Discovery Depositions

When an expert is deposed by the opposing side and is expected to testify live at trial, this is known as a discovery deposition.

Counsel who takes an expert witness discovery deposition has a series of goals she seeks to achieve. Understanding the goals of opposing counsel is the first step for experts to prepare for and be in the best position to excel at discovery deposition. The best lawyers usually find out as much as they can *without* tipping their hand to the other side as to what they might do at trial. As such, they will often ask very general questions. They also might not want to destroy the expert too early because the court may grant the expert's counsel leave to find another expert. Opposing counsel is trying to prepare herself, not the expert, for trial.

---

[2] Aron, *Cross-Examination of Witnesses: The Litigator's Puzzle,* Trial Practice Series (West Publishing Group: 1989) p. 500.

Opposing counsel's goals during a discovery deposition include the following:

- learn the opinions of the expert,
- learn the expert's qualifications,
- lock down the expert,
- size up the expert and his credibility,
- check to see if bias of the expert is an issue,
- discover the factual assumptions used by the expert,
- gather as much information as possible,
- use the expert to bolster the case of opposing counsel,
- intimidate the expert,
- learn what the expert did, and
- try to get the expert to express a new opinion off the top of his head.

Learn the Expert's Opinions
Counsel wants to learn and clarify the expert's opinion, the factual basis for the opinion, how the opinion was formed (i.e., the methodology used), when the expert arrived at the opinion, what future tests and evaluations the expert is planning, and whether the expert is willing to modify or change the opinion. Counsel may ask broad questions to start the opinion inquiry.[3] For example:

Q: Please tell me all of the opinions you may be offering at trial in this case.

and

Q: In addition to the opinions you just testified to, will you be offering any additional opinions at trial?

The idea is to lock the expert down, eliminate potential unpleasant surprises, and limit any new/additional opinions that may be offered at trial by the expert. Once the broad areas are covered, counsel may then hone in on specific opinion issues. Determining the exact nature, extent, and basis of an expert's opinion(s) is critical for the opposing attorney as he seeks to both prepare for trial and to evaluate the settlement value of the case.

Example 2.1: Pushing the expert on his willingness to change his opinion
Q: Is the opinion that you've expressed here today etched in stone?
A: Etched in stone? Would you want to define that?
Q: Are you willing to change your opinion?

---

[3] Broad, open-ended questions are characteristic of discovery deposition questions. This contrasts with the leading, tightly worded questions usually propounded at trial during cross-examination.

A: Am I willing to change it? I still don't grasp what you're getting at.

Q: Is your opinion inflexible?

A: I don't think my opinion is inflexible.

Q: So you're willing to change the opinion that you've stated here today?

A: I would be if the information convinced me otherwise.

Practice Pointer: Willingness to change your opinion if you are presented with new facts is important. Counsel may follow up this line of questioning by presenting just that—new and different facts. If the expert is unwilling to even consider new information, he may be perceived or portrayed as biased.

Example 2.2: Locking down the expert regarding opinions that he will *not* be offering at trial

Q: Are you going to offer opinion testimony with respect to the use of side impact air bags or side curtain air bags?

A: I don't think so. We haven't talked about it. I think I wrote in my opinion that it doesn't have them.

Q: So, no opinions with respect to side curtain air bags or side impact air bags—

A: Right.

Q: —other than to say this vehicle didn't come equipped with it?

A: Yes, right.

Q: You're not going to say the vehicle is defective because it did not come equipped with side curtain air bags?

A: Correct.

Q: Am I correct?

A: You're correct. I'm not going to say it would have saved this guy's life.

Q: You're not going to say it would have saved this guy's life?

A: Right.

Q: You have not done any testing with respect to side curtain air bags, I take it; is that right?

A: That's correct.

Q: So I won't hear at trial you testify with respect to side curtain air bags or roof rail air bags or some variation on that theme, that they should have been employed in this 1999 SUV and if employed would have prevented or mitigated Mr. Philldans's injuries?

A: Correct.

Q: Are you going to offer any opinion that those seat belts as equipped in the '99 SUV are defective?

A: No.

Q: Aside from glazing and roof design and performance, are you going to express opinions in any other subject areas at the time of trial?

A: Not directly, no. There are other things. You asked me a lot of questions about occupant kinematics and injury mechanisms and whatnot. If asked, I'll answer to the best of my ability the things that I've said so far here, but I'm not going to advance anything else.

Practice Pointer: Counsel in the above example relentlessly tries to pin the expert down on precisely what he will and will not be offering his opinions on. Note, however, how the expert leaves himself a little wiggle room when replying. He states: "I don't think so. We haven't talked about it…," "Not directly, no…," and "If asked, I'll answer to the best of my ability…."

The sophisticated expert does not usually want to absolutely commit to what opinions he won't offer. This is for two reasons:

1. things may change prior to the trial and
2. he may be asked questions by opposing counsel that necessitate additional opinions.

Learn the Expert's Qualifications
Opposing counsel wants to learn as much as possible about the expert's qualifications. Specifically, the expert may be questioned about her background, education, training, and experience. Counsel may question the expert thoroughly about her CV. Of particular importance is the expert's relevant experience with situations matching, or closely resembling, the current situation. Juries sometimes find experience, or lack thereof, to be the most important factor in weighing an expert's qualifications to give an opinion in a case. The information obtained during the expert deposition can be used at cross-examination during trial in an effort to lessen the expert's credibility. The strengths and weaknesses of the expert's qualifications are also important in opposing counsel's evaluation of the expert's likely effectiveness at trial and are points of discussion between counsel during settlement negotiations. Experts need to be very prepared to answer questions regarding their qualifications.

Counsel may start with open-ended questions in an attempt to encourage the expert to open up about qualifications that do not appear on his CV.

> **Q:** Leaving aside the material contained in your CV, what makes you qualified to offer an opinion in this case?

Counsel may later challenge the expert and try to mouse-trap him into claiming either a too limited or too broad area of expertise.

> **Q:** What areas do you think you are an expert in?

Example 2.3: Inability to answer routine questions about qualifications reflects poorly on the expert

When asked simple, routine questions about his qualifications at deposition, the prepared expert answers them simply and directly.

> **Q:** How long have you been licensed in the Commonwealth of Massachusetts?
> **A:** My license, I think, began in—shortly after medical school. I—it would have been sometime shortly after my graduation, probably in the early 1960s.

Practice Pointer: The expert in the above example did not distinguish himself with his reply to a *very* basic question. A more confident expert would have replied simply and directly:

> **Q:** How long have you been licensed in the Commonwealth of Massachusetts?
> **A:** Since 1964.

Example 2.4: Counsel tries to establish a lack of essential education

Q: Mr. Wilson, I'm going to hand you what has been provided to me and represented to be your current curriculum vitae. Is that in fact the most recent CV that you have?
A: I think so.
Q: Now, you graduated from the University of Illinois in metallurgy in 1978, is that correct?
A: The Department of Materials Engineering.
Q: When you were going to school at the University of Illinois, did you refer to yourself as a metallurgist?
A: No, I didn't.
Q: In your education, did you take any courses that would fall into the realm of engineering mechanics other than introductory-level statics and dynamics?
A: Yes.
Q: What courses?
A: I don't recall them, the courses. I took courses in machine design, a course in design called maybe Strength of Members or something like that.
Q: And it's your testimony that the courses you took that involved strength of members were classified as engineering mechanics courses?
A: I don't recall what they classified them as!

Practice Pointer: Counsel is attempting to establish a lack of a proper and relevant educational background, which may be relevant to the witness's qualifications to proffer an opinion in the case. Thus, the witness should carefully consider his answers. If counsel can get his hands on the witness's college transcripts (for example, as part of a licensing application that is public record), he will have precise evidence as to which courses the witness did and did not take.

Lock Down the Expert with the Threat of Impeachment
Counsel does not want any unpleasant surprises at trial. As such, an all-important goal of counsel during a discovery deposition is to lock in the expert's testimony. When experts are deposed they give testimony under oath. That testimony is recorded by a stenographer. Once the expert gives an answer to a question at a deposition it can be very problematic to give a different answer to the same question at trial. If she does, the cross-examining attorney can bring into evidence the inconsistent answer that the expert gave at the deposition. This process of using prior inconsistent deposition testimony during cross-examination at trial is called *impeachment.* Impeachment can have a severe adverse effect on a witness's credibility at trial. Locking down the expert's testimony so that she can be impeached if she contradicts it at trial is a primary goal of counsel.

Counsel may ask carefully worded questions in an attempt to "box in the expert" and make sure she does not change her opinions or testimony at trial.

Example 2.5: Expert boxed in by "all"
Q: You reviewed all of the police records in this case, correct?
A: Yes, I did.

Practice Pointer: The expert who answers in the affirmative can expect to be presented with numerous records she never saw. A seasoned expert utilizing active listening skills would have recognized the absolute nature of the word "all" and responded more cautiously and accurately.

> **Q:** You reviewed all of the police records in this case, correct?
> **A:** The records I reviewed are listed on page 2 of my 2/17/07 report.

Example 2.6: Counsel tries to lock down expert by requesting "full and final opinions"
Q: I take it you are prepared right now to give your full and final opinions relating to this incident?
A: Well, probably not. I need to read the deposition and make sure there are no errors there, and if anybody else submits some information that I am given, it may change my opinion or I might be adding to my opinion.
Q: Well, what other information do you anticipate receiving in this case before you can give me your full and final opinions?
A: I don't know. I'm sure it would be coming from you. You know, if you had any other experts or any other opinions or any other events happening that you supplied to Mr. Malloy who supplied it to me, then it might make me change or add to my opinion.

Practice Pointer: The expert here recognized that if he is supplied with additional information, his opinions may change or he may formulate additional opinions. The expert could have added that if he is asked different questions, answering them may involve offering new or different opinions.

Example 2.7: Locking down the expert with a narrowly worded, "If you were asked at trial..." question
Q: If you're asked at trial in this case, "Was Carolyn Newburg negligent in not riding with direct supervision?," are you going to give an answer?
A: Yes.
Q: And what's your opinion?
A: I believe she was.

Practice Pointer: The expert is now locked into her opinion regarding supervision. If she changes this opinion at trial, she will be confronted with and impeached by her prior inconsistent statement at deposition.

Example 2.8: Setting up grounds for impeachment
Q: Are you going to be postulating at trial an opinion that this child's cerebral palsy was caused by an infection?
A: I hope not.
Q: Are you going to be offering any opinion with respect to what caused this child's cerebral palsy?
A: I believe I'd like to be able to offer an opinion of what I conclude appeared to be going on in the delivery room related to the child, which might then have an implication for the status of the child at the time of delivery.

Practice Pointer: If the expert witness later testifies at trial that he believed the cerebral palsy was caused by an infection, he can be confronted with and impeached by his prior statement on this point at deposition.

Example 2.9: Expert locked in
Q: So the most significant lab value which one would need to know, the most significant laboratory test or blood test to take to establish metabolic acidosis at the time of delivery is taking an umbilical artery blood sample; is that fair to say?
A: I think that's fair.

Practice Pointer: The expert's deposition testimony will be used to impeach him at trial if he attempts to change his answer on this issue.

Size up the Expert and His Likely Effectiveness as a Witness
All trials come down to one issue and one issue only—credibility. A major goal of counsel at deposition is to determine the likely credibility of a witness when the witness will appear at trial in front of the jury and that how well that witness will

likely be received. Counsel wants to determine if the jury is likely to be sympathetic to the expert and will be likely to believe her. Factors such as demeanor and communication skills are very important in this analysis. Is the expert attractive and well groomed? Does she communicate well or does the expert speak with an unintelligible accent or talk over people? Is the expert arrogant or evasive? How does this person respond to surprise questions? Is the expert prepared and well organized? Does she speak loud enough so the jury will be able to hear? Even innocent sounding "jokes" or flip remarks by an expert during deposition may give counsel insight into how an expert's testimony will appear to the jury or fact finder. How an expert will play in front of a jury is crucial for determining cross-examination strategy and for evaluating the settlement value of the case. It is also crucial in determining how valuable a certain expert is.

Example 2.10: Trying to excite the expert to see how she reacts
Q: Your so-called on-line Ph.D. is really a mail-order degree, isn't it, "Doctor"?

Practice Pointer: An excitable expert is of less value than an expert who is unflappable. An excited, upset expert is more likely to say something that has not been carefully considered.

Example 2.11: Putting the expert "on the spot" to see how she performs when under pressure
Q: Could you take this yellow pad and run through the computations you did to determine that the vehicle was going 73 miles per hour?

Practice Pointer: The expert may or may not be able to do the computation with a yellow pad, but that is beside the point. The attorney here is testing how the expert responds to pressure. A calm, reasoned reply is called for.

> **Q:** Could you take this yellow pad and run through the computations you did to determine that the vehicle was going 73 miles per hour?
> **A:** No. I will need my computer, the appropriate accident reconstruction software, and one hour to do the computations, Counsel.

Example 2.12: Ill-advised jokes
Q: What is aggravation to a medical professional or to an orthopedic surgeon?
A: Something that an attorney does to a doctor.

Q: The next packet, I assume, sir, you looked at since it's the test results and it's six pages long.
A: I'll plead the Fifth.

Practice Pointer: Expert witnesses are well-advised to avoid flip, clever, or joking remarks. Such remarks lessen your credibility as a witness and will accordingly lessen your value to the attorneys who retain you.

Example 2.13: Defensive demeanor
Q: We are at the offices of Fair Market Associates, Inc.?
A: That's correct.
Q: Sir, I saw the sign on the door on the way in and I didn't see your name on it.
A: It's not—it's a group practice. My name will be put on the directory very soon.
Q: Okay. Maybe you can answer something, a mystery that I have, and I don't know that the jury can pick it up, but I see a bunch of certificates on the wall here that relate to some guy named Caleb Fisher.
A: Yes. We are using Mr. Fisher's office.
Q: Why aren't we using your office, sir?
A: I—well—I really don't have an office yet—but I hope to get one soon.

Practice Pointer: This witness was not calm and cool under fire. His demeanor suggests that he has something to hide or to be embarrassed about. If he has just joined the organization in question, he should have simply and directly stated so, without squirming, showing weakness, and appearing as though he has something to hide. This expert might not make a good witness in front of a jury.

Check to See if Bias of the Expert Is at Issue
The expert witness's credibility is a major issue in any trial. One fundamental way to destroy an expert's credibility is to show that the expert is, or could be, biased against or in favor of a party in the case. This is a legitimate area of inquiry because bias is always relevant to the credibility of the witness. Experts can expect to be questioned closely on the subject of bias. This is an integral part of being an expert witness. Areas of inquiry on the subject of bias commonly include expert witness fees and income, the propensity for testifying only for plaintiffs or defendants, and any personal interest in the subject matter of the litigation or the individual or corporate litigants. Even if bias is not apparent or does not exist, opposing counsel will try to fish around for and learn anything that can be used to imply, assert, or prove bias on the part of the expert.

Counsel may start his bias questioning by trying to "get the expert going" in hopes that she will reveal an underlying bias or prejudice.

Example 2.14: Attorney tries to establish bias with a carefully worded question containing a hidden pitfall
Q: You believe in getting injured workers back to work as soon as possible, correct?
A: Yes, what's wrong with that?

Practice Pointer: Here opposing counsel has tapped into what might be an admirable goal ("return to work") and has recharacterized it as a bias. Note how the "as soon as possible" characterization changes the dynamics. An experienced expert mindful of this trap might offer a more artful reply.

Q: You believe in getting injured workers back to work as soon as possible, correct?

A: I believe workers should be released to return to work when they are medically ready.

Example 2.15: Pointed question to establish bias

Q: You believe abortion is murder, correct?

A: Yes, I do.

Practice Pointer: When an expert has a long paper trail and track record supporting a position, she should not attempt to run away from her firmly held beliefs at deposition. Denying the truth can devastate an expert's credibility. Once an underlying belief, predilection, bias, or prejudice is revealed, counsel may leave exploration until the trial.

Another lesson from this example is the lesson of avoidance. Experts should not testify in cases where they are, or can reasonably be perceived to be, biased. For example, an OB/GYN who is a right-to-life activist should not become involved in a malpractice case against a pro-choice activist OB/GYN who works one day a week in an abortion clinic.

Example 2.16: Source of referrals

Q: Sir, you are being paid a fee for the time and the services you are providing in this case, are you not?

A: Yes.

Q: Does the fact that you're being provided a fee for your services affect the way that your opinion is going to go here today?

A: No, I'm provided a fee for other evaluations that I do.

Q: And sir, have you been asked to give evaluations both for plaintiffs and defendants in lawsuits?

A: Yes.

Q: The forensic psychiatric evaluations that you presently do, what are the sources of referral for those evaluations?

A: The sources of referral are attorneys or claims people from insurance companies.

Q: Of the forensic evaluations that you perform in civil matters, what percentage of those are for or in the behalf of plaintiffs?

A: I would estimate about 20 percent.

Q: Is the remaining 80 percent of referrals on behalf of defendants or insurance companies?

A: Yes.

Practice Pointer: Prudent experts insulate themselves from these types of challenges by working for both plaintiffs and defendants.

Example 2.17: Expert has testified against industry in the past
Q: Have you ever criticized any consumer products as being defective?
A: Oh. Yes.
Q: What consumer products have you criticized as being defective?
A: In my entire life?
Q: Yes, to the extent that you can recall as you sit here right now.
A: I was highly critical with a case with a butane-fired cigarette lighter that would do a reasonable imitation of a flame thrower right out of the box.

Practice Pointer: Most likely, this expert will be sized up to be a very effective witness at trial because:

- he answered questions directly and non-evasively,
- he was prepared,
- he was an active listener, and
- he used powerful and memorable language.

Discover the Expert's Factual Assumptions
The role of an expert witness in litigation is to offer an opinion relevant to one of the disputed issues in the case. This opinion will always be based upon an assumed set of facts. For example, if you are a physician testifying as to the disability of a plaintiff, one of the factual assumptions you may have made is that the plaintiff was being truthful when she told you about her pain. The expert's opinion is only as good as the factual assumptions it is based upon. If opposing counsel can prove that the assumptions the expert made were incorrect, she may be able to damage the credibility of the expert's opinion. The factual assumptions the expert has made in forming his opinion are, therefore, a legitimate area of inquiry at deposition and trial.

Counsel may first try to get the expert to detail each and every assumption he relied on in forming his opinion by using open-ended questions to elicit the assumptions.

Example 2.18: Open-ended assumption question
Q: Please tell me each assumption you utilized or relied on in forming each of your opinions.

Practice Pointer: When the expert omits any assumptions, counsel will use this omission later to attack the opinion of the expert at trial. A good response to the deposition question may include some hedge words, for example, "At this time, the assumptions that I can recall are as follows...."

Example 2.19: Assuming that relevant documents contain no useful information
Q: Wouldn't you agree that it would be useful to take a look at their underlying evaluation sheets in order to really get a handle on the total feedback they received?
A: I think the summaries tell you what you need to know. If you want to look at more and more paper—
Q: How do you know that the summaries tell you what you need to know? Have you ever seen any evaluation sheets created by the company's test riders?
A: No.
Q: How do you know and how can you be assured that riders didn't reach contrary conclusions that aren't included in the summary reports?
A: I guess I don't know that.

Practice Pointer: This is a very good line of questioning. Counsel has established that the witness has failed to consider potentially relevant information when forming her opinions. The expert would have been better served had she read the underlying evaluation sheets.

Example 2.20: Would opinion change if underlying assumptions changed?
Q: As a basis of one or all of your opinions, you've assumed as a fact on the date of the accident that Mr. Mobray was standing in line in a cash office area, is that correct?
A: Yes, I am.
Q: You've also assumed, in formulating one or more of your opinions, that he was kept waiting and I believe the period of time offered was for 15 minutes. Is that correct?
A: That's what the assumption was.
Q: If either of those assumptions is changed, would that affect your opinion in any way?
A: It might mitigate it some, but I'd still feel the procedure was incorrect.

Practice Pointer: Opposing counsel at deposition may attempt to get the expert to change, modify, or qualify her opinion. One of the techniques that counsel will use to "massage" the opinion is to attempt to shake the foundation of the opinion by modifying key assumptions.

The expert here correctly refused to instantly modify his opinion based on a nebulous change in an assumption. Note that counsel did *not* say how the assumption would be changed. If it was 14 minutes instead of 15 minutes, would that change the opinion? Experts can reply in a manner similar to the following:

> **Q:** If either of those assumptions is changed, would that affect your opinion in any way?
> **A:** I would consider any changes.

Or, alternatively:

Q: If either of those assumptions is changed, would that affect your opinion in any way?
A: It would depend on the changes.

Gather as Much Information as Possible

Discovery depositions are all about gathering as much information as possible about the expert, the expert's opinion, and the subject matter of the case. Experts are obligated to answer truthfully the questions put to them. They are not, however, required to volunteer information not asked for and do counsel's job for her. The best experts provide required information in response to the specific questions asked at the discovery deposition, but they do not volunteer information.

Included in counsel's attempt to gather information will be an effort to educate herself on the science involved in the expert's opinion. Questions concerning the science of an opinion serve a dual purpose. First, they educate counsel as to the underlying scientific principles or assumptions of the expert. Counsel can verify the validity of the scientific assumptions the expert is making with her own expert witness. Second, the questions help counsel get a better idea of how the expert may perform in front of a jury when attempting to testify about complicated technical matters. An expert witness is likely to perform well in front of a jury if he can explain complicated scientific or technical principles in terms a jury can understand.[4]

Counsel may play on the ego of the expert and his desire to "teach the world" all that he knows about his field. This is often accomplished with an open-ended, friendly, flattering question designed to get the expert talking.

Q: You testified that you didn't think this document was altered. You are an authority on altered documents. What are the different techniques used to alter documents?
Q: You literally wrote the book on detecting malingering. How many different tests are there available to detect malingering?

Example 2.21: Counsel has expert explain complex science

Q: What is an electronecessarystagnogram?
A: Nystagmus, N-Y-S-T-A-G-M-U-S, is the movement of the eyes, involuntary movement. An electronystagmogram is an electrical recording of that movement of the eyes.
Q: What, of what clinical significance, if any, is that test?
A: The nystagmus suggests that there is some abnormality in the neural network going from the vestibular, V-E-S-T-I-B-U-L-A-R, apparatus, the brain, or the eyes.

---

[4] For those interested in advanced training in this area, SEAK offers a one-day course on Persuasion Skills for Expert Witnesses. Please see www.seak.com.

Q: And if there is an abnormality on that test, what can it signify?
A: It depends, of course, upon what part of that neural network has been affected.

Practice Pointer: Counsel here may be sizing up the witness's ability to explain complicated technical principles to the jury.

Use the Expert to Help Counsel's Case

Counsel will attempt to use the opposing expert in an attempt to bolster his own case. This is commonly done in one of several ways. First, counsel will attempt to point out all the areas where you and the opposing expert are in agreement. This is a useful technique because counsel can then argue to the jury, "Even the defendant's expert agrees that…." Often, this technique is used when counsel cannot destroy the expert's credibility by showing bias or a lack of proper qualifications. Counsel may instead choose to concede your credibility and point out the many areas where your opinion supports his case.

Establish areas of agreement: Counsel may first attempt to use a series of brief direct questions that are intended to result in replies that are, or appear to be, beyond dispute. Why struggle to prove what the expert will admit? Counsel will ask questions to narrow the issues actually in dispute:

> **Q:** You do agree that the opposing expert is well qualified, correct?
> **Q:** Just because opposing experts disagree with you does not make them wrong, agreed?
> **Q:** You never visited the accident scene, correct?

Example 2.22: Narrowly worded "you would agree" question seeks concession from expert
Q: You would agree with me, according to the classification system, the way you used it, that a grade II fracture has a higher risk of infection than a grade I fracture?
A: I would say that's true.

Practice Pointer: Using the areas of agreement between the experts is an important technique to bolster the opposing expert's credibility.

Gain concessions: Counsel may attempt to get the expert to either make some concessions or appear to be inflexible. This may be done by asking questions to either elicit some concessions (usually minor) or, if all concessions are rejected, to portray the expert as rigid or biased:

> **Q:** Not every case of speeding results in an accident, correct?
> **Q:** In some cases, passengers with seat belts are more severely injured than they would have been if they were not belted, correct?
> **Q:** Sometimes airbags cause serious injuries, correct?

Changing assumptions to help opposing counsel's case: Counsel may attempt to show that if the expert's underlying factual assumptions are changed to match the facts that the opposing side asserts, the expert's opinion will change as well and support the opposing side's case. Many experts will not give an inch in this area, but they should. Experts should realize, and the jury will certainly realize, that an expert's opinion is only as good as the underlying factual assumptions, reports, correspondence, and test results upon which it is based. If those factual assumptions are changed, the expert's opinion may very well change to be favorable to the other side. If so, the expert should readily admit that if she assumes different facts, then her opinion *may* change. Failure to readily do so may make the expert appear evasive and may damage her credibility. Remember, it is the role of an expert witness to provide her best, honest opinion based upon the information that has been provided to her. It is not the expert's role to resolve all factual disputes in the case, nor is it the expert's role to act as an advocate for the party who retained her. Any perception that the expert is an advocate for the retaining party can severely damage her credibility.

Example 2.23: Expert is flexible
Q: Let's assume for the moment that the test results from the lab were inaccurate. Given this assumption, might you change your opinion?
A: Possibly, yes.

Practice Pointer: The expert handled this question well. It is unreasonable to state that you will not change your opinion no matter what the facts are.

Intimidate the Expert
Counsel may attempt to use the deposition as an opportunity to demonstrate to the expert the professional and personal price she will pay for continued involvement in the case. This price may be high as pointed questions about an expert's biases and qualifications (or lack thereof) are relevant to the expert's credibility. Counsel may use such pointed questions during deposition with the additional goal of keeping the expert off balance and making her apprehensive about her upcoming trial testimony. An expert who is off balance during a deposition is more likely to let slip a hasty answer that has not been carefully thought out and that may help the opposition. An apprehensive expert is more likely to be unsure of herself and thus be a less credible witness at trial. An expert who is concerned about her professional reputation may also be less likely to shade her testimony improperly.

The way to deal with this is to accept at the outset of the engagement that pointed questions about fees, biases, and qualifications are a legitimate and expected part of the case. The only way to avoid these questions is to decline to be involved as an expert witness. Seasoned experts keep cool during depositions and don't provide any hasty or ill-considered answers. The best experts do not fear a professional backlash from their testimony because they work hard to ensure that the testimony is truthful and based on accepted practices in their field.

Example 2.24: Trying to intimidate the expert with questions on past untruthful testimony and past mistakes

Q: Mr. Balzer, have you ever testified untruthfully?

A: I have testified on occasions and found that I had made a mistake.

Q: Could you tell me why Ken Dystra told the jury in the *Caldecott* trial that you were an embarrassment to yourself and to A-1 Auto Company?

A: I had run some tests that I found later were incorrect. The data I gathered was—I don't know whether it was accurate or not.

Q: And why did Mr. Dystra have to say you were an embarrassment to yourself and to A-1 if it was an inadvertent mistake?

A: Well, I was extremely embarrassed when I found that I had made a mistake in what I testified to and sat down on that evening, when I found the mistake, with Mr. Dystra and said, "I made a mistake here and it's something I shouldn't do. I'd like to recheck the data, recheck the testing, and present accurate information...."

Practice Pointer: The expert did a good job of handling this difficult line of inquiry. By being forthcoming and readily admitting his earlier mistake, he helped mitigate the damage done to his credibility. However, counsel's message has been delivered, namely, "If you testify incorrectly at trial, that black mark on your career will be front, center, and public."

Example 2.25: Threat of sending transcript to society's ethical section intimidates expert

Q: I want you to set aside rollovers in general—

A: Uh-huh.

Q: —and what I want you to do is to focus on this accident, Mr. Tabor's accident—

A: Uh-huh.

Q: What I want to know is if you have an opinion as to when the driver's door glass broke, keep in mind a copy of this transcript is being sent to your engineering society's section on ethical testimony, sir.

A: No, I'm not going to offer an opinion on when the driver's door glass broke.

Q: Okay. So, you've backed off of the opinion that it broke at the one-half to three-quarter mark then?

A: I'm not offering an opinion when it broke, and so if that means backed off, yes, I guess so.

Q: So you are backing off of that.

A: Yes.

Q: Okay. So, in sum, you cannot say when the driver's side window glass broke out, correct?

Practice Pointer: After 141 pages of transcribed deposition testimony, opposing counsel got the expert to "back off" some of his prior testimony. The threat of forwarding the transcript had the desired intimidating effect.

Learn as Much as Possible about the Opponent's Case to Evaluate Its Settlement Value

Counsel will attempt to clarify and learn as much as possible about the opponent's side of the case. This will enable counsel to evaluate the settlement value of the case more accurately. It will also help counsel prepare for the possible trial of the matter.

Counsel will take the opportunity to be educated by the expert (i.e., learn things he may not have been able to otherwise discover). Experts are well advised not to succumb to the temptation to show how much they know and go out of their way to educate counsel.

Friendly, open-ended questions playing to the expert witness's vanity and willingness to teach are used to obtain crucial information that may otherwise be unavailable to counsel. Seasoned experts don't give in to the temptation to provide more information than is asked for specifically.

Example 2.26: Expert's answers are longer than necessary

Q: How does weight distribution affect the handling characteristics of ATVs?
A: Well, weight distribution affects the development of the various forces that you're going to develop under various maneuvers under various terrains at the tires, which are part of developing, braking, acceleration and directional control. Weight transfer is a part of that, has to do with how that weight's transferred during various maneuvers, how the total design works in the weight transfer. And weight transaction is something that is a part of looking at little handling characteristics as well as a number of other factors.
Q: What other factors affect the handling characteristics of an ATV, other than weight distribution?
A: Power train design, acceleration characteristics, the nature of the tires, the nature of the suspension systems, operator location, operator movement, control inputs, position of the operator not only in movement but in terms of static sense. The nature of the interaction between the terrain and the tires. The attitude of the vehicle. There's a host of factors that go into handling. Those are just some of them.

Practice Pointer: Counsel has pumped the expert dry of information and has invited further questioning. The witness might have been better served had he responded more narrowly (but still responsively).

Learn What the Expert Did

Counsel here will get the expert to explain in as much detail as possible the process, procedures, tests, research, measurements, and the like that the expert used to reach his conclusions and opinions. The more detail the expert offers, the better opposing counsel will be able to understand the process for later cross-examination.

<u>What he did</u>
Q: What tests did you perform in this case prior to reaching your opinion?

<u>Why he did it</u>
Q: Can you explain the reason for performing each test?

<u>How he did it</u>
Q: Precisely how did you perform each test?

<u>The results obtained</u>
Q: Can you explain the results you obtained for each test performed?

<u>How the tests led to his conclusion</u>
Q: Please describe how each of the tests performed and the results obtained led to your opinions.

<u>What the expert did not do</u>
Q: Can you detail each additional test you could have performed but did not and tell me why you didn't perform each of these tests?

Get the Expert to Give an Opinion off the Top of His Head
Opposing counsel may try to add facts, alter facts, and pose hypothetical situations for the expert at deposition. Counsel here is trying to get the expert to give an "instant opinion" without having had the benefit of research, review, and thoughtful consideration. Please consider the following example.

Example 2.27: Expert refuses to give new opinion off the top of his head
Q: In your professional opinion, should the bank provide its guards with 2-way radios, so that the messenger guard could be in touch with the guard in the truck?
A: It certainly might help put the guard at ease, but I don't think it would necessarily prevent the incident. It's something I would have to study more than just give an opinion off the top of my head. I would look at a lot of data and a lot of facts and make that decision more scientifically than just off the top of my head today.

Practice Pointer: This expert faced additional facts and was asked to draw an instant conclusion/opinion based on these facts. He correctly pointed out that to formulate an opinion he would need to think about it and also study data and reconsider the facts before reaching an opinion. The expert may have been better served without his initial speculation ("It certainly might help put the guard at ease, but I don't think it would necessarily prevent the incident.")

Set the Stage for a Motion to Disqualify the Expert or Throw Out His Opinion
Many claims legally require expert testimony for them to be placed in front of a jury. An important tool attorneys use in litigation is to attempt to dismiss the case, or parts of the case, before trial by attacking the expert witness and his conclusions. One of the goals of opposing counsel may be to gather evidence that can later be used to disqualify the expert or to throw out the expert's opinion. This can be done in different ways:

1. The expert's qualifications can be closely examined to set up a motion to disqualify the expert from testifying at trial. Please see Section 5.2 for more on qualifications questions.
2. The expert's methodology can be closely questioned in an attempt to later legally exclude the testimony based upon Federal Rule of Evidence 702 and the *Daubert* line of cases. For more on likely methodology questions, please see Section 5.7.
3. The expert may be pushed hard on his opinions to determine one of two things:
   - The expert is not sufficiently confident in his opinion for that opinion to be admissible in court. For example, the expert phrases his opinion in terms of the possible, not the probable (please see Section 6.5).
   - The expert's opinion is not sufficient to satisfy a particular requirement of the case at hand. For example, in a medical malpractice case, the plaintiff's experts would need to testify that the doctor breached the standard of care *and* that that breach caused the patient harm. If the plaintiff's expert does not have an opinion on causation and there are not other plaintiff's experts, opposing counsel may be able to have the case dismissed through a motion for summary judgment for lack of proof on the element of causation.

2.6 Conclusion
Counsel's goals at a deposition will vary depending upon whether the deposition is a discovery deposition or a preservation of evidence deposition. The discovery deposition of an expert should help counsel prepare for trial. The expert's discovery deposition will also help each side evaluate the settlement value of the case more accurately. To excel during depositions, an expert needs to keep in mind the goals of counsel explained in this chapter and remember his role in the litigation.

Chapter 3 Preparing for Your Deposition

3.1 Introduction and Executive Summary

Experts who thoroughly prepare are far more likely to excel during their depositions. The benefits to diligent preparation include the following:

- increased confidence and peace of mind for the expert and
- increased likelihood that the expert will testify to the best of his ability.

The authors recommend several strategies for adequate deposition preparation:

- Hold a pre-deposition conference with retaining counsel.
  - During deposition, however, opposing counsel is allowed ask questions regarding the pre-deposition conference. It is unwise to be defensive or evasive when asked about the meeting.
  - The expert should request that retaining counsel hold an extensive mock deposition with him. This will help familiarize the expert with possible areas of questioning at deposition.
  - It is wise to go over other critical information such as the status of the litigation, housekeeping details, the pertinent legal standard, the amount of detail counsel would like the expert to provide, and any *Daubert* issues that counsel foresees.
- The expert should prepare thoroughly on his own. This involves the following steps:
  - Having a full, complete, and exhaustive knowledge of the facts in the case.
  - Knowing one's CV cold.
  - Possessing intimate and complete familiarity with any reports or other documents that the expert has authored or signed in the case.
  - Personally touching every piece of paper in the file.
  - Organizing the file oneself to allow quick and easy access to information even while under great stress.
  - Thinking of the most difficult questions that counsel might ask and being prepared to truthfully and artfully reply to them.
  - Being able to express and defend each and every opinion the expert has expressed in the case.
- Finally, if there is not enough time to prepare, the expert should *have the deposition rescheduled.*

3.2 The Importance of Thorough Preparation

Experienced and sophisticated expert witnesses understand the critical need for complete and thorough preparation prior to being deposed. An expert's reputation and credibility are on the line. The attorney who will examine the expert will most likely prepare thoroughly for the deposition. The best trial attorneys are not necessarily the smartest attorneys. They are usually the ones who work hard and prepare thoroughly. Expert witnesses must do the same to excel during deposition. The fact that an expert may be able to charge for his reasonable preparation time should remove any reason for not spending the time to become fully prepared.

The price of not being properly prepared may be high. Any oversights, mistakes, or errors made due to a lack of preparation will become a permanent part of one's "expert witness baggage." Not only is it likely to affect the result in the underlying case, but one's future as an expert witness could be damaged permanently as well.

Experts who prepare properly and exhaustively for deposition are in the best position to excel. Knowing that he is prepared will increase the expert's confidence and the likelihood that he will testify to the best of his ability. Opposing counsel will size up prepared experts as likely to be effective in front of a jury. Thoroughly prepared experts are valuable experts.

Example 3.1: Every case the expert is involved in becomes part of the expert's permanent record

Q: Okay. Mr. Rayend, have you ever been barred from testifying as an expert?
A: Well, let's see. Once in Virginia federal court.
Q: What was the name of that case?
A: Oh God. Something versus ACME Industries.
Q: Okay. It was a nail gun case?
A: Yes. You obviously seem to know about that one. So that, you know, that was—went up on appeal.
Q: And was reversed?
A: Reversed and retried.
Q: Any other cases?
A: And a case in Virginia where it was alleged that this—that relying on crash test data was hearsay evidence and that, therefore, I could not testify.
Q: Do you know the name of that case?
A: I can't remember that one.
Q: In how many other cases were you barred from testifying as an expert?

Practice Pointer: What happens in one case that you are involved in can and will be brought up in subsequent cases. To do the best job possible in your current case, you need to prepare thoroughly.

There is another important benefit of thorough preparation. That benefit is peace of mind. Giving an expert deposition can be stressful. There may be much anxiety in the period leading up to the deposition. A great way to reduce this anxiety is to prepare thoroughly. Another benefit is that a prepared expert is less likely to make a mistake at deposition that can be used against her if she is later called upon to testify at trial.

3.3 Conference with Counsel

Prior to being deposed, the expert should insist on a conference with counsel representing the party who retained her services. Counsel may, in an attempt to save time and money, advise the expert that no such conference is necessary and that he will come "a few minutes early" to the deposition to talk things over. While this may be expedient for counsel, it will almost always result in inadequate preparation for the expert. This type of last-minute review is a recipe for disaster and experts should refuse to participate in it. Experts need time to organize their files and their thoughts. Wise experts insist on a separate appointment with counsel days—not hours or minutes—prior to the date of the deposition.

To ensure proper preparation by retaining counsel, the expert should do the following:

- Consider a clause in one's retention agreement that allows the expert to withdraw from the case if not prepared properly.
- Ask, "Do you want me to be unprepared for my deposition in your case?"
- Take all reasonable steps to ensure that retaining counsel properly prepares the expert for deposition.

At the pre-deposition conference, counsel and the expert should discuss any areas or issues with which the expert is concerned. Areas to cover include the following:

1. Housekeeping details.
By definition, anything that the expert is concerned about may be a distraction and adversely affect her deposition preparation and performance. Upon receipt of the deposition notice/subpoena, thorough preparation calls for going over with retaining counsel the "little" but significant details:

- Anticipated length of the deposition.
- Where to park.
- How to dress.
- How many attorneys will likely be present.
- Will the deposition be videotaped?
- Who will pay for the deposition? Can payment be achieved prior to the deposition?
- Will the expert be paid for her time preparing for the deposition (approximate amount)?
- Will retaining counsel request the expert to agree to the usual stipulations and, if so, what are they?

2. The type of questions that opposing counsel will ask.
In complex or challenging cases, it is not unusual to have a "run-through" with a vigorous mock deposition by counsel or an associate. The most difficult questions will be asked. The expert will be given an opportunity to reflect on the questions and answers. Please see Chapter 5 for coverage of the types of questions experts should expect to be asked at deposition.

3. The questions (if any) retaining counsel will ask.

4. The pertinent legal standard for liability and causation.
A good way to obtain this information is to go over with retaining counsel the likely jury instructions.

5. Identifying any privileged information or work product contained in the expert's file.

6. A review of what the expert should and should not bring to the deposition.
This includes the expert's response to any subpoenas.

7. An update on the current status of the litigation.
Counsel may share documents, interrogatories, and pleadings with the expert. If these are not forthcoming, the expert may request them for review prior to deposition.

8. A discussion with counsel of any prior contrary opinions the expert may have rendered in other cases.
Problems are best dealt with when they are anticipated and disclosed to retaining counsel in advance.

9. A review of the expert's qualifications with a discussion of the bases for her opinions and how they fit into the case.
The expert should be prepared to "connect the dots" and succinctly and convincingly state why she is qualified.

10. Amount of detail to provide.
This will depend upon whether counsel is trying to settle the case or is anticipating a trial. Please see Section 6.4. Does counsel want to limit the expert's answers primarily to "yes," "no," or short but truthful replies? Are there particular areas of inquiry/questions that counsel would like answered with as much detail as possible? These could include:

- opinions,
- methodology,
- computations, and
- references relied upon.

11. Will there be a Daubert *issue?*

The expert and retaining counsel should discuss if a *Daubert* challenge to the expert's testimony is likely. If the expert is not very well prepared to defend his methodology, his opinion may be stricken later. Areas the expert should be prepared to address regarding his opinion include the following:

- the theories and techniques used and how and when they have been tested,
- the error rate or potential error rate,
- peer-reviewed literature that supports the conclusions and opinions,
- the reliability of the scientific data used and whether they are generally accepted in the scientific community,
- use of appropriate methodology, and
- whether the opinion is for litigation only.

A comprehensive pre-deposition conference has many benefits. First and foremost, the expert will be given a fairly good idea of the types of questions that may be asked. For more on this, please see Chapter 5. The expert will have an opportunity to think about the difficult questions posed and truthful and artful replies. Experts who are ill-prepared quickly reveal this at deposition. The expert will also be updated on the status of the case and will have counsel review the applicable legal standards and "magic words" that must be used when giving an expert opinion. Finally, there will be an opportunity for counsel to review the expert's file prior to it being produced at the deposition (if it has been subpoenaed).

Example 3.2: Expert ill-prepared for deposition
Q: When did you first get involved in this case?
A: I am uncertain of the date.
Q: Can you give me a broad sense?
A: Probably about six months ago, I believe, and it was informal discussions with Doctor Samuel Brinson.
Q: So you think that your first involvement in this case was about six months ago?
A: I believe so, and I'm not very confident in my memory on that.
Q: Now, if I told you that the initial report provided to us by Tucker and Co. is older than six months, would that change your view?
A: Well, yes. I mean it could have been as far out as a year and a half ago, and my memory over the last year and a half is—I've been very busy lately.
Q: Okay. Tell me about the first recollection you have about being involved in the Waltz case.
A: The first recollection I have is actually sitting down in Doctor Samuel Brinson's office and discussing what the occupant's likely movements would have been in this vehicle in the accident. It was an informal discussion.

Q: And do you have a reference date for when that sit-down with Doctor Brinson occurred?
A: I do not.
Q: Okay. Can you give me an approximate time on that?
A: No, sir, I really can't, no sir.
Q: So you're unsure when that occurred?
A: Yes, sir.
Q: It might have been six months ago or it might have been a year and a half ago?
A: Yes, sir.
Q: Okay. Was there anybody else in the room when that conversation occurred?
A: I don't believe so.

Practice Pointer: This is not the best way to start a deposition. The expert does not appear to have been properly prepared for his deposition. Expert witnesses need to prepare for deposition as if they were studying for a final exam in a difficult graduate-level course. While the expert is not expected to memorize each and every fact, a certain amount of familiarity with the case is important. The fact that the expert has admitted his memory is poor and then goes on to prove this does not bode well for the remainder of the deposition. The expert should either memorize or at least be able to ascertain when he was first contacted by looking at the file.

Example 3.3: Magic words
Q: Doctor, do you have an opinion as to whether or not the claimant's carpal tunnel syndrome was related to her employment?
A: Yes, I do.
Q: And what is that opinion?
A: To a reasonable degree of medical certainty, her carpal tunnel syndrome is related to her employment.

Practice Pointer: During the pre-deposition conference, counsel may have reminded the witness that in order to be legally sufficient, her testimony needs to be based on "a reasonable degree of medical certainty." The conference may have helped prevent the witness from stating something such as, "I think it's related."

Questioning about Preparation
There is a downside to a pre-deposition conference with counsel. Opposing counsel can and will inquire about the meeting and what was and was not discussed. Skillful counsel will attempt to turn a legitimate pre-deposition conference with counsel into a nefarious activity with conspiratorial overtones. One should be neither defensive nor evasive when asked about meeting with counsel prior to the deposition to discuss the facts of the case and one's opinions. This is a legitimate activity that will most likely also be used by the opposing side and its experts. An expert who responds defensively to questions about meetings with counsel plays into opposing counsel's

hands. However, if one is not defensive about having met with counsel, the significance of the meeting will most likely be downplayed. Experts are best served to keep in mind the maxim that "the cover-up is worse than the crime."

Example 3.4: Being asked about conversations with retaining counsel
Q: First of all, sir, are you here as a fair and impartial witness?
A: Yes.
Q: You indicated to Attorney Garcia that you don't care about the outcome of the case one way or the other?
A: Right.
Q: Okay. Would you explain why you met with Attorney Garcia behind closed doors for forty-five minutes before you gave your deposition today?
A: I generally do that. He requested to meet with me and I did that.
Q: Well, you were informed by your staff that I had arrived for the deposition, correct?
A: Yes.
Q: And you did not invite me in, did you?
A: No, I did not.
Q: During that private conference, you and Attorney Garcia had conversations about this case?
A: Yes.
Q: Please detail for the jury what you and Attorney Garcia discussed behind closed doors for forty-five minutes immediately prior to this video deposition taken in lieu of live testimony, sir.

Practice Pointer: This is a common and legitimate area of inquiry. The witness did a good job in not being evasive or defensive about the meeting. A truthful answer to the last question might be, "We discussed the procedures that will be used, the probable completion time of my testimony, and the probable questions I would be asked."

Example 3.5: Opposing counsel successfully shows that retaining counsel influenced the expert
Q: The report that you prepared that's dated February 17, 2007, were there any drafts of that report prepared?
A: No, I mean other than—I don't know what a "draft" is, but I used my computer. So, if there was a draft it was destroyed in the process of preparing it. I don't think there were any other copies.
Q: Was there any other version sent to Mr. Prahn other than the one dated February 17, 2007?
A: May I see that?
Q: Yes.

A: Yes.

Q: Do you have a copy of the other version?

A: No, but I can tell you exactly what the difference was.

Q: Okay.

A: That paragraph after item No. 6 was added.

Q: The portion where you say you would like to reserve the opportunity to amend your opinions?

A: Right.

Q: Was that inserted at the suggestion of counsel when you met with him?

A: Yes, I'd have to say he and I—

Q: He pretty much offered that paragraph for you?

A: I wouldn't say that. He said he had these other depositions which were referred to in my earlier correspondence that I was supposed to be reviewing and I hadn't received them yet. And so he said wait up on that until after I send you those depositions, but he had already committed to sending them to me prior to that particular day. So, yes, the answer is he wanted me to be sure to look at those.

Practice Pointer: You need to be prepared to testify about what was said and done during the pre-deposition conference with counsel. If counsel improperly influences your opinion, this will have a negative effect on your credibility.

Role-Playing with Counsel
Retaining counsel should be willing to subject the expert witness to at least one extensive session in which the expert is questioned as if he were being deposed. This session will greatly assist the expert to:

- be familiar with deposition questioning,
- face many difficult questions prior to the deposition, and
- become comfortable with issues and questions.

3.4 Preparing by Oneself
Although a preparation session with retaining counsel is extremely important, most of an expert's preparation time will be by himself. Successful experts set aside sufficient time to prepare alone. These experts develop and use a standard deposition preparation protocol that may include having the following at their command:

- an exhaustive knowledge of the facts in the case, including names and dates,
- thorough knowledge of the expert CV,
- an intimate and complete familiarity with any reports or other documents the expert has authored or signed in the case,
- personally touching every piece of paper in the file,
- organizing the file so the expert can access information quickly and easily even while under great stress (binders and tabs help greatly),

- thinking of the most difficult questions and being prepared to truthfully and artfully reply to them, and
- being able to express and defend each and every opinion the expert has expressed in the case.

The Facts of the Case

The expert needs to completely master the important facts of the case. These facts include names and dates. Remember, an opinion is only as good as the facts upon which it is based. If the expert gets the facts wrong during the deposition, his opinion may become worthless and his reputation and marketability as an expert witness may be severely damaged. The only way to master the facts of the case prior to deposition is to do one's homework and thoroughly prepare.

Example 3.6: Mastery of the facts

Q: Would you agree that Dr. Sohal could have just called home and stated, "I want to talk to you"?
A: You asked him that at his deposition and he explained the ethical reasons he did not do so.

Practice Pointer: There is no substitute for preparing so you have full command of the facts and the record. Without these facts and awareness, you will not know when opposing counsel is asking original questions, mischaracterizing testimony, or trying to create conflicts between experts and the parties.

There are many advantages to knowing the facts cold. The expert can fall back on the facts when asked a difficult question and he can recognize a question that is not based in fact. Because his opinions will be well-founded, the expert will make a powerful impression on opposing counsel. One of the main goals of opposing counsel is to size up the expert as a witness and determine how good of an impression he is likely to make in front of a jury. Thoroughly prepared experts are likely to make a very good impression in front of a jury. This fact will not be lost on opposing counsel.

Example 3.7: Falling back on the facts when asked a difficult question

Q: What specifically did Dr. Smith do to violate the standard of care?
A: As I detailed in my report, there were seven things. One…

Practice Pointer: Thoroughly prepared experts can be extremely effective.

Example 3.8: Calling counsel on a factually incorrect premise

Q: Did Dr. Smith violate the standard of care when he failed to order a CT scan on March 6, 2007?
A: According to the medical records, he did order a CT scan, Counselor.

Practice Pointer: Only a prepared expert can provide such an answer.

Example 3.9: Research indicates well-founded opinion
Q: Can you cite any research that supports your conclusions?
A: Yes, the following 12 peer reviewed papers support my conclusions. First,....

Practice Pointer: Prepared experts are ready to explain why their opinions are valid. They do not forget to mention key information, bases, facts, data, research, etc.

Review Important Dates
Successful expert witnesses review the crucial dates in the case. Many commit them to memory. These dates include the following:

- when the expert was first contacted by counsel,
- when the expert was retained as an expert,
- when the records were received and from whom they were received,
- when the expert formed his opinion(s) in the case,
- the date of the accident in question, and
- the date(s) key tests were performed.

Accurate testimony regarding dates greatly increases an expert's credibility. Failure to keep the relevant dates straight will damage one's credibility.

Example 3.10: Expert familiar with dates and facts
Q: What happened on July 17, 1998 in this man's life?
A: His brother died.
Q: When was the decedent born?
A: 1939.
Q: Who is Martha in this case?
A: Martha is the wife of the decedent.
Q: How many children did the decedent have?
A: Four living and one who died.

Practice Pointer: The expert here was intimately familiar with the dates and facts. Opposing counsel quickly saw that there was no advantage to be gained by continuing to test his knowledge of the dates and facts. The expert is not expected to memorize each and every fact in complex cases. However, the more familiar the expert is with the dates and facts, the easier his deposition will be.

Example 3.11: Inability to keep dates straight
Q: Do you know when you were first contacted by the attorneys for WeCare?
A: No.
Q: Do you keep a log of phone contacts related to this case?
A: There would be a log on the scheduling book, but for the most part, there's not a date associated with that.

Q: Do you recall if you had any conversations with the attorneys for WeCare before receiving the July 7, 2007, letter that you have in your file?
A: I can't recall any specific conversations....

Practice Pointer: How much credibility do you think a jury will give to an expert who cannot keep his dates straight?

Example 3.12: Date report dictated
Q: You don't know what date you dictated this report, do you?
A: Well, it would have to be right around March 26. I really don't know.
Q: You have no indication in the file as to the date?
A: No.
Q: There is no signature on the file copy or the copy that I've been provided of the report which has your father's name?
A: I do not have one in my file. I can't tell you if the original went to Memphis Associates with a signature or to the Board or to Murdoch.
Q: So there's no indication in your file that you ever reviewed this report of March 26 of 2007 after it was typed. Isn't that right?
A: There's no notation of that....

Practice Pointer: The failure of the expert to know when his report was dictated will lessen his credibility.

Know Your CV Cold
An expert should expect to have the contents of his CV carefully probed at deposition. As part of the preparation process, it is crucial for experts to update and fact-check the accuracy of their CVs carefully. Failure to do so can result in needless damage to one's credibility that could have been easily avoided through proper preparation.

If the expert's CV is subpoenaed, he will be required to bring it to the deposition and produce it to counsel. Experts should be very cautious about having multiple versions of their CVs (for example, long ones, short ones, and, worst of all, different CVs that emphasize various aspects of experience and expertise). Skillful counsel will portray this as an attempt to slant the CV to curry favor with the party who is considering retaining the expert.

Example 3.13: Current CV
Q: I'm handing you what I've marked as deposition Exhibit #1. Is this the current copy of your CV?
A: As far as I can tell. I don't know. I don't think it's been revised since this, but let me just check. It's hard to tell....

Practice Pointer: Experts can expect to be asked many difficult questions at deposition. Being asked if this is your current CV is not one of them. Experts should date their CVs so they can simply and promptly identify the latest version.

Example 3.14: Consequences of failure to update a CV

Q: Did you bring a copy of your curriculum vitae here today?
A: Yes, I did.
Q: The CV that you handed me dated February 1, 2006. Is this your current CV?
A: Yes.
Q: Do you know when the last time was that you updated your CV?
A: February 1, 2006.
Q: Since that time, you have published, correct?
A: Yes.
Q: Since February 1, 2006, you have lectured, correct?
A: Yes.
Q: Are these reflected in your CV?
A: No...I guess I really should update it.
Q: What other activities are not reflected in your February 1, 2006, CV, sir?
A: Well....

Practice Pointer: Failure to take the simple step of updating his CV has caused the witness to needlessly lose credibility.

Example 3.15: "Forgetting" to bring CV

Q: Did you bring a copy of your resume with you today?
A: No, I didn't.
Q: Well, I knew that was your practice, Mr. McDonald, not to bring it, so I brought one for you.

Practice Pointer: Experts who decide to be clever and leave their CVs home can anticipate this type of exchange.

Example 3.16: Different version of CV

Q: You have several different versions of your CV, do you not?
A: Well, I have a complete CV and a shortened version for faxing.
Q: I show you four different versions of your CV dated 2005. Are these your CVs?
A: Yes.
Q: Isn't it a fact that you have a "defense" CV you send to insurance companies and a "plaintiff" CV you send to plaintiff's counsel, sir?
A: No...well, I do have different CVs that emphasize different....

Practice Pointer: Having "defense" and "plaintiff" CVs should be avoided. If this is discovered, you will appear to be for sale to the highest bidder and your credibility will be lessened.

Example 3.17: Being able to identify latest CV

Q: Now, I did not receive, prior to today, a copy of your curriculum vitae.

A: Okay.

Q: I did pull one off the Internet, but it's dated from April of 2004. But have you brought a more recent curriculum vitae with you today?

A: Yes, sir.

Q: Thank you. Well, let's do this: since there are some differences in the CVs that you have brought and the one that was available on the Internet, I'm going to initially mark as exhibit number 2 a copy of the CV that you have brought, which is dated March 18, 2005. And your CV also includes a list of prior testimony. Is that correct?

A: Yes, sir.

Q: Okay. I show that to you and I ask you whether that is your current curriculum vitae, sir?

A: Yes, sir, I believe it is. Let's see. From what I can tell, this is fairly current.

Q: Well, you might want to take a look at this and just determine whether, for instance, there are any additional publications or presentations that you've been involved in or that you have prepared that are not included on this CV.

A: Yeah, that's—yes, sir, that's what I looked at. I looked to see if it had the most recent publication and the most recent deposition, and it did.

Q: It did?

A: Yes, sir.

Q: Okay. And is your prior testimony list up to date?

A: Yes, sir.

Q: So the last case in which you were deposed, or gave testimony, was on January 25, 2005?

A: That's correct.

Q: I'm going to mark as exhibit number 3 a copy of your resume dated April 16, 2004, which I took off the Internet, from Rogers Engineering, and I'll show that to you and just confirm for me whether that is, in fact, a copy of your resume.

A: Yes, sir.

Q: Now, I note when we compare your current resume from March 18, 2005 with the one from April 16, 2004, you have a whole new area of expertise that's not previously listed. Is that correct, sir?

A: Let me see it. To some extent it is considered new. I mean, until the time that I split this out, I really considered the occupant safety systems part of the occupant kinematics and injury biomechanics, as far as how the person perform—behaved as they related to those vehicles. So, it's more of a marketing tool to split out.

Q: Well, I don't see in your earlier resume, sir, where you talk specifically about occupant safety systems and analysis of seatbelts and airbags and interior impacts and crashworthiness.

A: That's correct.

Q: And it's not spelled out in your resume?

A: It's not spelled out, that's correct.

Q: So, this new area in your resume, which is current, is not spelled out in the prior resume, correct, sir?

A: That's correct. I wouldn't say it's a new area, though. I just—I feel like it's more one that's pulled out of another area.

Q: It wasn't declared previously. Is that correct?

A: That's correct.

Q: You didn't hold yourself out as an expert in occupant safety systems explicitly—

A: That's correct.

Q: —before?

A: That's correct.

Q: What has happened between April 16, 2004 and March 18, 2005, to ask you to declare these subjects explicitly, sir?

A: Well, like I said, I think that I just explained that. It's a continuation of expertise that I've actually been involved in all along. It's just that I separated it out from an area that I considered it to be part of before for the purpose of a more clear understanding.

Q: Thank you, sir. Now, your resume, your current resume which we've marked as exhibit 2, has nine publications, and you've already told me that that's complete. Is that correct, sir?

A: Yes, sir.

Q: Now, your earlier resume, which was April 16, 2004, has five articles on it, and the latest of those—I guess that's a publication list, and your current list is a publications and presentations list?

A: Yes, sir.

Q: Okay. So, since the earlier resume, you've added some presentations and perhaps—

A: At least one publication.

Q: —at least one publication. Which is the publication that you've added, sir? Do you want to take a look at that? I can show you both, if that helps out.

A: 8 and 9 both are publications that've been added. One's a comprehensive evaluation of NHTSA rollover test data for the use in computational model validation, and the other one is a peer review publication. An experimental examination of seatbelt webbing, loading marks on automotive plastic D-rings.

Practice Pointer: The expert should have his most current CV in hand and have the same CV posted on the company Web site. One good way of being able to quickly identify your CV is by putting a date on it. That would have avoided the reply, "From what I can tell, this is fairly current." The most serious problem created by the differing CVs is at least the implication raised by counsel that the expert modified his

CV at the last moment to increase his credibility and qualifications for the case at hand. Opposing counsel may have been saving that damaging accusation for the trial.

Other CV issues the expert should prepare to explain with retaining counsel include the following:

Publications
- What articles, book chapters, books, reviews, or abstracts have you written?
- Where and when were they published?
- Were there co-authors?
- Are any writings pending publication?
- Have any writings been rejected for publication?

Presentations
- Where have you spoken?
- What was the topic?
- What were the dates?
- Did you prepare written materials?
- Were you audiotaped or videotaped?
- Are the conference brochures or handbooks available?
- Do you have the materials from the presentations?
- Were these marketing talks or talks to educate colleagues?

Relevant practical experience
- What relevant practical (hands-on) experience do you have with regard to the issues in the case?

Litigation experience
- Have you testified in a lawsuit before?
- Where, when, and how often?
- How much of your income is derived from testifying and preparing to do so?
- Do you advertise your services? If so, where, when, and how?
- How did you get into this case?
- Have you served as an expert for this lawyer or firm before? If so, how often?

Accuracy
- Was your CV 100% accurate when written?
- Has anything changed since the CV was written?
- Was your CV 100% accurate when presented to counsel?

Timeline and gaps
- Have you listed your inclusive dates of work, education, and other activities?
- Do you have gaps in your CV timeline?

Prior CVs
- Are your prior CVs consistent with your current one?
- Are there material changes, omissions, or alterations that open lines of inquiry?

Multiple CVs
- Do you have more than one current CV?
- Are your multiple CVs prepared and used for different clients?

Professional societies and certifications
- Are the affiliations listed current?
- Have you removed those organizations in which you merely paid a fee and obtained the credentials?

Writings
- Are the dates, titles, and claims to authorship accurate?
- Have you listed co-authors?
- Have you exaggerated the importance of the publication or your role in it?

Self-serving comments
- Have you made self-serving comments that can be taken out of context and used to cross-examine you?

Previous cases
- Do you list the cases you have worked on?
- Do you list the cases' outcomes?
- Should you consider removing these from your CV?

Know Your Report Cold

Experts simply must know their own reports cold. Failure to do so is inexcusable and will result in avoidably ineffective deposition testimony. A thoroughly researched, thoughtfully reasoned, and well-written report can be of invaluable assistance in preparing to testify.[1]

Example 3.18: Lack of knowledge of facts and report

Q: In the Szabo test, how many exposures had a delta-V in excess of 6.1 miles per hour?

A: If you can direct me to it, that would save me a little bit of time....I'm sorry. I think I have it. Page 11?

Q: I think so.

A: Vehicle kinematics. The impact velos—well, I got the impact velocity for delta-V. I'm doing the calculation in my head. What is the number? I should have brought

---

[1] For more information on report writing, please see Babitsky and Mangraviti, *Writing and Defending Your Expert Report* (SEAK 2002) and SEAK's one-day Expert Report Writing Workshop (see www.seak.com for more details).

a calculator. It would appear only two of those tests were over the—that produce a delta-V of higher than 6.1 miles per hour.

Q: Which two are they?

A: Those are the two that are listed as kilometers per hour of 10. The 9.6 kilometers per hour is just about 6 miles an hour, so it's not quite 6.1.

Q: Okay. Can you tell me with regard to those two collisions in excess of 6.1 miles per hour, how many test subjects?

A: Well, now I'm trying to figure out which test subjects were in which test.

Q: Let me ask you, when you told me that there were two, you were looking at Table 3?

A: Yes.

Q: Under delta-V?

A: Correct.

Q: Okay. If we go over to the left, there's five—there's two sets of five tests with the letters A through E.

A: Okay.

Q: Do we presume that the first test that was 10 was subject D and the second test was subject A?

A: Probably.

Q: Okay.

A: Without checking the rest of the report to be sure of that, it would appear to be that way, but I'm, you know….

Practice Pointer: The expert must know the facts and her own reports cold. This expert did not and, thus, was a less valuable witness.

The Expert's File

The best experts touch every piece of paper in their file prior to being deposed. This helps the expert to be familiar with the file. It also serves to check to whether there is any extraneous information in the file.

Having a well-organized file is a must. It is preferable to place the file into three-ringed binders that are tabbed and have a table of contents. This serves two important functions. First, it allows the expert to quickly locate documents he may need to refer to in the deposition. Second, it gives the impression to opposing counsel that the expert is diligent and well organized. Remember that opposing counsel is sizing up what kind of an impression the expert is likely to make in front of a jury. An expert with an organized file is likely to make a much better impression than one who arrives with a sloppy, disorganized file.

Questions the Expert Is Likely to Be Asked
As part of the pre-deposition conference with retaining counsel, the expert will most likely go over some of the questions he is likely to be asked. One should also do this as part of one's preparation by oneself. The preparation process should consist of anticipating the questions that are likely to be asked *and* thinking about the truthful and artful answers that the expert will provide to each of these questions. The best experts have anticipated the questions they will face at deposition and have already thought about their responses. Please refer to Chapters 5, 6, and 11 for detailed coverage of the types of questions an expert can expect to be asked at deposition.

The Expert's Opinions
First and foremost, experts need to be prepared to express their opinions in a legally sufficient manner. The expert will also need to cogently explain the bases for these opinions and why he is qualified to give them. For more on opinion questions at deposition, please see Section 5.4.

Rest and Relaxation
Expert witnesses should come to depositions well rested. In addition, one's anxiety level can be reduced by leaving adequate time to be deposed. If the lawyers say it will take two hours, plan on four to be safe. Nothing is worse than a lawyer recognizing that an expert is time-pressed to finish his testimony. If counsel recognizes this, she may use it against the expert in an effort to have him concede contested points.

3.5 What to Do If You Are Not Properly Prepared
Adequate preparation is essential for proper performance during depositions. A failure to properly prepare may result in needless mistakes that will damage an expert's credibility and reduce his marketability as an expert witness in future cases.

The question arises as to what to do if the expert and the attorney do not have time to prepare properly. The authors have two recommendations. First, find the time. An expert should make preparation for the deposition a priority and insist that counsel take the time to talk with him prior to the deposition. This meeting can be done over the phone if necessary.

Second, the deposition can be rescheduled. *Depositions are very commonly rescheduled or "put over" for illness, scheduling conflicts, and even for no stated reason at all.* If an expert does not feel prepared for a deposition or does not have time to adequately prepare, he should ask his retaining attorney to try to reschedule it. It is likely that she will be able to do so. It is more likely that she will be able to do so the earlier the expert asks for the rescheduling. Depositions are scheduled by the parties and are often rescheduled. An expert should not be afraid to ask retaining counsel to attempt to reschedule the deposition if necessary.

Example 3.19: Ill-prepared expert
Q: You used the term "psychiatric or neuropsychiatric." What is the difference between psychiatric and neuropsychiatric?
A: I think neuropsychiatric usually would refer to some psychiatric problem that has a neurologic overlay or component. Neurobiologic.
Q: Is there a specialty in the field of psychiatry of neuropsychiatry?
A: No. Although, psychiatry is a part of—there's an American Board of Psychiatry & Neurology, you know, which accredits people in either specialty or both, but there is no—there is no specialty of neuropsychiatry *per se.* It's psychiatry and neurology.
Q: Would you say that you're a neuropsychiatrist?
A: I think so....

Practice Pointer: This expert appears ill-prepared to answer counsel's questions. As a result, the expert has made a poor impression. Maybe this expert would have been better served by requesting a postponement of the deposition until he could have better prepared himself.

3.6 Conclusion
The expert witnesses who generally perform best at deposition are those who are thoroughly prepared. Preparation is a great opportunity and equalizer for experts because it is something to a large extent within the expert's own control. If the expert works diligently to prepare, she will likely excel at her deposition.

Chapter 4 Subpoenas, Subpoenas Duces Tecum, and the Use of Documents at Deposition

4.1 Introduction and Executive Summary

Prior to being deposed, an expert will usually be served with either a subpoena or a subpoena duces tecum:

- Subpoena
    - Failure to appear when subpoenaed can result in sanctions and possible civil liability.
    - Inform counsel immediately if a scheduling conflict or emergency arises. Most times, depositions can be rescheduled to accommodate the expert's conflict.
- Subpoena duces tecum
    - The expert must produce designated documents at the deposition.

The authors suggest the following regarding producing and referring to documents during a deposition:

- Only bring requested documents to the deposition. Remove extraneous materials from the file (such as misfiled documents from unrelated cases).
- At deposition, confirm that you are referring to the correct document or exhibit.
- During the deposition, take time to read and review a document before answering any questions about it.
- Do not destroy, hide, "lose," or fail to produce notes, cover letters, or billing records.

4.2 The Subpoena

Depositions for expert witnesses are often scheduled by the attorney serving the expert with *a notice of deposition*. This legal document will specify the name of the case and give the time and date of the deposition. In many cases, a subpoena to appear will also be served on the deponent. One of the reasons that counsel issues a subpoena is to protect himself. If an expert witness is not served with a subpoena and does not show up at a deposition, counsel can be liable for court costs including attorney's fees.[1]

Failure to Appear

Expert witnesses who receive a deposition notice and subpoena and who fail to appear at their deposition may subject themselves to court costs, counsel fees, contempt of court charges, and, in rare instances, suit for malpractice or negligence.

---

[1] Fed. R. Civ. Pro. 30(g)(2).

Federal Rule of Civil Procedure 45(e), dealing with subpoenas, provides, "Failure by any person without adequate excuse to obey a subpoena served upon that person may be deemed a contempt of the court from which the subpoena issued...."

As a practical matter, as soon as an expert witness becomes aware of the fact that he cannot make the deposition due to a conflict, illness, inclement weather, a family emergency, etc., the expert should notify both retaining counsel and counsel who has issued the subpoena. In most cases, the deposition will be rescheduled without difficulty. The major exception is when counsel is up against a court-ordered time deadline. Deadlines may make postponement difficult for all parties.

The expert witness who does not note his calendar and fails to appear at deposition will incur the wrath of both counsel who has retained him and opposing counsel. The expert may be liable for stenographic costs and reasonable attorney's fees. If, due to time deadlines or discovery schedules, counsel is not permitted to reschedule the expert's deposition and loses the case, the expert may be liable for negligence or professional malpractice. It is a good idea to have the cell phone number and the home phone number of counsel should emergencies arise. Note that the expert witness who shows up late or makes the attorneys wait acts unprofessionally and detracts from his value as an expert. Rushing to get to the deposition on time will increase the expert's level of stress and likely reduce his effectiveness at the deposition.

The Subpoena Duces Tecum
In many cases, a subpoena of the type that requires the production of certain items will accompany the notice of deposition. This type of subpoena is a *subpoena duces tecum*. The subpoena duces tecum is a very powerful discovery tool because it forces persons or parties who are not parties to the lawsuit to "produce and permit copying and inspection of designated books, documents, or tangible things in the custody or control of that person."[2] Notice that the rule only provides that the person who is served with the subpoena permit the documents or things to be inspected and copied. The attorney is not allowed to retain the inspected original documents and books. Another limitation is that the documents must be in the expert's "custody or control." The expert is not required to produce anything that is not in his "custody or control." These are legal terms and experts should consult with counsel for advice regarding what they mean.

The "designated books, documents, or tangible things" are specified in an attached *schedule* or list. Appendix E provides a sample of such a schedule.

The expert should have counsel review the documents that the expert intends to produce pursuant to the subpoena. Some of the information requested may be objectionable because it is privileged, a trial preparation document, unduly

---

[2] Fed. R. Civ. Pro. 45(a)(1)(C).

burdensome to produce, or for other reasons. The expert who is served with a subpoena duces tecum should do the following:

1. In the pre-deposition conference, she should have counsel review her subpoena and her file to see if some of the information requested need not be produced under the discovery rules.
2. She should not remove or try to hide potentially damaging documents.[3]
3. She should not produce requested documents that are not properly discoverable under the rules of discovery.

If there is any question regarding what is legally required to be produced, the expert should obtain independent legal advice.

Experts who are served with a subpoena duces tecum are obligated to appear and produce the documents "as they are kept in the usual course of business or shall organize and label them to correspond with the categories in demand" in the schedule.[4] Thus, the expert is not allowed to intentionally disorganize the requested documents in an effort to make life miserable for the opposing attorney.

Many problems can arise for experts who are unfamiliar with the rules or who try to play "fast and loose" with documents in their possession or control. Such conduct is a serious error in judgment, can damage one's reputation and credibility, and may result in civil and, in some cases, criminal penalties. An untruthful response to the simple question, "Is this your entire file?" or "Was anything removed from the file by you or anyone else?" could be perjurious if done intentionally.

What kinds of things will counsel look for in an expert's file?

The expert should be instructed to bring the entire contents of his or her file to the deposition. This can be done either by agreement with opposing counsel or by serving a subpoena duces tecum. Carefully review the original file maintained by the expert witness, paying particular attention to any notes or diagrams made by the witness, which may reveal his or her thought process. Copies of depositions or other file materials should be inspected page by page to see if the expert has made any notes, highlighting or other markings on these documents. These markings may provide important insight into what the expert views as significant supporting or damaging facts.[5]

Example 4.1: Expert forthcoming about file

Q: I ask you to look at this notice entitled "Notice of Deposition." Have you seen any part of this notice before coming here today?
A: Yes, I have a copy of this.
Q: Do you see attached to that a Schedule A?

---

[3] Remember two things: 1) the best experts are transparent and 2) the cover-up is worse than the crime.
[4] Fed. R. Civ. Pro. 45(d)(1).
[5] David R. Geiger, et. al, *Deposing Expert Witnesses* (Boston, MA: MCLE, 1993) p. 68. See Section 4.4 for more on the expert's notes.

A: Yes.

Q: Was that given to you before you came?

A: Yes, it was.

(Stenographer marked Exhibit Number Three.)

Q: I will ask you to use your copy.

A: Sure.

Q: Before coming here today, did you make an attempt to put together the materials that were requested on Schedule A?

A: Yes, I did.

Q: How did you do that?

A: I touched every piece of paper in my possession to make sure I complied with the notice of deposition.

Q: Have you brought with you notes that you prepared in the course of your inspection of the 480 DM Screener in the course of research on this case?

A: Yes, I have.

Q: Would you please produce those?

A: It's in this file right here and in this file right here.

Practice Pointer: The deponent was forthcoming and responsive regarding the production of materials that the attorneys have a legal right to inspect under the discovery rules. He did not set off any red flags or warning bells by acting evasively.

Problems can occur when the expert does not personally supervise her production of documents or does not ensure that a highly competent person does so. Irrelevant documents dealing with other cases and containing confidential information should not be produced.

In some cases, experts are careless and produce documents in their file relating to *other* cases. This is a needless error that can be avoided with proper preparation. Consider the following example.

Example 4.2: Extraneous material in file

Q: Professor, in this case have you brought your entire file with you?

A: I have.

Q: I see a letter from Mr. Rolland to Neal Riley regarding the case *Browning versus Chicago and Northwestern.* Are you an expert in that case?

A: That doesn't belong in that file. I don't know how it got in here.

Q: But the question is: Are you an expert in that case?

A: Yes. Can we put that aside so that I can separate it out of there?

Q: Sure. Have you testified in that case yet?

A: No.

Q: Is your deposition scheduled in that matter?

A: Not that I'm aware of.

Q: Some more correspondence regarding *Browning.* From Judith Piquard, two of them. Those have nothing to do with this case, right?
A: They do not.
Q: Did you bring with you your file today?
A: Yes.

Practice Pointer: When preparing, make a final check of the file to make sure only documents that have been requested are in the file to be produced. Documents that have not been requested that pertain to other cases should not be left in the file.

Example 4.3: Missing information results in continued deposition and wasted time

Q: May I see your file, Doctor?
A: Sure.
Q: Also, for the record, Doctor, you said there were certain X-rays that are available but not here?
A: From the original—those would be from the original visits, in '96 and '98, I believe.
Q: Could you find those for me?
A: I can ask them to pull them. I don't know if I can find them. I'll have the other people look for them.
Q: Is she getting those X-rays, Doctor?
A: She's looking for them, yes. She had to pull up the number and everything.
Q: Do you know how long it will be?
A: I don't have a clue. In my office it would be about two minutes, but here I can't tell you.
    Opposing Counsel: Counsel, can we meet on Wednesday, July 31 at 10:00 A.M.?
    Retaining Counsel: Yes, I think I can be here.

Practice Pointer: A few minutes of preparation could have avoided needless delay and having to come back for a continued deposition.

Documents Covered by Protective Orders
Experts may occasionally be faced with the competing demands of the obligation to testify truthfully at deposition and the obligation not to reveal confidential information covered by a protective order. In these circumstances, it is crucial to remember that neither opposing counsel at the deposition, nor retaining counsel at the deposition, nor counsel who is trying to protect the confidential information is the expert's attorney. Please consider the following example.

Example 4.4: Dealing with a request to produce a document protected by a protective order

Q: I'll ask you if you've seen this or an earlier version of this deposition notice prior to today (indicating).

A: Yes, sir.

Q: Have you reviewed that duces tecum prior to today—

A: Yes.

Q: —what I call on here Exhibit A? You've done that before?

A: Yes, sir.

Q: Have you searched your files and brought everything to the deposition today upon which you're relying for your opinions in this case?

A: Yes, largely. There's one thing I wanted to bring for this case which was Autopia discovery, the 1988 minivan testing. I spoke to an attorney who said that's protected, so I'll meet with him tomorrow and talk to him about it because it was my impression it was not.

Q: So you did not bring an Autopia document on the minivan?

A: Right. It's a whole document of the test regimen and then a videotape which is on a disk, actually, of the impacts.

Q: So it's a test document and a video?

A: Yes, sir.

Q: What model year minivan?

A: 1988.

Q: What kind of a test is it?

A: I want to be general here—

Q: I understand that.

A: —I don't want to get into legal trouble.

Q: I don't want you to violate the protective order, but if you can, tell me what kind of test it was. I won't ask you what the results were, but if you can, tell me the kind of test it was. If you, in your own mind, can make a judgment as to whether or not you think that would keep you on the right side of the protective order, then please answer.

A: Yes, it is an impact test of a Hybrid III side-impact dummy into a high-g sled with a door on it and bilaminate glass. Brian Golden said that this has been in the glass collection for years which makes me think it's unprotected, but that's in dispute.

Q: Who is Brian Golden?

A: He is a retired Autopia employee who does significant amounts of expert witnessing for defense attorneys regarding glass.

Q: He's a defense witness?

A: He is.

Q: Is he a witness who testified in the Morales case in Texas recently?

A: I believe so. I had already busted camp by the time they had their expert.

Q: I'm sorry?

A: I had already left by the time—after my testimony was called for.

Q: By the time Autopia began putting on its witnesses?

A: Right, and I haven't seen trial transcripts, but I think that's a pretty reasonable assumption here.

Q: And Brian Golden, although a defense witness, is someone you correspond with or talk with, at least, from time to time?

A: Yes.

Q: And he advised you that he thought that this document was subject to a protective order?

A: No, an attorney, Collin Holly, told me that.

Q: Collin Holly out of El Paso?

A: Yes, sir.

Q: Did Brian Golden say anything with respect to whether he thought the document was protected?

A: He said that it has been in the glass collection for years, and it's my understanding that everything in the glass collection is unprotected, but I'm not a lawyer, so I have to be careful about what I say.

Q: When you say "in the glass collection," you mean an Autopia glass collection of documents?

Practice Pointer: The expert in the above example first says the missing information may be covered by a protective order and does not want to talk about it. The expert then testifies at length about the information. When faced with similar protective order problems an expert should consider:

- consulting with *his* attorney prior to being deposed and
- if that is not possible, saying as little as possible at the deposition until the issue is resolved.

Example 4.5: Refusing to answer questions until protective order issue is resolved

Q: So you did not bring an Autopia document on the minivan?

A: That's correct. I will not be answering any additional questions about this until the issue is resolved by counsel.

4.3 Referring to and Dealing with Exhibits

Referring to Exhibits

The attorneys who question an expert about documents usually will have those documents *marked* for identification. This usually involves the placing of a small sticker on the document in question. This sticker will contain a number or letter or both (such as "P-1"). Thereafter, the exhibit would be referred to as *exhibit P-1*. This is done for identification purposes in order to clarify the record (transcript) of the deposition. It has nothing directly to do with the admission of the document in question into evidence. Because exhibit nomenclature can often get confusing, the expert should always try to double check that the document to which she is referring is the one the attorney is asking about. Failure to take this simple precaution could result in the expert giving confused and erroneous testimony that can be used against her at trial. If such testimony is given, the record may not reveal that the expert was looking at the wrong document when asked the crucial question.

Example 4.6: How to ensure you are referring to the correct document
Q: Let me refer your attention to defense exhibit 17A. Do you agree with the conclusions set forth in this report?
A: Just to be sure which report we're talking about, is that the four-page EPA Site Report dated July 21, 2007?

Practice Pointer: The simple precaution of verifying the identity of the document in question and reading this verification into the record helped prevent the expert from giving potentially erroneous testimony.

Take Time to Read Documents You Are Questioned On
Experts are often questioned on documents. When questioned about a document at deposition, an expert should ask to take the time to read it and review it carefully before answering any questions. Experts should not concern themselves that they are slowing down the deposition or that counsel is getting impatient. That is the attorney's problem, not the expert's. If the deposition is not being videotaped, the time the expert takes to review the document will *not* be reflected in the deposition transcript. Because the transcript is what matters most, a careful review of the document in question is likely to have no downside.

Example 4.7: Taking the time needed to review the entire document in question
Q: Have you seen this document marked Exhibit #3, answers to interrogatories?
A: No.
Q: With reference to Question and Answer #4, will that be your opinion at trial?
A: I will need some time to read and review the document.

Practice Pointer: The expert asked to read the entire document, not just Question and Answer #4. Reading the entire document is always recommended to ensure understanding the context of various parts of the document.

4.4 Notes and Underlining
Experts are frequently questioned at length about notes, underlining, highlighting, and margin notes that appear in their files. Opposing counsel will focus like a laser beam on the expert's notes because these may provide insight into what the expert felt was important. Experts generally handle notes and underlining in one of four ways:

1. *Not taking any notes.* This may negatively affect the expert's ability to work.

2. *Taking notes and then "discarding" them when the report is written because they are no longer needed.* Aside from the legalities of not preserving evidence, this smacks of a cover-up. The cover-up allegations will likely do more damage to the expert and his opinions than whatever was in the notes.

3. *Making notes on Post-its and then dishonestly removing them from the file and discarding them (or other gamesmanship).* Again, aside from the legalities, the expert is likely to eventually get caught doing this and thus suffer a sudden and ignominious end to his forensic career.

4. *Preserving and producing notes and not hiding them.* The wise expert is transparent. Of course, the prudent expert is careful when taking notes not to write anything inflammatory or that may reflect poorly on the expert.

Of these four techniques, the authors strongly recommend #4. This is not just because it is the legal thing to do. It is also the most effective and wisest course of action. The most effective experts understand that transparency will usually help their credibility because the cover-up is usually worse than the crime.

Questions regarding notes should not be feared. These are often easily answered if the expert is well prepared. The expert is paid by the hour. If opposing counsel wants to spend time at deposition asking the expert why he underlined certain portions of records and what his handwritten notes mean, it's his nickel.

Example 4.8: Handwritten notes dictated and discarded
Q: Do you have your inspection notes?
A: Yes.
Q: May I see them?
A: (Witness indicates.)
Q: Thank you. Where are your handwritten notes?
A: There are none.
Q: Why is that?
A: While I was looking the vehicle over, I spoke into a Dictaphone and those notes were transcribed.
Q: Where are they?
A: In the report.
Q: Only in the report?
A: Yes.

Practice Pointer: The expert in the above example discarded his handwritten notes and thus opened the door for opposing counsel to argue that he was covering something up. He would have been better served to preserve his handwritten notes.

Example 4.9: Retaining all information
Q: Did you make notes to assist you in preparing your report?
A: Any notes that I made are in these binders. I didn't throw anything away.

Practice Pointer: The expert here follows a protocol (retaining all his notes) that completely blunts counsel's attempt to create doubts about the notes. This is an excellent example of an expert whose practice is completely transparent and, as such, is difficult to attack successfully.

Opposing counsel can be expected to have experts read and explain any handwritten notes they make. These notes can be written on the records themselves (typically in margins), on separate pieces of paper, or on small Post-it notes.

In these deposition exchanges, counsel is looking for inconsistencies, mistakes, changes of opinion, and creating a timeline for cross-examination purposes. Please consider the following example.

Example 4.10: Notes of expert
Q: Showing you what's been marked as Deposition Exhibit No. 6, for identification purposes, do you recognize that document, sir?
A: I do.
Q: Okay. And is that your writing?
A: That's my writing.
Q: Can you tell me when this document was written by you?
A: Before the last deposition.
Q: Was this done at one time or over the course of time?
A: I don't know. It looks like maybe it was done over two time periods, the top being one part and the latter part being together, but I don't remember.
Q: At the top it says "Defense." Is that "Kim" to the right of that?
A: Yes.
Q: And what does that refer to?
A: As I indicated to you, I try to see a case through both sides, and I try to see it through the other side before I try to see it through the side that's retaining me. So these are—not trying to do your work for you, sir, so I don't mean to be presumptuous, but these are the things that I thought were things that if I were in your position I would look at.
Q: Why?
A: I try to see things from both sides.
Q: For what purposes?
A: For the purpose of determining whether or not I can be retained as an expert in a testifying capacity.
Q: Well, you created this after you were retained already, did you not?

A: That's true, but I could be retained and, as I have in the past, tell people they don't have a case.

Q: What does it say under that, under where it says "Defense, Kim"? "Through a lot"?

A: Yeah.

Q: What does that refer to?

A: Kim was widowed. Her husband had a car accident. She was widowed. She had a son who was electrocuted and had some damage as a result of that. She marries a guy and appears happy for a year, and then he gets cancer. She looks after him during the time that he's down. That's what that refers to.

Q: How does that impact your opinions?

A: It would make me sympathetic to her.

Q: What's the next line down?

A: "Evidence that Nancy disinvited Gabor." This must have been done early on in the case because some of this stuff has been answered subsequently.

Q: In fact, there is a question mark before that, isn't there? Do you recognize this document?

A: I do.

Q: Okay. At the top it says "Plaintiff, Jim"?

A: Yes.

Q: This is your handwriting?

A: It's my handwriting.

Q: These are your notes?

A: And my notes.

Q: When did you create this?

A: Sometime before the last deposition.

Q: Okay. And the purpose of this document was what?

A: Looking at the other side of the coin from what we had discussed just a moment ago.

Q: So this is looking at it from Jim's point of view?

A: Right.

Practice Pointer: In the above example, counsel questions each and every mark and notation (question marks, etc.) that the expert has made. Counsel is interested in the expert's motivation, his thought process, and their ultimate impact on his opinions. Experts should be able to explain any and all notes they make on or off the record. The expert's explanation that he was looking at both sides of the case helps diffuse the impact of the notes. This expert was prepared to answer questions about his notes and did not make the mistake of trying to hide or discard his notes.

Example 4.11: Underlining questions

Q: Sir, I note that within this package, there is some blue underline. And I'd like to show you on a handwritten note of December 2, 2005, there is some blue underline, and ask you if you know who made those underlines.

A: I did.

Q: Why did you underline this particular passage?

Q: You've got the deposition of MaryBeth Hayden and again you've underlined, even dog-eared some things regarding her symptoms, when she started to work. Maybe I better let you look at that. Is there anything in that deposition that you've highlighted that you feel pertains to your opinions beyond when she started to work, her age, and her symptoms?

A: No. I think that probably summarizes it.

Practice Pointer: Be very careful about any handwritten notes or highlighting that you place on documents and be prepared to answer questions on these notes and underlining. You will almost always be questioned closely about such notes at deposition or trial.

Private Notes

Some experts mistakenly believe that their notes are "private" and should not have to be disclosed. ***There is simply no such thing as far as the law is concerned as a "private note" privilege.*** Notes can and will be discoverable as long as no exceptions to the discovery rules apply (for example, privilege, attorney work product, undue burden, etc.). The only way to guarantee that a note is never produced for discovery is to never create that note in the first place.

Example 4.12: Notes of expert are not private

Q: Now, your file or a file related to this is comprised of the two deposition transcripts and the offer of proof; is that correct? Is this one of the documents provided to you by ACME, the offer of proof?

A: Yes.

Q: And the rest of the documents are medical records provided to you by ACME?

A: Yes.

Q: Have you in preparation for today's depositions, apart from what you said about the two depositions, have you reviewed the medical records?

A: Yes.

Q: In addition to the medical records, do you have some notes related to this case?

A: I have one page of notes.

Q: Could I see those?

    Mr. Renya: Could I just look at them first?

    (Pause.)

    Mr. Renya: Okay.

Mr. O'Leary: Let's mark this as Exhibit No. 4.

A: Am I not entitled to the privacy of my own notes? These are not for submission.

Q: Sir, your work related to this case, because it's involved in litigation, is available to me.

A: I would not describe this as work. These are my notes. If I were preparing these to be copied or submitted, I would certainly not submit them in this form.

Q: I understand.

A: This is just me, just in terms of a quick rundown. I'd be happy to type them without changing them, but—

Mr. Renya: That's all right.

A: But that's certainly not representative of my style of work, to copy my scribbled notes.

Q: I understand. Are these notes that you made during your review of the case?

A: Yes.

Q: Could I see them, please?

A: Yes.

Practice Pointer: The answer to the expert's question is no. He is not entitled to the privacy of his own notes. They must be produced. Good experts do not fear the production of their notes and are prepared to answer questions regarding their notes.

4.5 Hiding Documents Is a Serious Mistake

An expert can expect to be questioned closely about whether anything has been removed from her file. Any attempt by the expert witness to "sanitize" her file is improper. A common example of this is the removal of cover letters, billing records, or notes. Such an attempt will make the expert look bad in the eyes of the jury or fact finder. If there are documents in the file that the expert feels are legally privileged, she should contact the appropriate lawyers and let the lawyers work it out.

A single act of removal of documents from a file can completely destroy the credibility of an expert witness. The problem of removal of documents is exacerbated if the removal is recorded on videotape. As has been evidenced by many corporate and legal scandals, the cover-up is always worse than the crime.

Example 4.13: Intentionally withholding information from file damages expert's credibility

Q: Sir, did you bring with you today your file regarding the *Christie* case?

A: Yes.

Q: May I look at it, please?

A: (Witness proffers file to counsel.)

Q: In addition, sir, I see that you've placed some documents on your desk. Are those documents included as part of your file in your office?

Counsel: Objection.

A: Yes.

Q: Could I see those, please?

A: (Witness reluctantly proffers to counsel.)

Practice Pointer: The witness has damaged his credibility by intentionally withholding information from the file.

Example 4.14: Attempt to hide documents captured on video

Q: Please give me your entire file.

A: I'm getting the part that you requested.

Q: I want—I'd like the whole thing, please. The whole paper. I'll take the whole file, in fact.

A: Here's the—

Q: Sir, may I see your whole file, please? I'm sorry. You just took some papers out in the presence—This is on film. Can you hand me the whole chart and the documents you removed from it?

Practice Pointer: The witness's attempt to hide documents has been caught on camera for the jury to see and hear. This attempt to hide documents has needlessly damaged the witness's credibility.

4.6 Cover Letters from the Expert's Client

One of the most frequent areas of controversy is the "cover letter" the expert receives from counsel or the party retaining her. ***The cover letter is generally not protected by attorney-client privilege and, generally, must be produced.*** In many cases, the cover letter is very revealing to counsel. Counsel should be very careful when drafting these cover letters. Experts should remember that counsel who send them sensitive material in a cover letter do so at their own risk. Experts should never participate in any attempt to hide damaging cover letters. Attempts to play "hide and seek" with these letters is both unethical and unwise and can result in sanctions.

It is not uncommon for skirmishes to break out at deposition between counsel as to whether a cover letter is privileged and need not be produced by the expert. The attorney-client privilege does not act in most states to shield an expert's communications with counsel. This is true because counsel is not representing the expert, she is representing someone else (the plaintiff or the defendant). When faced with claims of privilege and other evidentiary battles, the expert is well advised to do the following:

1. Let the lawyers sort out the dispute before turning over any documents.
2. Stay out of the dispute if possible.
3. Remember that counsel for the party who has retained you is *not* your lawyer and may be more concerned about winning the case than safeguarding your reputation.

Example 4.15: Missing cover letter in file reflects poorly on expert

Q: Was there a—I see you showed me a whole stack of records and a whole number are records or references in your report. Did those records come to you with some type of cover letter from either Mr. Verasco, his office, or A-1 Insurance Company?

A: They usually do come with a cover letter from the attorney's office.

Q: Can you find it for me?

A: This would be it. It's dated November 9, 2005.

Q: Now, in this letter—this letter was dated November 9, 2005, if we can have it marked P-1 for identification?

Q: Mr. Verasco indicates here in the letter that he's attaching a copy of Dr. Suh's letter. Do you have any idea why it would not be in your file?

A: No, I don't.

Q: Has anybody asked you to remove it from your file?

A: No.

Practice Pointer: By not having a complete file, the expert has given the attorney ammunition that can be used against the expert to lessen the expert's credibility.

Example 4.16: Letting counsel argue about privilege

Q: Can you produce the cover letter which accompanied the documents you received?

> **Mr. Ignatius:** Objection. My transmittal letter to him is privileged as attorney-client—attorney work product.
>
> **Mr. Norval:** Is this your client?
>
> **Mr. Ignatius:** It's attorney work product.
>
> **Mr. Norval:** Didn't you include this letter to the doctor? How can you claim attorney work product after you disclosed it to an independent expert? What's the basis of asserting that privilege?
>
> **Mr. Ignatius:** My communication to the doctor as an expert witness is not subject to discovery.
>
> **Mr. Norval:** Under what basis, sir? This is a witness that you have disclosed. This is not an independent consultant. You're now asserting a privilege here. What's the basis of that?
>
> **Mr. Ignatius:** My basis is that you're not entitled to see anything other than what he's referred to.
>
> **Mr. Norval:** Mr. Ignatius, on the basis that this is a consultant, that your work product is included in his chart, your work product is in his chart?
>
> **Mr. Ignatius:** Yes.
>
> **Mr. Norval:** Is that what you're telling this judge?
>
> **Mr. Ignatius:** Yes.

Practice Pointer: The expert was well advised to stay out of the attorneys' privilege discussion.

Example 4.17: Hiding the cover letter
Q: If there's a transmittal cover letter, I'd like that included, too, please. Would you hand it over to me, please?
A: This is the file.
Q: Would you please hand me the papers that you've just taken out of your chart?
A: I gave you the file. This is just a letter from counsel.
Q: Did you give me back the papers that you took out?
A: Yes, I did.
Q: Now, sir, have you given me your entire file including the transmittal letter?
A: Yes.
Q: I have before me Plaintiff's Number 1, which is an eighteen-page letter that you have taken out of your file; is that correct?
A: I only took it out of the file because....
Q: Yes or no, did you take it out of your file?
A: I merely removed it from the chart to review it—I had no intention of....

Practice Pointer: Cover letters are generally a legitimate area of inquiry. As such, attorneys and experts need to be very careful regarding what is placed in them. Attempts to be defensive about cover letters or to conceal them will most likely be counterproductive.

4.7 Billing Information
An expert should anticipate that counsel will look for information on fee schedules and the expert's bill for the case. Some experts may fail to include this information in the file they produce, even if it has been specifically requested. Sophisticated counsel can make the failure to include this information look like a pattern of deceit. Information regarding expert fees is discoverable because it may indicate bias. Sophisticated counsel will use the billing records to help create a timeline of what was done and when it was done. Counsel will then use this timeline at deposition to probe for inconsistencies. There is no point in trying to hide this information. Juries know and understand that expert witnesses are paid for their time. Finally, the expert witness retained by the opposing side is also being paid for her time. The fact that an expert is being paid will usually not taint his testimony.

Example 4.18: Failure to bring billing information
Q: Doctor, I would just like to, if you don't mind, have a look at your chart, because you've referred to it. Did you bring everything that you have relating to your work on this case here with you today?
A: Other than the X-ray films, yes.

Q: Okay. Are there other papers somewhere else in another file, in another office, that relate to the work that you did on Mr. Correly's case on behalf of this employer?
A: Not that I'm aware of.
Q: So, why don't you show that to me, if you don't mind?
A: (Handing the file.)
Q: Doctor, have you now just handed me your complete chart, as you know it, as it relates to Richard Correly?
A: As I know it, yeah.
Q: Okay. (Reading.) Now, Doctor, as I look through this chart here, I'm not sure that I find any billing information from you. Is your billing information kept somewhere different?
A: That's not something that I am involved with in my practice.
Q: That wasn't my question. Is your billing information kept somewhere different?
A: I presume so, because it's not in the chart.
Q: So, in fact, you haven't brought everything that you have related to Richard Correly here today. Do you want to change your answer that you gave me before?
A: Would you re—could I re-hear the original question again, please?
Q: Doctor, I asked you five minutes ago if you brought everything that you have as it relates to the work that you did on Richard Correly, right? Remember that question?
A: Well, I remember that you asked me a question. I don't remember the exact wording that you used. I'd like to hear that again. Do I have a right to hear that?
Q: Doctor, did you bring everything—I'll ask it again. Did you bring everything that you have—
A: And I asked you a question, Mr. Norval. Do I have a right to hear your question read back to me by the court reporter or not?
Q: No, Doctor. I'm asking you the question, and I'm going to keep going, and I'll rephrase it if you don't understand it. And maybe I should stop myself. If you don't understand one of my questions, would you tell me that? And I'll do my best to rephrase it.
A: All right. I will.
Q: Okay. But the question I asked was: Did you bring everything that you had as it relates to the work that you did on Richard Correly? Do you remember that?
A: Yes.
Q: And you told me that you did, right?
A: I told you that I brought everything that I had available, yes.
Q: Now, I've looked in your chart, and I don't find any billing information.
A: That's right, you didn't.
Q: That's kept somewhere else?
A: I would presume so, yes.
Q: But you don't know?

A: But I don't think it has anything to do with the medical part of this case. The fact that a billing record is not kept in the chart has very little to do with my opinion.

Q: Doctor, my question was: Did you bring everything that you have as it relates to him? And it appears that you did not, right?

A: I didn't bring the billing information, no.

Q: Okay. Do you have all the correspondence in that file?

Practice Pointer: The witness has caused himself much difficulty by his failure to bring the billing information and his inability to admit this directly.

4.8 Conclusion

Experienced experts produce all relevant, discoverable documents, take their time when testifying about documents, and are careful to create a clear record when referring to documents during a deposition.

Chapter 5 What Experts Can Expect to Be Asked

5.1 Introduction and Executive Summary

To excel during expert depositions, an expert witness must be able to answer counsel's questions directly and truthfully without making mistakes or falling victim to counsel's tactics, traps, or trick questions. The best way to do this is to anticipate and prepare for questions that counsel is likely to ask. A forewarned expert deponent is a forearmed expert deponent. This chapter will identify and give examples of the most common lines of questioning experts can expect to face. The expert witness who is aware of the common lines of questioning and tactics employed by counsel is in the strongest position to succeed at deposition. These include the following:

- Qualifications questions. These are relevant to the expert's credibility. The expert will probably be asked about the following:
  - Educational background
  - Grades
  - Degrees
  - Dates of attendance and degrees
  - Gaps in education
  - Additional training
  - Continuing education courses
  - Relevant practical experience
  - Membership in professional organizations
  - Certifications
  - If these certifications were earned, bought, or if the expert was grandfathered-in
- CV questions
  - Gaps
  - Mistakes
  - Inconsistencies with Internet CV
  - Sloppiness
  - Date prepared
  - Omissions
  - Multiple CVs
- Opinions
  - What the expert will and will not be testifying to (experienced experts usually leave themselves some wiggle room when they answer these types of questions).
  - Degree of flexibility in opinions (a totally inflexible expert may lose credibility because *nothing* would make her change her opinion).
  - Admissions—Areas of agreement that help opposing counsel's case.

- o Rationale for opinions. The most believable opinions are well reasoned and experienced experts are prepared to cite their rationale at deposition.
- o When was the opinion formed? Was there a rush to judgment? Did the expert have enough information at the time to form an opinion?
- o Did the expert rely on other experts' opinions? Were those opinions reliable? Were they reasonably relied upon?
- o Contrasting the expert's opinions with those of other experts.
- Interrogatory answers. Experts should sign off on these before they are signed and be familiar with them prior to deposition.
- Factual basis of opinion. The expert's opinion is only as good as the facts upon which it is based.
  - o Experts are well advised to master the facts as part of their deposition preparation process.
  - o Were the expert's equipment and testing reliable?
  - o How thorough was the expert's investigation? What didn't the expert do?
- Methodology. These questions may be extremely important at deposition because they may be relevant to both the weight and admissibility of the expert's testimony. In other words, the deposition may be used to support a motion to preclude the expert from testifying.
  - o Testability
  - o Peer review and publication
  - o Error rate
  - o Standards and controls
  - o Degree of general acceptance
  - o Was research independent of litigation?
  - o Unjustifiable extrapolation?
  - o Accounted for obvious alternative explanations?
  - o Is the expert being as careful in this work as he would be for work outside of litigation?
  - o Is the expert's field known to reach reliable results?
  - o Did the expert cherry-pick data?
- Potential bias of the expert
  - o Always testifying for one side. To blunt this, it is prudent to make a conscientious effort to testify for both sides.
  - o Always has same opinion regardless of facts? This is not believable.
  - o No flexibility in opinion?
  - o Personal/social relationship with a party to the case or with counsel.
  - o Professional witness?
  - o Expert acts like advocate?
  - o Fees? Do not be evasive.
  - o Bills?

- Impeachment with inconsistent statements. Experts should always tell the truth and not let opposing counsel take past statements out of context.
  - Prior sworn testimony
  - Reports from prior cases
  - Mistakes in prior testimony
  - Expert's publications and other writings

5.2 Qualifications

The expert should be prepared for counsel to use the deposition to discover and explore any weaknesses or shortcomings in her qualifications. The expert will probably be asked about her:

- educational background,
- grades,
- degrees,
- dates of attendance and degrees,
- gaps in education,
- additional training,
- continuing education courses,
- relevant practical experience,
- membership in professional organizations,
- certifications, and
- if these certifications were earned, bought, or if she was grandfathered-in.

Because the expert is a witness in the case, her credibility is a legitimate and important issue. The expert's qualifications, or lack thereof, are relevant to her credibility and are an area where there will be close questioning. To excel during depositions, expert witnesses need to be prepared to handle these questions properly. If asked the question, "Doctor, are you board certified?," the answer is either yes or no. Evasiveness can be far more damaging to an expert's credibility than an admission that she is not board certified because evasiveness may result in the perception that the expert is not honest.

An expert's qualifications will be judged ultimately by a jury or other fact finder. *It is the authors' opinion that jurors are far more influenced by an expert's relevant practical experience, perceived honesty, and demeanor than the expert's academic record or lack of publications.* If the jury likes an expert, thinks she is honest, and feels that she has a good amount of relevant hands-on experience, such an expert may be much more credible to them than an expert who is a professor with many publications, but who no longer does hands-on work and who has a pompous demeanor.

When asked simple, routine questions about qualifications at deposition, the prepared expert answers them simply and directly.

Example 5.1: Deponent unprepared to answer basic question about qualifications
Q: How long have you been licensed in the Commonwealth of Massachusetts?
A: My license, I think, began in—shortly after medical school. I—it would have been sometime shortly after my graduation, probably in the early 1950s.

Practice Pointer: The expert in the above example did not distinguish himself with his reply to a *very* basic question. A more confident and prepared expert would have replied simply and directly.

> **Q:** How long have you been licensed in the Commonwealth of Massachusetts?
> **A:** Since 1954.

Example 5.2: Not being evasive concerning critical hole in qualifications
Q: What is your occupation?
A: I am a mechanical engineer.
Q: What professional licenses do you possess?
A: I am not a registered professional engineer. I have a designation that is less than a professional engineering status…so, none.
Q: Again, do you have a license as an engineer?
A: No, I do not.
Q: What formal education have you had after high school?
A: I have a B.S. degree in mechanical engineering and I also have a Masters Degree in mechanical engineering.
Q: The B.S. in mechanical engineering was 1976 at the University of…Kentucky?
A: That is correct.
Q: Please tell us, what is mechanical engineering?
A: It's a course of study that broadly includes such topics as design, mathematics, heat transfer, fluid….
Q: Have you had any formal education in the nature of mechanical engineering or bioengineering since taking your Masters at the University of Kentucky?
A: No, I have not.
Q: Have you ever taken the test for an engineer's license in any state?
A: Yes, I have.
Q: Where was that?
A: In the State of Kentucky.
Q: Did you receive that license?
A: No, I did not.
Q: Why not?
A: I didn't pass the test.

Q: How many times did you take the test, sir?
A: Four.
Q: How many times did you fail the exam?
A: Four.

Practice Pointer: The expert did not try and hide his lack of a license. Counsel who has retained this unlicensed expert has made a conscious and informed decision. After the expert has disclosed any professional shortcomings to retaining counsel, it becomes the problem of counsel and not the expert. Counsel and the expert may realize that demeanor, perceived honesty, and relevant practical experience weigh more heavily with the jury than the absence of professional designations or licensures that the jurors don't understand.

Example 5.3: Counsel tries to show that the "expert" is not really an expert
Q: Doctor, have you ever attended a medical conference on head injury?
A: Not that I remember.
Q: Have you ever published an article on head injury?
A: No, I have not.
Q: Have you ever conducted any research on head injury?
A: No.
Q: Do you subscribe to any professional magazines or journals in the field of head injury?
A: No, I haven't.
Q: Doctor, I want to thank you for your time.

Practice Pointer: Note that the above physician, due to a lack of specific training and continuing education, may not have been well suited to testify about head injury. However, what he wasn't asked was what his experience with head injury had been. If this expert has been treating and diagnosing head injuries for forty years and appears believable and likeable, the jury may very well find him to be credible. Experts should, however, be cautious about being pushed by counsel into testifying in areas outside of their expertise. The expert's reputation, credibility, and standing in the profession are at stake. In addition, if the expert is found not to be qualified or his testimony is limited at trial, this will become part of the expert's "permanent record."

5.3 Curriculum Vitae
Experts should anticipate close questioning about their CVs. Counsel may try to show that an expert has been inconsistent or sloppy in putting together a CV. Opposing counsel will try to argue to the jury that they should not believe that the expert was accurate in her clinical methods and in formulating her conclusions and opinions if she was sloppy or inaccurate in formulating her own CV. Even a minor inconsistency in a CV can make a jury wonder why the expert has not corrected the CV. Is the expert lazy or just sloppy? If either conclusion is drawn by the jury, the

expert will lose credibility. To prevent this kind of damage to one's credibility, an expert needs to maintain an accurate and up-to-date CV.

Experts can expect to be questioned about and from their curriculum vitae at deposition. It is essential to bring and be able to recognize one's latest CV. This is easily accomplished by dating the CV at the end (for example, "Updated July 2007").

Example 5.4: Expert cannot determine how old CV is

Q: I'm handing you what I've marked as deposition Exhibit #1. Is this the current copy of your CV?
A: As far as I can tell. I don't know. I don't think it's been revised since this, but let me just check. It's hard to tell....

Practice Pointer: Experts can expect to be asked many difficult questions at deposition. Being asked if this is your current CV is not one of them. Experts should date their CVs so they can simply and promptly identify the most up-to-date version.

Example 5.5: Omissions from CV

Q: Doctor, we were also provided what is Exhibit Number 2, a CV. Do you know how that differs from Exhibit Number 3, which also purports to be your CV?
A: It's an earlier—it's an earlier CV.
Q: Doctor, you would agree that there are marked inconsistencies between the two CVs?
A: Well, when we did the most current version, we were trying to shorten it—that's what most people want—the short version. So we did omit certain unimportant activities and articles.
Q: So the omissions were intentional, is that your testimony?
A: Yes, I just explained that.
Q: I'm directing your attention to Exhibit Number 3, the current CV. I ask if you would turn to page 4, your bibliography. Have you published other articles under your name in addition to the six that are listed?
A: Actually, yes. There's a letter to the editor of the *New England Journal of Medicine,* which is not included.
Q: What was the subject matter?
A: Writing of prescriptions. It's not relevant to the current topic.
Q: Didn't you write a textbook that is not listed?
A: Actually, it was a chapter in a textbook which outlined the diagnosis and treatment of infection in total hip arthroplasty.
Q: Did it discuss the diagnosis and treatment of a septic hip short of a revision of the implant?
A: It may have. I can't actually recall. It's 14 years ago....

Practice Pointer: Counsel has taken a simple revision and shortening of a CV and made the expert look sloppy. In addition, counsel has raised the issue about why a key medical chapter was left off the CV.

Example 5.6: CVs and Web pages

Q: Now, I did not receive, prior to today, a copy of your curriculum vitae.
A: Okay.
Q: I did pull one off the Internet, but it's dated from April of 2004. But have you brought a more recent curriculum vitae with you today?
A: Yes, sir.
Q: Thank you. Well, let's do this: since there are some differences in the CVs that you have brought, and the one that was available on the Internet, I'm going to initially mark as Exhibit Number 2 a copy of the CV that you have brought, which is dated March 18, 2005.
Q: And your CV also includes a list of prior testimony. Is that correct?
A: Yes, sir.
Q: Okay. I show that to you and I ask you whether that is your current curriculum vitae, sir?
A: Yes, sir, I believe it is. Let's see. From what I can tell, this is fairly current.
Q: Well, you might want to take a look at this and just determine whether, for instance, there are any additional publications or presentations that you've been involved in or that you have prepared that are not included on this CV.
A: Yeah, that's—yes, sir, that's what I looked at. I looked to see if I had the most recent publication and the most recent deposition, and it did.
Q: It did.
A: Yes, sir.
Q: Okay. And is your prior testimony list up to date?
A: Yes, sir.
Q: So the last case in which you were deposed or gave testimony was on January 25, 2005?
A: That's correct.
Q: I'm going to mark as Exhibit Number 3 a copy of your resume dated April 16, 2004, which I took off the Internet, from Rogers Engineering, and I'll show that to you and just confirm for me whether that is, in fact, a copy of your resume.
A: Yes, sir.
Q: Now, I note when we compare your current resume from March 18, 2005, with the one from April 16, 2004, you have a whole new area of expertise that's not previously listed. Is that correct, sir?
A: Let me see it. To some extent it is considered new. I mean, until the time that I split this out, I really considered the occupant safety systems part of the occupant

kinematics and injury biomechanics, as far as how the person perform—behaved as they related to those vehicles. So, it's more of a marketing tool to split out.

Q: Well, I don't see in your earlier resume, sir, where you talk specifically about occupant safety systems and analysis of seatbelts and airbags and interior impacts and crashworthiness.

A: That's correct.

Q: And it's not spelled out in your resume.

A: It's not spelled out, that's correct.

Q: So, this new area in your resume, which is current, is not spelled out in the prior resume, correct, sir?

A: That's correct. I wouldn't say it's a new area, though. I just—I feel like it's more one that's pulled out of another area.

Q: It wasn't declared previously. Is that correct?

A: That's correct.

Q: You didn't hold yourself out as an expert in occupant safety systems explicitly—

A: That's correct.

Q: —before?

A: That's correct.

Q: What has happened between April 16, 2004 and March 18, 2005, to ask you to declare these subjects explicitly, sir?

A: Well, like I said, I think that I just explained that. It's a continuation of expertise that I've actually been involved in all along. It's just that I separated out from an area that I considered it to be part of before for the purpose of a more clear understanding.

Q: Thank you, sir. Now, your resume, your current resume which we've marked as Exhibit 2 has nine publications, and you've already told me that that's complete; is that correct, sir?

A: Yes, sir.

Q: Now, your earlier resume, which was April 16, 2004, has five articles on it, and the latest of those—I guess that's a publication list, and your current list is a publications and presentations list?

A: Yes, sir.

Q: Okay. So, since the earlier resume, you've added some presentations and perhaps—

A: At least one publication.

Q: —at least one publication. Which is the publication that you've added, sir? Do you want to take a look at that? I can show you both, if that helps out.

A: 8 and 9 both are publications that have been added. One's a comprehensive evaluation of NHTSA rollover test data for the use in computational model validation, and the other one is a peer-review publication. An experimental examination of seatbelt webbing, loading marks on automotive plastic D-rings.

Practice Pointer: Opposing counsel can be expected to closely scrutinize the expert's CV. Counsel will look for multiple CVs, inconsistencies between different CVs, CVs that may appear on a Web page, and recent additions to the CV. The expert should be intimately familiar with his own CV.

Example 5.7: Article not published when CV claimed it was

Q: Your CV states that you co-authored a paper entitled "Global Labor Standards." That was the *Contemporary Manufacturing* magazine, April 1997. Who was your co-author on that paper?

A: Jason Ardette.

Q: I am a little confused in reading the curriculum vitae. I would like you to clarify for me, are you saying the paper was published in the April 1997 issue of *Contemporary Manufacturing* magazine?

A: The paper was given at that date for a later publication.

Q: Was it ever published?

A: Yes….As far as I know, it was published in 1997. I think it was delayed for some reason.

Q: What issue?

A: I believe it was a, the, subsequent issue.

Q: Can you tell us what issue that was?

A: I don't recall specifically. I remember seeing the publication, but I don't recall.

Practice Pointer: When the expert's CV lists nonexistent or incorrectly cited articles, the expert's precision and credibility are quickly called into question. Was the assertion of publication a slip up, an exaggeration, or a lie?

5.4 Opinions

The main reason for the testimony of an expert witness is to give an opinion that will assist the trier of fact. Experts should anticipate close questioning concerning which opinions they will and will not be giving at trial. Most likely, there will also be close questioning about whether the expert is rigid and inflexible or if she would change her opinion if the facts are proven to be different. Counsel needs to know this information so that there won't be any surprises at trial. This information may also be helpful to counsel when he drafts pre-trial motions, such as motions for summary judgment. The line of questioning regarding opinions will usually include the following areas of inquiry:

- the opinions the expert will and will not be testifying to,
- the degree of flexibility in the opinion (that is, what would it take to get the expert to change her opinion),
- any admissions counsel can elicit from the expert,
- the rationale for the opinions,
- the facts and assumptions upon which the opinion is based (see Section 5.6),

- the methodology employed in deriving the opinion (see Section 5.7),
- when the opinion was first formed,
- other experts relied upon,
- experts who disagree with the expert's opinion,
- the deposition documents used by the expert in forming the opinion, and
- how the proposed opinion compares to answers previously given during discovery.

Opinions the Expert Will and Will Not Be Testifying To
One of the major goals of opposing counsel is to lock the expert into what opinions he will and will not provide at trial. A prudent expert leaves himself some wiggle room to offer additional opinions if he is asked an unexpected question, if there is subsequently reviewed information, or if one of the expert's opinions slipped his mind at the deposition.

Example 5.8: Trying to lock down the expert
Q: Now, Doctor, please state each and every opinion you intend to give at trial in this case.
A: Sitting here today, I intend to testify that Doctor Jones breached the standard of care in failing to order blood work on March 6, 2007, and that this breach resulted in the plaintiff's death. That may change if I am provided with additional information or if I am asked to opine on other matters.

Practice Pointer: The expert here has refused to let himself be 100% locked down.

Example 5.9: Overeager expert
Q: Doctor, in this case, it is agreed that Ricky Murphy had lumbosacral strain as a result of his injury at work. The question that we have here today is whether the injury at work resulted in a herniated disk. Do you have an opinion?
A: Yes. It did.

Practice Pointer: The doctor made two mistakes here. First, she was too eager to give her opinion. This may make her look biased and result in lost credibility. Second, she answered more than what was asked. Her answer to the question, "Do you have an opinion?" should have been, "Yes, I have an opinion." It is counsel's job to follow up with the question, "And what is that opinion, Doctor?"

Opposing counsel will also want to try to clarify and narrow the opinions that you are likely to offer at trial. Finding out which opinions you are *not* going to give may be as important to counsel as finding out which opinions you will proffer at trial.

Example 5.10: Locking the expert out of offering an opinion
Q: Will you be offering opinions in the area of occupant kinematics at trial?
A: No, I will not.

Practice Pointer: The expert essentially foreclosed offering opinions in this area. He may have been better served by leaving himself a little wiggle room as in the following interchange:

> **Q:** Will you be offering opinions in the area of occupant kinematics at trial?
> **A:** I have no plans at this time to do so.

Example 5.11: The expert leaves wiggle room on opinions

Q: Are you going to offer opinion testimony with respect to the use of side impact air bags or side curtain air bags?
A: I don't think so. We haven't talked about it. I think I wrote in my opinions that it doesn't have them.
Q: So no opinions with respect to side curtain air bags or side impact air bags—
A: Right.
Q: —other than to say this vehicle didn't come equipped with it?
A: Yes, right.
Q: You're not going to say the vehicle is defective because it did not come equipped with side curtain air bags?
A: Correct.
Q: Am I correct?
A: You're correct. I'm not going to say it would have saved this guy's life.
Q: You're not going to say it would have saved this guy's life?
A: Right.
Q: You have not done any testing with respect to side curtain air bags, I take it; is that right?
A: That's correct.
Q: So I won't hear at trial you testify with respect to side curtain air bags or roof rail air bags or some variation on that theme should have been employed in this 1999 SUV and if employed would have prevented or mitigated Mr. O'Neill's injuries?
A: Correct.
Q: Are you going to offer any opinion that those seat belts as equipped in the '99 SUV are defective?
A: No.
Q: Aside from glazing and roof design and performance, are you going to express opinions in any other subject areas at the time of trial?
A: Not directly, no. There are other things. You asked me a lot of questions about occupant kinematics and injury mechanisms and whatnot. If asked, I'll answer to the best of my ability the things that I've said so far here, but I'm not going to advance anything else.

Practice Pointer: Counsel in the above example is relentless in trying to pin the expert down on precisely what he will and will not be offering his opinions on. Note, however, how the expert leaves himself a little wiggle room when replying:

- "I don't think so. We haven't talked about it…."
- "Not directly, no…."
- "If asked, I'll answer to the best of my ability…."

The expert does not want to absolutely commit to what opinions he may offer because 1) things may change prior to the trial and 2) he may be asked questions by opposing counsel that necessitate additional opinions.

Example 5.12: Refusal to be locked down

Q: I take it you are prepared right now to give your full and final opinions relating to this incident?

A: Well, probably not. I need to read the deposition and make sure there are no errors there, and if anybody else submits some information that I am given, it may change my opinion or I might be adding to my opinion.

Q: Well, what other information do you anticipate receiving in this case before you can give me your full and final opinions?

A: I don't know. I'm sure it would be coming from you. You know, if you had any other experts or any other opinions or any other events happening that you supplied to Mr. Warburton and he supplied it to me, then it might make me change or add to my opinion.

Practice Pointer: The expert here recognizes that if he is supplied with additional information, his opinions may change or he may formulate additional opinions. The expert could have added that if he is asked different questions, answering them may involve offering new or different opinions.

Example 5.13: Possible future opinions

Q: To what extent, if you have an opinion as you sit here today, should the company's engineers have consulted those recommended practices and standards in the design of its ATVs?

A: As I sit here, I don't have an opinion on the extent.

Q: Is it fair to say that you would not be proffering an opinion with respect to Frederick's outcome based on a review of the films?

A: I hope not to proffer any opinion about his films.

Practice Pointer: In both of the exchanges above, note how the experts have not completely foreclosed the possibility of giving an opinion at a later date. These are truthful, yet artful, responses.

Example 5.14: Leaving wiggle room

Q: As I understand it, you will be testifying that Ms. Solomon is unable to work due to her herniated disk, is that correct, Doctor?

A: Yes.

Q: Are there any other opinions that you will be offering in this case, Doctor?

A: Yes.

Q: What other opinions will you be offering, Doctor?

A: Well, first, that her herniated disk was a result of her lifting at work on 1/3/07 and second, that she has developed a mild to moderate depression as a result of her back injury.

Q: So, we've got all of your opinions set forth in that report and you don't intend to prepare any more reports, correct?

A: Not at this point.

Practice Pointer: You need to be prepared for the open-ended, "Will you be offering any other opinions?" question. If you answer such a question with an absolute "No," presenting additional opinions at trial may be problematic. The "Not at this point" answer was a good one because it left the door open for additional opinions to be presented later.

Degree of Flexibility

Counsel will often probe the expert for information regarding how sure the expert is about his opinion and what it would take to get the expert to change his opinion.

Example 5.15: Opinion not etched in stone

Q: Right. That was horseplay, wasn't it?

A: It didn't sound like it to me.

Q: If it was, that would change your opinion, though, correct?

A: No.

Q: Is your opinion etched in stone here today?

A: Etched in stone?

Q: Yes.

A: No. I know of few things that are etched in stone.

Q: Well, will you change your opinion?

A: Would I change my opinion?

Q: Yes.

A: Not at the present moment, no.

Practice Pointer: The expert deftly deflected the attempt to portray his opinion as rigid (etched in stone) without actually changing his opinion. The expert did leave himself the option of changing his opinion at a later date.

Admissions

Often, sophisticated counsel will, prior to attacking the opinions of the expert, obtain crucial admissions from him. Such questions serve two purposes. First, they may serve to bolster the opinion of the expert for the opposing party. Second, they narrow significantly the contested areas of inquiry.

Example 5.16: Obtaining admissions

Q: Doctor, I'm going to ask a number of things about the opinion that you have just stated, and there, I believe, will be some areas where we have agreement and some areas where we have some disagreement. I would like to, if it's all right with you, find first some areas of agreement, okay?

A: Fine.

Q: You would agree with me that Mr. Lewis suffers from post-traumatic stress disorder?

A: Yes, I would.

Q: You would agree with me that post-traumatic stress disorder is a real entity?

A: Yes, I would.

Q: You would understand that when I ask you that question, there are persons in society that might think that post-traumatic stress disorder doesn't exist?

A: Yes. I understand some people find it controversial.

Q: Okay. In your opinion, post-traumatic stress disorder is a real psychological or psychiatric illness?

A: Yes.

Q: You would agree with me that Mr. Lewis's post-traumatic stress disorder has been exhibited through classic signs and symptoms, correct?

A: Yes.

Q: Those classic signs and symptoms would be those things as set out in the *Diagnostic and Statistical Manual,* fourth edition, correct?

A: That's correct.

Q: That would be known as the DSM-IV?

A: Yes.

Q: Would I be correct in assuming that you have made the diagnosis of post-traumatic stress disorder based on criteria in the DSM-IV?

A: Yes.

Practice Pointer: Here, counsel has obtained crucial admissions quickly and effectively from the expert. Counsel will go on to question the expert closely on the "cause" of the post-traumatic stress disorder. The expert understood and accepted the fact that the diagnosis was not really an issue and was compliant until the "cause" of the disorder was put in issue.

Rationale for Opinions

Counsel will always attempt to flesh out the precise rationale for the opinions of the expert. This information is critical if counsel is to prepare for trial and evaluate properly the settlement value of the case.

Example 5.17: Solidifying opinions of expert

Q: Do you have an opinion with respect to whether or not Barrett Hansen was negligent in this case?

A: I guess I don't have an opinion one way or the other. I don't know enough about what dealers should or shouldn't do.

Q: In this case was Carolyn Newburg negligent?

A: Yes.

Q: How was she negligent?

A: One, for failing to wear a helmet. Secondly, from riding without direct supervision, which was my understanding, at least from her mother's deposition, was what the family rule was. And then lastly, for operating the vehicle in such a manner to allow herself to drift off the road on the right-hand side to an area where there clearly is a hazard in terms of the waterway and ditch, so she could either have driven slower or stayed away from that side of the roadway.

Q: Anything else?

A: No.

Practice Pointer: Counsel has determined the expert's opinions and the reasons why she found one party was negligent. Should the expert change her opinions or her rationale, counsel will be able to impeach her at trial by confronting her with the inconsistent testimony from the deposition.

When the Expert Opinion Was Formed

The expert may be asked when he formed each opinion in the case. The date of the opinion frequently has significance because it can affect what information and evidence the expert did and did not consider in forming the opinion. Often, counsel will attempt to develop a timeline to indicate that crucial data could not have been considered because it did not come into the hands of the expert until after the opinion was formed. Counsel may also attempt to show that crucial evidence may have been altered or was no longer available at the time the opinion was formed.

Example 5.18: Date expert formed opinion

Q: I want to know what information you had when you wrote this report in November 2005 with regard to it being a minor collision; not with regard to the neurologic findings, with regard to the severity of the collision.

A: There are other things which were relied on when other studies—initial studies, including MRIs, were normal, he had an EEG done which was normal. All those things should be abnormal in a patient that has more severe injuries. All these would mean it was a mild injury.

Q: Can you just tell me, Doctor, what information you had with regard to how violent or nonviolent this collision was at the time that you wrote the report?

A: Just the things we talked about.

Q: Would it be fair to say that you had no information at the time that you wrote this report of November 2005 with regard to the speed of the vehicles involved in this accident?

A: To the actual speed? No, I did not.

Q: Do you know whether or not Mr. Allison's vehicle was stopped or moving?

A: No, I did not.

Q: Were you given any information from Mr. Allison or Mr. Lawton or any other source of how fast Ms. Adare was going at the time her vehicle struck Mr. Allison's vehicle?

A: No.

Q: Do you know how much property damage there was to either Mr. Allison's vehicle or Ms. Adare's vehicle?

A: No.

Q: So when you formed your opinion and wrote in your report in November 2005 that this was a minor collision, you had no information about the speed of either vehicle or the property damage to either vehicle. Correct?

A: Yes, that's right.

Practice Pointer: The date the opinion was formed is important because counsel will attempt to point out the information that was unavailable to the expert when the opinion was formed.

Other Experts

Counsel may attempt to discredit an expert opinion by showing that it is based primarily on the opinions of others. Sophisticated counsel will leave it to the jury or fact finder to conclude that the expert's opinion relies too heavily on conclusions reached by other experts. Relying on other experts' conclusions is, in many instances, allowed under the Federal Rules of Evidence,[1] but such reliance can and will be used to lessen the weight given an expert's testimony.

---

[1] Fed. R. Evid. 703, Bases of Opinion Testimony by Experts: The facts or data in the particular case upon which an expert bases an opinion or inference may be those perceived by or made known to the expert at or before the hearing. If of a type reasonably relied upon by experts in the particular field in forming opinions or inferences upon the subject, the facts or data need not be admissible in evidence in order for the opinion or inference to be admitted. Facts or data that are otherwise inadmissible shall not be disclosed to the jury by the proponent of the opinion or inference unless the court determines that their probative value in assisting the jury to evaluate the expert's opinion substantially outweighs their prejudicial effect.

In addition, opposing counsel may try to get the deponent expert witness to comment on the opposing experts, their qualifications, and their methodology. Counsel is trying to discover any criticisms or weaknesses of the experts prior to the trial. In addition, counsel may try to uncover any bias that the deponent expert has towards any of the opposing experts.

Example 5.19: Basing an opinion on another expert's opinion

Q: What objective factors did you rely upon in coming to your opinion that he was malingering?

A: Well, as I said, my opinion that he was malingering was based on my examination, my interview, my observations of him, and I think that my opinion was supported by Dr. Rudin's findings and those of Dr. Ingalls.

Q: Did you rely on Dr. Rudin's findings in coming to your conclusion?

A: Well, relied in the sense that I read it and I put some reliance on it since I found it supportive. It was not the only factor in my forming that conclusion, but, as I said, it was supportive of my opinion.

Q: If Dr. Rudin had concluded based on the neuropsychological testing that Mr. Allison had brain injury, would that have changed your opinion?

A: Well, that would be an entirely different situation.

Q: My question is had he done that, would that have changed your opinion?

A: Sure.

Practice Pointer: If the expert's opinion is based on another expert's opinion, it is only as good as that expert's opinion. This is a legitimate area of inquiry.

Counsel may compare the deponent expert's opinion with those of the other experts in the case. When doing this, she may be trying to have the jury or fact finder conclude that the deponent expert's opinion may be wrong because the other experts came up with a different conclusion.

Example 5.20: Contrasting your opinion with those of other experts

Q: So, I want to know, are you saying all his doctors are wrong in their diagnosis?

A: I would say that all of them are incorrect that believe, that think that he does have an organic brain syndrome, yes. I think my diagnosis is the correct one.

Q: All right. Dr. Miller diagnosed a concussion two or three days after the accident. That's an organic injury, is it not?

A: Yes.

Q: Was he wrong when he diagnosed a concussion?

A: I don't know because that's a time frame that is far beyond when I examined him.

Q: He was seen by Dr. Torlo shortly after the accident, who diagnosed a postconcussion and postconcussion syndrome. Was Dr. Torlo incorrect when he made that diagnosis?

A: He may have been. I don't know.

Q: Okay. He saw Dr. Stoller, I believe, in 2003 or 2004 and he made a diagnosis of organic brain injury. Was he incorrect at the time that he made the evaluation?
A: I do not know, but he made that diagnosis based on the history and the complaints offered by Mr. Allison.
Q: When Dr. Donya saw Mr. Allison at Hampton Hospital, he made a diagnosis of partial seizure disorder. Was he incorrect when he made that diagnosis?
A: I don't know.

Practice Pointer: Contrasting your opinion with that of several other experts can be an effective technique. Note also how counsel elicited a series of "I don't know" answers from the expert, which seriously call into question the validity of the expert's own opinion. If the expert doesn't know the answer to all these seemingly basic questions, how can he be so sure of his opinion?

Example 5.21: Commenting on other experts
Q: So far as your knowledge of the following people, I want to ask you if you have, or intend to offer an opinion as to the qualifications of and/or competency of the following individuals to address the agronomical issues involved in this case. Donald Brunn? I should say, offer an opinion, if asked. You're just not going to go into court and blurt out things, I understand that.
A: Yes.
Q: What would your opinion be?
A: I'm not sure that Don doesn't bring a little bit of a prejudice to his job with him.
Q: Why do you say that? Prejudice in what way?
A: Well, what is it, the WAC code, WAC 16-1020 and 1040, kind of exactly outline how an investigation is done. And, certainly, since Brunn became involved in this case, he has been kind of outside those guidelines.
Q: "In other cases," you're talking about—
A: That did involve Sinclair.
Q: What, the subsequent Sinclair investigation?
A: Right.
Q: Are you working with Sinclair in defense of the charges laid against them subsequent to 1999?
A: After 1999?
Q: Yes.
A: Yes.
Q: Other than that, anything else in regard to Mr. Brunn, your opinion as to his qualifications or his competency to address agronomical issues in this case?
A: Well, I don't think he's addressing agronomics. He's not addressing whether there was enough fertilizer or wasn't enough fertilizer. He's not offering an agronomic opinion, as far as I know.

Q: Then to address issues related to the matters involved in this case or his investigation?

A: What was the question again?

Q: Opinion as to his qualifications or competency to address—I said agronomical issues. I'll expand that to the pesticide issues involved in this case.

A: I have an issue with the agronomic issue. I don't think he's been asked to do that. I don't think he's qualified to do that. But he's certainly, as far as in his role as a pesticide investigator, he's certainly presumed to be able to interpret regulations and to perhaps take pesticide residue samples. I don't know as we sit here today if he's ever received any formal training on that or not.

Q: So, you really don't know about his qualifications or competency to do what he's charged to do?

A: Well, I've read what he said in his deposition, and I guess I would ask more specific questions, but that's neither here nor there.

Q: Tony Gaber, agronomical and pesticide?

A: I enjoy Tony a lot. Ten years ago I didn't have that opinion of him, but I do now. I enjoy Tony. I think that he is an individual who, if there's a way to amicably resolve some dispute, he certainly is in there with both feet working on that. My only criticism of Tony, as a generic criticism, would be that he still approaches his investigations from the aspect that he still works for the State Department of Agriculture. In other words, if there is, quote, a label violation, then that trumps everything else in the world, and that would be my generic criticism of him.

Q: Kind of a generic bias on his part?

A: I wouldn't say bias. I would just say, for example, if we both went into the same field to do an investigation, I would probably take a lot of soil samples and tissue samples and all this type of thing. Tony might read the label and go interview a few people. And I'm not a good enough people person—I'm not good at interviewing.

Q: Dr. Thomas Chatham?

A: Tom certainly has impressive credentials as a weed scientist. The caution I would have with Tom is he has to make sure that his weed science opinions and conclusions don't overlap into other fields, like pathology, in which he may or may not be qualified.

Q: Melvin A. DeSoto?

A: I think Mel's qualifications are extremely thin. I think he has really never done anything to upgrade his qualifications to any kind of a standard. I think he rides on his dad's reputation. But, as a person, he's very personable. I've never had a problem with him in the field or anything like that. But, professionally, you, one time, asked me in a case what I thought of Mel DeSoto's scientific technique, and I told you I thought he didn't have one.

Q: Eugene Morley?

A: Gene's a good, experienced asparagus fieldman. As far as any academic credentials, I don't have any idea.

Practice Pointer: When commenting on other experts, the deponent expert witness is best served by making objective statements backed up by objective facts. Whether the deponent likes the other expert or despises him is beside the point. The more opposing counsel can get the deponent to take cheap shots ("I think he rides on his dad's reputation") or otherwise reveal a dislike of the opposing expert, the less clinical, impartial, and scientific the deponent sounds.

If an expert is revealed to have an axe to grind with another expert, his opinion as to the opposing expert's qualifications may appear tainted at the least.

5.5 Interrogatory Answers

As part of the discovery process, counsel is allowed to propound written questions or *interrogatories* to other parties. These questions must be answered under oath. Included in almost all interrogatories are questions about the party's experts and their qualifications, opinions, and the factual bases for these opinions. Experts should expect to be questioned about the answers to interrogatories. As such, they should review them prior to the deposition and sign off on them before they are finalized. Counsel may use her questions regarding answers to interrogatories in an attempt to pin down and limit the opinions the expert will be giving at trial. In addition, counsel may test the expert's familiarity with the interrogatories.

Example 5.22: Lawyer uses interrogatory answers to lock down expert on areas of testimony

Q: Let me direct your attention to what we've marked as Exhibit No. 1. These are expert answers to interrogatories. I direct your attention to the page which has your name on it. (Pause.) Have you read that document before today?

A: No.

Q: Are those the opinions that you're going to render at trial?

　　Counsel: Objection in that that's a summary prepared by counsel. If you can answer the question.

A: I need some time to review this document. I think that the elements included here are well…reasonably my own viewpoint.

Q: Are there any other areas that you're going to render opinions about that are not listed on this document?

A: I have no preconception of the opinions that will be rendered at trial…I will try…and respond to the questions that are asked of me to the best of my ability.

Q: So are you saying that this does not include all the areas that you anticipate testifying on because you don't know what you're going to testify on? Is that right?

A: I anticipate to respond honestly to the questions asked of me.

Q: I wasn't questioning your integrity or your honesty. What I was asking you about was whether or not there are other areas you are going to render opinions on that are not listed here on Exhibit No. 1.

A: I have not reviewed that in detail, but I think the testimony will be referenced to the elements of this case in front of us. To the extent that that includes that, that's all I anticipate testifying about.

Practice Pointer: The expert witness has made some important concessions. In this deposition, counsel then went on to question the expert witness about the lengthy and detailed answers to interrogatories concerning what he was going to testify to at trial. Counsel repeatedly asked the question, "Is that your opinion and is that what you will be testifying to?" The expert witness was at a serious disadvantage due to the fact that counsel had not reviewed these answers with him before they were filed or immediately prior to the deposition. The expert made the situation worse by not taking the time during the deposition to review all of the answers carefully and fully *before* he started to give his crucial opinion testimony.

5.6 Factual Basis of an Opinion

An expert's opinion is only as good as the factual assumptions upon which it is based. Expert witnesses can expect to be questioned closely regarding the facts they assumed and the reports, tests, and other evidence they relied upon in forming their opinions. Counsel may use this information to help her dispute these facts at trial. If she can do so successfully, the expert's opinion may be invalidated. Counsel may also attempt to alter the facts and ask hypothetical questions based on a different fact pattern. To excel during deposition, an expert needs to handle questions regarding the factual basis of his opinion properly. The authors recommend the following:

1. Experts should master the facts of the case as part of deposition preparation.
2. An expert should not be evasive. Where appropriate, an expert should readily admit that *if* he were given false or inaccurate information, his opinion might be wrong. The truth of the facts underlying the expert's opinion is something the attorneys will fight about at trial. It's their problem, not the expert's. All the expert should do is make sure the opinion is based upon the best information available to him and that this information is reasonably reliable.
3. Experts should be prepared for hypotheticals and "Would it change your opinion if I told you that..." questions. These questions will most likely be based upon the opposing side's theory of the case. An expert witness can get this theory from retaining the counsel during the pre-deposition conference. For example, if their theory is that your patient was "faking it," you might expect the following hypothetical: "Doctor, let's assume for the time being that the plaintiff lied to you when she told you she had discomfort in her back.

Would that change your opinion?" Experts should be prepared for this kind of hypothetical.

4. An expert witness may be asked to formulate new opinions off the top of his head based on new or different facts or assumptions. Experienced experts neither shoot from the hip nor do they speculate.

Example 5.23: Knowing the facts and record makes a very favorable impression

Q: What happened on July 17, 1998 in this man's life?
A: His brother died.
Q: When was the decedent born?
A: 1939.
Q: Who is Martha in this case?
A: Martha is the wife of the decedent.
Q: How many children did the decedent have?
A: Four living and one who died.

Practice Pointer: The expert here was intimately familiar with the facts and the record. Opposing counsel quickly saw that there was no advantage to be gained by continuing to test his knowledge of the facts and record. The expert is not expected to memorize each and every fact in complex cases. However, the more familiar the expert is with the facts and record the easier time he will have at his deposition. Additionally, keep in mind that opposing counsel is sizing up how effective the expert is likely to be if called to testify at trial. An expert who has mastered the facts of the case and is thoroughly prepared will make a strong impression on all the lawyers in the case.

Example 5.24: Materials relied upon

Q: Please describe for me all documents, photographs, and other materials you have reviewed in the case.
A: They are listed in my report on page 7. They are....

Practice Pointer: Counsel here is trying to determine if the expert failed to review any key information. Experts who list this information precisely in the written report are in a very favorable position to answer such questions.

Example 5.25: Opinion inconsistent with facts and records

Q: What is the basis of your opinion that she had a depressive reaction prior to the date of the accident, June 2, 2006?
A: I based my opinion on her symptoms and the records.
Q: Doctor, prior to June 2, 2006, Ms. Allen didn't have a loss of energy, did she?
A: Not that I know of.
Q: Doctor, prior to June 2, 2006, she wasn't tearful, was she?
A: Not that I know of.

Q: Prior to June 2, 2006, she wasn't irritable, was she?

A: Not that I know of.

Q: Prior to June 2, 2006, she wasn't emotionally labile, was she?

A: Not that I know of.

Q: Prior to June 2, 2006, she didn't evidence sleep problems, did she?

A: Not that I know of.

Q: Prior to June 2, 2006, she didn't feel less of a person, did she?

A: Not that I know of.

Q: Prior to June 2, 2006, she didn't see herself as damaged, did she?

A: Not that I know of.

Q: Prior to June 2, 2006, she did not describe herself as not being herself, did she?

A: Not that I know of.

Q: You're not aware of her having any difficulty concentrating prior to June 2, 2006, are you?

A: I'm not aware of it.

Q: In fact, the medical records don't contain any reference to her having difficulty concentrating prior to June 2, 2006; do they?

A: I believe that's true.

Q: The medical records don't indicate, prior to June 2, 2006, that she was emotionally labile, do they?

A: That's my understanding.

Q: The medical records prior to June 2, 2006, don't evidence any irritability on her part, do they?

A: Not that I am aware of.

Q: Prior to June 2, 2006, she wasn't easily distracted, was she?

A: Not that I'm aware of.

Q: There's nothing in the medical records before June 2, 2006, indicating that she was easily distracted; correct?

A: That is correct.

Q: Prior to June 2, 2006, she didn't have any impaired social relations, did she?

A: Not that I'm aware of.

Q: Prior to June 2, 2006, there's no evidence that she had the feeling of vulnerability; correct?

A: Not that I'm aware of.

Q: Prior to June 2, 2006, there's no evidence that she had a concern over her bodily functions?

A: Not that I'm aware of.

Q: There's no evidence prior to June 2, 2006, that she had an inability to go on with her life; correct?

A: Not that I'm aware of.

Q: Doctor, in fact, there's no evidence of symptoms or medical records prior to June 2, 2006, that show Ms. Allen being depressed, is there?

A: I don't believe so.

Practice Pointer: Once the expert rendered an opinion that was inconsistent with the facts and records, he was in deep trouble. In the example above, counsel has effectively destroyed the credibility of the expert. Experts should be particularly careful about the assumptions and factual basis upon which they build their opinions. If the building blocks can be made to crumble at deposition, the entire testimony of the expert will fall.

Example 5.26: Research material used

Q: People who are trespassing who are mentally ill are potentially a violent crime danger, are they not, sir?

A: Not generally when they're the homeless. The homeless are less apt to do a violent act than homed people.

Q: Mentally ill people are more likely than non-mentally ill people to commit violent crimes.

A: Not when—not when they're homeless.

Q: Particularly Vietnam veterans.

A: Not when they're homeless. In fact, I don't know of a violent Vietnam vet. I know of a lot of them that are a little off, but I don't know of any them that have ever gone violent. I mean, there may be some, I don't know them. But when we know as criminologists that homeless people tend to be less violent than homed people in a trespass situation. And part of it is because they—they do have drug problems, they do have mental adjustment problems, but they're not violent offenders when you compare the two groups.

Q: Do you have any research to support that opinion, sir?

A: Yes—the Department of Justice Study dated 25 January 1999, a copy of which is Appendix "c" in my report.

Q: Did you rely on this so-called "Department of Justice" report in formulating your opinion?

A: In part, yes.

Q: Would you please read into the record the top of page ii?

A: Yes, sir, it says, "This document is a research report submitted to the U.S. Department of Justice. This report has not been published by the Department. Opinions or points expressed are those of the author and do not necessarily reflect the official position or policies of the U.S. Department of Justice."

Practice Pointer: Experts need to be intimately familiar with any research or reports they rely upon. A mistake at deposition like the one above can severely undermine the expert's credibility and opinion.

Example 5.27: Factual assumptions tested

Q: You're saying, nowhere in the medical record indicates that she lost consciousness?

A: That the Indiana General report was that she did not experience loss of consciousness.

Q: That's your recollection of the Indiana General Hospital report?

A: Correct.

Q: And if it did indicate a reported loss of consciousness, would that change your opinion?

A: If the Indiana General Hospital report was that she had experienced some loss of consciousness, then I would be influenced by that, yes.

Q: If eyewitnesses testified that she lost consciousness after this fall, would that change your opinion?

A: Well, I don't know that it would change my opinion, but it's something I would take into account.

Q: If eyewitnesses testified that she lost consciousness, would that affect your opinion?

A: Well, I would have to, you know, hear what they had to say and all. The—what I have at this point is that Mrs. Jules thinks that she might have experienced a few seconds of unconsciousness and the medical reports say no loss of consciousness, or the other doctor said that she was not knocked out.

Q: If there was evidence of loss of consciousness, would you consider changing your opinion?

A: If there was evidence that she had lost consciousness, then I would be inclined to think that she had lost consciousness.

Q: Would you consider changing your opinion?

A: Yes, I would.

Practice Pointer: The opinion of the expert in this example is only as good as the factual assumption upon which it is based (that there was no loss of consciousness). The attorney is attempting to attack the opinion by disproving the opinion's factual assumption. The expert has done a good job in admitting that his opinion may change if the facts were different. The expert realizes that the dispute about the underlying facts is to a large extent the attorneys' problem, not his. Note how the expert did *not* say he would change his opinion but that he would consider changing his opinion.

Equipment and Testing

Counsel who can show that the expert was sloppy in his use of equipment and testing can undermine the expert's credibility and cast substantial doubt on his results and opinion. Remember, an opinion is only as good as the facts, equipment, and tests upon which it is based.

Example 5.28: Expert unsure of methods and equipment

Q: How did you reach your conclusions on the exemplar fender?

A: I made certain measurements of features on the fenders that remained constant both in the photographs and in the flesh and then scaled those down to locate the location of the gouges.

Q: How did you do that?

A: Tape measure and the photographs.

Q: You just took the photographs and—you know, what type of ruler did you use?

A: Steel tape measure, a little six-inch rule, something like that.

Q: Do you know what you used?

A: I typically use a six-inch ruler. I may have used a—

Q: What was the degree of resolution on the measuring instrument used? You mean a sixteenth of an inch?

A: Hundredths of an inch, something like that.

Q: Excuse me?

A: Hundredths of an inch, something like that.

Q: Was it hundredths of an inch?

A: I would have been using a ruler and a caliper both to do that.

Q: You did use a caliper?

A: Yes.

Q: What type of ruler did you use? I want to know the resolution on it. Was it hundredths of an inch?

A: I don't remember. Caliper would go down to well less than that, but I don't remember what the ruler uses.

Q: So you don't know what the resolution was on the ruler that you used?

A: I don't know which ruler I used, offhand.

Q: Is it one you took with you?

A: No. I did this in the laboratory.

Q: Here in Newbury, Oregon?

A: Yes.

Q: And you have no way of going back and determining what ruler you used for your scaling?

A: Probably not. I mean, I've got half a dozen different types of measuring things in my desk.

Q: And you didn't detail the measurements that you took off the photographs of the accident vehicle either, did you…?

Practice Pointer: The expert in the above example may have done nothing wrong, but his "I don't remember" and "I don't know" replies do not instill confidence in him or in his opinion. The expert might have been better served by being better prepared to answer these questions.

Thoroughness

If counsel can imply that the expert was not thorough, she can challenge the factual foundation of his opinion. If the factual foundation of the expert's opinion is challenged successfully, the opinion may be easily discredited. Counsel will sometimes ask questions that at first sound innocuous but that get to the thoroughness of the expert's methods.

Example 5.29: No visit to accident scene
Q: Have you been to the accident site in this case?
A: No.
Q: Do you have any desire to go?
A: No.
Q: As far as you know, you're not going to go?
A: That's correct.

Practice Pointer: Counsel has quickly established at deposition that the expert has not, will not, and did not even have a desire to visit the accident scene. At trial, this may be portrayed by counsel as a lack of thoroughness on the part of the expert witness.

When the Case Was Accepted

Experts who are retained long after the accident or incident can expect to be questioned closely by counsel on this point. Counsel's motives could include attempting to show that the expert did not have adequate time to perform a thorough analysis and/or that counsel was shopping the case around and having difficulty finding an expert to take the case.

Another reason for the use of this line of questioning is to attempt to show that the expert's analysis may be flawed because its subject has changed or deteriorated during the time between the incident in question and the expert's retention. Counsel will often be developing a timeline for the case. The dates when the expert was retained and when he formed his opinion will be crucial parts of the timeline.

To excel during deposition, expert witnesses need to be prepared to deal with these types of questions. Experts should not be evasive about dates. These are hard facts and there is no role for evasiveness when asked a concise and direct question regarding the date one was first contacted or the date one first reviewed evidence in the case. To truly excel, an expert also needs to be prepared to discuss why his analysis was neither biased nor flawed as a result of the date of his retention and analysis. Without forethought, these justifications and rationales may slip one's mind at a crucial point in the deposition.

Example 5.30: Expert consulted 11 months after accident occurred

Q: Mr. Thierry, would it be correct to say that you were not retained as an expert in this case until some 11 months after the accident occurred?

A: I was brought into this case I believe I said in….

Q: March of 2005?

A: That's correct.

Q: And your understanding is this accident occurred in April of 2004?

A: April 30th of '04, yes.

Q: So it was approximately an eleven-month or ten-month interval?

A: That's correct.

Q: As a rule, do you think it's desirable as an expert evaluating a piece of machinery to look at the piece of machinery fairly close in time or as close in time as possible to the event that you are investigating?

A: Yes, it is.

Q: You said you read the complaint in this action so you know the complaint was filed in this case in September of 2004?

A: If that is correct.

Q: Do you know why you were not retained until some six months after the complaint was filed?

A: No, I do not.

Q: Are you aware of any other experts who have been retained previously by ABC Products prior to your coming in to the case?

A: No, I don't.

Q: You have no information on that at all?

A: No.

Q: Why is it desirable to be called into a case so soon after an incident as possible, sir?

A: Well, the machinery is in the same condition, the grounds and conditions would be as similar as possible.

Q: A lot might have happened to the machine in the intervening 11 months if it was in use, correct?

A: Yes.

Q: Was the machine in use during the intervening 11 months?

A: Yes, that's my understanding.

Q: How many hours of use and what maintenance and modifications did the machine undergo between April 30, 2004, and March 2005?

Practice Pointer: The expert properly admitted that it would have been better to be called in earlier. This is obvious to most people (and most jurors) and there is no point in trying to split hairs. Counsel is planting the seeds of doubt in the minds of the jurors about why there was a delay in calling in the expert. The jury is left to speculate. Note as well that counsel attempts to discover the existence of any consultants who have not been disclosed as experts. The expert's only possible mistake was in agreeing with counsel's characterization of "a lot" in the third-to-the-last question. Instead of accepting this broad characterization, a better response might have been, "There may have been some changes in the condition of the machine, yes." This response changes the response from "yes, there could have been 'a lot' of changes" to "yes, there could have been 'some' changes." Both responses are truthful and accurate, but the latter one is much better in that it implies less change.

5.7 Methodology

Experts can expect to be questioned closely regarding the methods used to form their opinions. If counsel can attack the methodology an expert used, he can ultimately challenge the validity of the expert's opinion and may be able to exclude it from evidence.[2] In addition, counsel may try and show that the expert cherry-picked selected data in an attempt to reach a specific conclusion. Expert witnesses need to be prepared to answer challenges to their fact gathering. More importantly, experts need to use a reliable and proven methodology that will withstand close questioning by counsel at deposition and trial.

An expert's deposition may be taken for the specific purpose of determining whether it meets the admissibility standards set forth in *Daubert, Joiner, Kumho Tire,* and subsequent cases. *Daubert* set forth a nonexclusive checklist for trial courts (i.e., trial judges) to use in assessing the reliability of scientific expert testimony. The specific factors explicated by the *Daubert* court are: (1) whether the expert's technique or theory can be or has been tested; that is, whether the expert's theory can be challenged in some objective sense, or whether it is instead simply a subjective, conclusory approach that cannot reasonably be assessed for reliability; (2) whether the technique or theory has been subject to peer review and publication; (3) the known or potential rate of error of the technique or theory when applied; (4) the existence and maintenance of standards and controls; and (5) the degree to which the technique or theory has been generally accepted in the scientific community.

Courts both before and after *Daubert* have found other factors relevant in determining whether expert testimony is sufficiently reliable to be considered by the trier of fact. These factors include the following:

1. Whether experts are "proposing to testify about matters growing naturally and directly out of research they have conducted independent of the litigation, or whether they have developed their opinions expressly for purposes of testifying." (See *Daubert v. Merrell Dow Pharmaceuticals, Inc.,* F.3d 1311, 1317 (9th Cir. 1995).)

---

[2] See *Daubert v. Merrell Dow Pharmaceuticals, Inc.,* 113 S.Ct. 2786 (1993).

2. Whether the expert has unjustifiably extrapolated from an accepted premise to an unfounded conclusion. (See *General Elec. Co. v. Joiner,* 118 (S.Ct. 512, 519, 1997). This decision notes that in some cases a trial court "may conclude that there is simply too great an analytical gap between the data and the opinion proffered.")

3. Whether the expert has accounted for obvious alternative explanations adequately. (See *Claar v. Burlington N.R.R.,* 29 F.3d 499 (9th Cir. 1994). Here testimony is excluded where the expert failed to consider other obvious causes for the plaintiff's condition. Compare *Ambrosini v. Labarraque,* 101 F.3d 129 (D.C.Cir. 1996). This decision holds that the possibility of some uneliminated causes presents a question of weight, so long as the most obvious causes have been considered and reasonably ruled out by the expert.)

4. Whether the expert "is being as careful as he would be in his regular professional work outside his paid litigation consulting." (See *Sheehan v. Daily Racing Form, Inc.,* 104 F.3d 940, 942 (7th Cir. 1997). See also *Braun v. Lorillard Inc.,* 84 F.3d 230, 234 (7th Cir. 1996). *Daubert* requires the trial court to assure itself that the expert "adheres to the same standards of intellectual rigor that are demanded in his professional work.")

5. Whether the field of expertise claimed by the expert is known to reach reliable results. (See *Sterling v. Velsicol Chem. Corp.,* 855 F.2d 1188 (6th Cir. 1988), where the court rejects testimony based on "clinical ecology" as unfounded and unreliable.)

All of these factors remain relevant to the determination of the reliability of expert testimony.

In the case of *Stasior v. National Railroad Passenger Corp.,* 19 F.Supp.2d 835 (N.D. Ill. 1998), the depositions of ergonomists were taken and then tested in a motion in limine under *Daubert.* The transcript of a portion of the lengthy deposition of Michael D. Shinnick, Ph.D., a highly regarded ergonomist, is provided in the example that follows.

Example 5.31: Unreliable methodology
Q: Did you quantify the number of key strokes per minute the reservation sales agents perform at the Chicago facility?
A: No.
Q: Do you know if Miss Stasior was using this wrist rest in 1991 and prior to that time?
A: I don't believe she was but I also know they had different keyboards at that point and I'm aware that keys would malfunction and I have—it's been reported to me that

the keyboards that they had prior to the ones they have now were—required more force.

Q: Do you know when those keyboards were used?

A: No.

Q: As you sit here today, Doctor, can you tell me what keyboard Miss Stasior worked on and for what period of time she worked on it?

A: No.

Q: Do you have any idea if that's what the job looked like and how she performed it in 1991 and prior to that time?

A: There was different equipment, but no.

Q: Let me interrupt you for a minute. You say there's different equipment. We might as well cover this while we're sitting here right now. Do you know the dimensions of the different equipment?

A: No.

Q: Do you know the height of the different equipment?

A: No.

Q: Do you know the height of the desk?

A: No.

Q: Do you know the width of the desk?

A: No.

Q: Do you know the height of the different chair?

A: No. They certainly didn't in the video and she said that's been her customary work posture. But prior to '91, no, I don't know.

Q: Do you know if she ever requested any different equipment prior to 1991?

A: No.

Q: Do you feel you have visited the Amtrak reservation sales office for a sufficient length of time in order to render opinions in this case?

A: Yes.

Q: How long was your visit at the Amtrak reservation sales office in January of 1997?

A: Don't know.

Q: Are you aware of any of the personal risk factors that Miss Stasior has which have been identified as having an association with carpal tunnel syndrome?

A: No.

Q: Did you feel it necessary to determine if she had any personal risk factors in arriving at your opinions in this case?

A: No, not once I looked at her job and her normal working position and the lack of ergonomic training, no.

Q: Did you quantify—and I apologize, I may repeat a little bit here—did you quantify the length of time Miss Stasior would spend with her wrists in a non-neutral position during the day?

A: No.

Q: As you sit here today, do you know for a fact what type of keyboard Miss Stasior was using in 1991 and before?

A: I do not know for a fact.

Q: As you sit here today, do you know for a fact what chair she was using in 1991 and before?

A: It's not relevant.

Q: So, in your opinion her job caused her condition?

A: From a[n] ergonomic perspective, yes.

Q: Tell me the methodology you used to reach that conclusion.

A: Well, I think we went—she was exposed to multiple risk factors.

Q: Which you did not quantify, right?

A: Don't have to.

Q: They're just there?

A: Yah.

Q: No matter what degree, they're there, that's enough.

A: We don't have thresholds.

Q: Do you have any idea what the prevalence rate of carpal tunnel syndrome is with not only the Amtrak—well, I'll limit it to the Chicago office with the reservation sales office.

A: The prevalence with—no, I don't.

Q: Do you have any idea what the prevalence is with the various reservation sales offices around the country for Amtrak?

A: No.

Q: Would that be a significant thing to know in determining whether or not the job caused carpal tunnel syndrome?

A: No.

Q: Is there any way to test your opinion that Miss Stasior's job caused her carpal tunnel?

A: Test it? Well, I think you can validate it by looking at what other industries have done as far as—and compare that to what Amtrak did not do.

Q: Can you tell me if they did provide the information she would not have developed carpal tunnel syndrome?

A: Well, I can tell you—I can say the probability would be reduced.

Q: But you can't tell me how much?

A: No.

Q: Have you in fact tested your hypotheses that Miss Stasior's work contributed to her carpal tunnel syndrome in any way?

A: No.

Practice Pointer: The court rejected the above deposition testimony, finding that it was not admissible. The rationale of the court is instructive.

The court holds that while Dr. Shinnick is qualified as an expert to render an opinion regarding causation, his actual testimony is not reliable under *Daubert* because he has not subjected his opinions to the scientific method.[3] Essentially, Dr. Shinnick "identified" the existence of risk factors and then concluded that these risk factors contributed to Stasior's CTS without performing any scientific tests or comparing the data he collected to scientific or epidemiological studies conducted by other ergonomists. Dr. Shinnick never observed the workstation Stasior used in 1991 and before, and he made no attempt to measure the awkward posture and repetition which are allegedly present at Stasior's current workstation in order to extrapolate what her pre-1991 conditions were like. (Shinnick Dep. 27-29, 17-20, 99, 44-45.) Dr. Shinnick simply assumes, without citing any corroborating authority, that because Stasior allegedly was not trained in the proper use of her equipment, the risk factors of awkward posture and repetition must have been present at Stasior's workstation in 1991 and before. (Shinnick Dep. at 21.) While Dr. Shinnick performed functional capacity and grip tests on Stasior, he does not cite any peer-reviewed scientific or epidemiological studies tying the results of his tests to the conclusion that awkward posture and repetition contributed to Stasior's CTS and tendonitis. The court also notes that Dr. Herrin did not base his proffered testimony on research he conducted independent of this litigation, but rather formulated his opinion expressly for the purpose of testifying. (Shinnick Dep. at 42-44.)

Dr. Shinnick defends his "methodology" by stating that any prudent employer does not care about quantifying a risk factor but rather about minimizing any risk factors that exist. (Shinnick Dep. at 99-100.) The court notes that this is a sensible assumption for an ergonomist whose job is to minimize the possibility of developing CTDs in a work environment. However, the analysis required to prospectively minimize the risk factors for CTDs is substantially different from the analysis required to determine specific causes of injuries that have already occurred. *Bennett,* 931 F.Supp. at 493. Because the allocation of legal and possibly substantial financial responsibility is at issue in this case, Dr. Shinnick must base his causation opinions on scientifically reliable methodologies. *Id.* at 493-494. Because Dr. Shinnick does not test his causation opinion in accordance with the scientific method, the court holds that his testimony is not reliable under *Daubert* and therefore is inadmissible.

…The court also holds that Dr. Shinnick's opinion as to forseeability is not reliable under *Daubert*. While Dr. Shinnick states "Amtrak could have known and should have known that the duties routinely performed by Mrs. Stasior placed her in danger of developing cumulative trauma injuries," (Shinnick Report at 4), he is unable to cite any studies from 1991 or before showing that the degree of posture, repetition and force at Amtrak's Chicago RSO was ergonomically unsafe. Therefore, it would be unreasonable to expect Amtrak to have foreseen that the workstation it provided Stasior would have contributed to her CTS and chronic tendonitis.

---

[3] Because the court finds that Dr. Shinnick's testimony is not reliable under *Daubert,* the court does not address whether Dr. Shinnick's testimony satisfies *Daubert's* relevance requirement.

Because Dr. Shinnick's testimony is not reliable under *Daubert* and therefore inadmissible under Rule 702, the court grants Amtrak's Motion to Bar Testimony of Michael Shinnick.[4]

Example 5.32: Cherry-picking data

Q: Okay. And in that note, Dr. McEllin says, "His foot looks fine." That's the third paragraph down?
A: Yes.
Q: He also says, does he not, in the final paragraph, that the foot—that "It was possible that that foot would always be somewhat uncomfortable given the degree of injury that he had." Do you see where he says that?
A: "It is possible,"—Yes, I do have that. Yes, indeed.
Q: Okay. And in March of '99, McEllin was saying that the foot looked fine, but it was possible that it might never be normal?
A: Never normal in terms of the total elimination of discomfort, I guess, is what he's saying here, yes.
Q: Right. Now, you didn't include that comment about the foot possibly being always somewhat uncomfortable. You did not include that in your report, did you?
A: I didn't.
Q: Do you recall—did you review an April of 1999 report—April 28, 1999 report from Dr. McEllin?
A: I have that.
Q: And you see in there that Dr. McEllin said that he was—that he felt, McEllin, that Mr. Strayve was "Not ready to return to his regular activity," and that he would, "expect many months before he was going to be able to tolerate that degree of work." Do you see where he says that?
A: I do see that.
Q: You didn't include that in your report—that quote, in your report, did you, Doctor?
A: I didn't, no.
Q: You say in your report, Doctor, on page eight, and that would be almost at the bottom of the last paragraph, you say in your report that Dr. McEllin had no explanation for Strayve's persistent symptoms?
A: Yes.
Q: And—but later—but in that report—that office note, Dr. McEllin diagnosed a chronic residual pain after right foot crush injury. Correct?
A: I have that page now and I see my quote, and then you're asking me about what he said?
Q: Your quote was—you quoted Dr. McEllin as saying the foot looks "great." Right?
A: Yes.

---

[4] *Stasior v. National Railroad Passenger Corp.*, 19 F.Supp.2d 835, 852-853 (N.D. Ill. 1998).

Q: But you did not quote him in terms of his assessment that Mr. Strayve was having chronic residual pain after right foot crush injury. You did not quote that?
A: I didn't quote it.
Q: And you also did not quote him, Dr. McEllin, that he concurred at that point that it was appropriate for Mr. Strayve to have a pain clinic evaluation and treatment plan. You did not quote that either, did you?
A: I didn't quote it.
Q: Okay. Now, you quoted Dr. Czycyk in your report?
A: I did.
Q: And that was, I believe, also on page eight of your report, in the end of that second to last paragraph.
A: Yes.
Q: And you quoted her as saying that Mr. Strayve had "some type of a syndrome"?
A: I did.
Q: And that was the extent of your quoting of Dr. Czycyk. Correct?
A: That was the extent of my quote.
Q: And what she actually said was—starting at the bottom of page one, "that he most likely had some sort of a pain syndrome." Correct?
A: "He most likely has some sort of pain syndrome going on, yes."
Q: And she also went on to opine that it might be "a combination of RSD with a nerve crush injury syndrome." Correct?

Practice Pointer: Opposing counsel in the above example pointed out time and again the "damaging or non-helpful" language that the expert left out of his report. The implication is that the expert tried to soften the damaging information by intentionally leaving out key parts of the underlying report. The expert could have stopped this line of inquiry in several ways:

> **Q:** You didn't include that in your report, did you?
> **A:** I reviewed hundreds of pages, Counsel, so I could not put each and every word in my 9-page report.

Or, alternatively:

> **Q:** You didn't include that in your report, did you?
> **A:** No, because I did not believe it was true.

Example 5.33: Cherry-picking from the record
Q: You specifically made mention of the plaintiff having been in a fight with a police officer when he was 17?
A: Correct.
Q: Now, you've chosen to make special mention of that in your 213 answers. I want to know why.

A: Two reasons. Number 1, this man seemed to have chronic problems with authority; and he had chronic problems with listening to authority. I'm not saying every day in every way or in the military or not, but certainly there was a pattern of noncompliance and not cooperating. So I'm inferring that that was an episode where there was some noncompliance with conformity, Number 1.

Number 2, it would raise the eyebrows of somebody looking at a lifetime pattern or certainly an adult lifetime pattern of bipolar illness. Whether it be unipolar or bipolar, it certainly is an affective illness. As to whether there might have been something going on in his adolescence, certainly the first is so that there is some authority problem there; and we certainly see that as time goes on.

Q: Are you saying he had bipolar disease when he was 17 years old?

A: No. I'm not saying that.

Q: Was he ever convicted of this crime?

A: I think he was arrested for beating up a policeman. That's what it said.

Q: Who said that?

A: It's in the social history of the hospital.

Q: In 1993?

A: Right.

Q: Taken by a social worker?

A: That's correct.

Q: Was it ever mentioned by any treating psychiatrist or physician?

A: No.

Q: So it couldn't have made any difference to anything, any difference to his diagnosis or treatment at that time, could it?

A: Only to the extent that I've already indicated, that there might be some—It suggests there might be some conformity problem with authority.

Q: And so what you're saying is that in order to, in order to deprecate this man's personality, I'm going to say that he was arrested when he was 17 years old and that that's going to make a bad impression on the jury, isn't it?

A: That's certainly not the case.

Q: You wouldn't do a thing like that, would you?

A: No, sir, I would not.

Practice Pointer: Opposing counsel here makes a frontal attack on the expert, his honesty, and, in essence, accuses him of advocating for the side that retained him. The expert was wise, after his simple denial, not to get angry and get in an argument with opposing counsel. The expert who loses his temper at this type of accusation and "goes off" magnifies the point and may appear defensive, thus giving some credence to the accusation.

Example 5.34: Unreliable methods

Q: Do you know the source of that hand drawing?

A: It was produced through Mr. Brown. Whether he actually made the drawing or not, I don't recall at this point.

Q: Do you know whether that drawing was produced by an engineer?

A: I have assumed that it was not.

Q: So, in order to make the conclusion that your exemplar wrench deformed to a curve which you described as being very similar to that of the subject wrench, you relied on a hand drawing that was prepared by a layman and a snapshot photograph of the wrench, is that correct to say?

A: Those are the two things I relied on. The photograph that I have is enlarged to eight by ten and there are various photographs of that particular wrench.

Q: Did you use any photometric process to determine the exact curve of the subject wrench?

A: No.

Q: You kind of did that by eyeballing, is that fair to say?

A: That is the term.

Practice Pointer: This was an effective assault on the methods relied upon to form the expert's opinion. The expert would have been wise to rely upon methods that the jury would see as more reliable.

5.8 Bias

Expert witnesses are routinely questioned during deposition by counsel to determine if they have any bias that may affect their credibility. The general evidentiary rule is that this line of inquiry is permitted because matters that affect bias are relevant to a crucial issue in the case—one's credibility as a witness. Counsel is given great leeway to discover any interest, bias, or motive for testimony that would serve to discredit the expert's testimony.

There are three things that expert witnesses can do to deal properly with questioning regarding their possible biases.

1. Tell the truth and "call them as you see them." This policy will enable experts to testify with confidence supported by the courage of their convictions.

2. State that the expert's opinion is independent and unbiased.

   The witness should make it clear, to the extent possible, that the engagement began without preconceptions concerning any issue and without any predisposition in favor of or opposed to any party or counsel. The expert was not told what opinion to come to but was asked to render an honest opinion and did so.[5]

---

[5] Gregory P. Joseph, *ALI-ABA's Practice Checklist Manual on Taking Depositions* (Philadelphia: American Law Institute, 1995) p. 89.

3. Try not to testify exclusively for only one side in cases. This may not be achieved easily because counsel and industry may peg an expert or refuse to use him if he testifies for the other side.

The following sections cover the standard areas of bias that experts are challenged on during their depositions.

Impartiality

Counsel can damage the credibility of the expert by showing that the expert is not being impartial. This may be done by showing that the expert only testifies for one side. For example, she only testifies for plaintiffs. Counsel is trying to show that the expert wouldn't want to put future referrals at risk by proffering testimony that her client wouldn't like. To excel during depositions, experts need to be able to handle this line of questioning. As always, it is best to answer the questions simply and directly. If an expert tries to cover up her propensities to testify for one side, these propensities will only be emphasized to the jury. The expert will also want to clarify in advance a rationale for why she usually testifies for one side. For example, an orthopedic surgeon might state that she usually testifies on behalf of plaintiffs because they are also patients she has treated and that she is the physician most familiar with their cases.

Example 5.35: Admits testimony for employers

Q: You have testified in other workers' compensation cases also on behalf of the employer?
A: Yes, I have.
Q: Do you recall each and every instance of testimony that you gave?
A: No, I do not.
Q: Is it true that in workers' compensation cases you testify mostly on behalf of employers?
A: I would state that's a fair statement; yes.

Practice Pointer: The expert was straightforward and did not try to mislead the questioner about his prior testimony. This ended this inquiry and counsel then went on to inquire about the expert's opinion.

Example 5.36: Good answer for why most work is for the defense

Q: Is there any specific reason why your plaintiff and defense percentage is skewed to the defense or is it merely that more defense lawyers call you or is there something else?
A: The percentages have to be based on the intersection of several factors, including number one, what you said, who calls me; number two, my turndown rate, which is the dismissal of a case as nonmeritorious depending on whichever side they are on;

and some of it is blind chance. If the next 20 or 30 cases are plaintiff cases that are valid, the percentage would shift.

Practice Pointer: The expert in the above example diffuses a potentially troublesome issue simply, directly, and, most importantly, without being the slightest bit defensive. Note how he also worked into his answer the ticking time bombs of "turndown rate" and "nonmeritorious cases." This was a prepared expert.

Example 5.37: Expert makes conscious effort for balance
Q: Of the 500 cases you've handled, approximately how many of them, by percentage, were on behalf—were you retained on behalf of the insurance company, and how many were you retained on behalf of the insured who was trying to get certain benefits from the insurance company? What has been your split on that?
A: Initially, I only did defense work on behalf of insurance companies only. I found out I was losing credibility because I was only doing one side. Since then I have represented the policy holder in many instances, and, despite coincidences, about half is for the companies and half is for the policy holder.

Practice Pointer: The expert, with the assistance of retaining counsel, was able to neatly and succinctly deal with this potential problem. It was the fact that the expert realized the problem and modified his practice of only accepting defense work that enabled him to easily overcome the issue. The expert would have been better served by not using the phrase, "I have represented." "I have been retained by" would be a more artful and truthful reply.

Example 5.38: Poorly prepared expert
Q: Is it true that in workers' compensation cases you testify mostly on behalf of employers?
A: No; for employers and for employees as well.
Q: Have you ever testified that an injured worker contracted carpal tunnel syndrome as the result of work?
A: Yes, I have.
Q: What was the name of the person that you testified on behalf of?
A: I can't—I cannot—obviously, patient confidentiality would restrict me from divulging—
Q: Don't give me that patient confidentiality, Doctor. I asked you if you testified on behalf of someone. You know very well there's no—
A: Testified—
Q: —patient confidentiality. I'm asking you—
A: Okay.
Q: —did you ever testify?
A: You define for me what testify means.
Q: Like here in a deposition or in court, did you ever give a deposition—

A: I've indicated in—I've indicated in—

Q: —on behalf of an injured worker?

A: —medical records that, and I've written letters to the effect that I felt an individual had developed carpal tunnel syndrome.

Q: So I can break your answer down, sir. The answer is, you cannot recall any instances where you testified on behalf of an injured worker that they contracted carpal tunnel at work, correct? Testified!

A: Define testified, please.

Q: Deposition or trial.

A: As I indicated, I cannot recall any specific incident that I've testified in court or on deposition, and my safe assumption is that it never had to go that far.

Practice Pointer: The expert in this case attempted to make his testimony sound more impartial than it actually might have been. This was a videotaped deposition intended to be used in lieu of live testimony at trial. The expert would probably have been better served by answering the first question with a simple yes. His evasiveness makes him look like he is an advocate and has something to hide. This encourages counsel to emphasize the point instead of moving on. This is far more damaging to his credibility than would have been an admission that he testifies mostly for employers.

Example 5.39: Always has same opinion

Q: Well, in your report you state that to a reasonable—I'm going to paraphrase it— to a reasonable degree of certainty Mrs. Gerald's job—

A: What page are you on?

Q: Why don't I just go ahead and get it for you so I can actually not paraphrase it? Page 4, second paragraph, what looks like about the third full sentence: "Within a reasonable ergonomic certainty a causal relationship exists between Mrs. Gerald's job duties and damage to the carpal tunnels." Other than this case, have you ever offered such an opinion?

A: Sure.

Q: Have you ever in a case in which you were retained to examine the workplace and possibly offer opinions in a carpal tunnel case, have you ever had a contrary opinion?

A: No. I've had different opinions but no, I haven't.

Q: In your opinion, the workplace has always caused the carpal tunnel syndrome?

A: Yes, but that's—yes, that's what I've found.

Practice Pointer: If you can be portrayed as always arriving at the same opinion, your impartiality and credibility may be very easily called into question. Note how this expert correctly refused to answer a question about a document (in this instance, his report) until he knew exactly what counsel was referring to in the document and he could review the exact language in question.

Inflexibility
If counsel can show during the deposition that an expert is inflexible (nothing would change her opinion), this is another indication of potential bias. If the underlying factual assumptions are changed and the expert still refuses to admit that she may have to change her opinion, her credibility will come into question. To refute these kinds of attacks on one's credibility, expert witnesses should demonstrate open-mindedness. This will go a long way in showing a lack of bias.

Example 5.40: Willing to consider new evidence
Q: If you were to learn that Aaron was different after the crash, that would change your opinion, wouldn't it?
A: If I had information indicating that, I would consider it.
Q: If you were to learn that after the car crash, Aaron Pharmer began to exhibit signs and symptoms that are the diagnostic of post-traumatic stress disorder, would you be willing to change your opinion?
A: Possibly. I will reiterate that Mr. Pharmer made it very clear to me that he had these classic symptoms from 1993 onward and indicated to me that they were unchanged in their intensity or frequency subsequent to the motor vehicle accident in 2003.
Q: If you were to learn that Mr. Pharmer was incorrect, or if your notation of his statements was incorrect, you would be willing to change your opinion, wouldn't you?
A: The notations of my—of his statements in my records are not incorrect. These are what he told me. If I learned that there was information indicating that his recollection of that was incorrect, I would consider it. I would not automatically change my opinion.

Practice Pointer: The expert psychologist demonstrated his willingness to consider new evidence and possibly change his opinion without actually changing his opinion. He handled these questions well.

Personal/Social Relationship with Party/Attorney
Another way to show potential bias is to establish that the expert has a personal/social relationship with a party or with the retaining attorney. The way to handle these questions is honestly and directly. Evasiveness can be more damaging to one's credibility than whatever point counsel is trying to make. However, expert witnesses should be careful to not agree with an attempt by counsel to mischaracterize a relationship. For example, if the party is an "acquaintance," the expert should not agree with counsel's assertion that she is a "close friend."

119

Example 5.41: Grudging admission of familiarity
Q: Are you a close personal friend of Attorney Burns?
A: I am a friend.
Q: Have you been to his home?
A: Yes.
Q: Have you been to his condominium in Vail?
A: Yes.
Q: Did you ski together?
A: Yes.
Q: Do you play racquetball together?
A: Yes.
Q: Are your spouse and his wife friendly?
A: Yes.
Q: How often do you see him socially?
A: Once or twice a week.
Q: Are you a close personal friend of Attorney Burns?
A: Yes—I guess I am.

Practice Pointer: If you disagree with counsel's characterization of your relationship with a party or attorney, you will need to prepare yourself to answer these types of questions.

Professional Witness
Counsel may try to portray the expert as a *professional witness*. A professional witness is a witness who testifies frequently and derives a large percentage of his income from forensic work. Counsel is trying to show that such a witness is biased by being consciously or unconsciously hesitant to jeopardize his livelihood by saying something that would hurt the party that retained him. The expert witness who can be portrayed as a *hired gun* due to the frequency with which he testifies can quickly be made to lose credibility.

Example 5.42: Expert not forthcoming and defensive
Q: Doctor, you are an experienced expert witness, are you not?
A: It depends on what you mean by "experienced."
Q: You testify quite frequently, don't you?
A: Again, Counselor, it depends on what you mean by "frequently."
Q: How many times have you testified in deposition in Massachusetts?
A: 60 to 80 times.
Q: In addition to depositions, you testified daily when you were a court clinic director?
A: That is correct.
Q: What superior courts have you testified in in Massachusetts?

A: Suffolk, Middlesex, Essex, Hampden, Worcester, I believe, Plymouth, Barnstable, Bristol. I think that's about it.

Q: Would you agree that you are an experienced expert witness?

A: It all depends on how you define "experienced."

Practice Pointer: Counsel has scored two major points with this witness. First, the doctor is clearly an experienced expert witness. Secondly, she is not forthcoming with any information. Both points will tend to make the jury or fact finder discredit her testimony. As a practical matter, the doctor would have been better off to admit that she was an experienced expert witness.

Example 5.43: Hired gun

Q: About 20 percent of your time is spent doing legal work, correct?

A: Probably. Yes, sir.

Q: And, you've been involved in cases involving medical legal questions in a number of states, haven't you?

A: Some 21 states.

Q: Well, would it be Vermont?

A: Yes, sir.

Q: New Hampshire?

A: Yes, sir.

Q: Massachusetts, obviously?

A: Yes.

Q: Is it actually more than 21, Doctor?

A: I thought it was 21, I could be wrong.

Q: Twenty-eight?

A: Sounds like I need to revise my list.

Q: And, that's ranged from the East Coast out to Colorado, correct?

A: Yes, sir.

Practice Pointer: The expert needs to know the number of states she has testified in. There is no reason for the expert to "lose count" as in the above example. Note that the expert was not initially asked the number of states she testified in:

> **Q:** And, you've been involved in cases involving medical legal questions in a number of states, haven't you?

A better, truthful, non-volunteering reply would have been a simple "yes." An inexperienced expert could have been tempted to fight back on this point.

> **Q:** Twenty-eight?
> **A:** You are probably right. I have been found qualified by judges in 28 states to testify.

However, a sophisticated expert would realize that it's best to save a response like this until trial and not waste it at deposition.

Advocate

The role of an expert is to state opinions. It is not to be an advocate for one side or the other. That's the attorney's role. If an expert starts to sound or act like an advocate, counsel can paint him as biased and he will lose credibility with the fact finder. In addition, if the expert generally advocates one position, this will be used at deposition in an attempt to discredit him.

Example 5.44: Expert acts like part of litigation team

Q: Your report is fairly detailed, it's an eight-page report to Mr. Hodge?
A: That's correct.
Q: Now, on page 3 of your report to Mr. Hodge, you state—I'll let you find it.
A: Yes.
Q: Quote, "That although sufficient witnesses have been present, they may not be unbiased witnesses in this particular accident."
A: That's what I stated.
Q: Why did you feel this was important to include in your independent medical report?
A: Mr. Saplich himself quoted that he had 30 witnesses or something so that it was witnessed that he had fallen. But I would challenge you to find one independent or one that would not be his co-worker, a friend with the same causes involved. So, yes, you have witnesses; and, yes, witnesses' recollections may or may not be shaded by whatever other circumstances go on. So, I felt that they would be witnesses, but the direct testimony you're going to get out of them may or may not be useful or entirely reflective of the situation.
Q: And why is it your function as the independent medical evaluator in this case to point that out to Mr. Hodge? That's what I'm trying to understand.
A: I'm not sure if it's my function to point that out. It might be my function to try to figure out why there are lots of complaints and lots of treatment and there were none before. And I see lots of secondary factors involved that would be probably more explained—more clearly explanatory of his clinical course than any medical issues involved.
Q: Well, right now we're talking about the witnesses that you're saying are biased in this particular case. Have you reviewed any of the witness statements in the case?
A: I'm not saying they're biased. I'm just commenting that they are probably not unbiased, and I have not reviewed any witness testimony here.
Q: So you really don't have any idea because you don't know what they said?
A: Don't have any idea, just had a feeling that they may not be as unbiased as one would like it to be.

Practice Pointer: The physician has left his role as an independent medical evaluator and unbiased expert and has become part of the litigation team for the defense trying to prove and win a case. As a result, it is likely that he will lose credibility.

Example 5.45: Well-known positions of expert
Q: Now, you have held rather passionate—a passionate position that trampolines should not be manufactured and sold to the public for the use—for recreational use in backyards. Is that a fair statement?
A: That's a fair statement.
Q: And how long have you held that opinion?
A: Probably my whole career.
Q: And you have advocated that opinion publicly. Is that a fair statement?
A: That's correct.
Q: And is it fair to say also that this has been a public position that to some extent has dominated the public positions that you've taken over the course of time?
A: I'm sorry, I missed you on that one.
Q: Let me ask you the question slightly different. You made this position known on national television?
A: Yes, sir.
Q: You've made it known in writing articles?
A: Yes, sir.
Q: You've made it known in speaking?
A: Yes, sir.
Q: You've made it known on ASTM committees that you've been on?
A: That's correct.
Q: Now, despite this position, it has not been embraced, has it, by the Consumer Product Safety Commission?
A: They haven't banned it, if that's what you mean, that's correct.
Q: Right. And if this product were to be banned, as you say, okay, one of the organizations, governmental organizations capable of doing that is the Consumer Product Safety Commission.
A: That's correct.

Practice Pointer: The expert here correctly does not try to run away from his strongly held beliefs. Any attempt, at this late date, to distance himself from long-held and widely expressed beliefs would be a disaster. Once the expert informs retaining counsel of his beliefs/positions and counsel decides to use the expert, any fallout from the beliefs will be the sole responsibility of retaining counsel. Of course, this expert's deposition would have been significantly easier if the expert didn't have such a lengthy "paper trail" indicating his belief. The most successful experts are usually careful to not create a potentially damaging paper trail.

Fees and Compensation

The fact that an expert is paid for his time (expert witnesses are never paid for their testimony, only for their time) is relevant to a possible bias toward the retaining party. Questions about expert witness fees and compensation are legitimate and relevant. The fact that the expert is being paid a fee is not something to be ashamed of because, as a professional, one's time is valuable. Furthermore, experts retained by the opposing side will also charge a fee for their time.

When questioning an expert about fees, counsel frequently attempts to get the expert to be defensive and, if possible, evasive. If the jury or fact finder gets the impression that the expert is trying to hide something, is doing something he is ashamed of, or is trying to conceal something, the honesty and integrity of the witness come into question quickly. In legal parlance, this is known as using a *red-herring* or making something out of nothing. Experts can protect themselves from such legal tactics by answering questions about fees in a straightforward manner.

The fee that an expert witness charges can be very high and still not damage her credibility. The key is to be able to justify the fee. For example, a plastic surgeon who charges $1,000/hour for her time can justify this by pointing out the surgical revenue she is foregoing by testifying and how her overhead costs remain extensive while she testifies.

Example 5.46: Defensiveness over fees a mistake

Q: Okay. How much did you receive in fees for doing your examination and report?
A: I received the usual and customary fee.
Q: And what is that?
A: I am not at liberty to provide that.
Q: Well, sir, you're under oath. At testimony here you're sworn to tell the truth. How much did you get paid for preparing the report and performing the examination?
   Counsel: If you know, go ahead and answer.
A: I would have to go look it up.
Q: Okay. How much are you charging for your time to testify here this morning?
A: Again, charging the usual and customary fee.

Q: Do you keep any records of how much you have made testifying as an expert witness on a yearly basis?
A: No.
Q: Do you have any estimate of what you have made as an expert witness in the last year, in 2006, since we all just finished our income tax returns?
A: No, we haven't. I sent an extension in.
Q: Do you have an estimate of what you made in the last year?
A: I don't.

Q: Do you have an estimate of what percentage of your income is derived from testifying as an expert witness?
A: Yeah, I think I could probably give you a guesstimate on that.

Practice Pointer: Note how evasive the experts appear over questions that could have and should have been answered simply and directly. Some experts honestly don't know how much they are billing because someone else in their office takes care of sending out the bills. To avoid such exchanges, experts should find out what their rates and incomes are before they testify at deposition.

Example 5.47: Defensive of fees

Q: What percentage of your personal time is devoted to forensic work?
A: My personal time. My full-time job is at the college.
Q: Okay.
A: I'm a chair and a professor. That's my 40-hour workweek. I work only when I get called for depositions or do work evenings and so forth. Personal time can vary during the course of a year. I can go two months without doing anything in consulting forensic work and then work for five weeks straight. I don't know. I don't know how to answer that one.
Q: If you—is there any way that you could provide for us what on average in terms of the number of hours per week or percentage of work that you do?
A: Well, see, it's the same thing. This week, for example, I had a deposition by phone on Monday for two hours, and then I'll be here for four hours, and that's it for this week. I have nothing scheduled again until February. So I don't know how to answer that.
Q: What percentage of your consulting work today is forensic?
A: Percentage of my consulting work today. It's this time here, the four hours for the deposition.
Q: Let me rephrase the question. You do consulting work apart from your work at Metropolitan through Consulting Services, Inc. What percentage of the consulting work today that you do through Consulting Services, Inc., is forensic?
A: Well, it's all of it today. I'm not doing any other consulting. I was at the college for my office hours, which ended at 1:00. That's why we set the depo at 2:00.
Q: What is the percentage of your personal income that is derived from forensic matters?
A: From forensic matters?
Q: Yes.
A: I would say it varies from year to year, anywhere from 40 percent to 50 percent of my total income. Including my Metro salary, you mean?
Q: Yes.
A: It varies. It can go between 30, 40, 45—
Q: Okay.

A: —percent, someplace in there.
Q: What is the amount of income that you earn from forensic matters?
A: You mean dollar amount?
Q: Yeah. Per year.
A: That varies, too. I've earned $20,000. I've earned $60,000.
Q: What did you earn last year, let's say?
A: Just gave that stuff to my accountant. I don't—
Q: So it should be fresh in your mind.
A: I don't know what it is. They figured it out. I don't have a clue.
Q: Okay. What was it in '04, then?
A: What is what?
Q: What was it in '04 then?
A: What was it—
Q: What was the amount of income that you personally made from forensic work in 2004, if you don't know it for 2005?
A: Probably gross, about $65,000, and that includes all expenses. That's gross.

Practice Pointer: The more directly the expert can answer these questions, the less time he has to spend explaining his situation. The less the expert explains, the less chance of sounding defensive or inadvertently revealing damaging information.

    Q: What percentage of your time is devoted to forensic work?
    A: It varies, but generally 20%.
    Q: What percentage of your personal income is derived from forensic matters?
    A: It does vary from year to year, but between 35% and 50%.

Example 5.48: Expert uninformed
Q: How much money was Pollin paid last year by FunBike in connection with ATV matters?
A: I don't know.
Q: You have no idea?
A: No.
Q: How much was Pollin paid last year by GoMotors in connection with ATV matters?
A: I don't know.
Q: How much did Pollin receive last year from FunBike as a result of work you did?
A: I don't know.
Q: You don't have any estimate of what your billings were to FunBike last year or to lawyers who were representing FunBike in litigation matters?
A: No.
Q: What were your billings to FunBike for the Feldman case?
A: I don't know what that is….

Practice Pointer: Expert witnesses who can be made to answer "I don't know" over and over again with regard to their fees or the fees of their company may look uninformed and, in extreme cases, evasive.

Example 5.49: Questioned about bills

Q: Have you billed Mr. Menno yet for your time?

A: Yes.

Q: How much time did you bill him for?

A: I have no idea.

 Counsel: Bob, I'd like a copy of that bill if I could.

 Attorney: Yeah, maybe I can have it faxed over to you.

 Counsel: You don't have to do it right now.

 Attorney: Might as well, otherwise it will get delayed and I can just have it faxed over.

Q: How much time did you spend preparing your opinions and your report?

A: If my invoice will be faxed over here it will have a chronological statement, and we can look at that.

Q: We'll go back to that. It's coming over.

 Attorney: My assistant is out to lunch and she's going to call here. I already left a message to fax the stuff, but I don't know if she's got your fax number and everything, so she'll give us a call and we'll get it.

A: If that occurs, I can respond specifically from that; if it doesn't, then I'll give you a guesstimate.

Practice Pointer: Your bills to the attorney who retained you are a legitimate area of inquiry. You should be prepared to be questioned closely about the content of these bills. Accordingly, experts should be careful about what they put in their bills.

Example 5.50: Hourly rate

Q: How much do you make an hour in connection with your litigation-related work?

A: All my time is billed by the company at the same rate, which is $450 an hour currently.

Q: Okay, and I know you've been asked these questions a lot in connection with litigation, and I've seen some printouts that you've done that have numbers on them and the whole bit. As you sit here today, do you have an estimate of how much your company's been paid by FunBike in connection with ATV-related cases—

A: For all—

Q: —and work?

A: It's certainly more than two million dollars. Maybe up to three million now. Something in—around there. I don't know exactly.

Q: I take it you hope to continue to testify on behalf of FunBike in the future—in these type of cases?
A: Absolutely.

Practice Pointer: The argument of bias is especially strong if counsel can show that the expert testifies a lot for a single client or industry. The argument that is made to the jury is, "Now, Mr. Expert wouldn't want to say or do anything that will jeopardize his little $3,000,000 business, would he?" The expert in this case did a good job of not being evasive when answering these questions. Had he been evasive, it only would have made a bad situation worse.

Financial Interest in the Case
Counsel may try to show that an expert stands to gain in the future from the outcome of the case. This gain may be the likelihood of future work as an expert witness or other forms of financial gain. Counsel who can imply that an expert has a financial interest in the outcome seriously undermines the credibility of the expert.

Example 5.51: Arrogant expert
Q: All right. Doctor, this procedure that you recommended that Miss Duff have with respect to her lower back, that's a surgical procedure, right?
A: Yes.
Q: Okay. And you were going to be the one that was going to perform that procedure, right?
A: If she wanted me to.
Q: Okay. And you weren't going to perform that surgery for free, were you, sir?
A: No.
Q: All right. You charge for your time as a surgeon, correct?
A: That's correct.
Q: Okay. What fee do you charge for performing the surgeries that you told counsel about that you do about five or ten times or eight to ten times a month?
A: That would depend on what the surgery was.
Q: All right. Let's talk about the garden-variety common laminectomy that you would perform to correct herniated disc at the L4-5 level. What is your fee for doing that procedure, sir?
A: I do not know.
Q: You do not know?
A: No, sir.
Q: Okay. How long have you been practicing as a surgeon, sir?
A: Working 10 years.
Q: All right. And how many surgeries have you performed over the years?
A: Thousands.

Q: All right. And you have no memory or knowledge of what you charge as a surgeon to perform a lumbar laminectomy at the L4-5 level?
A: No, sir.

Practice Pointer: Note how arrogant and foolish the expert sounds when he says he does not know how much he charges for surgery. This expert's credibility was further undermined because he would make money from the surgery he recommended.

5.9 Impeachment with Inconsistencies

Inconsistent Prior Sworn Testimony

An expert's prior sworn testimony in other cases may be used in an attempt to contradict and impeach her deposition testimony. Experienced expert witnesses who have testified frequently may be faced with the daunting task of attempting to explain, justify, recognize, and in some cases, defend their prior sworn testimony. Sophisticated counsel questioning the expert at deposition does not warn the expert of this line of attack. Counsel may attempt to "mousetrap" the expert by asking her opinion and then bringing up an alleged differing opinion in a prior case.

When the expert testifies at deposition to a fact or opinion that is inconsistent with her sworn statement in a prior case, counsel will first set the trap and then spring it. It is important to note that in today's information age, deposition and trial testimony transcripts are more and more readily available to attorneys. Furthermore, in federal court, the party that retained the expert witness is required to disclose to other parties "a listing of any other cases the witness has testified as an expert at trial or by deposition within the preceding four years."[6]

Example 5.52: Impeachment by prior testimony

Q: You've testified since 1998, almost 100 percent of the time on behalf of plaintiffs who have brought lawsuits against health care professionals, correct?
A: It runs 90 to 95 percent plaintiff work.
Q: Do you remember testifying in the Ralley case, and let me give you the date, Ralley versus First Health Hospital taken in July 22, 1998 down in West Virginia, that you testified almost 100 percent of the time for plaintiffs since 1998?
A: Since 1998 or before 1998?
Q: Do you remember testifying to that?
A: I don't remember it, but I would stand by my own testimony.
Q: You mentioned that you've testified four times, I believe, for Henry & Lopatkan?
A: I believe that's correct. This would be the fifth.
Q: When is the last time that you testified for Henry & Lopatkan, prior to today?
A: January, I believe.

---

[6] Fed. R. Civ. Pro. 26(a)(2)(B).

Q: Of '05?

A: Of '05.

Q: And, how about before that?

A: December of '04, that was two cases within a couple of weeks.

Q: Well, you testified three times in the Fall of 2004 alone for Henry & Lopatkan, correct?

A: Again, to the best of my memory there's been four other cases in Massachusetts with this law firm. This would be the fifth.

Q: Do you remember, though, in the Henriquez case, Henriquez versus some doctors at the American Medical Center, and you testified in, I believe, it was November of 2004? And, you testified in that case that you've testified for Henry & Lopatkan six times. That was as of November 2004.

A: That included two cases in New Hampshire.

Q: I didn't ask you by a state, Doctor. I said how many times have you testified for Henry & Lopatkan, and you told us four. So, the real answer is six?

A: Including the two in New Hampshire it would be six. Yes, sir.

Q: As of November 2004?

A: Yes, sir.

Q: And, then you told us about December of '04 and January of '05 and now we have April of '05. So, that's a total of nine times that you've testified for Henry & Lopatkan, correct?

A: No, it is not, sir.

Q: My question is: do you remember saying in the Henriquez case in November of '04, when attorney Loodins from Henry & Lopatkan asked you a question about how many times you'd testified that as of that time you'd testified six times? And, I think you told us a moment ago that that's correct, including two out of state.

A: Yes, sir.

Q: And, then you told us a moment ago that you've also testified in a case for Henry & Lopatkan in December of '04. So, that would be seven. And, then January of '05, that would be eight. And, then today is April of '05, that would be nine, correct?

A: Yes.

Practice Pointer: Opposing counsel in the above example demonstrates his mastery of the expert's prior testimony. Here the expert is forced into the awkward position of being defensive, admitting misstatements, and appearing not to have a command of prior testimony. By "dragging the information" out of the expert, the final admission is a more dramatic admission than it would have been if the expert admitted his misstatement earlier in the exchange.

Example 5.53: Impeachment with prior testimony/report

Q: Can you identify what Exhibit 73 is for me?

A: Yes. That's a report I wrote October 24, 2005, in the Lantz, L-a-n-t-z, versus Smith and Collins case to Mr. Leonard Welles in Bellefonte, Pennsylvania.

Q: And is that a case that Mr. Chester is involved in?

A: Yes. He deposed me in that case.

Q: Right. And can you just briefly tell me what the facts of the case were?

A: In that particular case, Laurel Lantz, on page 3, is actually what I talk about here, suffered a torn anterior cruciate ligament in her right knee and other tears when she fell through the springs on a trampoline, a backyard trampoline in the Smith home in May of 2002.

She was on the trampoline with other people. She jumped a few times. She decided to get off, was making her way across the trampoline, away from the center. She was planning on sitting down. She asked the other kids to stop but they didn't stop bouncing. She felt herself go off balance. She tried to get off the trampoline. One leg fell through the springs, the other leg on the mat, and then when she tried to get her leg out over the rail, that's when she fell and got seriously injured.

Q: Okay. Now, in that particular case and in this report, Exhibit 73, did you make a recommendation as to whether or not this particular trampoline should have had an enclosure?

A: I think I did.

Q: Okay. And do you recall that without reading the report?

A: I think if there was an enclosure there set up, she wouldn't have fell through the springs at the time because that's the purpose of the enclosure, to keep you on the trampoline.

Q: Well, do you recall in the report referring to the enclosure that you were recommending as a safety enclosure?

A: Don't know. I might have.

Q: Okay. Let's take a look at page 7.

A: Sure.

Q: At the very bottom. The trampoline—I'll read this. "The trampoline was further defective and negligently designed in that it was not sold as a single unit with safety enclosures that would prevent jumpers from being thrown off of the jumping surface either onto the ground or through the springs."

A: That's correct. I used the words "safety enclosures." I probably shouldn't have. That's correct.

Q: Going on to page 8, the next sentence following the one I just read in the record. You go on to say, "These safety cages have been manufactured and sold as separate units since at least the mid-1990s and could readily be utilized with the trampoline so that the likelihood of injury on these devices could at least be reduced." Did you write that?

A: Yes, that's correct.

Q: And you used the term "safety cages"?

A: Right. I didn't call the product a safety cage. I used a term.

Q: Safety cage?

A: Right.

Q: Is that a term that you use frequently?

A: I don't usually do that. I think when I was—and again, I can't remember when I wrote this report. I wasn't calling it—titling it a safety cage. I called them enclosures. In this particular case, what I was trying to say is that had she—had this enclosure been there, this kind of accident, would have saved it. It would have been safer for her to get out of the trampoline. And I think that's why I used "safety cages." Not as a title of the cage, because I used the word "cage" also here rather than "enclosure." It was just a term I used in the report.

Q: So it's quite possible that someone even as experienced as you might refer—

A: I used it again, by the way, on the bottom too.

Q: —might refer to an enclosure as a safety enclosure, okay, inadvertently even though the product may not be called a safety enclosure in terms of its formal name. Is that a fair statement?

A: Probably some people can call it a safety enclosure, sure.

Q: Now, if somebody informally referred to this on a regular basis as a safety enclosure, would the use of that term by that individual lead them to believe that the warnings on the trampoline bed were voided?

  Mr. Lester: Objection to foundation.

  A: I don't know.

  Mr. Fiore: Well, do you have an opinion on that?

  A: No. I've never been asked that question. I don't know if somebody inadvertently used any term, what that would mean in relationship to the warnings. I don't know how to answer that.

Q: Okay, so in terms of your opinion in this case, it is highly significant that the term "safety enclosure" is the name of the product as opposed to a term with which the user refers to the enclosure?

A: Right, that's my opinion. There's a big difference.

Practice Pointer: Experts should be prepared to testify about their prior cases, testimony, and reports at deposition. If counsel can establish that the expert tailors his opinions depending on who retains him, that will severely undercut the expert's credibility. In the example above, the expert was eventually able to distinguish his prior report and testify and show why there was *no* inherent inconsistency between his report in the prior case and his testimony in the case in which he was being deposed.

Example 5.54: Impeachment by prior deposition

Q: Agricultural engineering is a distinct profession, is it not…? The same as mechanical engineering, is that correct?

A: There are degrees listed as agricultural engineers, yes.

Q: Would you agree with the statement that agricultural engineering is a discipline all its own?

A: It has the title of a discipline all its own, yes.

Q: You don't agree with that fully?

A: I don't agree that it's unique unto itself, no.

Q: Didn't you on a prior occasion under oath state that in your opinion that agricultural engineering is a discipline all of its own?

A: I don't recall saying that.

Q: Do you remember giving testimony in the case of *Libby versus Sordino?*

A: Sordino…vaguely.

Q: I have before me a transcript of a deposition that was taken of you in that case in which you were testifying for a manufacturer. I ask you to look at it and tell me if you can identify it as your deposition.

A: It appears to be, yes.

Q: Would you please read your answer on page six beginning with line 12?

A: "Agricultural engineering is a discipline all of its own, one portion of which has to do with the design and construction of agricultural equipment and systems used in farming and agricultural food processing and that sort of thing."

Q: Was it true then and is it true today?

A: Yes.

Q: So it would be fair to say, correct to say, that at least as far as the design of agricultural equipment, agricultural engineering is a discipline all its own, is that correct?

A: Yes.

Practice Pointer: Had the expert listened carefully to the question, "Would you agree with the statement that agricultural engineering is a discipline all its own?," he could have anticipated an impeachment attempt based on the answer. The expert who tells the truth, takes his time, and does not tailor his answers to meet the needs of his client has little to fear from this type of impeachment at deposition.

Example 5.55: Prior inconsistent testimony

Q: Would you agree with the statement, "Keypunching, although it has high repetitiveness, you can punch keys all day long and look at a video display, it doesn't have static loading, it doesn't have force, it doesn't have vibration, it doesn't have all the components of the risk factors which research clearly state compound one another or certainly make the risk much higher"?

A: Yes, I disagree with that. We're talking about frequency.

Q: Do you remember giving trial testimony in the case of *Keller versus Southern Rail?*

A: Uh-huh. I see you have done your homework.

Q: And do you recall being questioned regarding the NIOSH study of the American Standard Communication System?

A: Not specifically, no.

Q: Would you disagree with me if it were in the transcript of your testimony?

A: No, probably not. I might have to read the context of it.

Q: Okay. Do you recall being asked these questions and giving these answers?

"Question: Are NIOSH studies something that you look at and rely on in your work that you do?"

"Answer: Yes. And in answering your question this is a summary of a study that was done on video display terminals. I am familiar with the fact there was a study that occurred relating to video display operators."

"Question: All right but they are evaluating so-called cumulative trauma disorders in people who purportedly use repetitive motions in their work, is that right?"

"Answer: In keypunching."

"Question: And that's something you would consider to be a repetitive motion?"

"Answer: Yes, can be."

And then he asked you to turn to page 12 of that report.

"Would you read the sentence starting with 'overtime'?"

"Answer: Overtime in the past year had a negative association with increasing shoulder symptoms. The increasing number of hours spent at a video display terminal or VDT work station per day had a negative association with increasing hand and wrist symptoms."

"Question: You see Dr. Robert Sans-Darnell's name over there?"

"Answer: It is Sands."

"Question: Is it Sands?"

"Answer: Yeah."

"Question: That's a fellow you mentioned a little bit ago on direct examination, wasn't it?"

"Answer: Yes. And what I think is significant is this is about video display terminal keypunch operators, which is not relevant to this case, to Mr. Keller. He didn't punch keys."

"Question: It's what you said is repetitive motion, isn't it?"

"Answer: Punching keys is repetitive motion, yes."

"Question: And that is what you say is one of the risk factors for cumulative trauma disorders?"

Practice Pointer: Your prior testimony is becoming increasingly easy for counsel to obtain. Prior inconsistent testimony can and will come back to haunt you. Experts who always tell the truth and who are careful not to let counsel mischaracterize their testimony have little to fear from questions on past testimony.

Prior Mistaken Deposition Testimony

Experts may be confronted with prior mistakes or errors that they have made while testifying. The fact that one has made mistakes in the past can affect an expert's credibility. Counsel is seeking to get these mistakes into the record and see how the expert will react. The best way to react is to admit the mistake if it occurred and not try to cover it up. Juries understand that everyone makes mistakes and may readily forgive this. If an expert tries to cover up a mistake, he may appear evasive or biased.

Example 5.56: Expert loses temper

Q: So your position is that systemic osteoarthritis is not trauma or an activity-related disease, correct?

A: That's correct. The pathophysiology is really not known.

Q: In one occasion in the Garland case you specifically cited an article to me, the *Journal of Bone and Joint Surgery,* 1985, New England edition, which you said supported your position.

A: Right.

Q: And the fact is, there is no such article in the 1985 New England edition of the *Journal of Bone and Joint Surgery;* is that correct?

A: Counselor, I'll make you a deal. You've done this to me three or four times on depositions. I'll have a Med-Line search done at the hospital and find the information that supports my contentions. There are a number of articles that support it. I don't know what article I quoted you there.

Q: I'll read it to you here, Doctor. You stated, quote: "I don't have it with me, but you're welcome to look it up, *Journal of Bone and Joint Surgery,* 1985, New England edition, they did a study on osteoarthritis of the spine, the hands, the extremities, and compared activity levels of individuals, such as coal miners, steel workers, et cetera, versus activity levels of attorneys, barristers and judges and doctors and those that do the heavy activity had the same incidence of those that don't in the same areas of the body with the same amount of complaints of pain."

A: Exactly.

Q: That was your testimony.

A: Exactly.

Q: There's no such article in the *Journal of Bone and Joint Surgery.*

A: There is an article, maybe not be in that magazine, maybe a different year. The article exists. I've quoted it more than once over a period of years. That's not happenstance. That was part of my education. I've read that article. I'll do everything I can to have the powers that be obtain those articles so I can waltz in here

135

every time we have a dep and demonstrate to you that the vast majority of accomplished physicians agree with that contention, because they do.

Q: Based upon your reading of the article you cannot find and may not even exist?

Practice Pointer: The expert made many mistakes in the above exchange:

1. He was imprecise with the earlier testimony.
2. Despite the fact that the issue keeps coming up, he hasn't bothered to locate the article.
3. He lost his temper.
4. His answers ramble.

The expert's cavalier attitude toward the facts and his prior sworn testimony may seriously affect his credibility with the jury and fact finder. A better way to handle this may have been, "I'm sorry if I made an error reporting the citation. I can try to get you an accurate cite if you like."

The Expert's Writings

Counsel at deposition may attempt to impeach an expert witness with an article or book that he has written. A comprehensive list of an expert's writings is readily available to counsel through a simple and easy Internet search. Experts should prepare for this type of impeachment by reviewing their published writings. A competent attorney will do her homework by reviewing an expert's writings. If the expert doesn't do the same, he may be trapped by the attorney.

Example 5.57: Impeachment by expert's own writings

Q: Is the textbook of Psychiatry by Kaplan and Sadock authoritative?
A: I certainly stand by my chapter in it.
Q: I thought you would.
A: I have to say it depends on what I read in it. It's a multi-authored book three years out of date when it appeared. You'd have to show me something and I'd tell you what I think.

Example 5.58: Expert impeached with his own book

Q: The normal range for a five-minute Apgar score is considered 7 and above in the predominant medical literature which you've reviewed?
A: Not necessarily.
Q: In your book, *Maternal Infant Medicine, Principles and Practice,* third edition, Wollin and Boyer, 7 and above is set forth as a normal five-minute Apgar, correct?
A: That's correct.
Q: Do you wish to retract the statement you made in your book?
A: No, I will stand by it.

Practice Pointer: Note how quickly counsel was able to cast serious doubt on the expert's "not necessarily" answer. The more accomplished the expert, the more she may have written. These experts are often hard pressed to remember everything that they have written if they don't review their pertinent writings. Contradiction by your own writings can be a very effective form of impeachment.

5.10 Conclusion

Experts are well advised to anticipate and prepare for the types of questions they will likely face at their depositions.

Chapter 6 Deposition Advice for Expert Witnesses

6.1 Introduction and Executive Summary

The authors recommend the following strategies for experts at depositions:

- Tell the truth.
- Prepare diligently.
- Consider not having the deposition in your office.
- Dress appropriately if the deposition is being videotaped.
- Do not argue with counsel because this will make you appear to be an advocate.
- Make requested drawings with extreme care.
- Do not exaggerate, speculate, guess, or estimate.
- Listen to the entire question before answering. This will ensure that you answer the proper question.
- Insist on finishing your answers—don't let counsel cut you off.
- Actively listen to the question.
- Pause before answering to give yourself a chance to think and to give retaining counsel a chance to object.
- Carefully consider whether you want to read and sign the transcript.
- Do not respond to pregnant pauses, wait for a question.
- Avoid gesturing because this is not recorded by the stenographer.
- Do not show weakness.
- Listen carefully to counsel's objections because these may contain valuable information. Don't get involved in bickering between counsel.
- Remember that "off the record" remarks can and will be used against you.
- Know the facts cold. Prepare.
- Be rested and alert before your deposition starts.
- Use a protocol for answering questions:
    - Do I understand the question?
    - Do I know the answer?
    - Do I remember the answer?
    - How do I phrase my answer in a way that is both truthful and artful?
- Exude confidence.
- Remain calm, cool, collected, and under control. Do not lose your temper.
- Act naturally and be yourself.
- Avoid jokes, sarcasm, and inappropriate remarks.
- Act dignified and polite.
- Do not be argumentative. If you are, you will appear to be an advocate and lose credibility.

- Avoid absolute words.
- Do not elaborate or volunteer.
- Be careful when using "hedge words." You'll need to state your opinion with reasonable certainty.
- Make concessions gracefully.
- If you don't know the answer, say so.
- If you can't recall the answer, say so.
- Answer only questions that you understand.
- Leave yourself some wiggle room on additional work and additional opinions.
- Do not ramble.
- Avoid slang.
- Do not answer with a simple "yes" or "no" if such an answer would be misleading.
- Correct misstatements as soon as possible.
- Force counsel to explain ambiguous questions.
- Occasionally break counsel's momentum.
- Encourage counsel to lose his cool.
- Use the clock to your advantage.
- Do not testify beyond your true area of expertise.

6.2 General Advice for Experts at Depositions

This chapter contains specific advice to assist experts in testifying at depositions. It is a good idea to read this section immediately prior to being deposed.

Tell the Truth

The single most important piece of advice for expert witnesses is to tell the truth, simply and directly. This cannot be overemphasized. An expert witness has a legal, moral, professional, and ethical obligation to tell the truth. Expert witnesses testify under oath. Experts who tell less than the truth run the risk of criminal prosecution for perjury, civil suits for negligence, and revocation or suspension of their professional licenses. Experts who do not tell the truth are discovered and discredited eventually. Experts who call them as they see them are respected, maintain their credibility, and have long expert witness careers. In addition, these experts are difficult to shake or undermine during cross-examination.

An expert is allowed, however, to state her truthful answers as artfully as possible. The mark of an experienced expert witness is one who answers in a way that prevents her opinion from being undermined.

Example 6.1: Failure to tell truth

Q: Sir, you did not really graduate from college with a B.A. as your CV indicates, isn't that true?
A: Well….

Practice Pointer: The expert who lies, embellishes, or doesn't tell the truth will be exposed and his career as an expert will end.

Example 6.2: Expert's honesty and objectivity will be called into question if he cherry-picks data

Q: Okay. And in that note, Dr. McEllin says, "His foot looks fine." That's the third paragraph down?

A: Yes.

Q: He also says, does he not, in the final paragraph, that the foot—that "It was possible that that foot would always be somewhat uncomfortable given the degree of injury that he had." Do you see where he says that?

A: "It is possible,"—Yes, I do have that. Yes, indeed.

Q: Okay. And in March of '99, McEllin was saying that the foot looked fine, but it was possible that it might never be normal?

A: Never normal in terms of the total elimination of discomfort, I guess, is what he's saying here, yes.

Q: Right. Now, you didn't include that comment about the foot possibly being always somewhat uncomfortable. You did not include that in your report, did you?

A: I didn't.

Q: Do you recall—did you review an April of 1999 report—April 28, 1999 report from Dr. McEllin?

A: I have that.

Q: And you see in there that Dr. McEllin said that he was—that he felt, McEllin, that Mr. Strayve was "Not ready to return to his regular activity," and that he would, "expect many months before he was going to be able to tolerate that degree of work." Do you see where he says that?

A: I do see that.

Q: You didn't include that in your report—that quote, in your report, did you, Doctor?

A: I didn't, no.

Q: You say in your report, Doctor, on page eight, and that would be almost at the bottom of the last paragraph, you say in your report that Dr. McEllin had no explanation for Strayve's persistent symptoms?

A: Yes.

Q: And—but later—but in that report—that office note, Dr. McEllin diagnosed a chronic residual pain after right foot crush injury. Correct?

A: I have that page now and I see my quote, and then you're asking me about what he said?

Q: Your quote was—you quoted Dr. McEllin as saying the foot looks "great." Right?

A: Yes.

Q: But you did not quote him in terms of his assessment that Mr. Strayve was having chronic residual pain after right foot crush injury. You did not quote that?
A: I didn't quote it.
Q: And you also did not quote him, Dr. McEllin, that he concurred at that point that it was appropriate for Mr. Strayve to have a pain clinic evaluation and treatment plan. You did not quote that either, did you?
A: I didn't quote it.
Q: Okay. Now, you quoted Dr. Czycyk in your report?
A: I did.
Q: And that was, I believe, also on page eight of your report, in the end of that second to last paragraph.
A: Yes.
Q: And you quoted her as saying that Mr. Strayve had "some type of a syndrome"?
A: I did.
Q: And that was the extent of your quoting of Dr. Czycyk. Correct?
A: That was the extent of my quote.
Q: And what she actually said was—starting at the bottom of page one, "that he most likely had some sort of a pain syndrome." Correct?
A: He most likely has some sort of pain syndrome going on, yes.
Q: And she also went on to opine that it might be "a combination of RSD with a nerve crush injury syndrome." Correct?

Practice Pointer: Opposing counsel in the above example pointed out time and again the "damaging or non-helpful" language that the expert left out of his report. The implication is that the expert tried to soften the damaging information by intentionally leaving out key parts of the underlying report. The expert could have stopped this line of inquiry in several ways.

> **Q:** You didn't include that in your report, did you?
> **A:** I reviewed hundreds of pages, Counsel, so I could not put each and every word in my 9-page report.

Or, alternatively:

> **Q:** You didn't include that in your report, did you?
> **A:** No. I did not because I did not believe it was true.

Prepare
Experts need to prepare fully with retaining counsel and by themselves prior to being deposed (please see Chapter 3 on preparation).

Do Not Have the Deposition in Your Office
Counsel taking the expert's deposition has the option of conducting the deposition at her own office, at the office of the expert, or at some neutral location. To save costs,

many busy experts have traditionally been deposed at their offices. By simply asking retaining counsel, an expert may be able to move the location of the deposition to or away from his office. There are *advantages* and *disadvantages* of having the deposition taken at one's office. The advantages include the following:

1. less travel involved,
2. more time available for other activities,
3. feeling more comfortable on "your own turf,"
4. control of logistics: seating, temperature, etc.,
5. staff available to assist, and
6. records available when needed.

While the advantages of being deposed in one's own office may seem obvious, the disadvantages are more subtle. These are discussed below:

Disadvantage 1: Interruptions
Interruptions may occur, which can be annoying and distracting. A distracted expert is unlikely to excel during his deposition.

Example 6.3: Distraction from having deposition in own office
Q: Do you want to answer that phone?
A: No, let it ring. The service will eventually get it.

Practice Pointer: If you are distracted, you will be far more likely to make a mistake and misspeak.

Disadvantage 2: Unwanted disclosure of information
Unwanted disclosure of information may occur inadvertently by being deposed in your own office.

Example 6.4: Expert's office used against her
Q: When we talk about a concussion of the brain, so as I understand it, you don't think that that term is synonymous with mild brain injury?
A: No.
Q: I see on the desk you have a green journal, *The Journal of Neurology.* Is that a journal that you utilize in your practice?
A: Yes.
Q: And is it not one of the hotter topics in neurology, concussion in sports?
A: It has been discussed recently, yes.
Q: In fact, I think in the March issue, Drs. Rosenberg and Kelly wrote an article with regard to concussion in sports?
A: There were several articles, yes.
Q: Have you read them?
A: Yes.

Q: And am I not correct that they used the term "concussion" and "mild brain injury" interchangeably?

Practice Pointer: Having the deposition in the expert's office was used against her. The attorney was able to determine that the expert used and read the journal in question.

Example 6.5: Diplomas on the expert's wall used against her
Q: I see from your diploma that you graduated from MIT in 1991. Your CV says 1989. Which is correct?

Practice Pointer: This question might never have been asked had the deposition not taken place in the expert's office.

Disadvantage 3: The time of the expert's staff
The expert and his staff will be responsible for cleaning the office and the staff may be called upon to assist at the deposition. This could cost business time, which translates into money.

Example 6.6: Costs of using office for deposition
Expert: Let me clean up my desk. Here, you take this chair. Let me get two more chairs. Is a stool okay? You need how many copies of this 29-page document? Here, let me see if I can get a staff member to help us.

Practice Pointer: There may be a cost to your business if you have the deposition in your office.

Disadvantage 4: Availability of on-site records
Experts may be called upon to produce additional records or documents that are available on-site. The expert may or may not be familiar with these documents and she may or may not be prepared to give testimony concerning these records or documents.

Example 6.7: Request for additional information
Q: I see the billing information is not in the file you provided. Could you have someone pull the records and bring them in?

Practice Pointer: This request would never be made in this form if the expert was not in her office.

Example 6.8: Producing more records
Q: There's a reference on page one, item number five, of a letter dated October 10, 2005, addressed to Kenneth Webber. Do you have that letter with you?
A: It must be around somewhere.
Q: Can you check your file for me?
A: Yes. Wait a minute.

Q: If you are buzzing your administrative assistant, I'd also like the letter of January 12th.

A: I'm going to tell her to bring everything in that is out there.

Q: Okay.

Practice Pointer: It may be disadvantageous to have a deposition held in your office.

Disadvantage 5: Distractions
Experts may be distracted by office noise, emergencies, and the usual anxiety about one's "to do" list. A distracted expert is much more likely to slip up.

Disadvantage 6: Less likely to prepare
Experts deposed in their offices may be less likely to prepare properly and to focus mentally. If the deposition is in one's office, it may subconsciously be considered less of an "event" than if it required travel. An expert might, therefore, spend much less time preparing for depositions held at her own office.

In the authors' opinion, an expert witness may be better served by having the deposition held in a neutral site out of the office. Counsel may be amenable to this and the expert's travel time may be billable. For the reasons discussed above, it may be to the expert's disadvantage to have the deposition held in her own office. If the deposition is conducted at the expert's office, care should be exercised to use a sterile/bare room so counsel cannot utilize books, articles, diplomas, certificates, or other materials to cross-examine the expert. The opposing attorney should not be permitted to sit in the expert's waiting room and listen to the conversations of the office staff. The attorney should immediately be isolated in the "sterile room" and encouraged to stay there until the deposition begins.

Dress Appropriately if the Deposition Is Videotaped
If the deposition is being videotaped, the expert will want to dress appropriately. What is appropriate depends upon how the deposition will be taped and who the jury is likely to consist of. If the deposition will not be videotaped, the jury will most likely never know or care how the expert dressed. In either case, it is wise to put in a quick call to counsel before the deposition and ask how to dress. For additional information on videotaped depositions, please see Chapter 9.

Avoid Arguing with Counsel
There is little, if anything, to be gained by arguing with counsel. Expert witnesses who get emotional and let counsel get under their skin frequently stop thinking clearly about the questions and answers. In video depositions, flashes of anger and quibbling with counsel can adversely affect the credibility of the expert. The more

the expert argues with counsel, the greater the risk that she will appear partisan and not impartial.

It is the role of the attorneys in the civil litigation process to argue with each other. The role of the expert witness is simply to answer the questions. The best experts remember these distinct roles and conduct themselves accordingly.

Example 6.9: Petty argument that should have been avoided
Q: Sir, would you have a seat, please?
A: If you will have a seat, I will have a seat.
Q: You're the witness here.
A: I would ask you to sit down, too.
Q: Sir, there's no requirement that says a lawyer has to sit when deposing a witness. Will you be seated?
A: Okay. (Expert reluctantly sits down.)

Practice Pointer: The expert has gained nothing by his petty dispute with counsel. He has risked distracting himself and has gotten off to a strange start to his deposition.

Make Drawings with Extreme Care
Counsel may call upon experts to draw diagrams, mark exhibits, or even draw sketches to demonstrate their theories or opinions at deposition.[1]

The sophisticated expert does these drawings or identifications with extreme care and precision to avoid later being impeached by his "own hand." When an expert witness is asked to draw (as opposed to identify), he is well advised to note for the record that this is done freehand, not to scale, and not with precision.

Example 6.10: Making drawing carefully
Q: In that installation you indicated that the support brackets were on the inside of the wheel—of the gear wheel and on the outside, correct?
A: Yes.
Q: And that they went down to a bottom bracket; is that correct?
A: A cross brace, yes.
Q: This is the cross brace here?
A: No, above that.
Q: Would you mark it, please?
A: Yes.
Q: This morning you put an X here.
A: Well—yes….But I was just approximating it. This is the correct location.

---

[1] David R. Geiger, et. al, *Deposing Expert Witnesses* (Boston, MA: MCLE, 1993) p. 7.

Practice Pointer: The expert's drawing can have as much, or more, impact than his recorded testimony. Drawings and markings should be done carefully with the disclaimer that they are "approximations" and "done freehand."

Example 6.11: Freehand disclaimer
Q: Could you by drawing show us on this bottom bracket where there are bolts?
A: On this bottom bracket?
Q: Yes.
A: Well, I will do the best that I can by freehand, understand.
Q: Do it right here over the conveyor (indicating).
A: Yes.
Q: And you are drawing here the overhead view which you have here?
A: They come through the end. You see the channels here and the holes at the end of the channel….

Practice Pointer: The witness's "freehand disclaimer" was a wise statement to make. She made the disclaimer but was cooperative and did not overplay her hand.

Don't Exaggerate, Speculate, Guess, or Estimate
Experts should not guess, speculate, exaggerate, or estimate. An expert witness who does not know an answer to a question should say so. Expert witnesses are under oath to tell the truth. They should not speculate but should testify with a reasonable degree of certainty. At deposition, many experts do not practice this principle and, in fact, speculate freely.

One of the most common forms of speculation by experts at deposition is the "I do not know, but…" reply. This response is usually a mistake. First of all, if the expert doesn't know, then any information she provides after the "but" is speculation. Secondly, the expert may volunteer damaging information after the "but."

Example 6.12: A simple "I don't know" might have been a better response
Q: Do you know whether or not the car manufacturer employed any other method to determine longitudinal velocity of test dummies?
A: I don't know if we compute longitudinal velocity based on accelerometers, but I suppose you could.

Practice Pointer: The simple, direct, and best response is, "I don't know." The throwaway statements that come after the "but" or "I don't know" reply help counsel by providing him with additional information. This type of reply frequently results in new lines of inquiry and detailed questioning by counsel.

Example 6.13: Volunteering and guessing with "I don't know, but…"
Q: Do you know, in this crash test, what causes the voltage drop and rise?
A: I don't know, but that's typically an indication that the switch is opening and closing.

Q: When you say opening and closing, sir, would you explain what you mean in this context?

Practice Pointer: By providing a "but," the witness has opened a new line of questioning. This was probably avoidable simply by answering the question, "I don't know" or "No."

Example 6.14: "I don't know, but..." should be avoided
Q: Why does crash test 4665 have such charts and the remaining frontal barrier tests do not?
A: Well, I don't know, but if you would like me to review the other tests to determine whether or not those tests have such—I can certainly do that, but I guess this one had switches and they must have been requested.

Practice Pointer: This witness has answered, "I don't know" and then made an offer to assist counsel. The simple, most accurate, and best reply is, "I don't know." Any comments made as an afterthought are unwise, unprofessional, and inconsistent with being successful as an expert at deposition.

Example 6.15: Guessing/estimating
Q: All right. You understand you've just taken the oath to tell the truth here today?
A: Yes.
Q: All right. And you understand the meaning of that oath is the whole truth and nothing but the truth; correct?
A: Correct.
Q: All right. You have testified in the past as to the number of times that you have been in litigation as a defendant. In a deposition on July 26 of 2002, you indicated under oath that at that point in time you had been a defendant in a malpractice case approximately a dozen or so times in 26 years. Did that sound about right for 2002?
A: That sounds about right.
Q: Okay. In September of 2002, you likewise gave a deposition that said that you thought you had been sued probably a dozen to 14 times over the last 26 years. Now, that's just about three months later. Does that sound about right for that time period?
A: Yes.
Q: All right. Eleven months later in a deposition you testified under oath that you have been a defendant some 20 or 22 occasions over 27 years. Were you sued over a dozen times between August of '02 and September of '03?
A: I believe the accurate number is probably close to 19 over the entire 28 years or so.

Practice Pointer: The expert in the above example does not come off too well in this example taken from the transcript of a videotaped deposition. It appears that he is either unconcerned about the precise number of times he has been sued or that he is getting sued so often he has trouble keeping track. A simple, direct, and precise reply could have avoided most of his difficulty:

A: I have been sued 21 times over the course of my 28-year career.

Example 6.16: Guessing
Q: Well, from your custom and practice in reading these forms, is it fair to say if either represents the time the culture was taken from the patient or the time it was received by the lab?
A: That would be my best guess.

Practice Pointer: Effective expert witnesses neither guess nor speculate. Instead, they form precise answers based upon their years of expertise. An expert's guess is not likely to play well to the jury. In fact, an expert's willingness to guess may damage his credibility.

Listen to the Entire Question before Answering and Insist on Finishing Your Answers
Expert witnesses are well advised not to interrupt questions and blurt out answers before the question is completed. By doing so, the expert may not answer the question the lawyer was going to ask. This may result in an incorrect answer that volunteers information unnecessarily. Additionally, interrupting the question may effectively deny retaining counsel an opportunity to object to the question.

Remember, too, that you are entitled to finish your answer to a question. You should not permit counsel to cut you off when some unexpected or unwanted testimony is about to be delivered.

Example 6.17: Insisting on finishing answer
Q: You testify for only defendants, isn't that correct?
A: No, that's not correct. As a matter of fact….
Q: Let's move on.
A: I have not finished my answer, Counsel. As I was about to say, a full 40% of my work is for plaintiffs.

Practice Pointer: The witness did a good job of not letting the attorney cut off his answer. He made sure he got his answer in the record.

Example 6.18: Opposing counsel cuts off expert
Q: What tells you, sir, that they got out from different sides of the SUV?
A: What I'm telling you is what is consistent with the physical evidence and what's inconsistent. There is not testimony—
Q: What is consistent—
A: —that the—
Q: —with the—

A: Excuse me. May I finish?
Q: What is—
A: May I finish?
Q: What is consistent with the physical evidence—

Practice Pointer: The expert here was not permitted to finish his reply. When faced with this tactic, the expert can be a bit more forceful:

> **A:** What I'm telling you is what is consistent with the physical evidence and what's inconsistent. There is not testimony—
> **Q:** What is consistent—
> **A:** As I was saying before you interrupted me—

If counsel persists in interrupting, the expert can just stop talking until counsel discontinues the tactic.

Actively Listen to the Question
Expert witnesses need to concentrate intensely on the questions being asked. It is only by listening, hearing, and understanding the question that one can reply honestly and directly. An expert who does not understand the question should reply, "I do not understand the question." Active listening skills are a must. The best experts don't answer the question they anticipate they are going to be asked. They answer the question they *are* being asked. It will be counsel's job to clarify or rephrase the question if she wishes to do so. Listening and answering the question directly can avoid turning a routine question and answer into a cat and mouse game with a final hesitant and reluctant concession.

Example 6.19: Reluctant admission
Q: You are an infectious disease doctor, correct?
A: I'm chairman of infection control at the Southern Presbyterian Hospital and I've had considerable experience in treating bone and joint infectious diseases during the last 22 years.
Q: Do you consider yourself an infectious disease doctor?
A: I consider myself to have extensive experience and expertise in the area of bone and joint infectious disease. I do not have boards in infectious disease.
Q: Do you consider yourself, though, an infectious disease physician?
A: Yes.

Practice Pointer: The jury or fact finder may give this "admission" additional weight due to the manner in which it was elicited. The expert probably would have been better off to answer "Yes" at the start of the questioning. Note as well the expert's mistake of volunteering that he was not board certified.

Pause before Answering

Witnesses should briefly pause before answering all but routine questions. *In transcribed depositions there are no points awarded for the speed of a reply because brief pauses do not show up on the transcribed page.* Pausing serves two important purposes. First, it gives the expert a chance to consider his response more carefully and thus reduces the risk of making a misstatement. Second, it gives counsel a better chance of objecting to the question if she so desires. Care should be taken not to overdo this technique, especially in videotaped depositions. In videotaped depositions, a pause is recorded and may be taken as a sign that the expert is hesitant, is unsure of his replies, or is lying. In any case, a pause of a second or two between the question and one's response is almost always a good idea.

Reading and Signing

Depending upon local rules, a deponent may have the right to review, correct, and sign the deposition after it has been transcribed. Under the Federal Rules of Civil Procedure, the expert witness has the right to review the transcript and make changes in "form or substance."[2] This right is not self-executing, however. To assert this right, the expert or the attorney must request reading and signing prior to the completion of the deposition.[3]

An expert witness may be asked to waive the right to read and sign. Experts, especially in high-profile litigation, are well advised not to waive the right to review the transcript. In lengthy technical depositions mistakes are not unusual. Experts will be given instructions on how to note corrections. It is imperative to follow the instructions precisely. In addition, reading and signing one's deposition is an excellent learning tool for the expert. It permits her to see in writing all of the mistakes she made and shows how she can improve for her next deposition. A sample errata sheet appears in Appendix G.

There is a competing school of thought proposing that experts should not read and sign their depositions. This is because if the expert has read and signed her deposition, she will have even less wiggle room to explain away later inconsistencies.

Do Not Respond to Counsel's Pregnant Pauses

Effective experts do not respond to pregnant pauses by counsel. This is a tactic that counsel may use to get or keep an expert talking. An expert should answer the question before him. After that, he should not say anything until counsel asks another question.

---

[2] Fed. R. Civ. Pro. 30(e).
[3] Fed. R. Civ. Pro. 30(e).

Avoid Gesturing

Expert witnesses should not use gestures, such as nodding or pointing, to respond to a question. Gestures cannot be recorded accurately by the court reporter.

Don't Show Weakness

While being deposed, experts should be careful not to give counsel an edge by demonstrating boredom, exasperation, or fatigue. Sophisticated counsel will use this information to his advantage. By showing weakness, the expert may prolong the questioning because counsel may keep hammering away until the expert breaks down and concedes all the contested points.

Example 6.20: Expert shows fatigue

Q: Did you, in fact, heed his suggestion here that you concentrate more heavily on design defect as opposed to warning in your opinions?

A: I'm sorry. It's getting late and I must be getting tired. I got in at 2:00 this morning due to the delays at the airport. Can you repeat the question, please?

Practice Pointer: The expert here has revealed that he is tired and weakening. This will likely inspire opposing counsel to press him even harder because he smells blood.

Listen Carefully to Objections, But Don't Get Involved in Disputes between Counsel

When an objection is made, the expert witness should stop talking and listen carefully to the objection. Counsel may, properly or improperly, be signaling the expert as to the importance of the question and its key elements. (This is called a "speaking objection." Although against the rules, this occurs very commonly.) Opposing counsel may note his displeasure, but this is often ineffective because the "cat is already out of the bag." If a dispute arises between the lawyers, the expert is well advised to stay out of it.

Example 6.21: Objection "advice" by retaining counsel

Q: When asked at trial, what is going to be your testimony in that regard?

A: Just what it says in my report. I don't know that information. It's a possibility, but I'm not going to jump up and down and say that he should have been operated on the day before.

Q: Is that opinion an opinion that you've reached to a reasonable degree of medical probability?

> **Retaining Counsel:** Objection. Which opinion? The one he doesn't know?
> **Deposing Counsel:** The opinion that whether or not the surgery would have worked.
> **Retaining Counsel:** Objection. There is no such opinion. Go ahead.

A: I don't have an opinion on that.

Practice Pointer: Retaining counsel objected twice in the above example and each time "spoke" his objection, tipping off the expert. While this type of "speaking objection" is against the rules, it occurs with regularity. The expert here picked up on the "advice" and framed his answer accordingly.

Note: It is the job of opposing counsel to object and put a stop to the "speaking objections." His failure to do so results in exchanges like the one above.

Example 6.22: Keeping your mouth shut during dispute between counsel

Q: I understand your answer, but my question is, if you were to learn that Mr. Jones flexed and extended his wrist, would you concede that his employment would be a risk factor?

    Retaining Counsel: Objection. How does he know what—

    Deposing Counsel: Please don't coach the witness.

    Retaining Counsel: I'm going to object.

    Deposing Counsel: Don't make a speaking objection, please, Mr. Halliday. State your objection and don't educate the witness. I don't appreciate that.

Practice Pointer: This expert kept his mouth shut and did not get involved in the bickering of the attorneys. After listening to the arguments and objections of the attorneys, he may be better able to answer the posed question accurately.

Don't Get Burned "Off the Record"

Experienced experts may start to feel like lawyers and ask to go "off the record" and say and do things while off the record. All that "off the record" means is that the court reporter is not recording what is said in the deposition transcript. Going off the record means nothing more than this. There is no implied promise, as with a source talking to a reporter, that the expert's off-the-record words will not be used against her. Counsel can and will bring up what was said off the record and not recorded. In addition, in video depositions, an attempt to go off the record can backfire and be portrayed by counsel as an attempt by the expert to hide something from the fact finder or the jury. Expert witnesses are well advised not to ask to go off the record. If and when an expert is off the record, she should not say or do anything that can be used against her.

Example 6.23: "Off the record" remark used against expert

Q: Welcome back, sir. Sir, while we were off the record taking a break, you told me that you really can't be sure what happened in this case, didn't you?

A: Ah….

Q: Sir? Did you state that to me?

A: We were off the record!

Q: Did you state that?

A: Let me explain, what I meant was….

Practice Pointer: Going off the record gives you no protection to make confidential comments. Anything you say can and frequently will be used against you later in the deposition.

Knowing the Facts Cold
Experienced experts enter their depositions with a full and encyclopedic knowledge of the facts. This knowledge permits the expert to quickly recognize when opposing counsel is modifying, mischaracterizing, or intentionally misstating the facts. This intimate knowledge of the facts is also an important refuge for the expert witness. These experts talk about the facts when they face adversity.

Example 6.24: Knowing the facts cold
Q: Okay. What were the physical effects of the emergency surgery, prior to execution of the September documents?
A: He still had—well, he still had an infection. He still had—you're talking about on September 1st or on September 2nd? I am not sure what date we're talking about.
Q: Well, it's got to be between the surgery and September 2nd, according to this sentence.
A: He was having uncontrolled—bleeding was uncontrolled. He had begun radiation therapy. He was dehydrated. He had pallor. He was—he had blood coming out of every orifice just about. He was vomiting blood. He had blood coming from his anus, blood coming from his nose. He had blood coming from his paracentesis.
Q: And you're getting this from the deposition testimony or medical records?
A: Medical records.

Practice Pointer: The expert's ability to either remember the facts in detail or locate them quickly and efficiently in the record made his reply effective and powerful. Counsel will size up the witness as one who is likely to be well prepared to testify at trial and thus be very formidable.

Be Rested and Alert
Experts need to be in peak physical and mental condition at deposition. Experts should:

- get adequate rest,
- clear their calendars,
- reduce or eliminate distractions,
- make sure they eat and hydrate, and
- relax for their deposition.

Experts who are tired, distracted, hungry, or rushed will not do their best at deposition.

6.3 Protocol for Answering Deposition Questions

Some attorneys prepare their witnesses for deposition by getting them in the habit of quickly analyzing each question by using a four-step process called "the form."[4] This process can be instructive and useful for expert witnesses as well.

I. Do I understand the question?

If you do not understand the question, say so and do not:

- guess what it means,
- help counsel rephrase the question,
- answer the question you think counsel might be asking you, or
- answer questions that are inconsistent with the facts.

A. Guessing

Q: Do you use the SMAC computer program in doing your analysis?
A: I think that may be the one I use.

B. Helping counsel rephrase

Q: Was the lifting incident an exacerbation of the patient's condition?
A: I think you mean aggravation, don't you, Counsel?

C. Answering the question you think counsel might be asking

Q: Would the facts you reviewed in this case indicate to you that the pump motor was defective?
A: By "defective" I assume you mean the manufacture and not the design?

D. Answering questions that are too broad or inconsistent with the facts

Q: In light of the failure of the backup alarm to function, was the driver negligent?
A: The backup alarm was functioning.

II. Do I know the answer to the question?

Experienced experts know and accept the fact that they do not know the answer to every possible question even if it is in their field. They do not hazard guesses and are comfortable saying they "do not know the answer to that question."

Q: What are the 14 potential causes of electrical fires?
A: I do not know.

---

[4] The form was developed by Dr. Martin Peterson, a trial consultant from Lincoln, Nebraska.

III. Do I remember the answer?

Due to the large number of facts, details, and information in litigated cases, the expert may not remember each and every fact and detail. Experts can reply in two ways. Either:

- they do not remember or
- they can refer to their written report for the reply.

Q: What was the size of the warning label in this case?
A: I do not recall.

Q: What was the size of the warning label in this case?
A: I have the precise measurements in my report, page 2, first paragraph. It was 2" long by 3.5" wide.

IV. How do I want to truthfully and artfully answer the question?

The expert takes a beat to think of the most effective way to truthfully respond to the question before him. Although all questions must be answered truthfully, they should also be answered artfully. That is, the answer should not be misleading such that it reflects poorly on the expert.

Example 6.25: Artful answer
Q: How much are you being paid for your deposition testimony here today?
A: I am not paid for my testimony. I am being paid by your firm $500/hour for my time.

Practice Pointer: This is a more artful answer than "$500 an hour" because it is less misleading.

6.4 Proper Demeanor at Deposition

Counsel is just as interested in *how* an expert responds to questions at deposition as in the answers themselves. The lawyers on all sides will evaluate the expert's demeanor to determine how effective and credible she will likely be before a jury or fact finder. The demeanor of the key expert witnesses and their likely effect on the jury are important factors when the lawyers evaluate the case for purposes of possible settlement. Because more than 90% of all contested cases are settled before trial, the demeanor of the expert witness at deposition will have a significant impact on the resultant settlement values. If the case is not settled, the expert's demeanor at deposition will help counsel prepare for her cross-examination at trial. When counsel evaluates the expert's demeanor at deposition, he will look first at the 5 Cs: *confidence, calmness, control, care,* and *coolness under fire.*

Exude Confidence

An expert witness should strive to achieve a professional tone of quiet, humble confidence. Confidence is important because if an expert does not appear to believe and trust her own opinion, how can the lawyers expect the jury to believe the opinion? Experts should be careful, however, to not cross the line from quiet, humble confidence to arrogance. Arrogance can damage one's credibility as much as quiet, humble confidence can bolster it.

Example 6.26: Quiet confidence of expert

Q: Now, Doctor, do you know when was the last time you updated your curriculum vitae?

A: I think it states on the upper right-hand—February 27, 2005.

Q: And your current position at Cortland County Hospital?

A: Chief of Obstetrics and Gynecology.

Q: How long have you been you the Chief?

A: I've been Chief of Obstetrics and Gynecology since the fall of '03 or so, over three years.

Q: Now your CV sets forth various publications that you've been involved in; is that correct?

A: Yes.

Q: How many published works—how many works have you published, do you know? Feel free to look at any exhibit.

A: Between 150 and 200 in total.

Q: And of those 150 and 200 published works, do you know how many refer to fetal distress issues?

A: I would say none.

Q: Have you ever written on any issues concerning fetal distress?

A: I would say no.

Q: And you've never written about fetal hypoxia?

A: That's correct. I've never written about fetal hypoxia.

Q: Have you ever written about fetal acidosis?

A: No.

Q: During the course of a year, how many deliveries are you actively involved in?

A: I personally do about 50 deliveries a year.

Q: And how long have you been doing 50 deliveries a year?

A: Since about 1986.

Practice Pointer: In reading the above exchange, one can almost feel the quiet, humble confidence of the expert. He has no problem in admitting that he has not written about fetal distress or fetal hypoxia. The attorney who cross-examined this expert at deposition did so almost deferentially due to the doctor's acknowledged expertise and quiet air of confidence. This is a valuable expert witness who will probably play well to the jury.

Remain Calm, Cool, and Collected
An expert witness will be a much more valuable asset to an attorney if he can stay calm, cool, and collected while under fire at deposition. Such a witness is difficult for counsel to shake. To stay calm, cool, and collected, one needs to understand and accept *at the outset of one's retention* that difficult questions will be asked and that not everything will go as planned. An ability to handle the unexpected while still maintaining a cool and calm demeanor helps make an outstanding expert witness. Experts who are flustered easily are less effective and successful at deposition because they may let their emotions take over and they may misspeak.

Example 6.27: Expert loses composure
Q: What are the factors one looks at under the DSM-IV for malingering?
A: Gee, I guess we'd have to get it. My memory, I don't have—you know, I know the DSM-IV, I don't have it memorized.
Q: Did you utilize the DSM-IV in coming to an opinion here that Mr. Allison was malingering?
A: Did I utilize it, no. That's a diagnostic manual. I don't think I have to use that as a reference to diagnose malingering. Can I take a break to look at the text?

Practice Pointer: The expert witness was caught off guard, lost his composure, and came off as weak and unsure of himself.

Example 6.28: Cool and calm expert
Q: At the time of the accident, do you know what Mr. Khan's age was?
A: No, I don't.
Q: Do you know what his height was?
A: No, I don't.
Q: His weight?
A: No, I don't.
Q: Past medical history with regard to any preexisting neck or back complaints?
A: No, I don't.
Q: I think you have indicated you don't know his position in the seat?
A: I believe he was the driver but beyond that, no.
Q: You don't know the relationship between Mr. Khan's head with the headrest?
A: No.
Q: Do you know whether the brake was applied?
A: No, I don't and to be perfectly honest, to me that doesn't matter.
Q: Whether a driver is applying a brake in a rear-end collision, would that factor change the length of time of the impact pulse?

A: If they were in fact applying the brake, it would change some circumstances and make the collision milder to the occupants of the vehicle. So, I have taken the worst case.

Practice Pointer: The expert, although under fire, maintains a cool and calm air about him. He is doing well by simply concentrating on answering the questions that are put to him.

Example 6.29: Consecutive "no" replies do not rattle expert

Q: Have you ever done any research or performed any studies on ECT plus continuation lithium?

A: No.

Q: Have you ever done any research or conducted any studies on the prognosis of bipolar disorders?

A: No.

Q: Have you ever done any studies or performed any research on continuation therapy in the prevention of relapse after ECT?

A: No.

Q: Have you ever done any research or written any studies or performed any kind of research on medication resistance during an index episode and its effect on the likelihood of sustained prophylactic effect?

A: Please repeat that again.

Q: Have you ever done any research or done any studies on medication resistance during an index episode and its effect on the likelihood of sustained prophylactic effect?

A: No.

Q: Have you ever done any research or done any studies on the length of remission after discontinuance of continuation therapy after ECT?

A: No.

Q: Have you ever been involved in any studies or done any research on the effect of the length of a period of remission on the likelihood of relapse of bipolar disorder after ECT plus continuation treatment?

A: No.

Q: Have you ever done any research or written any papers on the effect of long-term lithium continuation treatment on ECT remitters?

A: No.

Practice Pointer: The expert here was comfortable enough in his expertise and qualifications to continue to reply simply and directly "no" to these questions for as long as they went on. The expert stayed calm and collected and was not panicked into guessing or worse.

Maintain Control

Expert witnesses need to maintain strict control over their responses. To do this, one must concentrate and focus on the questions being asked. Remember, you are an expert, not an advocate. The expert's role at deposition is quite simple—to truthfully, simply, and directly answer the questions propounded to him. An expert who maintains control by simply and directly answering the questions asked will be a credible and highly valued expert witness.

Example 6.30: Focusing on questions keeps expert in control

Q: Do you know Dr. Callente?

A: I have met him on a couple of occasions.

Q: Are you familiar with ACME Research Corporation?

A: I'm aware of it.

Q: And they're a company that primarily does work for the insurance and defense industry? By "defense" I mean defense attorneys.

A: Actually, I don't know that. So I can't say that I know that one way or the other.

Q: Are you aware that over a five-year period in the '90's they were paid over seven and a half million dollars by InsurePlus Insurance in the low-impact collisions?

A: No, I wasn't.

Q: Knowing that fact or accepting that fact to be true, would that, in your mind, generate some question as to the validity of the Callente study?

A: No.

Practice Pointer: Despite being confronted with unexpected questions to which she did not know the answers, the expert maintained her control and did not volunteer any additional thoughts or rationale. She simply focused on the questions and answered them as truthfully and simply as possible. This was a good witness.

Avoid Sounding Arrogant

It is important for the expert witness to guard against any displays of arrogance. There is nothing that will turn off a jury or fact finder quicker than arrogance as evidenced in a video or transcribed deposition used at trial. Accordingly, experts need to be objective about their qualifications but should never be pompous. The weight to be given to an expert's testimony will ultimately be judged by a jury of lay persons. If they think the expert is arrogant, it can and will affect the expert's credibility with them. The testimony of an expert witness is worthless if it is not credible.

To avoid falling into the arrogance trap, experts should try going into the deposition with the mindset of meeting someone for the first time. If the witness appears arrogant or self-centered, the jury may become turned off quickly. If, on the other hand, the witness is honest yet humble, she is much more likely to make a good impression. A jury is just like a person you are meeting for the first time. They have little if any prior knowledge of an expert witness and they will form a positive or negative impression quickly. Many jury experts believe that in a battle of the experts, the expert who the jury likes and identifies with is the one they are most likely to find credible and convincing.

Example 6.31: Arrogant reply does not serve expert well
Q: Are you an expert in warnings, sir?
A: Am I an expert? I have written 197 articles and 4 books on warnings. I guess that would make me an expert.

Practice Pointer: "Yes" would have been a much better response to this question.

Act Naturally
All expert witnesses are best served by acting naturally and being themselves at deposition. While there is much to be gained by observing skillful and experienced expert witnesses live or on television, experts should not adopt the latest manner of answering questions. Thus, the best answer to the question, "When did you get your M.D. degree, Doctor?" is not, "To the best of my recollection, on or about June 1997." Likewise, the question, "Is Ms. Jones your associate?" perhaps should not be answered with, "The answer depends on how you define *is*." Credibility is an important issue. To maintain credibility, you should be yourself and try not to adopt another person's demeanor or style.

Avoid Jokes and Sarcastic or Inappropriate Remarks
Expert witnesses should not make any jokes, asides, or sarcastic remarks. These may be misconstrued by a jury or fact finder and could be used against the expert by counsel. In either case, the expert will probably come off looking unprofessional. Additionally, the jury may get the impression that the expert witness is not taking the litigation seriously.

Example 6.32: Joking reflects poorly on the expert
Q: Tell me about Ergo Master.
A: That's a computer program that utilizes—primarily utilizes—MODAPTS, but it also can use other systems in assessing work content and work motions and performing an ergonomic analysis based on the work content and the worker's motions and movements required to perform the work task.
Q: Again, is this something that can be used to analyze any job?
A: Yes, probably, except yours.
Q: Do you personally sell it or is it available through someone else?
A: It is produced by MindWize Software and I do sell it and MindWize Software sells it and there are a number of people that can—
Q: Do you know how much it costs?
A: $950. Would you like to order a copy?

Practice Pointer: It is completely inappropriate for the expert to attempt to sell counsel software in the midst of his deposition. Such an inappropriate remark serves no useful purpose and can only damage an expert's credibility. When this expert's deposition testimony is evaluated by counsel, his tendency to "crack wise" will not be looked on as an asset.

Act Dignified and Polite

An effective expert witness is polite and maintains her dignity. Experts who maintain their dignity and answer the questions politely are viewed as valuable expert witnesses. Such experts tend to play well to a jury and are less likely to misspeak. An expert who, on the other hand, continuously jousts with counsel may come off as a partisan who has an axe to grind. Perceived partisanship will damage such an expert's credibility with the jury.

Example 6.33: Biased, impatient reply reflects poorly on expert

Q: Please tell me in your own words every reason why you disagree with the OSHA investigator's conclusion as to how the accident in this case happened.

A: I think I have spent quite a few hours explaining it.

Q: Do you know what 40,000 PSI, using that figure, would do to the bones and soft tissues of a hand or arm that passed through such a configuration?

A: Under what condition?

Q: Under the conditions that you have a hydraulically driven conveyor belt with lugs on the under side that passes around a ten-inch-diameter stainless steel roller and the tissue, the hand and the arm passes all the way around that ten-inch roller under the belt?

A: Why don't we cut to the chase here and ask me why his hand wasn't crushed when it went through the roller because that is where you're trying to get. The questions that you're asking don't have a lot to do with engineering. I'll be happy to answer the question I just put to you.

Practice Pointer: The expert has moved away from his role as an impartial expert who should merely answer questions at deposition. This may suggest that he is biased and damage his credibility with the jury. He has also lost his cool and forgotten to simply answer the questions put to him.

Do Not Be Argumentative

Expert witnesses should not be argumentative. Experts who argue with counsel and who lose their cool and their appearance of impartiality are often ineffective. If and when an expert's deposition testimony is presented at trial, the jury may get the impression that she was so argumentative because she has an interest in how the case comes out. Sophisticated counsel is adept at getting under the skin of expert witnesses at deposition. Once the lawyer gets an expert to be argumentative, the expert is more likely to volunteer information or to phrase a response inappropriately.

Don't Lose Your Temper

Do not allow yourself to be goaded by counsel into losing your temper. If you lose your temper, you will give an emotional response to a question. Such an emotional response will not be carefully considered and will come back to haunt you.

Example 6.34: Showing temper

A: The question you're asking and, again, rather than dance around this for any length of time, is what my definition was of mild post-traumatic brain injury. If that's the case, then yes, he had one by definition. But, again, that's a much more encompassing term than is concussion. Yet subjective symptoms of headaches, dizziness, and within several days after the initial injury—so by definition, it's under the general classification of mild post-traumatic brain injury. Whether or not I think he had an initial cerebral concussion, no, I don't.

Practice Pointer: A cool, calm reply would have served the expert better.

Example 6.35: Expert loses cool

Q: How would you define HC's relationship to you, what are they to you?
A: They asked me to do this evaluation.
Q: I understand they asked you, what is HC to you?
A: They're an agency that, that wanted me to evaluate her.
Q: One word, can you think of one word that they are to you?
A: You want to give me a multiple choice? I'm not finding one word that you'd like. Why don't you just tell me what the hell you are looking for and let's get on with it.
    Counsel: I would like to take a break.

Practice Pointer: This is *not* the testimony of a cool, calm, collected, and unflappable expert. A better response might have been, "I'm sorry, but I can't answer that question the way it has been phrased."

6.5 Advice on Answering Questions

Carefully Listen to and Answer the Questions

Being careful is an invaluable asset for any expert deponent. Expert witnesses need to be very careful to actively listen to and understand the questions they are being asked. It is imperative to answer the questions accurately, without exaggeration or inaccuracy. If an expert is careful, he will be less likely to misspeak at deposition. Remember that for depositions that are not videotaped, there are no points given for speed. A delay of a moment or two between the question and the answer will not be reflected in the deposition transcript. Such a delay can help the expert witness to formulate a carefully considered response.

Example 6.36: Asking for a clarification before answering
Q: Do you know whether or not the Williams text, *Williams on Obstetrics,* sets forth criteria with respect to the pH testing as to whether or not a certain level indicates cesarean delivery?
A: Which text and which edition?
Q: The latest edition.
A: No, and I say that because the individuals who wrote the Williams text are not the strongest proponents of doing fetal scalp sampling.

Practice Pointer: The expert made the attorney clarify the question before answering it. The precision and care of the expert in listening to the question and formulating the response are characteristic of an effective and valuable expert witness.

Example 6.37: Answering the actual question asked
Q: In what instances would a sexual relationship between a lawyer and a client not constitute sexual misconduct, if you're able to give me an answer to that question?
A: Well, obviously number 1 would be if the lawyer is not involved in representing that person, although I guess "client" sort of implies representation. I mean, if you meet somebody at a party, it's not a problem. Number 2, if the legal matter is over with and time has passed, so that the issue is obviously resolved and finished, there probably would be no obvious or overt elements of exploitation in that situation.
Q: Anything else?
A: I suppose, for completeness, if the client was somebody else's client.
Q: Meaning you're not the person's lawyer?
A: Yes. You are an attorney and that person is a client, but they're somebody else's client.

Practice Pointer: Note how the expert in the above example answered the specific question he was asked. He did not answer the question that was intended but not asked. The expert, of course, did not help opposing counsel by rephrasing the question for him "Do you mean a sexual relationship between a lawyer and his client?" Experienced experts can "see" the question as if it were written and respond to the question "as written."

Example 6.38: Not answering the question asked leads to volunteering
Q: Give me the percentage of lawyers working for the plaintiffs versus working for the defense who have retained you.
A: In seatbelt cases?
Q: Yes.
A: The firm that I worked for or myself personally? There is quite a big difference.
Q: Well, let's take you personally first and then the firm you worked for.
A: I would say it's about 50/50 for me personally.

Q: Okay. Have you ever been retained by a lawyer representing an automotive manufacturer?

A: No.

Q: When you say you've worked 50/50, what types of lawyers have retained you representing what types of clients?

A: Prosecuting attorney, insurance company representing, well, the insurance interests, or railroads for worker compensation.

Q: Now, you also mentioned that the company you worked for might have a different ratio of plaintiff versus defendant.

A: Yes, sir.

Q: And you worked for Safety Engineering, correct?

A: Yes.

Q: And you've worked for them for how long now?

A: As a subcontractor, for six, seven years now; as an employee, two, three.

Q: Okay. And can you give me the percentage of plaintiff versus defendant cases, seatbelt cases that Safety Engineering has, if you know?

A: Not precisely, but I believe that it's probably over seventy to eighty percent for plaintiff's attorneys.

Practice Pointer: Note how the expert in the above deposition example helped counsel discover as much information as possible. First, he changed the question to narrow its scope to seatbelt cases. Presumably, answering the question actually asked might have resulted in a different, truthful reply. Second, he expanded the question and suggested to counsel that he inquire about both his personal caseload and then about the company he worked for. Had he answered the question "Give me the percentage…who have retained you," the direct and simple reply would have been, "50/50."

Avoid Absolute Words

It is wise to avoid, where possible, absolute words such as "always" and "never." Absolute words are frequently an invitation to, and fertile grounds for, cross-examination by counsel. Counsel will attempt to damage an expert's credibility by first getting him to make an absolute statement. She will then use counterexamples in an effort to show the falsity of the statement.

Example 6.39: Recovering from an absolute reply

Q: You testified previously that you have read *everything* written on warning labels, isn't that correct?

A: Yes, but that was some time ago.

Practice Pointer: The expert's response here was a good recovery.

Example 6.40: Absolute words
Q: Doctor, it's your testimony that acute stress cannot cause heart attacks under any circumstances, is that correct?
A: It is.
Q: So, Doctor, if I were to reach into my trial bag here (reaches into bag) and pull out a loaded .44 Magnum and point it at your head, and you then had an immediate heart attack, it would be your testimony that the heart attack was not related to stress?

Practice Pointer: The use of absolute words ("any" circumstances) opened the expert up to this sort of cross-examination.

Example 6.41: "Always"
Q: Is it always a mistake to speed and exceed the speed limit?
A: Yes.
Q: What about life-and-death emergencies?

Practice Pointer: The expert here is trapped due to his agreement with an absolute statement.

Example 6.42: "Always" and artful reply
Q: Is it always a mistake to speed and exceed the speed limit?
A: It would depend on the specific circumstances.

Practice Pointer: This is a more artful and accurate reply.

Don't Elaborate or Volunteer
Volunteering information can be one of the biggest mistakes an expert makes at deposition. Generally, an expert should answer only the questions she is asked and not volunteer information. Volunteering information will almost always result in new lines of cross-examination. It may also disclose information to which counsel otherwise never would have become privy. The one notable exception to this rule is where retaining counsel has asked the expert to be as forthcoming and detailed as possible in his replies in an attempt to position the case for settlement after the deposition.

Example 6.43: Volunteering information
Q: What objective findings of malingering did you make?
A: Lack of atrophy, good muscle tone, oil, and grease on his fingernails. There were plenty of subjective findings as well.
Q: Let's get into your so-called subjective findings.

Q: Would you agree with me that causation is a medical opinion?
A: Partially.
Q: Okay. (*Note:* No question was put to the witness, but he answers nonetheless.)

A: If there are idiopathic issues, then it's a medical opinion. If there are not any glaring idiopathic issues and if a person works in a job that exposes him to risk factors, then I can certainly analyze the job and determine what factors were present and if the person was exposed to those risk factors and barring any other, you know, medical opinion or medical opinion that says, well, there is an idiopathic issue here also, then we assume that the work caused it.

Q: Can you define for me idiopathic carpal tunnel syndrome?

A: Idiopathic causes would be, for example—can be related to diabetes, pregnancy, heart, circulation, even specific anthropomorphics like the size of a person's tunnel, carpal tunnel.

Q: The word idiopathic itself, what does that mean?

A: Well, we'll have to look up the definition.

Q: You'll defer to the dictionary for that.

A: Yes.

Practice Pointer: The experts' volunteering of information in both examples opened up new lines of questioning. They should have stopped their answers after their first sentences.

Use Hedge Words with Care

Care is necessary when using *hedge words* when expressing an expert opinion. Such words include "I guess," "I believe," "it seems," "it's possible," and "I would say." The main reason that an expert is testifying is to give an opinion. Hedge words and phrases can quickly undermine one's opinion and are an invitation for additional cross-examination. Worse, counsel may be able to make a motion to have the expert's entire testimony stricken because experts must be reasonably certain of their opinions under the rules of evidence.

Example 6.44: "Guess"

Q: That's your "guess," sir?

A: Well, what I meant to say, that it was my opinion that....

Practice Pointer: The expert needed to avoid the hedge words. If he had an opinion he believed in, he should have stated it without employing the hedge words.

Example 6.45: "Possible"

Q: You used the word "possible" in stating your opinion, correct?

A: Yes, I did, but what I meant....

Practice Pointer: Use of any one of a series of hedge words at deposition can result in the trial judge finding the expert's testimony legally insufficient and striking the testimony.

Make Concessions Gracefully

In answering questions honestly, an expert may have to make an occasional concession. An expert who makes a concession graciously and moves on will exude confidence, integrity, and flexibility. If, on the other hand, he doggedly refuses to give an inch, the expert may come off as rigid and partisan.

> The most common error the beginning expert makes in a deposition is the failure to concede an obvious and irrefutable point out of misguided loyalty to his or her side of the case....Quibbling over the possible exceptions or equivocating in some way helps no one.[5]

Example 6.46: Prompt concession lessens its negative effect

Q: Now, would you agree just because the Glasgow Coma Scale was 15, there were no focal neurological deficits, that one still cannot rule out whether or not Mr. Allison had suffered a concussion or mild brain injury?
A: That's correct. He could have.

Practice Pointer: When an expert makes a concession promptly without the necessity of a long series of leading questions, the concession's effect on the jury or fact finder is reduced.

Example 6.47: Making a concession shows the expert's honesty and fairness

Q: There's a point, I think it's in the addendum of your report, where you indicate an opinion that Carl Olan had refused a CT scan in relation to prior care, is that correct?
A: If you show me where you are reading, I will read it and see if that's what I said.
Q: I'm looking at the addendum, so the second part of your report. I'm going to find it here. Okay, on page 304 in your addendum there is a statement: Why no CAT scan? And you have a statement in there beginning 4 lines down at the sentence: evidently this is not the first time that Mr. Olan had refused a CAT scan.
A: Yes.
Q: What is the basis of that opinion?
A: Years earlier, one of his physicians in Arizona had ordered a CAT scan, and yet the CAT scan was not done.
Q: What, from that note, causes you to conclude that Mr. Olan refused the CAT scan?
A: I don't know, definitely, that he did refuse. But I'm saying, if he refused one then, it would maybe be explained why he refused one now.
Q: What would be the jump in your mind that you would make to reach that conclusion? If he had done it before, you say that he did it now?

---

[5] Thomas G. Gutheil, *The Psychiatrist As Expert Witness* (Washington, DC: American Psychiatric Press, 1998) pp. 69, 71–72.

A: Maybe he doesn't like CAT scans. Maybe he's claustrophobic or has heard that it's a bad experience.

Q: You don't have any facts which allow you to conclude that Carl Olan had refused a CT scan?

A: No.

Q: And so you wouldn't come into court and offer testimony to the jury that Carl Olan had apparently or evidently refused a CT scan in the past?

A: I would say that's a possibility based on the way I looked at the record. A CAT scan was ordered of his spine. He didn't have a CAT scan done according to the records that were given to me.

Q: Do you think that the statement contained within your addendum, "evidently this is not the first time that Mr. Olan had refused a CT scan" is a fair statement?

A: I think it would be a better statement to say perhaps.

Practice Pointer: The expert in the above example did make an appropriate concession. This concession will not hurt the expert in the eyes of the jury and, in fact, it may help show that he is willing to admit mistakes and actually help his credibility.

Note: The expert could have made the above exchange shorter and less painful had he made his concession earlier on in the questioning:

> **Q:** What, from that note, causes you to conclude that Mr. Olan refused the CAT scan?
>
> **A:** I agree. It would have been more precise to say "perhaps this is not the first time that Mr. Olan refused a CAT scan."

"I Don't Know"

If an expert witness is asked a question to which he does not know the answer, his answer should be, "I don't know." There is absolutely nothing wrong with this response if one genuinely does not know the answer to the question. There are probably thousands of questions that can be asked of experts in any discipline to which they do not know the answer.

Example 6.48: Expert not afraid to say "I don't know"

Q: What is the coefficient of friction for steel on cement?

A: I don't know.

Practice Pointer: The forthright admission of lack of knowledge was in the expert's best interest. Had the expert tried to talk around this, it would have only emphasized her lack of knowledge.

Example 6.49: Consecutive "I don't know" replies

Q: Were there any other instructions provided before Concrete Cutters came on-site to Mr. Rathje?

A: I don't know.

Q: Were there any telephone conversations where they discussed respective responsibilities?

A: I don't know.

Q: During the negotiation of the contract between Concrete Cutters and Henry Toohey was there any discussion about respective responsibilities?

A: I don't know.

Q: Was there any conversation about respective areas of expertise when it came to Concrete Cutters and Toohey?

A: I don't know.

Q: Are there any concrete pumping firms in this state that use the A.C.P.A. standards?

A: I don't know that.

Q: Let's go with this Henry Toohey Corporation. How big a company is that?

A: I don't know.

Q: What kind of on-site safety people do they have?

A: I don't know.

Q: Did they apply different standards to concrete pumping than you?

A: I don't know.

Practice Pointer: The expert in the above example had the confidence in his expertise and the fortitude not to speculate or guess. Just because opposing counsel is asking questions you do not know the answer to is no reason to panic or even be concerned. At deposition, most attorneys can ask experts hundreds of questions that they do not know the answers to. The simple solution is to answer each question, "I do not know" until counsel has exhausted these types of questions.

Example 6.50: Flustered expert

Q: If those wrist rests were unavailable prior to 2001, would you agree she had a higher probability then of being in a neutral position?

A: I don't know. That's an interesting question. I don't know. I mean I guess that's my answer, I don't know. But I think the wrist rests certainly emphasize, even though you have the Ridyard's ergonomic assessment of 2004, if Miss Gerald and/or her supervisor were trained, that would not have been a product of choice.

Practice Pointer: If you allow yourself to get flustered, your lack of knowledge will be emphasized to the jury. The expert in this example would have been better served by replying, "I don't know" and then sitting quietly and waiting for the next question.

"I Don't Recall"

When asked about a fact, situation, or occurrence that one honestly does not remember, the best answer is, "I do not remember" or "I don't recall." This is the only appropriate answer when an expert honestly has no recollection. If this is the expert's response, however, counsel may attempt to refresh her memory. This is permissible under the rules of evidence.

Example 6.51: Document doesn't refresh memory

Q: Doctor, do you have any memory, independent of the medical records, of any of the events that occurred on August 5 of 2005, regarding the treatment of Ms. Norbell?

A: I would say no. Can't really remember any real specifics on that particular day. I remember snatches of her. Over her two-year course, I recall her and various things over a two-year span, but that particular day I can't recall any real specifics.

Q: Have you reviewed the medical record of August 5, 2005, from the emergency room, the Green Mountain Medical Center?

A: Yes, I have.

Q: Does that medical record refresh your memory in any way as to where you were approximately the time that she was admitted to the hospital about 4 A.M. on that day?

A: She came in at 4 A.M. that morning. The reading doesn't refresh my memory.

Q: Does the record indicate approximately when you first appeared on August 5 at Green Mountain Medical Center?

A: Just looking at it very quickly now, looked at this in detail earlier, I don't see anything in the record in and of itself that refreshes my memory on when I physically was present, near Ms. Norbell. I don't see anything that would indicate an exact time.

Practice Pointer: As noted above, if the document does not refresh your memory or recollection, you are free to so testify. In this case, counsel was forced to drop this line of inquiry and move on.

Answer Only Questions You Understand

The expert witness at deposition should only answer questions he understands and to which he knows the answers.

Example 6.52: Request to rephrase vague question

Q: Should a company learn from its past mistakes?

A: I do not understand your question, can you rephrase it?

Practice Pointer: This expert correctly asks that the question be rephrased because the question is ambiguous and open to many interpretations:

- "A company": What kind of company? Large? Small?
- "Learn": Learn a lesson? Learn not to repeat it?
- "Past mistakes": What does this include? Honest mistakes?
- "Past mistakes": How far do you want to go back?

Example 6.53: Don't understand the question
Q: So you wouldn't relate to the extent of the evidence of cystitis within the bladder to whether or not that UTI may result in gas formation?
A: Would you mind repeating that? Would you please read it back?
Stenographer: So you wouldn't relate to the extent of the evidence of cystitis within the bladder to whether or not that UTI may result in gas formation?
A: I don't understand the question.

Practice Pointer: The expert in the above example made a thoughtful good faith effort to understand a very poorly worded question. Having the question repeated gave him a second opportunity to hear it. When he still did not understand it, he stated so simply and directly.

Note: The expert did not make the mistake of assisting counsel in rephrasing the question or, even worse, guessing at what the question meant.

Do Not Lock Yourself Down or Commit to the Future Unnecessarily
Opposing counsel at deposition will try and tie all loose ends together and "lock-down" the expert on:

- any additional work she may do on the case and
- any additional opinions that the expert may offer at trial.

Counsel wants to avoid any last-minute surprises and trial by ambush.

Additional work: The key is for the expert not to lock herself down by her deposition testimony.

Example 6.54: Leaving wiggle room
Q: Are you planning to do any additional work on this case prior to the trial?
A: Not at this time.

Practice Pointer: This simple reply leaves the expert wiggle room should the need arise to do additional work prior to trial.

Note: Savvy counsel will ask for assurances on the record that opposing counsel will inform him of any additional work that is done after the deposition. While counsel is aware of the continuing obligation to supplement discovery under Rule 26, he wants to make sure he is not sandbagged at trial.

Example 6.55: Possible additional work
Q: Have you been asked to do any additional testing or work other than what you've already completed through today?
A: No.

Q: Do you have any intention of doing additional testing between now and the time of the trial in October?

A: I don't have any intention of doing it. If something comes up that implies, or I'm requested to do that, I will do that.

Q: If you perform additional tests, would you do that, unless you were requested to do so by counsel, so that your attorney would be aware of it, is my concern?

A: In the past, we may have made quite a few tests, as you can see. But from here on out, I will confer with Mr. Dennis regularly to make sure we don't do anything that he's not aware of.

Q: So we're clear, can we have an agreement that if you perform additional tests, you'll advise Mr. Dennis or Mr. Windsor so that they can make me aware of any additional testing you do between now and the time of the trial?

A: Yes.

    Attorney: Counsel, can we have an agreement that if he does additional testing, I can be made aware of that prior to trial?

Q: I want to make sure that I have the opportunity to ask you about any new opinions or additional testing that you have before we get to trial, because I don't want to be in a position of hearing it for the first time with the jury.

A: Sure.

Q: Does that make sense to you?

A: Yes.

Q: Is that agreeable, Counsel? We have that obligation under Rule 26. Yes. And if you would agree to reciprocate with regard to Ihler and Cooper, because I understand that they were looking at, maybe, doing some more experimentation after this deposition. We just wanted to be reciprocal and make sure that we're taken care of. Absolutely. With that, I'll pass the witness.

Practice Pointer: The expert here left open the possibility of doing additional work prior to trial if requested. If and when the expert undertakes additional work, he should inform retaining counsel who has a continuing obligation to inform opposing counsel prior to trial.

Additional opinions: Opposing counsel will also want to make sure that the expert will not spring new or additional opinions on her at trial.

Example 6.56: Different questions/different opinions

Q: Are these all the opinions you will be offering at trial?

A: These are the opinions I have today. If I am asked different questions, I may have additional opinions.

Practice Pointer: Here the expert does not commit to limit his opinions. He is aware that additional questions may be raised for the first time at trial.

Example 6.57: "I will continue to study the case"
Q: Have we covered all areas that you will testify to at trial?
A: We have covered the major areas. However, I will continue to study the case and may have additional opinions in the future.

Practice Pointer: Here the expert points out that the study or work in the case is ongoing and that new opinions may be formulated.

Do Not Ramble
Experts who ramble when answering open-ended questions at deposition lack the demeanor of an effective expert witness. An expert who rambles may come off as not being focused and will almost certainly volunteer damaging information. In an attempt to get the witness to ramble, counsel might ask open-ended questions near the end of a deposition when the witness is tired.

Example 6.58: Rambling reply
Q: Who is going to have the final say about the care and treatment of Ms. Jones?
A: I'll tell you what my experience is. I see many, many injured workers. I see many individuals with knee problems and I help counsel those individuals as to whether or not they should get certain types of treatment.

Now, I consider myself in a unique position in that I will see a hundred, you know, hundreds of knee injuries come in the door that range from minor to moderate to, you know, more significant to severe and that may include some ligament strains and tears, bursitis, a whole host of things. And I think we'd all agree that probably 90 to 95 percent of them never even get to the orthopedist or the Dr. Millers of the world that are standing across the table from me.

Oftentimes I think that because I see such a wide variety of injuries and see the 90 to 95 percent that never get to the surgeon, that oftentimes I'm in a better situation or better position to have a perspective on it to say, hey, this one we've treated conservatively, you know, maybe an injection, some physical therapy, some anti-inflammatories, some bracing, some restricted activities, and they get better whereas some orthopedics, and it's not their fault, obviously, they're going to see a skewed population. They are only seeing the ones that people like me refer to them.

And, for the most part, by the time I have referred them to an orthopedist, you know, the wheels are set in motion that they're going to have surgery because I have already talked with my patient and I feel that they need surgery. That's why I have called the orthopedist in.

So, I don't know, to answer your question, I think it's a difficult question to answer. Who's going to have the final say? I would like to think that at least in my working with orthopedists that I work with, we both have input into it. Obviously I'm not going to do the surgery. So the orthopedist is going to end up scheduling, you know, talking the patient into it or out of it, whatever, for the final decision, and is going to be involved with the scheduling and all that.

I would say probably a more appropriate answer is the patient ultimately decides whether or not they are going to have surgery. We give them recommendations, but ultimately they decide.

Practice Pointer: The expert would have been better served by answering, "The patient ultimately decides himself," rather than rambling.

Example 6.59: "Do you have anything to add?"
Q: Please tell me in your own words every reason why you disagree with the OSHA investigator's conclusion as to how the accident in this case happened.
A: I think I have spent the last twelve hours explaining it.
Q: Would you add anything to what you already said?
A: I have jotted down some notes that I would like to refer to relative to that question and to the extent that I disagree with the OSHA inspector's report that will be responsive to your question.

If you excuse me some of these things we have covered. I am looking to see if there is any that we have not.

Okay, I also would like to express the opinion that the wrench has been reported to be on the nut and I find that very unlikely that the wrench can be. The jaws of the wrench can be closed tightly enough on its own or generate enough friction or clamping force to get the needed torque that it would take to bend the wrench as we see here.

Therefore I again don't believe it was on the nut. Also, there has been an opinion expressed most recently by Mr. Cabric that well perhaps the wrench had slipped between the nut and the frame of the take-up assembly.

I find that from the photographs it is my opinion there is not a sufficient space there for the wrench to fit in that area and if it did it would remove it further from the end of the wrench further from…Decreasing the likelihood the wrench in fact made contact with the hinge pin.

One opinion that I don't think has been mentioned today or one issue is that the center line of the threaded rod is three inches below the top most edge of the take-up assembly and based on the theory that Mr. Abbingdon was holding the wrench by the head of the wrench at the time it's unlikely that holding it in that position would allow any portion of his thumb to come in contact with the upper most portion of the take-up assembly.

Further, I would express the opinion that based on the reported scenario that the stanchion or the vertical member that we have referred to we know from photographic evidence that it's approximately 12 inches. The closest edge is approximately 12 inches back from the center line of the threaded rod and therefore

175

the stanchion would have likely contacted Mr. Abbingdon's arm above the elbow not some three or four inches above the juncture with his wrist as reported by Mr. Cabric.

I also found that the stanchion did not act. Or it's my opinion that the stanchion did not act as a guillotine or any type of shearing action for the reason that I have stated and for the fact that it is a single member and there is no cutting action associated with the stanchion.

Additionally, if the thumb had been trapped against the top of the take-up frame the palm of the hand would have been away from the direction of travel of motion of the conveyor and the top portion of the wrench and it was unlikely that the arm would have been pulled at all since the arm in effect was lodged against movement by the pinning action against the take-up frame and let alone there was sufficient force to in fact rip the arm off in that position. I also expressed the opinion that the wrench became dislodged following the energy buildup as reported by Mr. Cabric and others that the direction of travel of the head of the wrench when Mr. Abbingdon was positioned holding it would have been back towards Mr. Abbingdon due to the actual crimping action of the top portion of the take-up assembly.

I believe we have covered in sufficient detail my opinions relative to the three OSHA regulations that have been cited…1910.212, 1910.147 and 1910.219 relative to their applicability in this case.

It is further my opinion….Because we have covered I think in detail what my opinions are relative to the accident scenario….Hand on the wrench to the roller assembly….

But in addition to that it would be my opinion that the adjustment of the wrench has not been, as shown in the police photos, has not been changed immediately following the accident.

I know we touched on that briefly but I want to express that point again….

Practice Pointer: A better answer might have been, "No, not at this time." That would have probably been the end of the deposition. By letting his frustration get the better of him, the expert rambled, revealed damaging information, boxed himself in at trial, and showed that he can be goaded easily.

Example 6.60: Long, rambling reply
Q: What documents have you provided to counsel in this case?
A: I was the recipient of the report that I had, that I had requested the members to submit documentation to, which was the NULCA damage survey report. I would like to put it in some context, though, if I could, with you.
Q: All right.
A: And the documents that I am referring to are not mine, are findable, should you wish to. But roughly about the same time this happened there was two other reports published, one from the Energy Company Alliance, ECA, and another from the Utilities Solution Unit, which reports to the National Reliability Council out of

Washington. Energy Company Alliance is a trade association. Both of them examined damages. Now, we're talking about three already published things, the CAN report, ECA report, and now this report. ECA report actually used empirical data gathered from their gas company reporters about how many damages were done in a given year. I think it was '96, '97, roughly around that time. And they, to the best of their ability, realizing the fact this was data gathered in different ways by different companies, reported in different ways, how many damages we had, what cost. The Utilities Solution Unit deals with damages, which I also sat on at the time. And we reported to the FTC, or FCC. It reports and analyzes all communications outages that affect more than 30,000 people more than 30 minutes. So they're big guys. They're the 911s, the airports getting shut down, those sorts of things. Both of those came back with a statistical background that was actually quite interesting. One of which still bears today, as far as I know, is that 50 percent of all damages in America are still today caused by people not calling before they dig, just simply not making that phone call to the dig center, for instance, and going ahead to dig. Another 35 percent are caused by excavators not paying any attention to the markings that are existing on the ground. Taking too many chances, digging too deep, digging too close, for whatever reason. And roughly about 14 to 16 percent of damages are caused by marking error. Now, within that marking error there's a number of things. One of which may be, maybe the line couldn't have been located, maybe it's a gas line that's plastic, it has no metallic conductor with it, just couldn't find it at all, maybe there's no records to it. Maybe the locating device can give you a ghosting signal and put it in a different area. Or maybe the locator just plain screwed up. So, anyway, within that context this was published.

Practice Pointer: The expert in the above example goes on for three pages in the deposition transcript when presumably answering a very simple question: "What documents have you provided to counsel in this case?" A simple reply could have been: "The documents are listed on page 6 of my report."

Interestingly, even after this lengthy reply counsel knows enough to ask: "Did you finish your answer?" The expert replies "not quite" and goes on again.

While it is tempting for scientists and experts to show everything they know, replying to the question simply and directly is often preferable.

Beware of Open-Ended Questions

Experts should be cautious when dealing with open-ended questions. These questions invite long, rambling answers. Counsel may be trying to get the expert to volunteer information not called for by the question. Volunteered information is likely to be used against an expert during cross-examination. It is wise, therefore, to answer open-ended questions as concisely as possible, being careful not to provide information that was not asked for.

Example 6.61: Open-ended question yields rambling response

Q: What do you consider to be the unsafe uses of an ATV?

A: Oh....I can give you some highlights. There are many, many unsafe uses, but classic unsafe use is as a mobile transport form to transport you and a loaded firearm. This is not a motorized attack vehicle. It is not a multi-passenger transport vehicle, although it has to be conceded that because of its stability and because of its wide platform, you can safely transport a passenger on it. You just have to be more careful. But that is not a correct use of the vehicle, so depending—it's like everything else. You could probably even transport a loaded firearm safely if you took enough precautions, so when I say unsafe use, it's not a recommended use, not that you can't pull off that maneuver safely with enough care.

Certainly you could easily find loads and pulling tasks like stumps that just by their nature the vehicle was not designed to do, and people will try and use the dynamics of the vehicle to run up against the rope and jerk on something really hard and say—but that's not a good idea.

It is not for transport on paved roadways. I mean, you can drive it. It will run. The traffic cops in Hawaii write all their parking tickets on three-wheeled ATVs with tires scrubbed smooth, and you can do that safely, but that's just not a recommended use. I mean, you are—you are....

I think it's fair to say unless you know what you're doing, it is not a competitive speed machine. I mean, there are...people race it and, and...most people don't have any business racing cars. It doesn't mean they don't do it, but that is potentially a hazardous use.

They are not vehicles...for—I don't know how to characterize this...I'm going to say not very well thought out horseplay. That's an inelegant statement, but you see uses of these vehicles for games like chicken and...sort of it's horses substitutes for games. I mean, they are not a horse. I mean I don't mean that pejoratively. Horses, because they have their own will, they have their own unique set of problems, but an ATV is not a horse, and attempting to use it like one can be a misuse of it.

And finally, I guess, an ATV is not a toy. Anything with a multiple horsepower engine is not a toy in the sense that classic things people think of as a toy is something you can drop—drop in the crib or playpen, and, you know, it ain't one of those. It's a vehicle that has the capability of putting energy at the command of anybody...tall enough to reach the handle bars and the accelerator and the gear shift or long enough legs to reach the gear shift, and the people who ergonomically fit that envelope do not overlap totally with the people whose judgment is appropriate for operating one of these, and so use of it as a toy, as a toy substitute, is not appropriate.

Now, obviously, every one of those categories has bits of infinite detail, numerous scenarios.

Practice Pointer: Note the numerous areas of inquiry opened up by this long, rambling answer to a single open-ended question. Experts are better served by brief, succinct replies to open-ended questions. If counsel has follow-up questions, let her ask them. Don't do the lawyer's job for her.

Avoid Slang

Effective experts avoid slang expressions when replying to questions. When slang expressions are transcribed and read back to a jury, they diminish the value of the reply and can make the expert sound almost illiterate. Most slang expressions slip from experts unintentionally. To avoid making such a slip, experts must maintain their concentration and focus.

Example 6.62: Slang reflects poorly on expert

Q: Now, sir, you took a history from Harold Bellamy, right?
A: Yup.
Q: And the history is the story that he tells you, correct?
A: Yup.
Q: Is that a yes?
A: Yes, it is.
Q: And you told us that Mr. Bellamy told you that he hurt himself while lifting some boxes at work?
Q: Uh-huh, I mean, yes.
Q: Are you familiar with an organization called ABC, Inc., sir?
A: Nope.

Practice Pointer: The expert's use of slang cheapens his testimony and diminishes his credibility.

Watch for Counsel's "Bumble and Fumble" Gambit

Wise experts do not help counsel when he apparently bumbles or fumbles with some type of technical question. Experts are frequently tricked into volunteering key information by such real or feigned ignorance. Let counsel bumble or fumble all he wants. Expert witnesses are there to answer questions, not to assist counsel in framing them correctly.

"Yes" or "No" Responses

Opposing counsel usually does not want to limit the replies of expert witnesses at deposition. The strategy is to get the expert talking and have him reveal as much information as possible. Occasionally, counsel may want to completely control the expert and his replies. This may be done when a videotaped deposition is being taken and will be used at trial. In these limited circumstances, opposing counsel may try to get the expert to answer the questions simply "yes" or "no."

If counsel asks for a "yes" or "no" response and the expert can answer the question with such a response, she should endeavor to do so. If counsel attempts to insist on a "yes" or "no" answer to questions that cannot be answered in that fashion, the expert can state, "I cannot answer that question with a 'yes' or 'no' reply without my answer being misleading." It will then be up to counsel to either let the expert explain her answer or he will need to rephrase his question.

Example 6.63: Getting the expert to agree to answer "yes" or "no"
Q: If the questions call for a "yes" or "no" answer, it would save us an awful lot of time if you answer them that way. If you don't answer it that way and you give me a long answer, I'm going to have to go back to the same question again, and it's going to cost us a lot of time. You can explain anything that you want to explain either at the end of your deposition or at the time of trial. So, if we can get my questions answered, then we will be out of here. Okay?
A: If I can answer them "yes" or "no," I'll be happy to do that.

Practice Pointer: By agreeing to essentially answer all questions "yes" or "no," this expert has given up the right to explain his replies. This trap is called "The Deal" and is most frequently used to control the witness under cross-examination at trial. When asked to limit his answer to "yes" or "no," the expert can properly refuse to do so:

Q: Will you agree to answer all questions "yes" or "no"?
A: No. A "yes" or a "no" answer may be misleading and I have sworn to tell the whole truth.

Correct Misstatements as Soon as Possible
Expert witnesses are not expected to be perfect. During a long and arduous deposition, an expert may misspeak or make a mistake or error. If this happens, the expert should correct the error on the record as soon as she recognizes the error: "I want to correct a statement I made a few minutes ago. I stated that the 2005 EMG was related to the surgery. That is incorrect." Counsel may challenge the expert on the mistake before she has an opportunity to correct it. In that case, the expert should admit the error graciously.

After making a mistake, the expert needs to avoid making the matter even worse by an inability or unwillingness to admit the mistake. This could make the expert look biased. If the expert discovers a mistake after the deposition concludes, she should notify counsel and correct the deposition transcript when it comes for her signature.

Example 6.64: How to admit a mistake
Q: You only treated her for a 2005 accident, correct?
A: You know, it's interesting. I'm looking at what we wrote down here and it says "2001–2004 motor vehicle accident, recovered." I may have misinterpreted what this

note was. The accident was in '01, but we saw her in '04; and I apologize if I misled you.

Practice Pointer: The expert has done a good job handling his mistake. He comes off as human and, above all, honest.

Watch Out for the Word "Hoping"
Sophisticated counsel may attempt to trap the expert witness by using the word "hope." If the expert inadvertently agrees with a characterization, she may allow the lawyer to successfully call into question the reliability of her opinion. When confronted with an "And you are hoping…" question, it may be best to actively refute that characterization. When an expert is passive and agrees to an attorney's characterization or mischaracterization, she is, in effect, letting the attorney put words in her mouth.

Example 6.65: "Hoping" for an accurate history
Q: Doctor, one more thing. Your opinion here today that Mr. McKenney has asked you about, in part, is based on the history that you get from the patient, isn't that correct, and your training, obviously?
A: Yes, sure.
Q: And you're hoping, of course, as most doctors, that the patients are accurate when they give you a history and tell you what's wrong with them. Is that a fair statement?
A: Yes.

Practice Pointer: Counsel has raised questions in the minds of the jury or fact finder regarding the reliability of the history (i.e., assumptions upon which the expert's opinion was based). "Hoping" may be made to seem akin to "guessing." A better answer might have been, "I don't 'hope' that I was provided an accurate history, I assume so unless I have reason to suspect otherwise."

Don't Be Tricked into Speculating
Expert witnesses should not permit themselves to be tricked, cajoled, or forced into speculating when answering questions under oath at deposition. There is nothing wrong with the response, "I'm sorry, but I'm not going to speculate on that."

Example 6.66: Expert correctly refuses to speculate
Q: So what you're saying here is that this coated cable itself is what deflected?
A: That is correct.
Q: And is it also correct to say that when you ran that test that a portion of that coated cable was left outside of the interlocking portion of the lacings?
A: It would be correct to say that that assembly as purchased was assembled based on our understanding and also whatever instructions that came with it so there was an equal portion sticking out of either end. The exact length of the cable beyond the

lacing what we refer to as the hinge device, I can't give you a dimension on that. I don't really recall.

Q: Was there some portion of it?

A: My recollection that the washer was crimped on the metal cap and to what extent the cable stuck out, I couldn't theorize at this point.

Q: Can you say whether it did or whether it didn't to any extent?

A: I can't with any accuracy.

Q: I am not asking for any millimeters.

A: I understand. I can't speculate that it did or did not at this point.

Force Counsel to Explain Ambiguous Questions

Experts at deposition are best served by forcing opposing counsel at deposition to explain ambiguous questions.

Example 6.67: Expert forces counsel to explain vague terms in question

Q: Was the patient better before the accident?

A: Can you explain what you mean by "better" and "before"?

Practice Pointer: The expert here did not guess at the meaning of the question. Instead, he forced counsel to specifically tell him what he meant by the ambiguous terms.

Example 6.68: Falling into counsel's trap by answering a vague question

Q: Are you familiar with the literature in the field?

A: Yes, I am.

Q: Look at this list of 1,700 articles and tell me which ones you have read.

Practice Pointer: The expert here opened himself up to this standard line of attack.

Example 6.69: Forcing counsel to explain a vague term

Q: Are you familiar with the literature in the field?

A: There is a lot of literature, can you be more specific?

Practice Pointer: The expert here demands more information before replying.

Break Opposing Counsel's Momentum

The expert here understands that there are numerous ways to break or disturb the momentum of opposing counsel. Breaking counsel's momentum will give the expert a needed chance to pause, think, and regroup. Additionally, it may throw counsel off track. Experts should use this technique judiciously. Some techniques to break counsel's momentum include:

- asking for clarification of an ambiguous portion of the question,
- answering a question with a question to make sure you know what counsel is asking,

- asking for a question to be rephrased because it is confusing or misleading,
- asking that the question be repeated to be sure it was heard correctly,
- requesting a break to use the facilities, do some quick research, or just stretch and refresh,
- sipping water, then asking for the question to be repeated, and
- referring to a document.

Encourage Opposing Counsel to Lose His Cool
Experienced experts can get under counsel's skin by doing the following things:

- Telling the truth. Opposing counsel wants to catch the expert in a lie so he can destroy her credibility. A scrupulously honest expert takes many lines of attack away from counsel and can be quite disappointing.
- Maintaining one's cool. Nothing frustrates a trial lawyer like an unflappable witness.
- Being prepared. A prepared expert can be very frustrating to depose because she generally makes very few mistakes.
- Maintaining a high level of concentration. Experts who can do this are not worn down and do not fall for counsel's tricks and tactics.
- Picking up on things that annoy counsel and pushing counsel's buttons by using these things strategically.
- Pushing back where necessary and letting counsel know that he can't browbeat you into unreasonable concessions like not breaking for lunch.
- Occasionally breaking opposing counsel's momentum.
- Pointing out mistakes and mischaracterizations counsel makes.

Use the Clock to Your Advantage
By rule, statute, or stipulation, many depositions are conducted under a strict time limit. Experienced experts realize that it is good practice to take their time when answering questions. Experts should not be concerned about opposing counsel running out of time and not getting to the most important questions. If counsel runs out of time, that's his problem, not yours.

Do Not Testify Beyond Your True Area of Expertise
Opposing counsel can be expected at deposition to drag or nudge the expert outside his true area of expertise. If the expert leaves his comfort zone (his "sandbox"), then he becomes particularly vulnerable to cross-examination. Experienced experts refuse to testify outside their true area of expertise. Please consider the following example.

Example 6.70: Refusal to stray from true area of experience
Q: Do you have any opinion whether or not Dr. Lee violated the applicable standard of care in this case?

A: I don't know that. He's a general surgeon. I'm a neurologist. I couldn't offer an opinion whether or not he violated any standard of care.

Practice Pointer: The expert here refuses to go beyond his true area of expertise. Experienced experts prepare with retaining counsel and decide prior to deposition how far they will go in offering opinions, i.e. which opinions they will and will not be offering. Leaving this type of decision to the moment the question is asked can result in the expert being led outside of his true area of expertise.

6.6 Conclusion
Experts should consider employing the techniques and strategies described in this chapter when testifying at deposition.

Chapter 7 Understanding and Defeating Counsel's Deposition Tactics

7.1 Introduction and Executive Summary

Because the goals of opposing counsel differ at deposition from those at trial, the tactics employed by counsel differ as well. Generally, at deposition, counsel will try to elicit as much information as possible from the expert witness by:

- being open and friendly,
- playing dumb,
- asking how and why questions,
- asking open-ended questions, and
- seeking long, detailed answers.

To excel at deposition, experts need a full understanding of the tactics employed by opposing counsel and the effective methods of dealing with these tactics:

- Beginning a deposition with a pointed, challenging question in an attempt to rattle you.
  - Be prepared to address key issues at the outset.
- Attempting to make you appear shifty or untrustworthy on camera.
  - Watch the camera setup. Remember that you are on camera.
- Requesting that you waive reading and signing of the deposition transcript.
  - Carefully consider whether you want to do this.
- Making the deposition uncomfortable for the expert.
  - Demand a reasonable environment.
- Conducting a lengthy deposition in an attempt to wear you down.
  - Get an agreement up front as to how long the deposition will last.
- Jumping to different topics.
  - Concentrate on each question and don't try to out-think counsel.
- Asking about notes.
  - Answer the questions. Don't ditch your notes.
- Asking if anything has been removed from your file.
  - Do not remove anything. Do not misfile extraneous documents into the file.
- Intimidating you with an unfriendly demeanor.
  - Do not soften your opinion or get nervous as a result of the attempted intimidation.
- Asking about conversations you had during the break.
  - Don't discuss the case with counsel during the break.

- Trying to get an answer that contradicts your report or the interrogatories.
  - Know your report and the interrogatories cold.
- Trying to lock you down on how critical a factual assumption is.
  - Hedge your responses to these types of questions.
- Questioning about newly presented documents.
  - Insist on time to adequately review the new document before answering any questions.
- Attempting to get you to unwittingly attest to the authenticity of a document.
  - Listen carefully to the questions and carefully phrase your response. For example, you could state, "It purports to be…."
- Asking about key names and dates.
  - Know this information cold.
- Trying to get you to lose your cool.
  - Remember that counsel wants you to lose your temper. Take the high road.
- Asking unintelligible questions in an effort to get you to volunteer information.
  - Don't take the bait.
- Remaining silent after you finish answering a question to try to elicit more information.
  - Remain silent after you finish your reply.
- Getting you in a rhythm.
  - Carefully listen to and answer all questions.
- Asking convoluted questions.
  - Don't answer any questions unless you understand them.
- Asking "catchall" questions to limit your future testimony.
  - Answer truthfully, but leave yourself some wiggle room. For instance, state, "Not that I can recall at this time."
- Using your own office against you.
  - Don't have the deposition at your office.
- Bringing the opposing party to the deposition.
  - Do not let the appearance distract you or make you sympathetic.
- Counsel asking if you have anything else to add.
  - You can state, "Not that I can recall at this time."
- Using abusive conduct.
  - Warn counsel on record and, if necessary, terminate the deposition and file for a protective order.
- Counsel playing the "wide-eyed student" in an effort to get you talking.
  - Answer the questions asked fully but narrowly.
- Using hypothetical questions designed to turn you against your client.
  - You should offer a very carefully considered response.

- Helping the opposing expert prepare for trial.
  - o All criticisms should be objective.
- Trying to get you thrown off the case.
  - o Be prepared to explain why you are qualified and why your methodology is reliable.
- Questioning "magic word" legal standards.
  - o Recognize them and use them correctly.
- Scheduling a deposition over multiple days to get you to contradict yourself.
  - o Have retaining counsel resist this.
- Getting you to criticize co-defendants.
  - o If you don't have an opinion or haven't looked into an issue, say so.
- Mischaracterizing your testimony or opinion.
  - o Actively listen and do not agree to counsel's characterization unless it is 100% accurate.
- Getting you to agree that a text is "authoritative."
  - o Hedge your response and state that, although you agree with some things in the book, you do not agree with all of it.
- Asking if the expert turned in a colleague he was critical of for professional discipline.
  - o Carefully word criticism about colleagues.
- Pushing the expert to give an absurd opinion.
  - o Don't over-testify.

7.2 Tactics Employed by Opposing Counsel

Tactic 1: Starting off with a pointed, challenging question
This tactic is designed to catch the expert witness off guard before he is warmed up and ready for difficult questions.

Example 7.1: Pointed question at outset of deposition
Q: You do not know what caused the failure of the 750KVA transformer. Isn't that true, sir?

Practice Pointer: This tactic is defeated by preparation and being ready to address the key issues in the case at the outset of the deposition.

Q: You do not know what caused the failure of the 750 KVA transformer. Isn't that true, sir?
A: That's not correct. The unbalanced load caused the individual phase windings to overheat, which led to the failure.

Example 7.2: Starting off with pointed question to keep expert off guard

Q: Good morning, Mr. Mason. As you know, my name is Bruce Stein. I represent Vijay Khan with regard to this motor vehicle collision. It's my understanding that it's your opinion that the speed change of Mr. Khan's car was no more than 6.1 miles per hour; is that correct?

A: That is correct.

Q: As a result of that change of speed, the average forward acceleration of Mr. Khan's car was no more than 2.8 g's for a duration of approximately 100 milliseconds; is that correct?

A: That is correct.

Q: You used the term "average acceleration." What was the peak acceleration for Mr. Khan's car?

A: Well, I don't technically compute that; however, you would expect it to be approximately two point two times the 2.8, or 5.6g's.

Q: Did you calculate the average or peak g's that were applied to Mr. Khan's neck or head?

A: No.

Q: Why did you not do that?

A: I'm working on the car rather than the person.

Q: Could you calculate the peak or average g's that were applied to Mr. Khan's head?

A: That's normally done by the biomechanist, in these cases, and not by me. And to be perfectly—I, you know, if somebody gave me the equation, yes, I could punch them in the calculator and compute them. But, no, I don't normally do that and I don't normally know those code equations.

Practice Pointer: Counsel has established the expert's opinion and put him on the defensive almost immediately. An experienced expert should be prepared for this tactic.

Tactic 2: Setting up unflattering camera angles during videotaped depositions
The idea here is to set the room so that the expert does not look at the camera when giving her responses. This makes the expert look untrustworthy to jurors who may view the videotape at a later date.

Practice Pointer: This tactic is defeated by the expert and retaining counsel taking pains to make sure the room is set up so that answers are delivered into the camera.

Tactic 3: *Playing games to make the expert look shifty on camera*

Examples include opposing counsel pacing when questioning the expert witness and opposing counsel throwing a pen up and down in the air.

Practice Pointer: This tactic is defeated by asking opposing counsel to refrain from the activity in question and by constant awareness that the camera is on at all times.

Tactic 4: *Asking the expert to waive reading and signing of the deposition transcript*

The expert may waive his right to read and correct the deposition transcript. This may be ill-advised because the transcript can contain errors and reviewing the transcript is an excellent learning tool for the expert.

Practice Pointer: This tactic is simply defeated by the expert refusing to waive his right to read and sign the transcript, if that is what he thinks is in his best interest. Note that there is a competing school of thought arguing that it is in the expert's best interest to waive reading and signing because that gives the expert more flexibility to deal with impeachment at trial.

Tactic 5: *Providing an uncomfortable deposition environment*

Opposing counsel will make the deposition room uncomfortable (too hot, cold), the chair hard, or provide inadequate space for the expert to spread out her file. This is done to make the expert consciously or subconsciously want to get out of the room as quickly as possible.

Practice Pointer: This tactic is defeated by objecting to the uncomfortable environment and demanding a reasonably comfortable environment.

Tactic 6: *Conducting a lengthy deposition*

The goal of this tactic is also to wear down the expert. Opposing counsel expects that the more tired the expert gets, the more likely he is to misspeak, make a mistake, get angry, or become frustrated.

Practice Pointer: This tactic is defeated by having an agreement as to how long the deposition will go on, but the expert may agree to extend the deposition to accommodate the other side. If the expert cannot extend the deposition, it can be continued at a later date. Many jurisdictions by rule limit the length of depositions. Employing this tactic is likely to be very expensive for opposing counsel because the longer the deposition continues, the more opposing counsel will need to pay the expert for his time.

Tactic 7: *Questioning on the notes the expert takes at the deposition*
This tactic is defeated by simply not taking any notes beyond the names of the people in the room. Experts who do make notes do so with the understanding that they will likely be asked to read the notes into the record and may have the notes marked for inclusion as part of the deposition.

Tactic 8: *Jumping around to various topics*
This tactic is designed to confuse the expert witness and to make it difficult for the expert to anticipate where opposing counsel is going.

Example 7.3: Jumping from topic to topic
Q: You have a second degree of Bachelor of Science in agronomy?
A: That's correct.
Q: It says you were focused on plant protection chemistry?
A: Yes.
Q: How does glyphosate work? How does it cause symptoms in any target species?
A: Well, it depends on whether it's a sensitive plant or not.
Q: When you say you're certified, that's the CP Ag.?
A: Yes.

Practice Pointer: This tactic is defeated by taking one's time, answering each question truthfully, and not trying to outguess counsel. The more the expert tries to anticipate the question, the less focused he is on the question at hand.

Tactic 9: *Asking about notes made to documents in the expert's subpoenaed file*
Opposing counsel will invariably ask the expert about any and all notes the expert has made on the documents produced.

Example 7.4: Notes taken by expert
Q: Showing you what's been marked as Deposition Exhibit No. 6, for identification purposes, do you recognize that document, sir?
A: I do.
Q: At the top it says "Plaintiff, Jim"?
A: Yes.
Q: That is your handwriting?
A: It's my handwriting.
Q: These are your notes?
A: And my notes.
Q: When did you create this?
A: Sometime before the last deposition.
Q: Okay. And the purpose of this document was what?

A: Looking at the other side of the coin from what we had discussed just a moment ago.

Q: So this is looking at it from Jim's point of view?

A: Right.

Practice Pointer: Opposing counsel can be expected to have experts read and explain any handwritten notes they make. These notes can be on the records themselves (typically in margins), on separate pieces of paper, or on small Post-it notes.

In these deposition exchanges, counsel is looking for inconsistencies, mistakes, changes of opinion, and creating a timeline for cross-examination purposes.

This tactic is defeated by not making any notes or, alternatively, by simply answering the questions to the best of one's ability. This tactic should not be defeated by hiding, misplacing, or "losing" notes. Such dishonest actions can easily destroy an expert's credibility.

Tactic 10: *Asking point-blank whether the expert or anyone else removed anything from the file prior to it being produced*

In response to a subpoena: Counsel will try and determine if the expert has in fact brought his entire file with him to the deposition.

Example 7.5: "Is this your entire file?"

Q: Is this your entire file, sir?

A: Yes, it is.

Q: Where are your billing records?

A: Well, I keep the billing records in a separate file. I didn't know….

Practice Pointer: This tactic is defeated by the expert fully complying with the subpoena and bringing his entire file to the deposition. It is also good practice to be careful when filing and not to misfile any unrelated documents into the case file.

Example 7.6: Expert produces complete file

Q: The court reporter has just marked as Exhibit 215—it's a deposition subpoena for the personal appearance, and production of documents and things, directly to you. Please take a look at the—Exhibit 215, please.

A: (Complying.)

Q: Did you receive a copy of this subpoena?

A: Yes.

Q: Did you review the documents that it requested that you produce?

A: I did.

Q: The documents that you handed to me at the outset of this deposition, were all those documents responsive to the categories of documents that we requested to be produced?

A: Yes.

Q: We're copying those right now, and we'll mark those as exhibits and talk about those later. But just so I'm clear, have you withheld any documents from production that would have been otherwise responsive to the categories here?

A: No.

Practice Pointer: Experts who fully and completely comply with any subpoenas they receive in conjunction with their deposition remove the "compliance issue" from the radar screen. Failure to comply or, even worse, attempts to cover up invariably lead to disaster.

Tactic 11: Intimidating the witness with a professional but notably unfriendly demeanor

Counsel may try to unnerve the expert through the absence of any pleasantries beyond "good morning" and a firm, adversarial demeanor at the beginning and throughout the deposition.

Example 7.7: Intimidation with discussion of perjury

Q: I want to go over a couple of these preliminary matters with you. Do you understand that your testimony here is given under oath and subject to the penalty of perjury?

A: Yes.

Q: And do you understand that your testimony here today becomes part of a permanent record of your testimony. That is, that unless there is an order by the court sealing the deposition, that's there is potential that it is part of a public record that can be reviewed, for example, by other lawyers or by your peers?

A: Yes.

Q: And, I had mentioned that it is also permanent. That is, that it would be preserved and that other lawyers or your peers may in the future have an opportunity to review their testimony and compare it with testimony you have given in past cases or may give in future cases?

A: Yes.

Q: You understand that?

A: Yes.

Practice Pointer: Here counsel raises the specters of perjury, permanent records, peer review, publicity, and future impeachment. While this is unlikely to affect experienced experts, inexperienced experts may soften their opinions or get nervous and make mistakes as a result of the attempted intimidation. This tactic is defeated by being prepared for it and by not cracking under this psychological pressure.

Tactic 12: *Asking about conversations with retaining counsel during breaks*
Counsel here will try to imply that the expert was coached by retaining counsel at the break.

Example 7.8: Questions about conversations at the break
Q: Did you talk to Attorney Tierney during the 10-minute break?
A: Yes.
Q: Tell me everything you talked about.
A: Where the best place to have lunch is.

Practice Pointer: This tactic is defeated by not discussing the case at the break or not talking to retaining counsel.

Tactic 13: *Questioning designed to elicit a different response than those contained in answers to interrogatories or in the expert's written report*
Counsel is trying to show inconsistencies and raise the expert's anxiety level.

Example 7.9: Inconsistency with report
Q: Does the insurance company have a definition section and a table of contents in its policy?
A: Yes, it does.
Q: Didn't you say in your expert report dated 4/15/06, page 17, "the insurance policy does not contain a definition section"?

Practice Pointer: This tactic is defeated by knowing one's written report and answers to interrogatories *cold,* by testifying truthfully, and by not testifying in a way that is inconsistent with the report and the interrogatories. This will also help correct counsel if he is taking statements out of context.

Tactic 14: *Trying to lock down the expert on the crucial nature of her factual assumptions*
Counsel will try and show that the assumptions are the foundation of the expert's opinion and if the assumptions change, so will the opinion.

Example 7.10: Changing assumption
Q: You assumed that the plaintiff was not limping prior to the accident, correct?
A: That's true.
Q: If in fact the plaintiff was limping prior to the accident, would you change your opinion on causation?
A: I would consider this new fact.

Practice Pointer: This tactic is defeated by carefully listening to the question asked and hedging your response as to whether you would change your opinion if it turned out an assumed fact was not true. The general response to defeat this line of inquiry is, "I would consider any new factual assumptions." Experienced experts understand that changing one fact or assumption often may not be enough to change their opinion.

Example 7.11: Proposed change in assumption(s)
Q: As a basis of one or all of your opinions, you've assumed as a fact on the date of the accident that Mr. Keith was standing in line in a cash office area, is that correct?
A: Yes, I am.
Q: You've also assumed, in formulating one or more of your opinions, that he was kept waiting and I believe the period of time offered was for 15 minutes. Is that correct?
A: That's what the assumption was.
Q: If either of those assumptions changed, would that affect your opinion in any way?
A: It might mitigate it some, but I'd still feel the procedure was incorrect.

Practice Pointer: The expert here correctly refused to instantly modify his opinion based on a nebulous change in an assumption. Note that counsel did *not* say how the assumption would be changed. If it was 14 minutes instead of 15 minutes, would that change the opinion? Experts can reply:

> **Q:** If either of those assumptions changed, would that affect your opinion in any way?
> **A:** I would consider any changes.

Or, alternatively:

> **Q:** If either of those assumptions changed, would that affect your opinion in any way?
> **A:** It would depend on the changes.

Tactic 15: Questioning about new and lengthy documents
Counsel may try to spring additional new and lengthy documents on the expert during deposition. The idea is to elicit a response that has not been carefully considered.

Example 7.12: Springing a new document on the expert
Q: Had you seen and considered this 3/14/06, 87-page investigative report prior to forming your opinions?
A: No.
Q: Why don't you take a look at it now so we can discuss how it might impact the opinions you have expressed?

A: OK. I estimate that will take me approximately 3 to 4 hours because it is single-spaced. Would you like me to start reading it now?

Practice Pointer: This tactic is defeated by insisting on all the time necessary to thoroughly review and digest a document before commenting on it.

Tactic 16: Attempting to get the expert to unwittingly vouch for the authenticity of a document
Part of the reason opposing counsel may ask an expert about a document is to attempt to have him unwittingly vouch for its authenticity.

Example 7.13: Unwittingly vouching for document
Q: I am handing you the contract dated 4/1/05 and signed by Orson Poole, correct?
A: That is correct.

Practice Pointer: This tactic is defeated by very carefully phrasing responses regarding documents (for example, "it appears to be…" or "it purports to be…").

Tactic 17: Asking questions about key names and dates
Here opposing counsel probes the expert to see how familiar he is with the facts.

Example 7.14: Probing on facts and dates
Q: What were the dates you did sampling at the farm in question?
A: April 20, 2006, April 24, 2006, and June 6, 2006.
Q: What did Dr. Oates do at the farm in 2006?
A: He took tissue, soil, and water samples.

Practice Pointer: This tactic is defeated by knowing key names, dates, and facts cold.

Tactic 18: Trying to get the expert to lose his cool
This is often done through pointed *ad hominem* attacks designed to make the expert lose his cool and thus help break his concentration and reduce the effectiveness of his testimony.

Example 7.15: Pushing the expert's buttons
Q: What kinds of medications are you on?
A: You dirty SOB….

Practice Pointer: This tactic is defeated by being aware of the goal of counsel and not losing your temper or cool.

> **Q:** What kind of medications are you on?
> **A:** One baby aspirin and 2 Tylenol I took at the last break.

Tactic 19: Fumble and bumble gambit
Opposing counsel may try to appear confused in an effort to encourage the expert witness to volunteer information.

Example 7.16: Counsel sounding confused elicits more information
Q: Did you comply with all of your ethical standards—I mean the ones you agreed to comply with when you joined professional organizations?
A: I belong to 6 engineering associations and they have ethical standards covering competence, honesty, conflicts of interest, truthfulness, fees, confidentiality, and impartiality. Which ones are you asking about?
Q: Why don't you go through all of them one at a time?

Practice Pointer: Experts should not assist opposing counsel in formulating their questions. This tactic is defeated by requiring counsel to ask specific questions.

Tactic 20: The silence gambit
Opposing counsel may just stare at the expert witness following a response. The goal is to psychologically encourage the expert to elaborate and, thus, possibly volunteer damaging information. Experts can defeat this tactic by simply stopping talking when they have finished their reply. Eventually, counsel will be forced to ask the next question or conclude the deposition.

Tactic 21: Getting the expert witness into a rhythm
Opposing counsel may try to get the witness into a rhythm by asking a series of questions to which the answer is the same, such as "yes," "no," or "I don't know." The idea is to break the expert's will to independently answer each question and to make each similar response easier to make. Alternatively, counsel may try and get the witness nervous about successive "I don't know" replies, forcing the expert to end the series by speculating or guessing.

Example 7.17: "I don't know" rhythm
Q: Were there any other instructions provided before Concrete Cutters came on-site to Mr. Rathje?
A: I don't know.
Q: Were there any telephone conversations where they discussed respective responsibilities?
A: I don't know.
Q: During the negotiation of the contract between Concrete Cutters and Henry Toohey, was there any discussion about respective responsibilities?
A: I don't know.
Q: Was there any conversation about respective areas of expertise when it came to Concrete Cutters and Toohey?

A: I don't know.
Q: Are there any concrete pumping firms in Vermont that use the A.C.P.A. standards?
A: I don't know that.
Q: Let's go with this Henry Toohey Corporation. How big a company is that?
A: I don't know.
Q: What kind of on-site safety people do they have?
A: I don't know.
Q: Did they apply different standards to concrete pumping than you?
A: I don't know.

Practice Pointer: This expert had the confidence in his expertise and the fortitude to not speculate or guess. Just because opposing counsel is asking questions you do not know the answer to is no reason to panic or even be concerned. Most attorneys can ask experts hundreds of questions at deposition that they do not know the answer to. This tactic is defeated by just answering each question "I do not know" until counsel has exhausted these types of questions. Alternatively, you can break the momentum of counsel by asking a question or taking a break. See Section 6.5.

Tactic 22: Asking convoluted questions
Opposing counsel may ask a compound question which, in effect, asks two separate questions. This is done in an attempt to confuse and rattle the expert witness and, perhaps, to have the expert answer incorrectly.

Example 7.18: Convoluted question
Q: With respect to center markings, do you agree that there is a difference of opinion among professionals as to whether or not center markings would be helpful or might, in fact, encourage people to do somersaults and other unsafe maneuvers?
A: That's a compound sentence and I'm not sure I totally understand that.

Practice Pointer: This tactic is defeated by recognizing compound questions and requesting that they be split into separate individual questions.

Tactic 23: Asking catchall questions
Opposing counsel may try to ask a final "catchall" or series of "catchall" questions designed to lock the expert into limiting future trial testimony to only what was presented at the deposition.

Example 7.19: Catchall question
Q: So you will not be offering any testimony at trial about the use of air bags, correct?
A: I have formulated no opinions on side air bags, but if I am asked about them at trial I will answer to the best of my ability.

Practice Pointer: This tactic is defeated by recognizing such questions, answering truthfully, but hedging your responses to them such that you leave yourself some room for unanticipated questions that may be presented at trial.

Example 7.20: Refusal to be boxed-in by catchall question
Q: Do you recall any other information which bears on this case?
A: Not at this time.

Practice Pointer: This is an artful, yet truthful, answer. It is, therefore, a good answer.

Tactic 24: Using the expert's office against her
Opposing counsel will carefully peruse the expert's office in an effort to discover information (such as textbooks) that can be used against her.

Practice Pointer: This tactic is defeated by not having the deposition in your office or, if you do, by isolating opposing counsel in a sterile (empty) conference room with no books, diplomas, etc.

Tactic 25: Encouraging the party to attend the deposition
Opposing counsel may ask his client to attend the deposition (they have a right to attend) to make it psychologically difficult for the expert witness to give an opinion that may have severe adverse consequences on the party.

Practice Pointer: This tactic is defeated by determining from retaining counsel who will be in attendance. If a party does appear, do not let the appearance distract you from telling the truth simply and directly.

Tactic 26: Asking "anything else" questions
Opposing counsel may attempt to limit the expert's trial testimony by asking questions such as, "Is that everything?," "Do you remember anything else?," and "Did you do anything else?"

Example 7.21: "Anything else" question
Q: Did you do anything else we have not yet discussed?
A: Not that I can recall at this time.

Practice Pointer: This tactic is defeated by diligent preparation and a carefully worded response that answers artfully without unnecessarily limiting one's trial testimony.

Tactic 27: Rattling the expert with abusive conduct

Here counsel will act obnoxiously in an attempt to browbeat the expert into submission or to force him to lose his cool, get angry, and say something ill-advised.

Example 7.22: Obnoxious questioning

Q: Are you an aficionado of pornography?

A: No, I am not.

Q: Do you believe in military solutions to political problems?

A: I don't understand…

Q: Do you want time to think about it, Doctor? Because I mean there seems to be a habit in this case of witnesses who don't know what to say to simply sit there and think and come up with some cockamamie response to a very serious question. Now, I'd like you to answer the question without thinking about it for the next five minutes.

Practice Pointer: This tactic is defeated by staying calm and being sure to document on the record what is occurring. If the deposing counsel has a reputation for obnoxiousness, consider getting the deposition videotaped. Nothing brings civility to a proceeding like a camera and microphone. If the abuse continues after a warning, consider terminating the deposition and then immediately filing for a protective order.

Tactic 28: Playing the wide-eyed student

Counsel may act as a student and seem very interested in and ignorant of the expert's field. He may seem very respectful and may never challenge the expert. He may encourage the expert to teach him. What counsel is doing is feigning ignorance to pump the expert dry of damaging information.

Example 7.23: An expert who likes to hear himself talk can get himself into trouble

Q: Tell me more if you could, I find this fascinating. Are there other reports in this area that you are aware of?

A: Yes, roughly about the same time this happened there was two other reports published, one from the Energy Company Alliance, ECA, and another from the Utilities Solution Unit, which reports to the National Reliability Council out of Washington. Energy Company Alliance is a trade association. Both of them examined damages. Now, we're talking about three already published things, the CAN report, ECA report, and now this report. ECA report actually used empirical data gathered from their gas company reporters about how many damages were done in a given year. I think it was '96, '97, roughly around that time. And they, to the best of their ability, realizing the fact this was data gathered in different ways by different companies, reported in different ways, how many damages we had, what cost. The Utilities Solution Unit deals with damages, which I also sat on at the time. And we reported to the FTC, or FCC. It reports and analyzes all communications outages that affect more than 30,000 people more than 30 minutes. So they're big guys. They're the 911s, the airports getting shut down, those sorts of things. Both of those came back with a statistical background that was actually quite interesting. One of which still bears today, as far as I know, is that 50 percent of all damages in America are still today caused by people not calling before they dig, just simply not making that phone call to the dig center, for instance, and going ahead to dig. Another 35 percent are caused by excavators not paying any attention to the markings that are existing on the ground. Taking too many chances, digging too deep, digging too close, for whatever reason. And roughly about 14 to 16 percent of damages are caused by marking error. Now, within that marking error there's a number of things. One of which may be, maybe the line couldn't have been located, maybe it's a gas line that's plastic, it has no metallic conductor with it, just couldn't find it at all, maybe there's no records to it. Maybe the locating device, can give you a ghosting signal and put it in a different area. Or maybe the locator just plain screwed up. So, anyway, within that context this was published.

Practice Pointer: This tactic is defeated by remembering that the expert's role is to briefly and truthfully answer the questions asked, not to teach opposing counsel. This tactic is an act designed to get the expert to open up and provide damaging information. A better response to this question would have been a simple "yes."

Tactic 29: Turning the expert into opposing counsel's witness through hypothetical questions
Opposing counsel will ask the expert to answer questions that assume different facts than those the expert assumed. The idea is to get the expert to agree with the opposing side's theory of the case.

Example 7.24: Hypothetical questions
Q: Can excessive stress contribute to the acceleration of cancer?
A: That is a hypothetical question and my general reply is it may be possible to have some relationship to cancer.

Practice Pointer: This tactic is defeated by being very careful when responding to hypothetical questions and not providing more of an answer than is called for or than you are able to give in good faith.

Tactic 30: Helping the opposing expert prepare for trial
Opposing counsel will ask the expert to critique the opposing expert's deposition testimony or the opposing expert's report. This helps the opposing expert prepare for trial.

Example 7.25: Critique of expert or report
Q: Anything else in regard to Mr. Theopholous, your opinion as to his qualifications or his competency to address agronomical issues in this case?
A: Well, I don't think he's addressing agronomics. He's not addressing whether there was enough fertilizer or wasn't enough fertilizer. He's not offering an agronomic opinion, as far as I know.
Q: Opinion as to his qualifications or competency to address—I said agronomical issues. I'll expand that to the pesticide issues involved in this case.
A: I have an issue with the agronomic issue. I don't think he's been asked to do that. I don't think he's qualified to do that. But he's certainly, as far as in his role as a pesticide investigator, he's certainly presumed to be able to interpret regulations and to perhaps take pesticide residue samples. I don't know as we sit here today if he's ever received any formal training on that or not.

Practice Pointer: This tactic is defeated by not being over-eager to critique (and therefore greatly help) the opposing expert and resisting the urge to trash him.

Note: When commenting on other experts, the deponent expert witness is best served by making *objective* statements backed up by *objective* facts. Whether the deponent likes the other expert or despises him is beside the point. The more opposing counsel can get the deponent to take cheap shots or otherwise reveal a dislike of the opposing expert, the less clinical, impartial, and scientific the deponent sounds.

Tactic 31: Trying to get the expert thrown off the case
In this tactic, opposing counsel will ask questions to build a record to show that the expert witness should be thrown off the case for not being qualified, not using a reliable methodology, proffering an opinion that invades jury functions (e.g., an opinion on credibility) or that jurors do not need expert help with (e.g., how much pain and suffering damages should be), or having a conflict of interest (e.g., previously working for the opposing party and being privy to confidential information).

Practice Pointer: This tactic is defeated by being scrupulous in only agreeing to testify in cases where you are well qualified, using a reliable methodology, and avoiding cases where you have a conflict of interest.

Tactic 32: Questioning "magic word" legal standards
Opposing counsel will use the deposition to show that the expert used the wrong standard when applying a legal standard (such as "defective," "standard of care," "open and obvious," "aggravation," and "reasonable degree of medical certainty"). This is a set-up to later challenge the expert's opinion because if it can be shown that

the expert used a personal standard rather than the correct legal standard, the court may throw out the opinion.

Example 7.26: "Magic words"
Q: The plaintiff fell into a hole that was open and obvious, correct?
A: No, if it was open and obvious he would not have fallen in.

Practice Pointer: This tactic is defeated by doing your homework, preparing with retaining counsel, and knowing and understanding the correct legal standards and "magic words."

Tactic 33: Trying to schedule or take the deposition over multiple days
This may be done in an attempt to make the expert contradict earlier testimony and give opposing counsel more time to prepare additional areas of inquiry.

Practice Pointer: This tactic is defeated by working with retaining counsel to get an early start and resisting attempts to stretch the deposition to a second day.

Tactic 34: A house divided
Opposing counsel's dream in a case with multiple defendants is to get one defendant to criticize the other defendants.

Practice Pointer: This tactic is defeated by recognizing this goal and being extremely careful before criticizing other defendants. Often, you may not have formed an opinion as to the conduct of other parties or are not in a position to do so.

Tactic 35: Making mischaracterizations
Opposing counsel will often mischaracterize the testimony or opinions of an expert witness.

Example 7.27: Mischaracterization of assignment
Opposing counsel may try to set a tone early on in the deposition by mischaracterizing or putting the expert's assignment in a bad light. Please consider the following example:

> Q: Who employed you as a witness in this case and when was that employment?
> A: Well, I wasn't initially employed as a witness. I was initially employed to just investigate the claim. And I think I have the actual date. According to my records, it was on August 24, 1999.

Practice Pointer: The alert expert does not permit counsel to mischaracterize her assignment and gently corrects him. While the above exchange is not a major issue, it lets opposing counsel know that he will not be permitted to get away with these types of comments.

Example 7.28: Mischaracterization of facts

Counsel may intentionally or, in some cases, unintentionally misstate facts, prior testimony, or even the nature of exhibits at the expert's deposition. Experts should be alert to this and not answer questions that subsume incorrect factual information. Please consider the following example:

Q: Have you written any correspondence to Mr. Nolan's office other than what we have marked as Deposition Exhibit No. 1?
A: I didn't send that to his office.
Q: Well, let me restate my question. Have you written any correspondence to Mr. Nolan's office?
A: No.
Q: Have you submitted any type of—anything in writing to his office?
A: No.

Practice Pointer: Note how the expert in the above example is alert to counsel's misstatement. Had the expert just answered the first question with a "No," he would have left the incorrect impression that he did send Exhibit #1 to retaining counsel.

Example 7.29: Mischaracterization of role in case

Opposing counsel may subtly or not so subtly mischaracterize the expert's role in the case during the deposition. Counsel hopes to "slip it by the unwary expert." Please consider the following example:

Q: Now, how many cases like this do you currently have pending, that is, security cases where you're a security expert?
A: One other.
Q: OK. And where is it?
A: It's in Houston.
Q: And are you representing the defendant or the plaintiff in that case?
A: Plaintiff.

Experienced counsel may follow-up on this question with a series of similar questions:

Q: Who did you represent in *Meyers vs. Galina Security?*
A: Plaintiff.

And then the trap:

Q: Now, when you represent the victim in a security case, do you look at the same information you do and use the same methodology when you're representing the defendant?

Practice Pointer: The expert needs to carefully listen to and hear each question. The above could have easily been avoided.

Q: And are you representing the defendant or the plaintiff in that case?
A: I was an expert. I did not represent any party.

Example 7.30: Mischaracterization of prior testimony
Q: Wouldn't someone with mechanical aptitude be most likely to…Given a choice…to have used that screwdriver for the cleaning function?
A: I don't believe there was any testimony that the screwdriver was available at the time of his accident. Clearly, it's in this photograph. We know that certain things have been placed on that fender after the accident, so I don't know that in fact that screwdriver was available.
Q: So it's your testimony that you believe that the screwdriver was placed there by someone after the accident occurred?
Counsel: Objection.
A: That wasn't my testimony.

Practice Pointer: The expert handled this lawyer tactic well. He quickly corrected the "state of the record" and the mischaracterization of his testimony by counsel.

Example 7.31: Mischaracterization contained in summary question
An expert witness should pay particular attention to counsel at deposition when she attempts to summarize one's entire testimony in one question, answer, or statement. Frequently, counsel will attempt to trick the expert into making an error or may intentionally or unintentionally mischaracterize the prior testimony. When confronted with questions of this type, it is acceptable to respond, "I don't agree with your characterizations" if you don't agree with them. It is also important that the expert witness have counsel clarify any broad or ambiguous terms that the jury can interpret differently later on:

Q: You have just been asked a series of questions to offer an opinion about the causal relation between Mr. Easton's employment and his occupational disease. Do you no longer have an opinion as to the cause of this disease?
A: I would state that I have not testified as to what the cause of Mr. Easton's carpal tunnel syndrome or cumulative trauma disorder is.
Q: Is that because you don't know?
A: In this case, I don't know.
　　Counsel: I will therefore move to have the doctor's entire testimony stricken from the record as he has just stated that he does not know the cause and therefore his opinion as stated earlier has absolutely no merit and is without any basis.

Practice Pointer: Counsel in the above videotaped deposition was able to call into serious question the entire testimony of the expert as a result of the expert's reply to one summary question. You need to be especially careful when answering these broad "sound-bite" type of questions.

Tactic 36: Getting the expert to agree that a text or other reference is "authoritative"

Counsel may attempt to get an expert's admission that a certain text or reference is authoritative with the purpose of setting up the expert for later cross-examination from the reference.

Example 7.32: Refusal to endorse textbook

Q: Would you consider Campbell's *Urology* an authoritative text, with respect to the field of urology?

A: I don't know of any text that I consider absolutely authoritative. There are some parts of Campbell's, the last 8th edition, that I agree with, and others that I don't agree with. And I think most urologists think the same way.

Q: Would you consider Campbell's a reliable authority?

A: We rely on Campbell's as a reference as we do Dr. Gilamorter's text and several other texts. There can be things in Campbell's that I would read that I would totally disagree with and, in that regard, I would call it unreliable, but I rely on the book to refer to from time to time.

Practice Pointer: This tactic can be defeated by using measured language when referring to the text. The expert in this example did not endorse the text as completely authoritative. He correctly and truthfully pointed out that while he used the text as a reference, he totally disagreed with portions of the text. When opposing counsel tries to later cross-examine the expert from the text, the expert can without contradicting himself say, "I do not agree with the text on that issue."

Tactic 37: Requesting professional discipline for criticized colleague

The professional discipline tactic is one frequently employed by counsel to back the expert witness into an untenable position. When using this tactic, counsel will attempt to turn a disagreement between experts into a flagrant ethical violation. To defeat this tactic, the expert witness needs to be extremely careful when responding to questions about another expert's actions. Consider the following example:

Example 7.33: Criticism of colleague

Q: And Dr. Edwards found that this person, Rita Landers, had a psychiatric disorder, correct?

A: Yes.

Q: And Dr. Edwards offered the opinion that the psychiatric disorder was a result of the occupational asthma?

A: Yes.

Q: You would also agree with me that Dr. Warren found the presence of psychiatric disorder in Rita Landers?

A: Yes.

Q: So, Doctor, we're clear, Rita Landers was able to fool two other doctors, right?

A: I don't know if it was fooling.

Q: She wasn't able to fool you, was she?

A: I don't know.

Q: Well, Doctor, here's this lady with a ninth-grade education and low to normal intelligence and it appears that she was able to convince a psychiatrist and a psychologist that she has a psychiatric condition. What happened?

A: What happened? Well, there's a number of things that, that happened. Dr. Edwards relies in part on the psychological test and does not go through criteria for DSM-IV.

Q: So Dr. Edwards didn't do it right, that's why he's wrong, correct?

A: He didn't do it the way to evolve to a DSM-IV diagnosis.

Q: So he misdiagnosed Rita Landers' condition?

A: I guess so.

Q: Were you shown the treatment notes by Dr. Edwards?

A: No.

Q: Do you know that he's treated her?

A: Yes.

Q: Do you know that he's treated her for several years?

A: No.

Q: Did you know that he's seen her on multiple occasions?

A: Yes.

Q: So, he's treating her essentially for a condition that doesn't exist, correct?

A: I don't know.

Q: Well, you say it doesn't exist.

A: I, I don't know what he's treating her for.

Q: Well, if he's treating her for depression or post-traumatic stress disorder, he would be treating her for a condition that doesn't exist?

A: At the—right, at the time that I saw her, right.

Q: Now that you know this information, are you going to turn him into the state licensing board?

A: No.

Q: So, you're going to let a doctor go ahead and treat a person for a condition that's not there?

A: Right. Okay. So, am I going to turn him into the board? No.

Q: Are you aware of your legal duty to turn in fellow physicians who are engaged in fraud or who are incompetent?

A: No—I am not.

Q: And Dr. Warren made a misdiagnosis as well, correct?

A: It seems that way.

Q: Are you going to turn him in?

A: No.

Q: So, you think it's okay for a doctor to blow the diagnosis and then still get to go out in the world and treat people and not be called to task for it?

A: Yes.

Practice Pointer: The doctor has been forced to answer with a reply that may be unacceptable to him and the jury. He should have been more artful in his criticism of his colleague's methods and actions. For example, he could have stated, "Just because a doctor makes a misdiagnosis does not mean he is incompetent. If that were the case, every doctor in the world would be incompetent."

Tactic 38: Pushing the expert into an untenable position

Counsel may attempt to push the expert into stating an extreme opinion. Experts are well advised not to state extreme, unbelievable opinions.

Example 7.34: Expert expresses ridiculous opinion

Q: And given what you know about the tendency of the vehicle to roll over and given what you know about the vehicle's handling characteristics, you think it's good design practice to have manufactured and sold three-wheel ATVs that could go as fast as 25 miles an hour for use by children as young as three years old?

A: Oh, yes.

Practice Pointer: Extreme opinions may be difficult for the jury to believe. If counsel can push you into giving such an extreme opinion, she may lessen the weight that your opinion will have with the jury.

7.3 Conclusion

Experts should be prepared to defend against the lawyer tactics described in this chapter.

Chapter 8 Setting and Collecting Your Fee

8.1 Introduction and Executive Summary

The party deposing an expert witness is usually responsible for paying the expert's deposition-related fees. These fees must be *reasonable*. Expert witnesses should charge the retaining and opposing parties the same hourly rate for their time. Experts should also charge for:

- preparation time,
- travel time,
- travel expenses, and
- waiting time if the deposition starts late.

The authors recommend that, rather than having a higher deposition charge, the expert charge a slightly higher hourly rate for *all* time spent on the case.

It is the best practice to collect one's fees in advance and to employ a reasonable cancellation policy to protect oneself against last-minute cancellations.

8.2 Setting and Collecting One's Fee

Who is responsible for paying the expert's fee?

Under the Federal Rules of Civil Procedure, the party seeking to depose an expert witness (usually the opposing party) is liable for the fee.[1]

How much can the expert charge?

The Federal Rules provide that experts must be paid a reasonable fee for depositions. What is a *reasonable* fee for being deposed? In the case of *Anthony v. Abbot Laboratories* (106 F.R.D. 461), the court used 10 factors to determine a reasonable fee.

1. Location of the deposition was chosen to suit the convenience of the witness;
2. A timely objection was made to the amount of the fee;
3. The credentials possessed by the witness;
4. Whether the deposition was being obtained on very brief notice or with adequate lead time;
5. The going rates in the area where the deposition was being taken;

---

[1] Fed. R. Civ. Pro. 26(b)(4)(c) states: Unless manifest injustice would result, (i) the court shall require that the party seeking discovery pay the expert a reasonable fee for time spent in responding to discovery under this subdivision; and (ii) with respect to discovery obtained under subdivision (b)(4)(B) of this rule the court shall require the party seeking discovery to pay the other party a fair portion of the fees and expenses reasonably incurred by the latter party in obtaining facts and opinions from the expert.

6. Whether the witness was one of few persons with qualifications and expertise to testify on the matters in issue (in this case, the causative effects of diethylstilbestrol);
7. What the witness charges or has charged a "friendly litigant" as opposed to the adversary;
8. Whether there was any showing of manifest inconvenience;
9. Whether there was any showing of consequential loss; and
10. Whether the witness has any discernible overhead.[2]

Other courts have used similar factors:

In determining whether an expert's fee is reasonable, courts have considered the following factors: 1) the expert's area of expertise, 2) the expert's necessary training and education, 3) the prevailing rates for comparable expert witnesses, 4) the nature, quality and complexity of the discovery provided, 5) the cost of living in the relevant community, 6) the fee being charged by the expert to the party who retained him, 7) fees traditionally charged by the expert on related matters, and 8) any other factor likely to be of assistance to the court in balancing the interests implicated by Rule 26.[3]

The expert who attempts to charge a fee that is unreasonable is subject to counsel moving for a protective order and obtaining a strict limit on his hourly fee. This is especially true if an expert tries to charge a higher fee for the deposition than he is charging the party that retained him for other time in the case. For example, in a case where the expert charged retaining counsel between $150 and $250 an hour and tried to charge opposing counsel $500 an hour, the court reduced the fee to $250 an hour for the deposition.[4]

Example 8.1: Same rate for opposing and retaining counsel
Q: Do you have an agreement generally for compensation for your services in this case?
A: Mr. Yoder is aware of what I charge for my services, if that constitutes an agreement.
Q: With whom do you have an agreement?
A: With Mr. Yoder.
Q: What are your normal charges?
A: $250 an hour.
Q: Are they any different for the deposition?
A: No, sir.

---

[2] James L. Branton and Jim D. Lovett, *Depositions* (Ft. Worth, TX: Knowles Publishing, Inc., 1998) W10.
[3] *Cabana v. Forcier,* 200 F.R.D. 9 (D. Mass. 2001).
[4] *Jochims v. Isuzu Motors, Ltd.,* 141 F.R.D. 493 (S.D. Iowa 1992).

Practice Pointer: The expert charges the same hourly rate for the deposition as she charges counsel for the party who has retained her. There is no dispute or problem.

If you decide to raise your hourly fee because opposing counsel is taking the deposition, this may create problems. An attempt to gouge opposing counsel is ethically and legally suspect and may result in intense cross-examination. It could also damage your credibility at deposition.

Example 8.2: Charging opposing counsel an increased fee

Q: All right. What is the scale that you charge for depositions that are taken here at your offices in Pennsylvania, Doctor? You can look at the exhibit that gives a breakdown of your deposition fees, sir.
A: Oral deposition, first hour $600.
Q: Okay. And what is the cost for attorney time?
A: Attorney conference, first half-hour $150.
Q: And what is the cost of a video deposition, sir?
A: The first hour $800.
Q: And what is the cost for each additional hour after the first hour?
A: Will be charged at the same rate as the first hour but will be charged in 15-minute increments.
Q: Okay. And Doctor, you require a deposit of $500 in advance of taking your deposition, correct?
A: That's correct.
Q: And if that $500 is not paid in advance of the time that your deposition is scheduled, the deposition will be cancelled, correct?
A: That's correct.
Q: All right. You said that you do not recall the fee that you required that I pay to take your discovery deposition a few weeks ago, Doctor, and I want to hand you this and ask if you recognize this as being part of the stationery from your office, sir?
A: Yes.
Q: All right. Is that a bill?
A: It's one of the sheets of a bill, yes.
Q: Okay. And that bill is made out to who?
A: Lawrence & Petri, Attorneys at Law.
Q: Okay. And you recognize that as being my firm, correct?
A: Yes.
Q: Okay. And the charge at the bottom here says what?
A: $750.
Q: So, in fact, you raise your fees when opposing counsel takes your deposition?
A: That's ridiculous.
Q: You attempted to overcharge for this deposition also, did you not?
A: I charged a reasonable fee.

Q: Didn't you receive any of the correspondence from the court regarding the issue that we had about your fees for deposition?
Counsel: Objection.
Q: Cost of services, sir?
Counsel: Objection.
A: I had looked at it before referring it to my attorney, yes.
Q: Okay. You referred the matter to your attorney, right, Doctor?
Counsel: Objection.
A: That's correct.
Q: And the court reduced your fee pursuant to my request, correct?
A: That's correct.

Practice Pointer: This is not the recommended way to start a discovery deposition. Had the expert charged a reasonable fee instead of attempting to charge opposing counsel an increased amount, the above interchange could have been avoided. Experts should check to see if local court rules or practices dictate the parameters for what constitutes a reasonable fee.

What can the expert charge for?
In addition to the time spent at the deposition itself, experts should be able to charge *reasonable* amounts for:

- Preparation time. (See *Collins v. Village of Woodridge,* 1999 WL 966455 (N.D. Ill. 1999) where the court allowed the expert to collect for preparation time at 1.5 times the length of the deposition.)
- Travel time. (Generally at half the expert's rate.)
- Actual reasonable travel expenses. (The expert is well advised to keep receipts.)
- Waiting time if the deposition does not start on schedule.

Practice Pointer: In case a court denies or limits any of the expert's charges to opposing counsel, the expert may consider a clause in his fee agreement that retaining counsel will make up the difference.

The following case is instructive on how courts handle disputes over expert fees at depositions.

Example 8.3: Expert should be paid while lost traveling to deposition, for preparation time, and for waiting for deposition to begin, but travel expenses will not be paid without proof and a flat fee for deposition was unreasonable
Mannarino v. U.S., 218 F.R.D. 372 (E.D.N.Y. 2003)
In this case the court was forced to address many issues regarding the expert's requested fee, including travel time, preparation time, waiting time, flat fees, and travel expenses. The key portion of the court's opinion is reprinted below:

> In determining the reasonableness of an expert's requested fee, courts weigh the following factors: (1) the witness's area of expertise; (2) the education and training that are required to provide the expert insight that is sought; (3) the prevailing rates for other comparably respected available experts; (4) the nature, quality, and complexity of the discovery responses provided; (5) the cost of living in the particular geographic area; (6) the fee actually being charged by the expert to the party who retained him; and (7) fees traditionally charged by the expert on related matters. See *Mathis v. NYNEX,* 165 F.R.D. 23, 24-25 (E.D.N.Y.1996); *Adams v. Memorial Sloan Kettering Cancer Ctr.,* No. 00 Civ. 9377, 2002 WL 1401979, (S.D.N.Y. June 28, 2002). Additionally, courts consider "any other factor likely to be of assistance to the court in balancing the interests implicated by Rule 26." *Mathis,* 165 F.R.D. at 24-25. As a general rule, "[t]he party seeking reimbursement of deposition fees bears the burden of proving reasonableness....If the parties provide little evidence to support their interpretation of a reasonable rate, the court may use its discretion to determine a reasonable fee." *New York v. Solvent Chem. Co.,* 210 F.R.D. 462, 468 (W.D.N.Y.2002) (citations omitted).
>
> Here, defendant seeks payment of a flat fee of $3,000 and travel expenses of $64. The reasonableness of these requests will be reviewed in turn.
>
> The Flat Fee. Dr. Storace affirms that the $3,000 fee "represents an amount equal to twelve hours at $250/hour." (Storace Aff. ¶ 9.) Although the flat fee does not, by definition, correspond to actual hours expended in connection with a deposition in any particular case, Dr. Storace affirms that the twelve hours assumed by the fee "is based on experience regarding the actual time expended in meeting deposition and court requirements." *(Id.)* He argues, in effect, that the set amount is fair even when he performs fewer than twelve hours' work on a particular case, because he does not charge more than this amount in cases when he performs more than twelve hours' work. *(Id.)* In any event, he affirms that he in fact spent twelve hours in connection with his deposition in this case. *(Id.* ¶ 7.) Dr. Storace avers that he spent four hours attending the deposition as well as traveling to and from it, and an additional eight hours "reviewing the case materials and preparing for the deposition." *(Id.)* Thus, the Government argues, "[i]f plaintiff's attorney had been charged on an hourly basis, based on the hourly fee of $250.00 for twelve hours of work, the fees would still total $3,000.00." (Freeman Ltr. at 3.)
>
> As a flat fee, I find $3,000 unreasonable. Courts expect "some reasonable relationship between the services rendered and the remuneration to which an expert is entitled." *Anthony v. Abbott Labs.,* 106 F.R.D. 461, 464 (D.R.I.1985); see also *Hurst,* 123 F.R.D. at 321 ("[A] reasonable fee should cover the expert's time spent complying with

the requested discovery"); *Luddington v. Sec'y of Dep't of Health & Human Servs.,* No. 90-2351V, 1992 WL 206287, at *1 (Cl.Ct. Aug. 5, 1992) (fee requests by expert witnesses "should be substantiated by a detailed summary of the time and activity records of each expert witness"). By its nature, a flat fee runs counter to this principle. It is simply not reasonable to require parties in every case to pay the same amount regardless of the actual "services rendered" or "time spent complying with the requested discovery." The flat fee charged by Dr. Storace effectively compels parties in relatively simple cases, such as this one, to subsidize parties in complex cases requiring a much greater expenditure of the expert's time. This is unfair, and I therefore find that $3,000 cannot be justified as a flat fee.

In rejecting the flat fee, I note that I am unpersuaded by the fact, offered by the Government, that other clients of Dr. Storace have willingly paid this amount. (Freeman Ltr. at 3; Freeman Decl., Ex. D.) That other parties in other cases have not objected to Dr. Storace's billing scheme has no bearing on whether it is fair to plaintiff in this case. [FN1] Additionally, I note that the fee charged by a different company, Exponent, for an expert in engineering (Freeman Decl., Ex. C)—a fee the Government cites as that of a "comparably respected expert[ ]" (Freeman Ltr. at 3)—does not support the imposition of a flat fee. On the contrary, the bill from Exponent is explicitly based on an hourly rate. (Freeman Decl., Ex. C (invoice showing $2,925 charge for thirteen hours of expert's time at $225 per hour).) That the bottom line of the Exponent bill approximates the amount sought here is purely coincidental, and does not make Dr. Storace's flat fee any more reasonable.

The Government also tries to justify the fee as the product of the hours Dr. Storace actually spent on this case—purported to be twelve—and the hourly rate of $250. (Freeman Ltr. at 3.) Plaintiff does not object to paying a $250 hourly rate, but contends that the twelve hours Dr. Storace claims he spent in connection with the deposition are excessive. (Rosenstock Ltr. at 3-4) (suggesting that Dr. Storace be paid for two hours at the $250 hourly rate).

It is true that when plaintiff first objected to the $3,000 flat fee, Dr. Storace's office offered to bill him at an hourly rate of $375 with a four-hour guaranteed minimum. (Storace Aff. ¶ 4; Rosenstock Ltr. at 2.) Dr. Storace asserts that this rate was contingent upon the deposition's taking place at InterCity, because this supposedly would have limited the disruption of his work schedule. (Storace Aff. ¶ 4.) Plaintiff disputes that any such condition was placed on the rate. (Rosenstock Ltr. at 2.) However, because the deposition did not take place at InterCity, and, more importantly, because Dr. Storace does not seek this hourly rate now, the dispute is irrelevant. In any event, the court notes that, as discussed below, Dr. Storace is being compensated for his travel time and the consequent interruption of his other work.

As mentioned, the deposition lasted approximately one hour and five minutes. Dr. Storace obviously should be fully compensated for this time. Dr. Storace asserts that he also spent approximately eight hours "reviewing the case materials and preparing for the deposition." (Storace Aff. ¶ 7.) Although caselaw supports compensating an expert for preparation time (see, e.g., *Silberman v. Innovation Luggage, Inc.,* No. 01 Civ. 7109, 2002 WL 1870383, at 2 (S.D.N.Y. Aug. 13, 2002)), the court finds eight hours excessive. No one knew in advance that the deposition itself would last only one hour, but counsel for plaintiff did indicate beforehand that she expected it would last only about three hours. (Duffy Ltr. at 1.) Moreover, as plaintiff points out, Dr. Storace had prepared his expert report only a few months prior to the deposition, and he testified that in preparing for the deposition he did not review anything that he had not already reviewed in preparing the report. (Rosenstock Ltr. at 3; Freeman Decl., Ex. F. at 17-18.) Based on these factors, and on the fact that the issues in this case are not complex, I find that four hours of preparation time would have been reasonable. Cf. *Silberman,* 2002 WL 1870383, at *2 (finding eight hours' preparation for six-and-a-half-hour deposition reasonable); *EEOC v. Johnson & Higgins, Inc.,* No. 93 Civ. 5481, 1999 WL 32909, at *2 (S.D.N.Y. Jan. 21, 1999) (finding twenty-three hours' preparation for thirteen-hour deposition excessive, and reducing compensable preparation time to thirteen hours). Dr. Storace is therefore entitled to compensation at his full rate for four hours, plus an hour and five minutes for the time spent at the deposition itself. At the rate of $250 per hour, this comes to $1271.

Travel Time and Expenses. Dr. Storace states that "the total time for the deposition, including the deposition, travel, time lost due to inaccurate directions and time lost due to a disruptive work schedule[,] was four hours." (Storace Aff. ¶ 7.) As mentioned, one hour and five minutes of this time was spent at the deposition itself. It is undisputed that Dr. Storace got lost on his way from his office to Mr. Rosenstock's office, where the deposition took place. Dr. Storace asserts that he was "repeatedly given inaccurate directions" by Mr. Rosenstock's office. (*Id.* ¶ 5.) Mr. Rosenstock states that his office is easy to find and that Dr. Storace seemed incapable of following directions. (Rosenstock Ltr. at 3.) Dr. Storace's deposition was scheduled for 10 a.m., but because of his lateness, plaintiff's counsel began the deposition of Dr. Meyer at that time. (*Id.* at 2-3.) Upon Dr. Storace's arrival, he was given the choice between waiting until the completion of Dr. Meyer's deposition, and returning at noon, and chose the latter. (*Id.* at 3.)

Regardless of whether plaintiff's attorney's directions or Dr. Storace's navigation skills were responsible for the delay, the fact remains that Dr. Storace was unable to work during the period he was lost. Because Dr. Storace obviously did not intentionally get lost, the court finds that he is entitled to be compensated for this time. In addition, the court finds it somewhat troubling that both Dr. Storace's deposition and Dr. Meyer's were scheduled for the same time. (Rosenstock Ltr. at 2.) It seems reasonable to hold plaintiff responsible for the additional disruption in Dr. Storace's work schedule caused by this "double booking." See *McHale v. Westcott,* 893 F.Supp. 143, 151 (N.D.N.Y.1995) (Pooler, J.) ("[T]he expert certainly should be reimbursed for any time during which he was unavailable to do other work, such as time spent waiting at the deposition").

Plaintiff asserts that, based on his own experience, travel time between his office and Dr. Storace's should not have been more than twenty minutes. (Rosenstock Ltr. at 3.) Dr. Storace does not say how long his initial trip took him, nor does he indicate how long each of the three subsequent trips took. In the absence of any such information from Dr. Storace, the court will accept plaintiff's estimated time for a normal trip between the two offices. The court will also assume that the initial trip, during which Dr. Storace got lost, took twice as long as it otherwise would have. Accordingly, the court finds that Dr. Storace is entitled to compensation for forty minutes for his initial trip to Mr.

Rosenstock's office, plus twenty minutes for his first return trip, plus forty minutes for the round trip he made in connection with the rescheduled deposition.

The general rule, which this court follows, is that compensation for travel time should be half the regular hourly amount charged. See, e.g., *Silberman,* 2002 WL 1870383, at *2; *Grdinich v. Bradlees,* 187 F.R.D. 77, 83 (S.D.N.Y.1999). Therefore, Dr. Storace is entitled to $125 per hour for the hour and forty minutes he spent traveling to and from the deposition, or $208.

Dr. Storace also seeks $64 in travel expenses but does not offer any explanation of what these expenses were, much less an itemization thereof or any supporting documentation, such as receipts. Without such guidance, the court cannot assess the reasonableness of the $64 charge. Further, the accuracy of this amount is questionable, given that it was set before any expenses were actually incurred. From his affidavit and the Government's submissions, the only expense the court can fairly assume Dr. Storace incurred is gas. Accordingly, the court finds that Dr. Storace is entitled to only $5 in travel expenses, which represents the court's best guess as to his expenditure on gas.

For the reasons stated above, plaintiff is entitled to reimbursement of $1,271 for Dr. Storace's time spent preparing for and attending his deposition, $208 for Dr. Storace's travel time, and $5 for Dr. Storace's travel expenses. Accordingly, within ten (10) business days of the date of this Order, plaintiff is directed to pay to Dr. Storace $1,484 for the fees and expenses reasonably incurred in connection with Dr. Storace's deposition. SO ORDERED. At 374–377.

Practice Pointer: This court reaffirmed the expert's right to be paid for travel time, waiting time, and preparation time. All such time is time spent on the case when experts cannot focus on other work. As such, experts should charge for these items.

Should time spent at depositions be billed at a premium rate?
Many experts routinely charge a higher hourly rate for being deposed than they do for their other work such as file review, investigation, conferences, and report writing. The rationale is that the deposition:

- often interferes with regularly scheduled work and
- it is difficult and anxiety-provoking.

Some courts have dismissed these rationales as illogical. For example, the court in *Kirby v. Ahmad* (63 Ohio Misc. 2d 533, 635 N.E.2d 98 (Ohio Com. Pl. 1994)) rejected as incomprehensible an expert's fee schedule that set forth fees of $500 an hour for a discovery deposition and $750 per hour for a video deposition. In addition, some courts find that depositions conducted in the expert's office do not warrant a "premium fee" as there is no disruption or inconvenience to the expert's regular practice. (See *Hose v. Chicago & North Western Transportation Co.,* 154 F.R.D. 222 (S.D. Iowa 1994).)

Many experts are moving away from separate deposition charges and are charging a slightly higher hourly rate for all of their work. The authors recommend such a uniform rate. A uniform hourly rate has 3 main attributes:

- It is simple to explain.
- It is easy to bill for.
- It results in increased overall billing for the time spent on the case because the vast majority of work experts do is not testifying at deposition or trial.

How are fees collected?

Many experts request full payment for the deposition to be paid in advance. This eliminates collection difficulties. Some experts will not even agree to schedule a deposition until a deposit is in hand. Many attorneys commonly agree to this, although some may push the issue with the court. Where the deposition time exceeds the prepaid amount, experts commonly request counsel to agree on the record to pay the outstanding balance within 7 business days.

If an expert is not paid in advance for the deposition, she should *promptly* submit her bill for payment. This is helpful in securing collection for two reasons. First, if the expert is not paid, she can attempt collection while the litigation is ongoing. She will have the most leverage to collect while the matter is still pending before the court. Second, attorneys are more likely to pay experts who bill promptly. When a bill is sent late, especially after a case has been lost, collection problems may arise.

Practice Pointer: Some experts include a provision in their contracts with retaining counsel stating that retaining counsel will be responsible for:

- collecting fees for their deposition from opposing counsel and
- payment of the fees if opposing counsel fails to pay promptly or if their fee is reduced below their standard rate.

What is a wise cancellation policy?

Problems sometimes arise for experts due to last-minute cancellations of depositions. Such cancellations can be costly to the expert as they waste the expert's time. As such, many experts inform opposing counsel of their written cancellation policies when requesting their advanced fees. These cancellation policies usually call for a forfeiture of all or a part of the attorney's deposit for last-minute cancellations or postponements of depositions. Once again, the key to such policies being upheld by the court is their reasonableness. What is and is not reasonable will depend upon the facts of the case and the judge's discretion. A good rule of thumb is to design a cancellation policy in good faith as a legitimate tool to compensate for wasted time, not a windfall provision.

8.3 Conclusion

Experts should understand the rules concerning fees and should be paid a reasonable fee for their time and expenses related to giving a deposition.

Chapter 9 Videotaped Depositions

9.1 Introduction and Executive Summary

Videotaped depositions of expert witnesses are being used with increased frequency because they leave a dramatic impression with the jury. Effective witnesses are aware of how to maximize their impact during videotaped depositions.

The Rules of Civil Procedure prohibit the misrepresentation of appearance or demeanor using recording techniques. Attorneys, however, may attempt to distort the expert's appearance by:

- pacing to force the expert's eyes to move back and forth,
- using lighting to wash out the witness,
- using extreme close-ups to emphasize facial expressions, and
- getting the expert angry.

Videotaped depositions may be shown to the jury and can be used to cross-examine and impeach the expert if he appears as a witness during trial. The authors recommend several strategies for increasing the effectiveness of a videotaped deposition:

- Prepare with counsel and practice in front of a video camera to correct annoying or unfavorable mannerisms.
    - These practice tapes, however, may be discoverable.
- Dress conservatively.
    - Wear a suit without flashy or excessive accessories.
    - Do not wear white, black, or red.
- Be aware of your body language.
    - Effective non-verbal communication includes leaning forward, listening attentively, and using minimal hand gestures.
- Avoid eating, smoking, drinking, chewing gum, or chewing on pencils or pens.
- Speak clearly and distinctly.
    - Stop speaking when someone else is talking.
- Look directly at the camera when testifying.
- Avoid long pauses that make you look evasive or uninformed.
    - "Dead air" will suggest to jurors that you do not know the answer.
- Turn off pagers, cell phones, and beepers.
    - Do not take phone calls.
- When handling exhibits, hold them so they can be appreciated by both the judge and jury.

- Do not be goaded into flashes of anger, arrogance, and combativeness.
- Review your prior videotaped depositions to learn how you can improve your performance.

9.2 Use of Videotaped Depositions

Videotaped depositions of expert witnesses are being used with increased frequency to preserve testimony at trial. In some cases, these depositions are used in lieu of live testimony:

- to comply with an order of the court,
- to save the expense of presenting live expert testimony,
- due to the unavailability of the expert witness, and
- to make a more powerful record for use as impeachment at trial.

Impact of Videotaped Depositions

Research has shown that videotaped depositions are more revealing and have a much more dramatic impact than reading into the record traditional stenographically recorded depositions. Videotaped depositions permit the jury or fact finder to better evaluate the credibility of the expert witness.

> Taking a deposition by visual means such as videotape is advantageous if the deposition is introduced at trial, because the fact finder at the trial often will gain greater insight from the manner in which an answer is delivered and recorded by audiovisual devices and will avoid the tedium that is produced when counsel reads lengthy depositions into evidence at the trial. A videotaped deposition provides the best means for the court and the jury to judge the demeanor of the witness....[1]

In today's computer and television age, jurors are used to seeing dramatic developments on television. In addition, more and more accidents, crimes, and national events are captured on video. A videotaped deposition can capture the nuances of a witness who is:

- uncomfortable,
- sweating,
- embarrassed,
- searching for answers, or
- engaging in nervous mannerisms.

> Jurors are more likely to be influenced by a video presentation than a deposition transcript. Jurors remember what they see and hear more than what they merely read. Videotape tends to capture and hold the attention of a jury. A deposition

---

[1] 10 Fed. Proc. L.Ed., p. 657.

transcript, by contrast, can be quite boring. Jurors who are used to television as a medium of communication tend to be comfortable with the presence of a television screen in the courtroom.[2]

Videotaped depositions also provide better ammunition for impeachment if the deponent does testify at trial because the cross-examiner can play the video of the allegedly inconsistent statement. Videotaped depositions usually result in less coaching by counsel as well because the camera (and jury) can pick up on such techniques.

In addition, videotaped depositions permit demonstrations including tests or large machinery not feasible in the courtroom. Often counsel prefers to videotape these demonstrations to avoid the risks of "live" demonstrations.

> Taking a deposition by visual means such as videotape is advantageous if the deposition is introduced at trial, because the fact finder at the trial often will gain greater insight from the manner in which an answer is delivered and recorded by audiovisual devices and will avoid the tedium that is produced when counsel reads lengthy depositions into evidence at the trial. A videotaped deposition provides the best means for the court and the jury to judge the demeanor of the witness.[3]

9.3 Rules and Procedures
Federal Rule of Civil Procedure 30(b)(4) provides the following.

Fed. R. Civ. Pro. 30(b)(4)
Unless otherwise agreed by the parties, a deposition shall be conducted before an officer appointed or designated under Rule 28 and shall begin with a statement on the record by the officer that includes (A) the officer's name and business address; (B) the date, time, and place of the deposition; (C) the name of the deponent; (D) the administration of the oath or affirmation to the deponent; and (E) an identification of all persons present. If the deposition is recorded other than stenographically, the officer shall repeat items (A) through (C) at the beginning of each unit of recorded tape or other recording medium. The appearance or demeanor of deponents or attorneys shall not be distorted through camera or sound-recording techniques. At the end of the deposition, the officer shall state on the record that the deposition is complete and shall set forth any stipulations made by counsel concerning the custody of the transcript or recording and the exhibits, or concerning other pertinent matters.

---

[2] Paul Michael Lisneck and Michael J. Kaufman, *Depositions: Procedures, Strategy, and Technique* (St. Paul, MN: West Publishing, 1995) pp. 7–11.
[3] 10 Fed. Proc. (ED p. 65).

Rule 30(b)(4) provides only general parameters on what cannot be done. The distortion of the appearance or demeanor of a deponent through camera or sound recording techniques is the only specific prohibition. The 1993 amendments to 30(b)(4) encouraged increased use of videotaped depositions by no longer requiring counsel to obtain permission of the court or agreement from other counsel before videotaping a deposition.

Notice of Videotape
Federal Rule of Civil Procedure 30(b)(2) requires that the deposition notice specify if it is going to be videotaped.

Fed. R. Civ. Pro. 30(b)(2)
(2) The party taking the deposition shall state in the notice the method by which the testimony shall be recorded. Unless the court orders otherwise, it may be recorded by sound, sound-and-visual, or stenographic means, and the party taking the deposition shall bear the cost of the recording. Any party may arrange for a transcription to be made from the recording of a deposition taken by non-stenographic means.

An expert should review the deposition notice carefully to see if the testimony is going to be videotaped. If the deposition is going to be used as evidence at trial in lieu of live oral testimony, the notice should state this.

9.4 Looking Good for the Camera
The videotape of a deposition may ultimately be played to the jury. It is important, therefore, that the expert witness make a good impression on camera. Normally, the expert will rely on retaining counsel to ensure that the taping is done fairly, impartially, and without operator bias or distortion. Nevertheless, to avoid disaster and professional embarrassment, a basic understanding of the technical aspects of the taping is helpful.

Camera Shots and Angles
Gregory P. Joseph notes in *ALI-ABA's Practice Checklist Manual on Taking Depositions* that there are four basic camera shots used in depositions:

- The full or establishing shot, which is a wide-angle view which establishes the scene showing all participants;
- The two-shot, which includes head and shoulders of two people, the deponent and the examining attorney;
- The medium shot, which includes only the head and shoulders of the deponent; and
- The close-up, which is a tight shot which focuses on an exhibit or a limited area of an individual's body, such as the head.[4]

---

[4] Gregory P. Joseph, *ALI-ABA's Practice Checklist Manual on Taking Depositions* (Philadelphia: American Law Institute) p. 92.

The four basic moves of the camera are:

- zooming (closing in),
- panning (moving the camera horizontally),
- tilting, and
- trucking or dollying (moving the entire camera).

Lawyer Tactics

Despite the admonition in the Rules against distortion of the appearance or demeanor of the witness, tactical advantages may be sought by counsel. Techniques used by counsel at videotaped deposition may include the following:

- pacing to force the expert's eyes to move back and forth, thus making the expert look shifty,
- pointing the camera up at the expert to make him look sinister,
- lighting to wash out the witness or placing the expert in shadows,
- using an extreme close-up to make the expert look harsh and to emphasize facial expressions and movements, and
- getting the expert angry or upset so the jury or fact finder can see his "true nature."

While there is little an expert can do to prevent these actions by counsel, being aware of them can minimize their impact on one's testimony. It will ultimately be up to retaining counsel to make sure that the expert's image is not distorted.

9.5 Use of Videotaped Depositions for Impeachment

It is important to understand and remember that a videotaped deposition may be used to later cross-examine and impeach the expert if she appears as a witness at trial. (See *Warner v. General Motors Corp.* 357 N.W.2d 689 (1984).) Prior to being impeached by a videotaped deposition at trial, the expert need *not* be afforded any advance notice or warning by counsel. Because the tape of the deposition can be used against an expert during trial, it is important to try to excel when giving a videotaped deposition. Rule 613 of the Federal Rules of Evidence governs and is printed below.

Fed. R. Evid. 613 Prior Statements of Witnesses
(a) Examining witness concerning prior statement. In examining a witness concerning a prior statement made by the witness, whether written or not, the statement need not be shown nor its contents disclosed to the witness at that time, but on request the same shall be shown or disclosed to opposing counsel.

In litigation involving expert witnesses and a lot of money, lawyers are making more and more sophisticated use of videotaped depositions. With the permission of the trial judge, they can edit and compress the testimony of the expert to compare it with live testimony, documents, and other exhibits. The impact of such techniques can be devastating.

9.6 How to Excel During Videotaped Depositions

It is especially important to excel during a videotaped deposition. This videotape could be the only means by which the jury receives an expert's testimony. In addition, one's reputation, credibility, and effectiveness as an expert may be based on videotaped depositions. The expert will need to look and sound good. If the expert does testify at trial, the videotaped deposition may be used at trial to impeach her. The authors recommend the following:

1. *Prepare with counsel and practice before a video camera to correct annoying, distracting, or unfavorable mannerisms, methods of answering questions, or nervous habits.* Prepare with counsel and practice before a videotape camera. Upon reviewing the tape, you should be able to note your annoying, distracting, or unfavorable mannerisms, methods of answering questions, or nervous habits. Correction of these mannerisms can make the difference between an expert who appears nervous and anxious to the jury and one who is calm, collected, and professional.[5] Note that these "practice tapes" may be discoverable.

2. *Dress conservatively.* Do not appear with gaudy or flashy jewelry, cell phones, or pagers. Image is extremely important. You don't want to turn the jury off or lose credibility. Thomas Vesper suggests the following:

   > *Conservative clothing is a must for a video deposition.* A dark business suit with light blue shirt is appropriate for men, and a suit or long sleeve sedate dress with jewel neckline for women. Avoid excessive, glitzy or gaudy jewelry, accessories, or dangling earrings: they will distract video viewers from your testimony. Avoid red clothing, herringbone or tight plaid patterns. Makeup and hair should be simple and neat.
   >   *Choose your clothing colors carefully.* Try to choose colors to wear in the middle range: blue, brown, tan, green, maroon, wine, gold, gray, and purple. Bright colors also work well. Your hair color should be considered: Light (gray or blonde) hair—clothing color should be light, beige, pink, light gray, light blue or other pastels. Dark (brown or black) hair—clothing should be medium to dark (avoid black), royal blue, forest green, burgundy, brown.
   >   Do not wear white—the camera darkens your face unnaturally. Do not wear black—the camera will adjust to lighten the picture and wash out your complexion. Do not wear red—the camera will also wash out

---

[5] Be aware, though, that this preparation session can be a subject of inquiry at the deposition. "Did you meet with counsel prior to giving this deposition today…? What did you do and discuss?"

your facial color. Avoid plaids, stripes, herringbone or loud patterns—besides distracting the camera, they tend to make you appear at least ten pounds heavier.

   Personal note: Women—no frills, scarves, or "busy" accessories."[6]

3. *Watch out for your nonverbal behavior and body language. Avoid the following:*

- Appearing impatient
- Clearing your throat excessively
- Drumming on the table
- Eye blinking
- Fidgeting with pens and pencils
- Gritting your teeth
- Head nodding or shaking
- Looking at your watch
- Looks of disgust
- Playing with your hair
- Rocking back and forth in your chair
- Shifting your eyes
- Slouching
- Smirking
- Touching your face
- Wringing your hands

Regarding nonverbal behavior and body language, Thomas Vesper notes:

> Effective non-verbal communication includes leaning forward, listening attentively, and using only minimal hand gestures. Do not sit in a swivel chair or you will undoubtedly swivel in it! Eye contact should be directed toward the questioner, not at the camera directly. (Note: the camera can be placed such that it is shooting over the shoulder and slightly to the side of the deposing attorney; or it can be set for a side shot of both the deposing attorney and the deponent, or just the deponent. The over-the-shoulder shot is preferable if the tape will be used in court because it will allow the jury to see your facial expressions.)
>
> Sit comfortably but upright and alert. You should be relaxed and comfortable. Do not fidget. However, your forthright demeanor and sincerity may become suspect if you slouch or become so lax that you appear to be nonchalant, unconcerned and bored with the solemnity of this serious

---

[6] Thomas Vesper, *ATLA Deposition Notebook*, 3rd ed., (Thompson/West: 2005) pp. 123, 124.

court proceeding. Your testimony is important, therefore please give it the dignity it deserves.[7]

4. *Avoid eating, smoking, drinking, chewing gum, or chewing on pens or pencils.* This may distract the jury, make you look bad, and may make the audio portion of your testimony harder to understand. If the jury is distracted or has to listen closely to understand you, it is likely that they will daydream and not listen to you at all.

5. *Speak clearly and distinctly.* Depending on the quality of the sound recording equipment, your voice may not always be audible with background noise. *Stop* speaking if and when someone else is talking, *wait,* and then resume your answer if you were interrupted. Do not interrupt or rush to answer when the questioner is still speaking. Please speak clearly, out loud, and with careful enunciation so that your words are not slurred or mumbled.

6. *Look directly at the camera when testifying.* You will keep the jury more interested and appear more credible.

7. *Avoid long, pregnant pauses that make you look evasive or uninformed.* Vesper suggests the following:

    Avoid "dead air." Be aware that real time has greater significance in a video deposition. Our customary instruction for a witness is to pause and take time before answering. On videotape your pauses will seem longer. Pauses or "dead air" may suggest to jurors that you do not know the answer. Therefore, in a video deposition, you should answer as quickly as you can after listening carefully to the question. Please try not to play with or linger over documents after you have reviewed them. Rather you should look up and listen for the attorney's next question.[8]

8. *Turn off pagers, cell phones, and beepers and do not take phone calls.* You want to appear as though your entire focus is on the questioning and that you are taking your responsibility seriously. If you don't focus on your testimony, why should the jury?

9. *When handling exhibits, make sure you hold them so that they can be appreciated fully by the viewers, the judge, and the jury.*

10. *Avoid making unnecessary and distracting noise by rustling papers, touching the microphone, or moving furniture.* Again, you want to make it easy for the jury to listen to and receive your testimony. If it is hard for them to hear, they may mentally "turn you off."

---

[7] *Ibid.* at pp. 123, 124.
[8] *Ibid.* at pp. 123, 124.

11. *Avoid being goaded into flashes of anger, arrogance, and combativeness.* This may quickly turn off the jury or fact finder and make you seem biased. You may also say something that was not carefully considered that can come back to haunt you.

12. *Use make-up and powder (men and women) to avoid shiny noses, heads, and a washed-out look.* Image may be 90% of the battle with a jury. You need to look good.

13. *Try to not appear evasive, suspicious, nervous, or anxious.* You will be less credible if you seem ill at ease. Smiling can be very effective and disarming. Do not let yourself be distracted by counsel. This does not look good on camera.

14. *Prepare by reviewing other videotaped depositions taken by opposing counsel.* This preparation will expose you to the tone, tactics, questions, and techniques of opposing counsel. Ask retaining counsel to help you obtain these videotapes.

15. *Review your prior videotaped depositions to learn how you can improve your performance.* While watching yourself on videotape may be difficult, it is an excellent learning tool. This review will help you eliminate or reduce your nervous mannerisms and help you improve your presentation skills.

9.7 Conclusion
Remember you are always "on" in a videotaped deposition.

You are constantly on stage. "The camera never blinks!" Witnesses must look credible at all times: not only during responses, but between questions, answers, and during any delays. Giving video deposition testimony means a witness must develop a level of self-awareness beyond that required for a transcribed deposition.[9]

---

[9] *Ibid.* at pp. 123, 124.

Chapter 10 Handling Abuse

10.1 Introduction and Executive Summary

Experts may be exposed to different types of abuse when giving depositions. Following are types of expert abuse and strategies for dealing with such abuse:

- Refusal to prepare the expert
  - Insist on full preparation by retaining counsel.
- Abusive questioning (such as, vulgarity, ethnic slurs, extreme and repeated sarcasm)
  - Have thick skin.
  - Remember that the vast majority of pointed deposition questions are proper because the expert's credibility is an issue in the case.
  - Warn counsel on the record.
  - If all else fails, terminate the deposition and immediately file for a protective order.
  - An expert witness who improperly terminates a deposition may be liable for sanctions.
- Repetitive questions
  - Exercise tireless patience and politeness and answer the questions.
- Hostility
  - The expert should maintain her demeanor and remain calm and collected.
- Non-payment of fees
  - Collect expert fees prior to the start of the deposition.
- Wasted time
  - Charge by the hour and bill for travel time.
  - Have a reasonable cancellation policy for last-minute cancellations.
- Providing an uncomfortable environment
  - Insist on "reasonable accommodations" and threaten to terminate the deposition if these are not made.
- Threats of opposing counsel
  - Ignore or have retaining counsel stop opposing counsel's threats.
- Lack of breaks
  - Have retaining counsel set up the timing of periodic and lunch breaks at the beginning of the deposition.

10.2 Refusal to Prepare the Expert

The vast majority of abuse takes place at the deposition by opposing counsel. However, retaining counsel's refusal to prepare the expert can be abusive. Lack of preparation can lead to a bad result in the case and a ruined reputation for the expert.

In this type of abuse, retaining counsel advises the expert to meet him a half hour to an hour immediately prior to the deposition to prepare. When the expert requests a meeting to be properly prepared, counsel refuses. The reasons why retaining counsel may in some cases be reluctant to fully prepare the expert include:

- lack of time because counsel is too busy,
- reluctance to pay the expert for his time for a preparation meeting, and
- lack of understanding of the expert's need to be fully prepared.

Experts can and should insist that retaining counsel fully prepare them. This preparation should include a review of:

- the key issues in the case,
- any "magic words" or words of art,
- the discovery (especially those involving the expert),
- the procedure, and
- a complete mock deposition.

Experts who are fully prepared for their depositions will invariably do better than those experts who are unprepared.

Practice Pointer: If retaining counsel is showing reluctance to properly prepare you, ask her this question: "Do you want an unprepared expert?"

10.3 Abusive Questioning

The American legal system is an adversary system. This means, in part, that parties to a dispute are allowed to cross-examine witnesses aggressively in an attempt to determine the truth. As an expert witness, one can expect to be examined aggressively. Most of this aggressive questioning will be appropriate, legal, and ethical. *If you are thin-skinned and do not want to subject yourself to aggressive questioning, your best course of action may be to choose not to involve yourself in the case as an expert witness.*

Expert witnesses who testify at deposition must be prepared to deal with occasional abusive questioning by counsel. The expert who understands his legal rights and remedies is in the strongest position to deal with abuse. However, aggressive examination is generally allowed. Fed. R. Civ. Pro. 30(d)3 deals with what is *not* allowed.

> **Fed. R. Civ. Pro. 30(d)3**
> At any time during a deposition, on motion of a party or of the deponent and upon a showing that the examination is being conducted in bad faith or in such manner as unreasonably to annoy, embarrass, or oppress the deponent or party, the court in which the action is pending or the court in the district where the deposition is being taken may order the officer conducting the examination to cease forthwith from taking the deposition, or may limit the scope and manner of the taking of the deposition as provided in Rule 26(c).

Experts, with the assistance of retaining counsel, will have to decide which questions are truly abusive. Is a repetitive question abusive enough to seek judicial intervention? Normally, it would not be considered abuse. The expert is best served by smiling, answering the question yet again, and not getting flustered (which is what opposing counsel is trying to achieve). What will normally be considered abusive in a deposition context includes:

- vulgarity,
- ethnic or racial slurs,
- throwing things,
- physically threatening the expert, and
- repeated sarcastic and demeaning remarks.

It will be up to retaining counsel to object. If retaining counsel does not do so, the expert can ask that the abuse stop. The request to stop the abuse should be followed by a warning on the record. If the abuse continues unabated, retaining counsel or the expert can terminate the deposition, but they must immediately file for a protective order with the court.

Practice Pointer: Appendix C contains an example of abusive behavior.

Practice Pointer: If the court determines the deposition was improperly terminated, the expert/retaining counsel may be liable for the costs of the proceeding. Thus, you want to be sure that opposing counsel has crossed the line and refuses to stop the abuse prior to your termination of the deposition.

10.4 Repetitive Questions
It may be annoying for counsel to repeatedly and deliberately ask the same questions over and over again. This tactic is designed to trip up the expert by obtaining different responses and getting the expert upset. In most cases, counsel will be granted substantial leeway by a judge regarding repetitive questions and these will not be precluded for being abusive. Thus, the most appropriate way for the expert to respond is by simply answering the questions.

Remember that expert witnesses are compensated for their time. They should, therefore, exercise tireless patience and politeness. Once counsel realizes that he is getting the same answer over and over again and that the expert will not become flustered, he will move on.

In many instances, retaining counsel will interject an objection because she is losing her patience. Let counsel argue amongst themselves. If they want the expert to answer the question, he should do so and force opposing counsel to move on.

Example 10.1: Repetitive question upsets expert
Q: Why did you join the American Society of Agricultural Engineers?
A: I have already answered that question. How much more of this do I have to take?…You know, I do have other things to do besides sit here and answer your inane questions.

Practice Pointer: Counsel has obtained the desired result—she has gotten the expert flustered and upset. If the expert does not calm down quickly, he will be less effective in answering additional questions. Furthermore, in videotaped depositions, these flashes of anger may put off the jury or fact finder. A better answer might have been, "To obtain their newsletter and publications."

10.5 Hostility

Opposing counsel does not have to be nice when deposing an expert. Some counsel may raise their voice, get angry, or otherwise show hostility toward the expert. Most of the time, this is done to intimidate, anger, or upset the expert.

Experts may be faced with many hostile questions at deposition. The best way to deal with these questions is to maintain one's demeanor and simply answer the questions. Remember that counsel is frequently role-playing his hostility. A calm and collected answer will make the lawyer look like a bully and should bolster the expert's credibility. If the question is so blatantly personal, hostile, or vulgar that the expert can in no way dignify it with a response, the expert should suspend the deposition and consult an attorney immediately.[1] Otherwise, the expert should answer the question in a calm, professional manner and force counsel to move on.

Practice Pointer: If you are going to be deposed by a notoriously obnoxious attorney, consider having retaining counsel arrange to have the session videotaped. This can be quite effective at toning down an attorney's behavior.

---

[1] For example, "You're nothing but a fucking whore for the insurance companies, aren't you?"

Example 10.2: Dealing with a hostile question

Q: When you do a medical/legal examination for someone, like this insurance company, it doesn't matter if the claimant gets better or takes their medication, does it? Because all you care about is doing the exams, and satisfying your client, and getting more medical/legal work in the future, isn't that correct?

Practice Pointer: The best way to deal with this question is to simply answer it "No."

10.6 Personal Attacks: Demeaning and Sarcastic Remarks

Some lawyers taking depositions go too far with personal attacks and extreme sarcastic and demeaning remarks. The clearest examples of such questioning would be sexist comments, racial or ethnic slurs, vulgarity, or other clearly inappropriate comments. Experts need *not* take this type of abuse at deposition. Counsel should be given a warning "to make a record." For example, the expert might state on the record, "I will have no choice but to terminate this deposition. This is your final warning." If the improper conduct persists, the expert witness should terminate the deposition and *immediately* have an attorney file for a protective order with the court.

> If the opposing attorney is hostile or uses intimidating questions and tactics, he should be cautioned on the record, and if the deposition is not being videotaped, the party cautioning the abusive attorney should clearly state on the record what it is that is being objected to and make repeated nonantagonistic requests that the abusive conduct be ceased. After making as clear a record as possible, clearly inform the abusive attorney that you will seek judicial protection if the activity continues.[2]

Example 10.3: Crossing the line

Q: You testified that you obtained your degree in India. Did they have an accredited medical school there or was it instruction mainly for medicine men?

Q: Your hobbies listed on your CV are bird watching and dancing....What about home decorating? Do you do any of that, as well, sir? How about vacationing in San Francisco or Provincetown?

Practice Pointer: In the authors' opinion, a judge would probably find that these questions have crossed the line. The expert should warn counsel on the record. If the personal abuse continues and you do not want to take any more, terminate the deposition and have an attorney immediately file for a protective order.

---

[2] James L. Branton and Jim D. Lovett, *Depositions* (Ft. Worth, TX: Knowles Publishing, Inc., 1998) p. 28.

Counsel who go too far may be subject to legal action. For example, in the case of *Florida Bar v. Schaub* (618 So.2d 202 (Fla.1993)), a prosecutor was suspended for thirty days after he insulted a defense expert, elicited irrelevant information from the expert, and expressed his own derogatory opinions of the expert's field.

The key to success for an expert who is faced with abusive questioning is when to start to push back. The test of how much counsel can get away with is one of reasonableness.

> The deponent has no redress unless the annoyance, embarrassment, or oppression will be unreasonable, and the seeking of information is not unreasonably annoying, embarrassing, or oppressive if the information is material and relevant.[3]

Remember that as a witness in a case, the expert's credibility is a major issue. Thus, questions about licensing, criminal convictions, fees earned, suspensions, exclusion of prior testimony, prior expert witnessing work, etc. are all fair game and should be answered without hesitation. *If you do not want to be subjected to such questioning, you should choose not to involve yourself in the case as an expert witness.*

Example 10.4: Embarrassing but not abusive questions
Q: Did you flunk the exam for certification three times before you finally passed it, sir?
A: Yes.
Q: You were convicted of tax evasion in 1997, correct?
A: Yes.
Q: You have earned over $1.5 million in performing IMEs in the last ten years, correct?
A: That's correct.
Q: Your license was suspended for how many years starting in 1991?
A: Two years.
Q: Your testimony on hedonic damages was excluded in six different cases, correct?
A: That's correct.
Q: According to your CV, you have testified over 500 times in depositions in court, correct?
A: Yes.

Practice Pointer: As an expert witness, your credibility is a legitimate and important issue. All of the above questions and answers may be embarrassing and annoying, but they are permissible because they relate to your credibility.

---

[3] *Federal Procedure,* Lawyer's Edition (Rochester, NY: Lawyers' Cooperative Publishing, 1994) p. 654.

10.7 Non-Payment of Fees

Under the Federal Rules of Civil Procedure, the party seeking to depose an expert is liable for his reasonable fees.[4] Under this form of abuse, counsel will schedule the deposition and not arrange for payment of the expert.

Experienced experts use the following methods to avoid this abuse:

- have a clause in their retention agreement holding retaining counsel responsible for payment or collection of their fee prior to their deposition and
- insist on being paid prior to the start of the deposition.

If the deposition goes longer than was estimated (which is not uncommon), sophisticated experts have counsel agree on the record (recorded by the stenographer) to make the additional payments required, ask for the check then and there, or ask for the deposition to be continued until additional payment is received.

An expert who has not collected her fee up front should bill the person or entity responsible for paying the fee immediately after the deposition. If the bill is not paid, the expert should call and ask that it be paid. Experts should not let attorneys browbeat them into waiting for payment or accept excuses (which may often happen). If the bill is not paid, the expert may threaten or file legal action.

Experts who are proactive in collecting their money prior to being deposed rarely fall prey to this type of abuse.

10.8 Wasted Time

During depositions, there are four ways that the time of expert witnesses is frequently wasted. First, experts may be asked a seemingly endless series of repetitive questions. Second, a deposition may be cancelled on short notice and the expert may lose the profitable use of the blocked-out time. Third, the expert may be called upon to conduct lengthy and wasteful travel. Fourth, the deposition may not start on time.

The authors recommend three simple solutions to these problems. First, charge by the hour. Experts are very likely to be taken advantage of through lengthy questioning if they charge a flat fee for a deposition. Second, wise experts insist up front on a nonrefundable deposit for the late cancellation of a deposition. This is easily justified because late cancellations can be very

---

[4] Fed. R. Civ. Pro. 26(b)(4)(c) states: "Unless manifest injustice would result, (i) the court shall require that the party seeking discovery pay the expert a reasonable fee for time spent in responding to discovery under this subdivision; and (ii) with respect to discovery obtained under subdivision (b)(4)(B) of this rule the court shall require the party seeking discovery to pay the other party a fair portion of the fees and expenses reasonably incurred by the latter party in obtaining facts and opinions from the expert."

costly to an expert. Finally, ask for an agreement up front to bill for travel time portal to portal. Counsel is not likely to ask an expert witness to drive all over the state if she is paying the expert $350 per hour for his travel time.[5]

10.9 Providing an Uncomfortable Environment

Opposing counsel may seek strategic advantage by making the expert as physically uncomfortable as possible at the deposition by:

- using a small, poorly lit room,
- setting high or low temperatures,
- providing uncomfortable seating, and
- failing to provide a desk or surface to write on.

When faced with these or other uncomfortable environments, the expert or retaining counsel can insist on "reasonable accommodations." If opposing counsel refuses to alleviate the untenable situation, retaining counsel can threaten to terminate the deposition.

10.10 Threats of Opposing Counsel

Opposing counsel may attempt to bully the expert into answering improper questions (questions asked in bad faith to annoy or embarrass or oppress the expert). Counsel will usually threaten to "go to the judge" and seek sanctions and court costs if the expert refuses to answer. The expert is usually best served by being thick skinned and letting retaining counsel do battle with opposing counsel. If the expert is unsatisfied with the assistance of retaining counsel and opposing counsel is going way over the line, the expert can, after warnings on the record, terminate the deposition and seek immediate judicial relief.

10.11 Lack of Breaks

Opposing counsel may attempt to wear down the expert or distract him by conducting the deposition for hours on end without taking or permitting a break. Experts and retaining counsel are permitted and can insist on taking reasonable periodic breaks. Experts should, however, not request a break when a question is pending nor should they discuss the case at break. The first question after a break will always be: "What did you discuss with counsel at the break?"

---

[5] See, e.g., *Haarhuis v. Kunnan Enterprises, Ltd.,* 223 B.R. 252 (D.D.C. 1998). (The expert was entitled to be paid $300 per hour portal to portal for travel time from his office in Baltimore to Washington, DC. The deposing party insisted the deposition take place in Washington rather than at the deponent expert's office in Baltimore.)

Practice Pointer: A good way to avoid problems arising from breaks is to have retaining counsel make an agreement with opposing counsel in advance as to when and for how long breaks will be (for example, for 10 minutes at 50 minutes past each hour and for one hour from 12:00 to 1:00). This way, retaining counsel can act as a timekeeper and enforce these breaks without you needing to get involved.

10.12 Conclusion

Experts who understand their legal rights and the kinds and amount of abuse that go with the territory are best positioned to properly draw a line in the sand that opposing counsel crosses at his peril.

Chapter 11 Truthfully and Artfully Answering Trick and Difficult Questions at Deposition

11.1 Introduction and Executive Summary

The key to answering trick and difficult questions at deposition is *not* to memorize answers to questions. Because there is an almost endless supply of these questions, the key is to hone your techniques for answering these questions.

First: Each question must always be answered truthfully.

Second: Memorizing answers to questions is not what experienced experts do. These experts listen very carefully to every word of the question, analyze the question, deconstruct it, and look at its potential impact on the jury and on their own credibility.

Third: Experts look for the techniques used by counsel in these types of questions and develop their own methods for dealing with these and similar questions.

Fourth: Experts can be asked an endless number of difficult questions. The questions in this section are for demonstration purposes only and are designed to help prepare experts for tough new questions they will face in their cases.

Fifth: What works for one expert in one case against one lawyer may not work for his colleague in a different case. Every case is different and the best experts are able to judge the most appropriate responses to give *under the particular circumstances of the case at hand.*

11.2 Trick and Difficult Deposition Questions

1.   **Q:** What is the one question you are most afraid of being asked in the trial of this case?
   A: Anything about my late wife. It's very painful to talk about.
   Lesson: Sometimes tough questions boomerang against opposing counsel.

2.   **Q:** What opinions do you plan to present in court?
   A: Those that are in my report and possibly some other opinions depending upon what questions I am asked.
   Lesson: The expert leaves himself the option of presenting additional opinions.

3.   **Q:** Other than the opinions you have expressed in your report, will you be expressing any other opinions at trial?
   A: I have no plans to do so at this time.
   Lesson: The expert refused to box herself in.

4.   **Q:** Will you be doing any additional work between now and trial?
       A: Possibly.
       Lesson: The expert leaves himself some room to maneuver.

5.   **Q:** Is this a copy of your college grades transcript?
       A: It appears to be.
       Lesson: The expert does not vouch for the authenticity of the document.

6.   **Q:** How long did you live in Cleveland Circle?
       A: I can't recall exactly. That was over 30 years ago when I was in grad school.
       Lesson: The expert is not ashamed that he can't remember everything.

7.   **Q:** How many other wops did they let into Harvard that year?
       A: Counsel, that's an inappropriate ethnic slur. If you don't cease from making such inappropriate remarks, I'll be forced to terminate this deposition and seek a protective order.
       Lesson: One way to handle an attorney who crosses the line.

8.   **Q:** Do you know why the plaintiff didn't do that?
       A: No.
       Lesson: The expert refuses to speculate.

9.   **Q:** Here's the report in question. Do you agree with it?
       A: Counsel, you've presented me with a 10-page report. It will take me at least an hour to review this before I can respond. Would you like me to start now?
       Lesson: One way to handle new documents presented to you.

10.   **Q:** What continuing education courses have you attended in the last 10 years?
       A: Many. We are required to have 30 hours per year.
       Lesson: The question is answered narrowly.

11.   **Q:** How old was the plaintiff at the time of the accident?
       A: Fourteen.
       Lesson: The expert is prepared and has memorized key facts.

12.   **Q:** Can you name any peer-reviewed studies that support your opinion?
       A: Yes.
       Lesson: The expert is prepared for the follow-up questions about which studies support his opinion.

13.   **Q:** Is your methodology generally accepted in your field?
    A: Yes.
    Lesson: The expert is prepared for the follow-up questions by citing evidence that proves that his methodology is commonly accepted.

14.   **Q:** Is this your personal or professional opinion you are expressing?
    A: It is my expert opinion.
    Lesson: Experts need not accept the characterizations of opposing counsel nor do they have to repeat words in the question when answering it.

15.   **Q:** What exactly are you an expert in?
    A: Mechanical engineering.
    Lesson: Simple, direct replies are often called for.

16.   **Q:** Can you tell me what the industry standards are in this case?
    A: Yes.
    Lesson: The expert here answered the question and did not volunteer information, such as "The standards are...."

17.   **Q:** Did you use your common sense in formulating your opinion?
    A: I used my 25 years of experience, which includes my common sense.
    Lesson: Denying the obvious often leads to a series of more pointed questions.

18.   **Q:** Would new or different facts change your degree of certainty in this case?
    A: It would depend on what the new or different facts were.
    Lesson: The expert remains open to consider new information.

19.   **Q:** Did you use the same degree of precision and certainty in formulating your expert opinion as you do in your non-forensic work?
    A. Yes, I did.
    Lesson: Experienced experts understand the need for precision, accuracy, and following their standard protocol.

20.   **Q:** Do you know the history of the industry standards in this case?
    A: Can you identify the industry standards you are referring to?
    Lesson: The expert refuses to answer a vague question and breaks the momentum of counsel.

21.   **Q:** Do you know what a net opinion is?
    A: No, I do not.
    Lesson: The expert is not afraid to admit he doesn't know the answer and forces counsel to explain or move on.

22. **Q:** Did you list in your report everything you relied on to formulate your opinion?
    A: No.
    Lesson: The expert is cautious about a positive reply to an "all-or-nothing question."

23. **Q:** What is your degree of confidence in the opinion you are expressing?
    A: To a reasonable degree of certainty.
    Lesson: Counsel may slightly change the words of questions (for example, "degree of confidence" and "degree of certainty") to confuse the expert.

24. **Q:** Mr. Jones, the opposing expert, has an excellent reputation, does he not?
    A: I am not that familiar with Mr. Jones or his reputation.
    Lesson: The expert is cautious in vouching for the reputation of another professional.

25. **Q:** What are the reliable texts in this field?
    A: I would not rely on any one textbook, nor would I agree with everything in it.
    Lesson: The expert is reluctant to vouch for any entire textbook because he frequently disagrees with portions of the texts.

26. **Q:** What do you think your purpose and function are in this case?
    A: I was asked to examine the facts and records and offer my expert opinion, which I have done.
    Lesson: The expert does not fall into the trap of arguing with counsel over his comment "What do you think…?"

27. **Q:** Have you made any credibility judgments as part of your analysis in this case?
    A: No.
    Lesson: The expert does not vouch for the credibility of witnesses or parties.

28. **Q:** What is your margin of error in this case?
    A: Plus or minus 3%.
    Lesson: The expert makes this concession only when he has precise numbers to support it.

29. **Q:** Are you stating your opinion with absolute certainty?
    A: I have stated my opinion to a reasonable degree of certainty.
    Lesson: The expert does not repeat the term "absolute certainty."

30.   **Q:** You are here today as an advocate, correct?
       A: I am an advocate for my opinion and the truth.
       Lesson: The expert does not run away from his being present to advocate for his opinion.

31.   **Q:** Do you think the party that retained you should prevail?
       A: That is the jury's decision.
       Lesson: The expert respectfully defers to the jury who may be hearing his deposition testimony.

32.   **Q:** At trial you will try and persuade the jury, correct?
       A: I will answer the questions posed by counsel for both sides; counsel's job is to persuade the jury.
       Lesson: The expert defines her role and defers to counsel.

33.   **Q:** Did you have all the records in this case when you formed your opinion?
       A: The records I had are listed on pages 2 and 3 of my report.
       Lesson: The expert states the records he had available and avoids the "all the records" characterization.

34.   **Q:** The lawyer who retained you is your client and is paying your substantial bills in this case, correct?
       A: Actually, you are paying my bill for this deposition.
       Lesson: The expert tweaks counsel and may force him to explain.

35.   **Q:** Do you believe the opposing expert is being dishonest in offering a different opinion than yours?
       A: No, I do not.
       Lesson: The expert understands that all experts who disagree with him are not dishonest.

36.   **Q:** What percentage of forensic work do you reject?
       A: I accept appropriately 50% of the expert witness work I am contacted on.
       Lesson: If he is questioned further on this point, the expert has the records to prove the above assertion.

37.   **Q:** Your fee schedule is designed to maximize your expert witness income, correct?
       A: My fee schedule is designed to let retaining counsel know of my hourly rate.
       Lesson: The expert waits for the follow-up question about "maximizing" and is ready for it.

38.   **Q:** If you discovered you made a mistake in this case, how would you go about correcting it?
A: I would inform retaining counsel in writing.
Lesson: A truthful reply that also indicates that retaining counsel will be forced to follow-up on the correction.

39.   **Q:** Are you trying to help retaining counsel win the case?
A: It is counsel's job to try and win cases, not the job of the expert.
Lesson: This is a far better answer than a "yes," which may be misleading.

40.   **Q:** Did you use the same intellectual rigor in this expert witness assignment as you do in your professional work?
A: Yes, I did.
Lesson: Note how this is a reformulation of Question #19 above.

41.   **Q:** There are experts who are more qualified in this area than you are, correct?
A: I am the most qualified expert to opine in this case.
Lesson: The expert takes a general question and makes it more case-specific and also invites a follow-up question.

42.   **Q:** Should the jury be suspicious of expert witnesses who offer diametrically opposed opinions?
A: The jurors will be instructed by the judge on how they should evaluate all the testimony presented.
Lesson: The expert does not take the bait and refuses to get led into a discussion of which expert is "right."

43.   **Q:** What protocol did you follow in this case?
A: The standard protocol I follow in each and every case. Would you like me to explain?
Lesson: The expert points out that she follows the same protocol in each case and invites an additional question.

44.   **Q:** In the past, when you made mistakes, were you able to correct them?
A: Yes, I was.
Lesson: The expert did not deny any past mistakes nor did he become defensive about admitting past mistakes.

45.   **Q:** Please answer the question with "yes," "no," or "I can't answer it yes or no," okay?
A: I cannot promise to answer questions in a way that may be misleading to the jury.

Lesson: The expert points out the problem with "yes" or "no" answers and provides a reasonable rationale for his refusal to agree in advance to answer questions in this fashion.

46. **Q:** How often have you been sexually aroused by a patient?
A: That is an offensive question that I think is beneath you, Counsel.
Lesson: Some deposition questions cross over the line to harassment and embarrassment and need not be answered.

47. **Q:** How do you justify charging $750 an hour?
A: That is my hourly rate.
Lesson: The expert replies simply and directly and does not try to justify his fee.

48. **Q:** As your testimony is based on a 51% degree of certainty, there is a 49% chance you are wrong?
A: My testimony is based on a reasonable degree of certainty.
Lesson: When possible, the expert refuses to get into a numbers game, which is usually a losing proposition.

49. **Q:** What are the weakest parts of your case?
A: I do not have a case, Counsel.
Lesson: The expert refuses to accept the mischaracterization of counsel.

50. **Q:** You testify mostly for plaintiffs, do you not?
A: Yes, I do.
Lesson: The expert does not deny the obvious nor does he act defensively and try to explain or justify it.

51. **Q:** You do make mistakes, don't you?
A: Yes, I do.
Lesson: The expert answers honestly and increases her credibility.

52. **Q:** Have you ever lied?
A: Yes.
Lesson: The expert does not try to deny the obvious, justify it, or explain it away.

53. **Q:** Is your opinion engraved in stone?
A: No, it is not.
Lesson: The honest expert is always willing to consider new information and the impact of the information on his opinion.

54. **Q:** Why did you spend an hour preparing with counsel if you were just going to tell the truth?
A: We reviewed the procedure and the questions I would likely be asked.
Lesson: The expert does not run away from being prepared by retaining counsel.

55. **Q:** What was your forensic income last year?
A: Approximately $110,000.
Lesson: The expert has the information available and is not defensive about the amount.

56. **Q:** You do forensic work for the money, don't you?
A: I do want to be paid for my time and I also enjoy the intellectual challenge in forensic work.
Lesson: There is nothing wrong in the expert admitting that part of the reason he does expert work is for the money.

57. **Q:** Please explain the difference between "possible" and "probable."
A: "Possible" is less likely than not, "probable" is more likely than not.
Lesson: The expert has basic definitions at his fingertips.

58. **Q:** How did counsel who retained you learn about you?
A: I don't know.
Lesson: The expert is not reluctant to reply "I don't know" when it is appropriate.

59. **Q:** How many times have you been sued for medical malpractice?
A: Three times over the past 30 years.
Lesson: The expert softens the reply by putting the number in perspective.

60. **Q:** Isn't it possible that you are wrong?
A: Yes, but it is highly unlikely.
Lesson: The expert answers directly but softens the blow.

61. **Q:** If the factual assumptions you based your opinion on were incorrect, would you change your opinion?
A: I would consider any new facts.
Lesson: The expert is open to new information, but it would not necessarily change his opinion.

62. **Q:** How many times have you testified in depositions or trials in the last 5 years?
A: At deposition 14 times and at trial 7 times.
Lesson: The expert has this basic information at his fingertips and relates it simply and directly.

63.　**Q:** You testify for the party that pays you, correct?
　　A: No, as a matter of fact, you are paying me for my time at this deposition.
　　Lesson: The expert points out that opposing counsel is paying his deposition fee.

64.　**Q:** Other experts might have a different opinion, correct?
　　A: Yes.
　　Lesson: The expert makes the above meaningless concession without hesitation.

65.　**Q:** Are there diagnostic tests that accurately measure how much pain someone is in?
　　A: No, there are not.
　　Lesson: The expert answers the question without making an attempt to qualify or explain the answer.

66.　**Q:** Will you be accepting new cases from the attorney who retained you in this case?
　　A: I may, depending on the case.
　　Lesson: The expert offers a truthful reply.

67.　**Q:** How much are you being paid for your testimony here today?
　　A: I am not being paid for my testimony. I am being paid $400 an hour for my time.
　　Lesson: The expert does not let opposing counsel mischaracterize his financial arrangement.

68.　**Q:** What are the authoritative textbooks in this area?
　　A: There are several excellent textbooks, however, I do not consider any one of them to be completely authoritative.
　　Lesson: The expert does not vouch for entire textbooks when he may disagree with some passages.

69.　**Q:** You do advertise that, for a price, you are available to testify, correct?
　　A: I list myself in several professional directories and I do expect to be paid for my time.
　　Lesson: The expert here reframes the question and then answers it.

70.　**Q:** When did you first form your opinion?
　　A: I formed my opinion on August 4, 2006, the date of my expert report.
　　Lesson: The expert does not raise the issues of preliminary opinions or future work and changes in her opinion.

71.   **Q:** Have you ever given an erroneous opinion?
      A: Not that I'm aware of.
      Lesson: A simple, direct reply to a straightforward question.

72.   **Q:** If the assumptions on which your opinion is based were to change, could that change your opinion?
      A: I would consider any new facts.
      Lesson: This is almost exactly like a prior question (#18 above).

73.   **Q:** What is your fee to date for work on this case?
      A: Approximately $16,000.
      Lesson: The expert has this information at his disposal and offers it without an explanation.

74.   **Q:** What is your understanding of the term "reasonable degree of medical certainty"?
      A: It is more likely than not.
      Lesson: The expert avoids the slippery slope of percentages.

75.   **Q:** Do you still have a substance abuse problem?
      A: No, I have been in A.A. for the past 14 years without a relapse.
      Lesson: The expert does not get indignant or excited and offers a well-reasoned reply that discourages additional questioning in this area.

76.   **Q:** If you were to assume the examinee lied to you, would that change your opinion?
      A: I would consider any new or different information provided to me.
      Lesson: The expert is open to new information, but does not agree to change his opinion without knowing what exactly the information is.

77.   **Q:** Did you verify the facts provided to you by Attorney Smith?
      A: Yes, I did.
      Lesson: The expert replies directly and invites further questioning about how he went about verifying the information.

78.   **Q:** You do disagree with recognized experts in this field, don't you?
      A: In some cases.
      Lesson: The expert replies vaguely to this general catchall question.

79.   **Q:** Who are the national experts in this field?
      A: I don't understand the question.
      Lesson: The expert does not assume that counsel is looking for "nationally recognized experts."

80.   **Q:** Did you discuss with counsel what you would testify to?
       A: We discussed my direct testimony.
       Lesson: The expert replies and points out that it would be difficult to discuss the answers to questions that he has not been asked yet.

81.   **Q:** What changes in the medical history of this case would alter your opinion concerning the existence of causation, Doctor?
       A: I would have to consider any changes.
       Lesson: The experienced expert does not give "seat of the pants" new opinions at depositions.

82.   **Q:** What research, if any, did you review in conjunction with this case?
       A: I reviewed the texts and articles cited in my report of February 14, 2006.
       Lesson: The expert is not afraid to reference specific research he has done.

83.   **Q:** If the history you had to work with changed, would that alter your opinion?
       A: I would consider any new history.
       Lesson: This is another take on "if something changed, would you change your opinion?"

84.   **Q:** Have you ever been disqualified from testifying?
       A: No, I have not.
       Lesson: Simple question, simple reply.

85.   **Q:** How many hours have you spent reviewing this case?
       A: I have spent approximately 36 hours to date on this assignment.
       Lesson: Note how the expert answers the question she wants to answer.

86.   **Q:** At what time did they allow you to be listed as an expert witness in this case?
       A: I do not understand the question.
       Lesson: The expert refuses to answer this confusing question.

87.   **Q:** What precisely are you an expert in, Doctor?
       A: Orthopedics.
       Lesson: The expert has a simple and direct reply ready for this standard type of difficult question.

88.   **Q:** Are physicians who disagree with you usually wrong?
       A: Sometimes they are.
       Lesson: The expert here replies indefinitely and invites additional questioning about the case at hand.

89. **Q:** You advertise yourself as an expert for hire, is that correct?
     A: I list myself in several professional directories and I do expect to be paid for my time.
     Lesson: This is another variation of "advertise for a price…" (see Question #69 above).

90. **Q:** You promote yourself as an expert witness by using a Web site?
     A: Yes, I do.
     Lesson: Any attempt at denial will result in a series of promotion/advertising questions that will help portray the expert as a businessman.

91. **Q:** You are represented by an expert witness referral agency that obtains work for you through advertising, e-mails, sponsorships, and bulk mail solicitations, is that correct?
     A: Yes, I am.
     Lesson: The expert makes this concession and does not permit counsel to drag it out of him in a dramatic fashion.

92. **Q:** Do you consider the latest edition of the *Diagnostic and Statistical Manual of Mental Disorders* to be authoritative?
     A: No, I do not.
     Lesson: The expert does not vouch for a large textbook that is being constantly changed and revised and invites the "why not?" follow-up question.

93. **Q:** Do you consider any text authoritative in the field of the evaluation of permanent impairment?
     A: No, I do not.
     Lesson: The expert again refuses to vouch for any textbook and will gladly explain why specific texts are not authoritative.

94. **Q:** Did you evaluate both sides of this case?
     A: I consider all aspects of the assignment before forming my opinion.
     Lesson: The expert reformulated the question and then answered it.

95. **Q:** In all of the other forklift cases in which you have testified, you have always blamed the operator for the accident, correct?
     A: No, that is not correct.
     Lesson: The expert refuses to accept the characterization "blamed" and is ready to respond to follow-up questions.

96. **Q:** You stated in your opinion that the defendant was negligent. Would you please define "negligence"?
A: Yes. It is the failure to use the reasonable care that a prudent person would have used under similar circumstances.
Lesson: The expert does not use terms he cannot define at deposition.

97. **Q:** Can you explain what you mean by reasonable degree of scientific certainty?
A: Yes, it is more likely than not.
Lesson: The expert avoids the slippery slope of percentages.

98. **Q:** You have testified that Dr. Breck failed to properly diagnose cancer in this case. When exactly did the cancer begin?
A: The cancer started approximately one year before Dr. Breck's missed diagnosis.
Lesson: The expert reframes the question into one that he feels comfortable answering.

99. **Q:** Is it possible that the plaintiff became drowsy and fell asleep at the wheel from one baby aspirin he took that morning?
A: No.
Lesson: The expert answers the very narrowly drawn question simply and directly.

100. **Q:** Were there any other potential causes of the explosion?
A: Yes.
Lesson: The expert acknowledges the other potential causes and is prepared to discuss them.

101. **Q:** There is a disagreement amongst cardiologists concerning whether stress can cause, precipitate, or aggravate a myocardial infarction, correct?
A: A small minority of cardiologists believes stress is unrelated to myocardial infarction.
Lesson: The expert replies and puts the "disagreement" into perspective so that his answer is not misleading.

102. **Q:** You estimated the rate of the speed of the vehicle at 54 miles per hour. What is your margin of error, sir?
A: Plus or minus 5 miles per hour.
Lesson: The expert makes this concession only when he has the factual numbers to support it.

103. **Q:** You do make mistakes, don't you?
      A: Yes.
      Lesson: The expert does not even try to deny the obvious.

104. **Q:** What is the most recent mistake that you made?
      A: Last year when I let my teenager Joselyn use my car.
      Lesson: A little self-deprecating humor can help humanize the expert.

105. **Q:** Why didn't you report your findings of an unreasonably dangerous product to the Consumer Products Safety Commission?
      A: I reported my findings to retaining counsel and he sent a copy to you as well.
      Lesson: The expert indicates that both counsel were given the report and does not apologize or justify not sending the report to the commission.

106. **Q:** Would you explain why you didn't list your attendance at the University of Iowa on your curriculum vitae?
      A: I only attended for one semester.
      Lesson: The expert explains as succinctly as possible.

107. **Q:** Do you still have a substance abuse problem, sir?
      A: No, I have been drug-free for 7 years.
      Lesson: The expert tacitly admits a prior problem and encourages opposing counsel to move on.

108. **Q:** How do you justify charging $300 an hour?
      A: That is my hourly rate.
      Lesson: The expert does not attempt to justify his hourly rate.

109. **Q:** You charge $400 an hour for testifying in court as an expert. Do you make $400 an hour in your regular place of employment?
      A: No, I make more than $400 an hour.
      Lesson: The expert answers the question and makes sure his reply does not leave any misunderstandings.

110. **Q:** What is your fee to date for your work on this case?
      A: Approximately $14,000.
      Lesson: The expert has the information on hand to answer this standard question and replies simply without being defensive.

111. **Q:** You testify in these cases for the money, don't you?
      A: I testify when requested by counsel and I do expect to be paid for my time.
      Lesson: In this slight variation of Question #56, the expert is not ashamed to admit he expects to be paid for his time.

112. **Q:** Why were you not provided with a complete set of records to review before you formed your opinion?
A: I do not know.
Lesson: The expert does not try to "cover for" or justify the actions of retaining counsel.

113. **Q:** Are you aware that the plaintiff had a 2-year history of chiropractic care?
A: No, I am not aware of that.
Lesson: The expert who is given an incomplete or false history does not try to cover up this fact.

114. **Q:** If the plaintiff had a prior back injury, would you change your opinion on causation in this case?
A: I would consider the nature and extent of the prior back problem in formulating my opinion on causation.
Lesson: The expert remains open to new information, but she does not immediately agree to change her opinions.

115. **Q:** Where are the notes you made when you visited the accident scene?
A: In my file here.
Lesson: The expert does not try to hide or ditch his notes.

116. **Q:** Your opinion is based on the assumption that the road was dry, correct?
A: My opinion is based in part on a dry road.
Lesson: The expert points out that the dry road was just one of the factors he considered when formulating his opinion.

117. **Q:** What additional information would get you to change your opinion?
A: I would consider any new information provided.
Lesson: Experienced experts do not offer "seat of the pants" new opinions at deposition.

118. **Q:** Your opinion is subject to change if you are provided with additional information, correct?
A: Yes, and I indicate that fact in the last paragraph of my report.
Lesson: The truthful expert always reserves the right to consider new information and change his opinion.

119. **Q:** Can you explain why, when you were initially deposed, you testified under oath that the machine guard was manufactured by AMBS, Inc. and now you are saying IDEX, Inc. manufactured it?
A: Yes, I was provided with additional information after my initial deposition.
Lesson: The expert explains his differing answers without being defensive.

120. **Q:** Are you certain about your opinion?
A: Yes, I am.
Lesson: The expert has expressed his opinion with a reasonable degree of certainty and thus is certain.

121. **Q:** You would agree that an expert should consider every relevant factor before arriving at an opinion?
A: Every significant factor, yes.
Lesson: The expert narrows the scope of the question, explains, and then offers his yes reply.

122. **Q:** What other potential causes of the accident did you consider and reject before you arrived at your opinion?
A: I considered 4 other possible causes. Would you like me to explain?
Lesson: The expert admits he considered alternative causes (a positive) and is more than ready to discuss why they are in fact not the cause.

123. **Q:** You stated that your opinion was supported by "the literature." What literature are you referring to?
A: The literature I cited on page 7 of my 4/14/06 report.
Lesson: The expert avoids all-encompassing claims ("based on the literature") that are difficult to explain and defend and cites specific literature relied upon.

124. **Q:** Professor DeBlois is from Yale and Dr. Padilla is a professor from Columbia University and their opinions are completely different from yours. What is your explanation for this discrepancy?
A: They have not spent 3 years and 274 hours studying this issue.
Lesson: The expert makes a general qualification question into a case-specific one and then replies.

125. **Q:** You have expressed your opinion. Would you defer to an expert with more experience and who is more qualified than you are?
A: No, as I have studied this problem for 2 ½ years, I am the most qualified expert to render an opinion in this case.
Lesson: The expert does not admit that other experts are more qualified to render an opinion *in this particular case.*

126. **Q:** What research did you do before you formed your opinion in this case?
A: I updated my research since the time of my 2006 textbook.
Lesson: The expert acknowledges he updated his research and slips in a mention of his textbook.

127. **Q:** Do you often testify as an expert witness?
A: I testify approximately 5 times a year.

Lesson: The expert does not answer this vague question ("often testify"), but she replies factually.

128. **Q:** How many times have you testified in the last four years?
A: Approximately 14 times.
Lesson: The expert includes his deposition and trial testimony and does not encourage counsel to drag out this line of questioning.

129. **Q:** You have testified in 38 different states as an expert witness, sir. Is that correct?
A: Approximately 38 states, yes.
Lesson: The expert does not run away from his vast experience, but he adds a little wiggle room to his reply.

130. **Q:** You spend 100% of your professional time consulting with attorneys and working on lawsuits, correct?
A: No, that is not correct.
Lesson: The expert is able to explain the other work he does (for example, research, writing, and teaching).

131. **Q:** You are a professional expert witness, correct, sir?
A: This is not a field for amateurs, Counselor.
Lesson: A little humor can occasionally be used to deflate opposing counsel.

132. **Q:** Do you enjoy being an expert witness?
A: Yes, I do.
Lesson: The expert does not hide his enthusiasm and the intellectually challenging nature of expert witness work.

133. **Q:** How many times did you meet with your lawyer before you came into court today to testify?
A: I met with attorney Johnson 4 times.
Lesson: The expert refuses to accept the mischaracterization ("your lawyer"), but he replies to avoid looking cute or defensive.

134. **Q:** Did you discuss with retaining counsel what you would be testifying to today?
A: I discussed my direct testimony with counsel.
Lesson: The expert implicitly points out it would be difficult to discuss questions that have not yet been posed.

135. **Q:** Did you rehearse your testimony here today?
A: No.
Lesson: The expert refuses to accept counsel's "rehearse" characterization.

136. **Q:** Did you discuss with retaining counsel whether to write a report in this case?
A: Yes, I did.
Lesson: The expert admits this very routine discussion and is not defensive.

137. **Q:** You were served with a subpoena duces tecum to bring your entire file, weren't you?
A: Yes, I was.
Lesson: Because the expert has brought his entire file, he is not in the least concerned about this question.

138. **Q:** Where is the correspondence to and from retaining counsel?
A: In binder number three.
Lesson: Experienced experts retain all correspondence and have it at their fingertips at deposition.

139. **Q:** You have testified about the defects in the lawnmower. How many lawnmowers have you designed, sir?
A: None.
Lesson: The expert makes this concession without being defensive.

140. **Q:** You have testified as an expert on 45 different products over the past ten years, correct?
A: Approximately 45, yes.
Lesson: The expert acknowledges this fact (and is able to explain that's what engineers do) and leaves himself a little wiggle room.

141. **Q:** You don't claim to be an expert on who is telling the truth in this case, do you?
A: No, I do not.
Lesson: The expert normally will not opine on veracity.

142. **Q:** There are highly qualified experts, articles, and texts that support a position different from the opinion you reached in this case, correct?
A: Not based on these specific facts.
Lesson: The expert takes a general qualification question and makes it case-specific.

143. **Q:** Is the opposing expert qualified to render an opinion in this case?
A: That is for Her Honor to decide.
Lesson: The expert understands his role and the role of the judge.

144. **Q:** Are you more qualified than Mr. Binder (the opposing expert) to determine the cause of this accident?
A: Yes, due to the time I have spent working on this accident.

Lesson: The expert avoids making any disparaging remarks and makes the qualification issue case-specific.

145. **Q:** What is Mr. Steven Suh's reputation in the field of electrical fire causation analysis?
      A: I do not know.
      Lesson: The expert who is not intimately familiar with the opposing expert does not comment on his reputation.

146. **Q:** You are the kind of doctor people call when they are going to court, not when they need medical treatment, correct?
      A: I retired after practicing medicine for 41 years, so I no longer treat patients.
      Lesson: The expert reframes the question, softens it a bit, and then replies.

147. **Q:** You believe the tort system should be reformed, do you not?
      A: Yes.
      Lesson: The expert does not run away from his expressed views.

148. **Q:** Are you acting as an advocate for the plaintiff here today?
      A: No, I am an advocate for the truth and my opinion.
      Lesson: The expert replies and refuses to leave any misimpressions.

149. **Q:** You as an expert are holding yourself out as an authority for the side that's presenting a particular proposition in this legal case, correct?
      A: I am testifying at the request of counsel for the plaintiff.
      Lesson: The expert reformulates the question and then replies.

150. **Q:** Do you think the defendant in this case should prevail?
      A: That is for the members of the jury to decide.
      Lesson: The expert understands his role in the legal process.

151. **Q:** Is your curriculum vitae current, complete, and accurate?
      A: Yes, to the best of my knowledge.
      Lesson: The expert replies but leaves himself a little wiggle room.

152. **Q:** You list on your 17-page curriculum vitae the positive highlights of your career, articles and books written, and lectures given. You intentionally omitted the mistakes you made and the low points in your career, correct?
      A: That is not correct.
      Lesson: The expert is ready to point out the college he flunked out of is listed on his CV.

153. **Q:** You list on your CV the cases you testified in, whether you were successful, and the amounts of the verdicts or settlements, correct?
A: I listed the results of the cases.
Lesson: The expert refuses to accept the "you were successful" characterization.

154. **Q:** You failed to list the 37 cases you have testified in on your 24-page CV, correct?
A: I do not list cases on my CV.
Lesson: The expert refuses to accept the "failed to" characterization and invites further inquiry. He is confident in his explanation of why he omits the cases.

155. **Q:** Why were the depositions in this case withheld from you?
A: I do not know why they were not provided to me.
Lesson: The expert replies but moves away from the "withheld" characterization.

156. **Q:** You testified at deposition that you only reviewed the "relevant" portions of the deposition transcripts you were provided. How did you decide what was relevant?
A: I only reviewed the portions dealing with disability.
Lesson: The expert explains the limited role he played.

157. **Q:** Who is your client in this case and what duty do you owe your client?
A: The client is Attorney Goldwell and I owe him the duty of honest, accurate opinions.
Lesson: The expert replies in a strong, confident fashion.

158. **Q:** Did you review your professional canons of ethics before you prepared your expert report?
A: Yes, I did.
Lesson: The expert is prepared to explain how he periodically reviews the canons of ethics.

159. **Q:** If the other side in this case called you first, would you have accepted the assignment?
A: No, because I do not believe in the position they are advocating.
Lesson: The expert moves away from the hired gun portrayal.

160. **Q:** Did the opposing expert depart from the standards of the profession?
A: No—but he is mistaken.
Lesson: The expert replies and points out that the expert can be mistaken without departing from the standards.

161.   **Q:** Are some lies permissible in your own personal code of conduct?
A: In extreme cases, yes.
Lesson: The expert is ready with a devastating example ("I told my cancer-stricken father he looked good") if he is asked.

162.   **Q:** Your expert witness practice is a business, correct?
A: It is a professional practice.
Lesson: The expert resists the business characterization of his expert witness practice.

163.   **Q:** What is the best way to explain your fee structure?
A: I charge $400 an hour for my time.
Lesson: The expert can explain his hourly rate fee structure in one simple sentence.

164.   **Q:** Do you keep 1099s for your expert witness testimony?
A: Yes, I do.
Lesson: The expert answers this simple question directly and with confidence.

165.   **Q:** If the plaintiff loses this case, will you still be paid the fee due to you?
A: I have already been paid for my time.
Lesson: The expert's answer helps explain that his testimony is not in any way influenced by any outstanding bills.

166.   **Q:** How do you promote your expert witness practice?
A: By word of mouth and listings in professional directories.
Lesson: The expert is not defensive about his very professional promotional activities and does not try to run away from them.

167.   **Q:** Is this a copy of the ad you use to promote your expert witness business in *Trial* magazine?
A: Yes, it is.
Lesson: The expert does not act defensively when asked about his advertising.

168.   **Q:** Do you solicit expert witness work from both plaintiffs and defendants?
A: I make myself available to both plaintiffs and defendants.
Lesson: The expert rephrases the question and then replies.

169.   **Q:** Did you assist retaining counsel in preparing his case?
A: No, I did not.
Lesson: The expert replies simply and directly.

170. **Q:** Could you tell me the number of conversations you had with retaining counsel and what you discussed in each conversation?
A: Approximately 12 conversations according to my billing records and each record contains what we discussed.
Lesson: The experienced expert has a transparent record system.

171. **Q:** Did you review with retaining counsel the answers to interrogatories and disclosures pertaining to your proposed expert testimony here today?
A: Yes, I did.
Lesson: The expert understands that working with retaining counsel is expected and is nothing to be defensive about.

172. **Q:** Did you go over with retaining counsel the questions he was going to ask you and the answers you were going to give?
A: We discussed the questions and answers.
Lesson: The expert helps soften the affirmative reply.

173. **Q:** Is there anything you requested from retaining counsel that you did not receive?
A: No.
Lesson: The expert answers this question directly, leaving no ambiguity.

174. **Q:** Doctor, what is confirmatory bias?
A: Finding what you are looking for.
Lesson: The expert is not afraid to admit that he knows what the term is.

175. **Q:** Have you reviewed any books, treatises, articles, or other written works in connection with your work in this case?
A: Yes, they are listed on page 3 of my report.
Lesson: The expert's report is complete and is a significant help when testifying at deposition.

176. **Q:** What did you do to prepare for your testimony here today?
A: I touched and read every piece of paper in my file and met with retaining counsel.
Lesson: The expert is not reluctant to admit she worked hard to prepare for her deposition.

177. **Q:** Are you using the same standards of scientific validity and certainty testifying here today as you use in your practice?
A: Yes, I am.
Lesson: This is yet another iteration of the same standards questions (see #19 and #40 above).

178. **Q:** Did you personally do all the work that led you to your opinions?
A: Yes, other than typing my report.
Lesson: The expert answers simply and, if others assisted him, he acknowledges their contributions.

179. **Q:** Is your opinion subjective?
A: No.
Lesson: Because the expert's opinion is based on records, history, and analysis, it is generally not subjective.

180. **Q:** In forming your opinion on causation, how much weight did you give to the time sequence between the alleged exposure to the chemical and the alleged illness?
A: It was one of many factors I considered.
Lesson: The expert admits that he considered the temporal factor among others, but she does not attempt to assign weight to each factor as this could be a slippery slope.

181. **Q:** Can you point to a single error that the opposing expert made in this case?
A: Yes, the conclusions he reached.
Lesson: The expert at deposition is not afraid to say that the opposing expert reached the wrong conclusion. He is prepared to explain how and why that happened if asked.

182. **Q:** You would agree with me that there are circumstances in which employees who are under the influence of intoxicating alcohol or substances have poor judgment in terms of the safety that they use on a work site?
A: In some cases.
Lesson: The expert at deposition does not deny the obvious, but he leaves himself plenty of wiggle room to distinguish specific cases if requested.

183. **Q:** What assumptions did you make in reviewing the records in this case?
A: That the records were genuine.
Lesson: The expert is not afraid to concede that this was one of his assumptions.

184. **Q:** You have stated your opinion. Is it possible that you are just plain wrong?
A: It is possible, but it is not likely.
Lesson: The expert concedes the possibility of error, but he puts the concession into context.

185.   **Q:** Would you agree with me that the healthcare providers that were involved in this patient's care would be in a better position to give information with regard to her level of weakness as it was observed than you are based on the record?

A: Not necessarily.

Lesson: The expert at deposition refuses to concede this point because he was not present and does not know what the providers did or did not see. He is prepared to explain this if requested.

186.   **Q:** You reviewed and endorsed the book *How to Excel During Cross-Examination: The Comprehensive Guide for Experts,* correct?

A: No, I read and reviewed the text.

Lesson: The expert refuses to accept the "endorsed" characterization and reframes the question (which softens her reply).

187.   **Q:** Are you nervous?

A: Yes, Counsel, your reputation precedes you.

Lesson: An honest reply with a little jab at counsel.

188.   **Q:** You enjoy the adversarial questions and answers in depositions, don't you?

A: Yes, I do.

Lesson: The self-assured expert is not afraid of cross-examination and enjoys the intellectual challenge.

189.   **Q:** Do you agree that the consequences of your testimony here today could have a serious impact on the life of the plaintiff?

A: Yes.

Lesson: The expert does not deny the obvious importance of his testimony.

190.   **Q:** When was the last time you actually treated a patient?

A: Two weeks ago at the clinic.

Lesson: The expert who stays active by teaching, volunteering, etc. is best positioned to answer a question of this nature.

191.   **Q:** Do you agree with the following statement? "Myocardial blood flow is necessary to properly oxygenate the heart and brain in addition to reestablishing a normal pulse rate. Defibrillation alone has not been proven to have significant success rates outside of a three-minute initial window in which CPR is begun."

A: Generally, yes.

Lesson: The expert agrees, but she leaves herself latitude to distinguish case-specific questions that are likely to follow.

192. **Q:** Are you a nationally known expert?
      A: I am known by many of my colleagues in the profession.
      Lesson: The expert takes some pains to neither brag nor suggest that the entire nation knows who he is.

193. **Q:** Do you know why counsel hired an expert witness who lives 1,500 miles from here to testify in this case?
      A: No.
      Lesson: This simple reply should force counsel to move on to a new line of questioning.

194. **Q:** Please go to the board and demonstrate how you calculated the probability that walkers will not slip and fall using equation #9.
      A: I cannot do that without my computer, software, and about one hour of time.
      Lesson: The expert does not agree to do demonstrations without the proper equipment.

195. **Q:** Has your testimony ever been limited or rejected in any way by any judge, court, or administrative body?
      A: No.
      Lesson: The experienced expert takes great pains to avoid this type of "record."

196. **Q:** Do you consider yourself smarter than the average juror?
      A: No.
      Lesson: The expert understands there are all kinds of "smarts" and respects the collective wisdom of the jury.

197. **Q:** When was the last time you lost a case?
      A: I don't have cases, Counsel.
      Lesson: The expert points out that it is not his role and reminds the jury that "counsel" have cases.

198. **Q:** Have you ever built a prototype of the alternative design you suggested for the snow thrower?
      A: No.
      Lesson: A simple and direct reply.

199. **Q:** Have you written any articles or books on the specific subject you are testifying about today that have been published?
      A: Yes.
      Lesson: The expert will point out where they are in his CV if requested.

200. **Q:** Do you keep current with the literature in your field?
A: I read approximately 6 journals a month.
Lesson: The expert does not want to make an all-encompassing admission because counsel will drag out hundreds of articles to question him about "the literature."

201. **Q:** Not only is there nothing in the literature to support your conclusion, but you haven't written anything or published anything to give the scientific community an opportunity to review your conclusion, have you?
A: I do not agree with that statement.
Lesson: The expert is not afraid to disagree with counsel and is prepared to back up his statement.

202. **Q:** You gave retaining counsel an oral report before he told you to write a written report, correct?
A: Yes, we discussed the case.
Lesson: The expert makes the concession and softens the blow.

203. **Q:** How many draft or preliminary reports did you do before you finalized your report in this case?
A: None.
Lesson: Many experienced experts refuse to write drafts or preliminary reports to avoid the "why did you change this?" line of attack.

204. **Q:** Are you aware that you are under oath and that your responses will in essence become part of your permanent record that can be brought up in all future cases that you testify in?
A: Yes, I am.
Lesson: The expert is not intimidated by this transparent tactic.

205. **Q:** Do you know of any materials counsel did not provide you?
A: I don't understand the question.
Lesson: The expert does not respond to vague questions and forces counsel to rephrase them.

206. **Q:** Do you in any way suspect that counsel did not provide you all of the materials in his possession?
A: No, I do not.
Lesson: Experienced experts do not work with counsel who intentionally withhold information from expert witnesses.

207. **Q:** Did counsel ever discuss his trial strategy with you?
A: Yes, he did.
Lesson: Counsel who reveal trial strategy to their experts do so at their peril.

208.   **Q:** What is your understanding of how you fit into counsel's trial strategy?
    A: I am testifying exclusively on causation.
    Lesson: The expert does not repeat the words "trial strategy" and softens his function.

209.   **Q:** What is your understanding of the facts and events that led to this lawsuit?
    A: The plaintiff was hit by a drunk driver.
    Lesson: The expert does not attempt to summarize numerous facts.

210.   **Q:** Please tell me everything you did to come up with your opinion.
    A: Generally, I read the pleadings, reviewed the documents, visited the accident scene, viewed photos, conducted tests, and formulated my opinions.
    Lesson: The expert leaves herself a little wiggle room by starting with "generally," indicating she is *not* trying to list each and every thing she did.

211.   **Q:** Do you agree with [statement from a text or article]?
    A: No, I do not.
    Lesson: The expert is cautious about agreeing with general statements in books or articles.

212.   **Q:** Did you ever ask for any additional material to review?
    A: Yes, I did, and it was furnished.
    Lesson: The experienced expert has a transparent practice and thus all letters requesting materials are made available to opposing counsel when requested at deposition.

213.   **Q:** Have you done everything necessary to give your final opinion?
    A: Yes, but my opinion is always subject to modification if new pertinent material is made available to me.
    Lesson: The expert is always open to receiving and reviewing additional pertinent information.

214.   **Q:** What else do you need to see or do?
    A: I don't understand the question.
    Lesson: The expert does not answer vague, unintelligible questions.

215.   **Q:** Which journals are the most authoritative in this area?
    A: None that I can think of.
    Lesson: The expert is concerned about vouching for journals and refuses to rank journals in order of their authoritativeness.

216.   **Q:** Are your opinions universally accepted in your field?
    A: I don't understand the question.
    Lesson: The expert refuses to try and guess what counsel and the question are calling for.

217. **Q:** Why did you leave your last job?
      A: For better working conditions.
      Lesson: The expert does not go into a long tirade about his former employer.

218. **Q:** Please name every person who knows why you left your last job.
      A: I don't know.
      Lesson: The expert would have no way to know who his employer talked to, so he is unable to answer this with any degree of accuracy.

219. **Q:** Have you ever failed a test since graduating college?
      A: No.
      Lesson: Short and sweet reply.

220. **Q:** How did you come to be involved in this case?
      A: I was contacted by retaining counsel.
      Lesson: The expert answers directly and is prepared to answer additional questions if questioned further.

221. **Q:** Will you agree to provide me copies of everything you have written on this topic?
      A: I don't understand the question.
      Lesson: The expert understands that "this topic" and "everything written" are too vague to reply to accurately.

222. **Q:** Which peer-reviewed publications support your opinion?
      A: I do not know.
      Lesson: The expert does not have any way of knowing which of thousands of publications may support his opinion.

223. **Q:** Do you agree to let me know at any time before trial if there are any changes to your report or opinion so that we may reopen your deposition?
      A: Yes. I will report the same to retaining counsel.
      Lesson: The expert agrees to cooperate, but she would prefer to deal with retaining counsel (who will be under a continuing obligation to pass this information along to opposing counsel).

224. **Q:** Did anyone else help you write your report?
      A: No.
      Lesson: The expert acknowledges any assistance he received in writing his report.

225. **Q:** Whom have you spoken to about this case?
      A: Retaining counsel, my assistant, and you.
      Lesson: The experienced expert is cautious about discussing confidential case material.

226. **Q:** Whom have you spoken to in conjunction with forming your opinion?
A: The plaintiff and the police officer.
Lesson: The expert is organized and thorough. She has this information in her file.

227. **Q:** Do you have any criticism of my expert's report or opinion?
A: I do not agree with his conclusions.
Lesson: The expert does not use the word "criticism," but he gets the idea across.

228. **Q:** Have you told me everything?
A: I don't understand the question.
Lesson: The expert refuses to answer this vague question.

229. **Q:** Is that all?
A: Can you rephrase the question?
Lesson: The expert does not try to guess what the question is and certainly does not provide a long, rambling response in an attempt to "cover everything."

230. **Q:** How do you define "standard of care"?
A: Generally, how the average prudent physician in a given community would practice under the same or similar circumstances.
Lesson: If the expert is a standard of care expert, he needs to know this definition and be able to repeat it at deposition. However, this expert wisely leaves himself some wiggle room.

231. **Q:** How do you define "defective"?
A: In terms of a product, one that is unreasonably dangerous to the user.
Lesson: The expert narrows the question and then replies.

232. **Q:** How do you define "aggravation"?
A: A permanent worsening of a condition, generally speaking.
Lesson: The expert, at deposition, is conversant with these commonly used terms of art.

233. **Q:** Do you receive a bonus for testifying in court?
A: No, I do not.
Lesson: Being able to reply no to this question is just one of the advantages of a simple uniform hourly rate fee structure.

234. **Q:** Would you like your side to win this case?
A: I do not have a side, Counselor.
Lesson: The expert understands his role in the legal process and does not permit opposing counsel to portray him as an advocate.

235. **Q:** Has a case ever been decided by a judge or jury contrary to an opinion you gave?
A: Yes.
Lesson: The expert makes this concession freely without being defensive.

236. **Q:** What is the most important case you have ever worked on?
A: Each case is very important to the parties.
Lesson: The expert does not "rank" cases by level of importance.

237. **Q:** Are you an expert?
A: Yes.
Lesson: A simple question calls for a simple reply.

238. **Q:** Please describe the practical training you have had in your field.
A: I have 25 years of hands-on civil engineering.
Lesson: The expert replies and is willing and able to be more specific if questioned further.

239. **Q:** Why are you not certified?
A: Because I did not take the exam.
Lesson: The expert makes the concession and encourages counsel to move on.

240. **Q:** Did you collaborate with anyone else in forming your opinion?
A: No, I did not.
Lesson: The expert acknowledges any assistance he received in his written report.

241. **Q:** What do you think of [opposing expert]?
A: I like him.
Lesson: The expert points out that he has no personal animosity toward the opposing expert.

242. **Q:** Whom do you represent?
A: I do not represent anyone.
Lesson: The expert knows his role and resists the attempt by opposing counsel to portray him as an advocate.

243. **Q:** Why did you delegate that task?
A: It was more efficient to do so.
Lesson: Experienced experts often delegate routine tasks to others under their direction and control.

244.   **Q:** What do you see as the biggest weaknesses in my client's case?
       A: His version of the facts.
       Lesson: The expert understands the facts are often an issue and many times versions are inconsistent with documents and witness statements.

11.3 Conclusion
Experts should develop their own techniques for truthfully and artfully answering trick and difficult deposition questions.

Chapter 12 Sample Annotated Expert Deposition Transcripts

12.1 Introduction and Executive Summary
This chapter contains two complete annotated expert deposition transcripts. These have been provided:

- to show the reader typical expert depositions,
- to see how questions arise in the context of a deposition as a whole, and
- to reinforce many of the practice pointers provided in this text.

12.2 Sample Annotated Medical Expert Transcript
Many of the concepts and techniques discussed in this book are demonstrated in the following complete deposition transcript. The deponent in this case was a psychiatrist retained by the defense. At issue was the extent of the injuries sustained by the plaintiff after being rear-ended in a low-to-moderate speed motor vehicle accident. As you will see, both plaintiff's counsel conducting the deposition and the expert witness are very well prepared and very experienced. The deposition is conducted civilly and there is never even a hint of inappropriate behavior. There is no bickering between counsel. The expert demonstrates highly advanced active listening skills and a command of the facts of the case. He also readily makes concessions where appropriate and hedges his responses so that they are not misleading. The expert was also very transparent in all areas—except his forensic income. He probably would have been better served by being more forthcoming in this area.

STIPULATIONS
It is stipulated by and between counsel for the respective parties that the deposition transcript is to be read and signed by the deponent under the pains and penalties of perjury; and that the sealing and filing thereof are waived; and that all objections, except as to form, and motions to strike are reserved to the time of trial.

GREG S. DAVIS, M.D.
a witness called for examination by counsel for the Plaintiff, being first duly sworn, was examined and testified as follows:

DIRECT EXAMINATION
BY MR. GLENN:
Q. Good afternoon, Dr. Davis.[1]
A. Good afternoon.
Q. Would you state your full name, please?
A. My name is Greg S. Davis, D-A-V-I-S.

Curriculum vitae and publications
Q. And are your current business addresses listed on Exhibit 1, which is your CV?[2]
A. Yes, they are.
Q. Is Exhibit 1 a current resume or curriculum vitae?
A. Correct. It was completed in '03. I don't have any newer one. I don't think that there are any substantial additions to it, but I usually double-check that sometime in January of each year. But that's the January—February '03 edition.
Q. Do you believe there are any additional publications since you've published Exhibit No. 1?
A. I don't think so. I don't believe so.[3,4]

Inquiries about past testimony—counsel looks for dirt
Q. Doctor, Exhibit No. 2, which you were kind enough to copy for me, is a list of cases, and it's dated 2002, 2001, 2000 and 1999. Is there also a similar list for the year 2003?[5]
A. Not yet. I usually do that in January of '04 for—you know, so I haven't compiled that list, but I anticipate doing that in the next few weeks when things settle down a little bit when I have time to.
Q. How do you go about compiling the list of cases?
A. I usually go through my appointment book and look for—Since it's—The list is testimony at trial or deposition, so I go through my appointment book and look for January 7, 2004, deposition, and the case. And that's how I would do it.
Q. So the list of cases here include only those cases where you've given testimony in the form of either a deposition or trial or both?
A. Correct. That's in accordance with the federal rules basically, which basically say that witnesses should provide cases that they've testified in the past four years.[6]

---

[1] Most depositions are conducted cordially and professionally.
[2] Counsel makes sure that there is nothing he should know about that is not listed in the expert's CV.
[3] Counsel wants to know everything the witness has written because the witness's writings can provide potent ammunition for cross-examination.
[4] Note that counsel doesn't waste time (and his client's money) by asking questions that are apparent from the CV. Also, if he has dirt on the expert, he doesn't want to tip his hand at the deposition.
[5] Notice how professional the attorney is. This is the norm in most expert depositions. There is also a practical benefit because attorneys can usually pump more information out of the expert by being nice.
[6] The expert demonstrates a correct understanding of the federal rule.

Q. With respect to Exhibit No. 2, can you tell me in looking at the exhibit whether you testified or were retained for any plaintiff whose name is listed on exhibit No. 2?

A. Emily Vella. I don't know how to characterize an estate that was in contention, plaintiff versus defendant. I think that that was the person initiating the challenge to a—an estate situation.

Q. Was that the Vella case or is that another case?

A. That's another, Richard Stewart. Board of Registration versus someone. I was working for the Board of Registration. I don't know how to count that one, but I was retained by the Board of Registration in that matter.

Q. Was that a—

A. Board versus Chapman. That was 2001.

Q. Was that a matter involving some disciplinary action against a physician?

A. Yes. Violet Welch versus Chelsea Housing, a 1999 case. Harvey Albert versus Schlossberg Funeral Home, a '99 case. Some of these cases I'm not specifically remembering, but I think those are the ones that I have a clear recollection that it was for the plaintiffs.

Q. Fair to say that the remaining cases listed on Exhibit No. 2 you were retained by the defense?[7]

A. No, because there's criminal cases there, so U.S. Attorney, for example, and— With regard to the civil cases, that probably is correct.

Q. Okay. I'm going to make a request of you that when that list is prepared for the year 2003 of the cases which you've testified on, if you would provide that to Attorney Smith.

A. Sure. [8]

MR. ONG: Do you mean Ong?

MR. GLENN: Ong. Off the record.

(Discussion off the record.)

Inquiries into the doctor's practice and time spent on forensic work

Q. Doctor, do you maintain a private practice?

A. Yes, I do.

Q. Where do you maintain a private practice?

A. At this office, Suite 254, Lamb Street, Lemont.

Q. With respect to the private practice, do you treat patients?[9]

A. Yes.

Q. On average in the year 2003, how many patient hours did you average?

---

[7] Plaintiff's counsel is trying to establish that the expert is biased toward the defense.

[8] This sophisticated expert has nothing to hide.

[9] Trying to establish that the expert is a "professional witness."

A. It's—On a weekly basis when here, okay, it probably ranges from 10 to 15, occasionally 17, 18.

Q. What do you mean when you're here?

A. Well, if you ask something over a yearly basis, there are times when I'm away on vacation and things of that sort. On a weekly basis it's 10 to 17, 18 hours depending on the week.

Q. And that 10 to 15 hours you devote to psychotherapy of patients?

A. Yes.

Q. That is outside of your forensic work?

A. Correct.

Q. On average, on a yearly basis, how many hours do you devote to your forensic psychiatric work?

A. Again, it's hard for me to answer in that form. It's about a third of my time, so— and it's gotten to be a little bit more in recent years, but it's probably about 40 percent of my time. So it would be 15 hours to 20 hours in a working week, a full working week.

Q. So you average 15 to 17 hours of psychotherapy, 15 to 20 hours a week of forensic psychiatric work; would that be fair?

A. No. 10 to 17 for practice, 15 to 20 depending on the week in forensic work. 20 is a bit high. It probably is closer to 15.

Q. Does that amount of hours cover all of your professional work for which you get paid?

A. No.[10]

Q. What additional amount of hours do you spend in some other professional activity for which you get paid?

A. I'm at the Youngstown Hospital approximately eight hours a week, usually most of it on Wednesday. I was there this morning. I'm there. I teach and see patients. I saw patients this morning, participated in the transplantation team, did rounds with the psychiatric residents and fellows. And I teach courses to psychiatric residents and occasionally medical students, but in the fall semester primarily.

Fees

Q. What is your current fee for your forensic work?

A. It is $400 per hour, except for public payers, Board of Registration in Medicine, U.S. Attorney's Office, District Attorney's Office, Mass. Defenders for the Committee for Public Counsel Services. I preferred it when they were the Mass. Defenders. It was easier to say. That's $350 per hour.

Q. With respect to civil matters, do you charge both plaintiff and defense counsel or insurance companies the same $400 per hour?[11]

---

[10] The expert answers the narrow question asked and does not volunteer additional information.
[11] Again, counsel is trying to establish bias.

A. Yes.[12]

Q. The charge for your work in the forensic area of $400 an hour, is that inclusive of reviews, testimony, deposition testimony at trial?

A. Correct, one fee.[13]

Q. How much money did you earn in the year 2003 from your forensic work both criminal and civil?

A. I don't basically keep track of that number. I—More than half of my income comes from forensic work.[14]

Q. If you don't keep track of the amount, how do you know it's approximately one half?

A. Because the insurance companies pay anywhere from $56 per hour to the good payers 100 bucks an hour, and so—and my forensic work pays $350 to $400 per hour.

Q. When you say insurance companies, are you referring to for medical services that you render? Is that what you're referring to?

A. Yes. I don't do work directly for insurance companies in the forensic area. I'm called by people, defense attorneys or plaintiff attorneys.

Q. I don't understand how you can approximate your forensic income as being one half of your annual income based on the relative disparity between the hourly fees of forensic work versus insurance payers.

A. I said it was well over—Go ahead.[15]

MR. ONG: There wasn't a question. You said I don't understand—

Q. Can you explain that?

A. It's just that the rates paid are just far in excess of what I get paid either by the Youngstown Hospital or the health insurers or individuals who may be paying out of their pocket.

Q. Yes. What you're saying is there's a disparity between the two payers, the forensic area and the insurance area. Also there's a factor of the number of hours that you devote either per week or annually for forensic work versus other work. I assume and that's how—Is that how you approximate that it's one half of your annual income, that is your forensic work?

A. I said it was well over half.

Q. How much over?

A. I don't know.

---

[12] This expert wisely charges plaintiffs and defendants the same fee.

[13] The authors recommend such a uniform fee structure.

[14] The authors do not like this answer. Even if it's true, most jurors will not find it believable that a person does not know how much money he makes. Experts should track this information, be prepared to answer the percentage of income question, and force counsel to move on.

[15] Here the witness responds to a statement, not to a question. He should have said nothing and waited for a question.

Q. Between well over one half and what is your best approximation?

A. I don't understand your question.[16]

Q. Well, you said that your income from forensic work is well over one half of your total annual income; is that correct?[17]

A. Professional income, yes.

Q. And I'm asking you, can you approximate for me how much over one half your forensic income is of your total income?

A. I just know it's well over half. It might be 60 or 70 or 75 percent.

Q. Is it possible it's as high as 90 or 95 percent?

A. No.

Q. So it's somewhere between 70 and 75 percent up to 90 percent; is that fair?

A. I don't know the number, so I can't answer the question.

Q. And that number, that is the percentage of your gross income that's devoted to forensic work, that's something that would be reflected in your tax returns, would it not?

A. Not directly.

Q. Well, indirectly would it be?

A. I report all my professional income on whatever schedule it is, and it has my private practice psychotherapy, it has insurance, it has individual payers, people who pay, it has income from forensic work from law firms, it has income from organizations I might do consultations or teaching kinds of things.

Q. So that if you're unable, for example, to approximate what percentage of your total gross income in 2003 is from forensic work, your tax returns and other documentation would reveal that approximate percentage?[18]

A. I don't think it's fair—I gave you an estimate of what I thought my income was from forensic work, so I don't think it's correct that I'm, quote, unable to do it. I just have had no particular reason to do it. And the money that I get from my professional activity is all the same to me. Okay? I just report my professional income from all sources to my accountant, and he prepares the...

Q. But if an individual were to look at your tax returns in the documentation of your forensic work as well as the documentation in the return of your gross income, those records would document, would they not, the amount of forensic income you had in a given year; is that true?

A. You'd have to go through my records in a way I have never had had a reason to go through and figure out what the—if I sent, for example, a 1099, what was the source of it, what was it for, was it for forensic work, was it for clinical work.

---

[16] The expert prudently refused to answer an unintelligible question.

[17] This is not serving the expert well. If he testifies as much as he claims, he should find out the answer to this question that he will be asked in almost every case. The expert comes off as evasive here.

[18] If the expert would have just answered the question, counsel wouldn't start down the road of going after the expert's tax returns. There would be no need for this.

Sometimes they're mixed because one insurance company can do both kinds of things. So it would involve going through various documents, but—And they may not even give a fair representation of what the monies were for, I mean, because I don't track them that way.

Q. Doctor, if you went to your tax returns and the back-up documentation, for example, with respect to the year 2003 or 2002, would you be able to give me an approximation of how much the percentage is of forensic income versus your gross income?

A. What do you mean by back-up documentation?

Q. Well, you indicated that the tax records would indirectly indicate what your sources of income were or words to that effect, correct?

A. The tax return has the total professional income on whatever schedule those kinds of things go in. It gives a total amount of professional income from all sources. I get a W-2 from Youngstown, which is a kind of separate item, but all the rest of the professional income would be reported on whatever the appropriate schedule. That is made up of monies that come in from Blue Cross & Blue Shield and Signa and Harvard Pilgrim and Options and John Hancock which might be for health care or might be for forensic work, as well as 1099s or records of income directly from law firms and the like, so that it's—when—For example, this is the season of 1099s. They come in. I put them in an envelope. I don't make a particular distinction about who's paying me for what. I have no reason to know that. So I don't know if that answers your question.

Q. A question I have for you is, Doctor, if you went to your tax records and the back-up documentation that you keep for that, would you be able to give me an approximation of the percentage of income from forensic work versus your total gross income on an annual basis, let's say, for the year 2003 or 2002?

A. With a great deal of effort, probably. And it may vary from year to year too.

Q. Now, Doctor, I appreciate that you've copied for me, made readily available for me various documents related to the Lytle case. Do you also have readily available for yourself your tax returns as ordered by the court?[19]

A. My tax records are in this office suite, yes.[20]

Q. And in compliance with that court order, they're readily available?

A. Yes.

Q. How much total income did you earn in the year 2003 from your work in the forensic psychiatric area?

A. I don't know exactly.

Q. Would that information in response to that question be available in those tax records for the year 2003?

---

[19] Such a court order is usually not granted if the expert is forthcoming about his forensic income.

[20] An example of one reason why the expert may not want to have the deposition in his own office.

A. I don't understand how this is different than what we just went through with regard to questions. Yes, if I went through all my financial tax records with a great deal of effort, I could figure out approximately—or fairly accurately, but not exactly accurately, what portion of it came from doing forensic work.

Q. And just so that the record is clear, you could go back to the tax records for prior years, 2003, '02, '01 and 2000, look at the tax returns and the back-up documentation, and you would be able, would you not, to answer my question as to the amount of forensic income you had in that given year, correct?

A. Probably.

MR. ONG: Objection just to the extent that 2003 information isn't available yet.

MR. GLENN: I don't know that, and the doctor hasn't indicated whether it is or it isn't.

MR. ONG: You haven't asked either. You've assumed. That's why I'm objecting. This is the end of the year. They haven't come through from a lot of providers.[21]

Q. Well, Doctor, obviously when you receive the necessary documentation, that information would be readily available to you, would it not?

A. Yes.

Q. Also with respect to going—

A. What is readily available?

Q. Counsel for the defense here has indicated that perhaps your 2003 tax returns and back-up documentation is not yet available. Is that accurate that it's not yet available?

A. Correct.

Q. And that's because we're in January, and you understand, do you not, that W-2s and 1099s are not due until the 31st of January?

A. I don't know that, but I have no reason to doubt that that's the case.

Q. Now, also going back to your tax returns for 2002, '01 and 2000, and 2003 when they're available, you could go back to those returns and back-up documentation and answer me as to your gross income for those years and figure out the percentage that came from forensic work, correct?

A. Yes, with great effort.[22]

Q. But without that effort, without that documentation, without those returns, you're unable to tell me with respect to 2003 and 2002 the approximate percentage of income that you derive from forensic work except to say it's well over half of your annual income, correct?

A. And likely—I can say with great confidence that it's well over half. Whether it's 60 or 75 percent, I can't say.

---

[21] The expert is probably listening closely to these objections. The content of the objection may have reminded the expert that the 2003 returns are not available.

[22] The doctor wisely qualified his response.

Q. Can you tell me whether it's 80 or 85 percent?
A. No.

Testifying history

Q. Now, with respect to the civil work that you've done during the year 2003, with respect first to the gross number of cases, how many cases have you been retained on during the year 2003?
A. If we could have a brief—I have that info right in my desk around the corner.
Q. Sure.
(Discussion off the record.)
A. Was the question—
MR. GLENN: Robert can read it.
(Record read.)
A. I can't answer for 2003 because I haven't kind of tallied things up, and it would be basically the same process. I can do 2002, 2001, and 2000, but I haven't gotten to the tallying up of the ones in 2003.
Q. And the tallying up that you do is going through your appointment book and, if you will, while you make the list, which is different than you're testifying, you could make a list, could you not, on cases that you've been retained on and come up with a gross figure?
A. Yes.
Q. And you'd come up with a gross figure on civil matters?
A. Yes.
Q. And in doing that, have you done it for the year 2002, 2001?
A. Yes, 2001 and 2000. 2000, 2002—The last three years before 2003.
Q. Could you tell me what those figures are?
A. Starting?
Q. Whatever year you have.
A. You want civil and criminal or just civil?
Q. Civil, please.
A. 2002 civil cases, defendants 43 cases, plaintiffs five. 2001 civil cases, defendants 54, plaintiffs nine.[23]
Q. I'm sorry. Did you say nine?
A. Nine, that's correct. The year 2000 civil cases, 56 for defendants, eight for plaintiffs.
Q. And when we add obviously those together, we get the total number of civil cases that you were retained on, some of which you actually testified on, correct?
A. Correct.
Q. With respect to those particular years, 2000, 2001, 2002, what's the total number of criminal matters that you were retained on? Do you have such a list as well?

---

[23] This expert can easily be characterized as a professional witness who is biased toward the defense.

A. Yes. 2002 criminal side, nine times for the prosecutor, four times for defendants.
2001, 11 times for the prosecutor, seven times for the defendants. 2000, the year
2000, criminal side, prosecutor 14 times, defendants three.

Q. Are there any other additional types of cases that you were retained on for those
years beyond the civil and criminal matters, for example, being retained by an
administrative board?

A. The Board of Registration in Medicine, yes.

Q. BBO?[24]

A. I have in the past. I don't know that I was in these years, but I have been.

Q. For those same years, do you have any numbers for any additional cases for which
you were retained in which you did forensic work?

A. I don't—The ones that came to testimony are in the list. Okay? I don't think that
I counted them up because that's not the kind of question I've been asked before.
That would be five to ten cases a year average, or no more than ten, but a few cases
directly for an organization or an agency, and sometimes it is not even, quote, a case.
It may be a consultation about an agency and a problem it's having within itself, if
you will.

Q. With respect to the number of cases on the civil side that you gave me for those
years, do those cases include, for example, a case that you were retained on and
turned down, meaning you reviewed the case for one side or the other and you turned
it down in the sense that it didn't—your opinion did not support the party that
retained you—

Let me withdraw the question and ask you this: What does this figure for 2000, 2001,
2002 represent when you gave me those cases retained by the defense, those for the
plaintiff?[25]

A. They were all cases. Okay? They were cases in which I may have said, In my
opinion, I—Well, my opinion may not have been in the common perception of the
interest of the person retaining me. I happen to think that's unfair to both—to people
who ask opinions of experts. But sometimes for plaintiffs I will review materials. I
will charge and I will say, as I did earlier this week, that I don't think you—that I can
testify or write a report that would say something that you—Again, I hate to use the
word—would—other people might assume you're interested in. For example, this is
from this week. A defense attorney sent me a lot of material on an individual, and I
told her, I think this case, his deposition and all the records support his having
psychological damages related to a motor vehicle accident. So—But I will bill for
that and it would be counted on my defense—retained by defendant's tally for next
year.[26]

---

[24] Board of Bar Overseers. The entity that disciplines attorneys.

[25] Counsel wisely rephrases his question into one that calls for a broader answer and that will likely
result in more information being divulged.

[26] A good answer supporting the image of an expert who calls cases as he sees them.

Q. When do you anticipate putting together your 2003 list or numbers of the civil and criminal matters that you were retained on, not just testified on?

A. I usually do it in January. A little bit depends on the flow of things. You need a little quiet time to get together the material and organize it. So—But I usually do it in January.

Q. I would again request for the record that when that is completed, if you would give it to defense counsel. We'll make a request through him for that list.

A. Sure.

Questions on clinical practice

Q. Thank you. Is there a particular business entity under which you perform your forensic psychiatric work?

A. No.

Q. Is your forensic psychiatry work listed on your CV?

A. I don't know if I understand the question.[27]

Q. Sure. Well, let me ask you a different question. Maybe we'll get to it. What is Lemont Consultation Center?

A. This group of offices.

Q. Do you have any type of professional relationship with any other individuals who are members of Lemont Consultation Center?

A. Sharing expenses only.

History of expert witnessing

Q. You've described for me the forensic psychiatric work that you do. And my question is, when did you first start performing forensic psychiatric work?

A. In the early '70s.

Q. Is your work with respect to the forensic work listed here on your CV, in other words from the 1970s to the present forensic psychiatrists consulting to attorneys' organizations, agencies, something along those lines?

A. I think there is. Just let me see. This CV is in the form of the Harvard Medical School format, and so it—they pretty much tell you the categories. Here on page 3, particularly at the top.

Q. Which lists some of the agencies for which you've rendered consulting services. It doesn't indicate anything about being retained by attorneys in civil matters, does it?

A. Nor defense attorneys or the like. I mean it—What the CV wants to know is do you have a connection with organizations in part for conflict of interest reasons. And so within the format of an academic CV, that wouldn't be appropriate to mention criminal—defense attorneys, civil attorneys, plaintiffs, defendants. It just wouldn't— But consultant to organizations, state organizations and things is relevant.

---

[27] A completely appropriate response if the expert does not understand the question.

Q. Do you maintain any other type of CV or resume?
A. No, I do not.

Expert does not advertise or have a Web page
Q. Do you have any, for lack of a better word, promotional material that describes the forensic work that you do? In other words, some people have a brochure or have a Website or something like that. Do you have any of that material?
A. No, I do not. When you said promotional, I was thinking academic promotion kind of thing. No, I don't have a Web site or…

Training in related fields
Q. In your education and training as well as your professional experience, have you ever been trained as a neuropsychologist?
A. As a neuropsychologist?
Q. Right.
A. No.
Q. Have you ever taken any courses in psychological testing?
A. Yes.
Q. When did you take those?
A. In the course of my residency.
Q. Ever been trained interpreting psychological tests?
A. In terms of formal training, no, but I've worked over the years with a number of neuropsychologists.
Q. I understand. But you're not trained—You aren't trained, are you, in interpreting raw data from neuropsychological testing, are you?
A. How do you mean trained? I've not been formally trained, that's correct.
Q. Are you a trained interpreter of the raw data of an MMPI?
A. Formal training, no, but I do have the capacity of scoring.
Q. To score it?
A. (Witness nodded.)[28]
Q. Do you have the professional experience to interpret those scores?
A. I believe I do.

Factual investigation
Q. And in this particular case, Alfred Lytle, did you interpret his raw data from his MMPI?
A. I didn't score it myself, no.
Q. In my mind I have a distinction between scoring and interpreting scores. And what do you mean by, I didn't do the scoring in the Lytle MMPI?
A. I sent out his answer sheet, a copy of which you made earlier, to NCS, and had it scored by them and received their interpretation.[29]

---

[28] The expert should have responded verbally and thus assured an accurate transcript.

Material reviewed

Q. Since you wrote your report of December 17, 2002, which is Exhibit No. 3, have you reviewed any additional material with regard to the Lytle matter?[30]

A. Yes.

Q. Do you know what additional material you have reviewed?

A. I think I remember most of it. It involved some depositions of co-workers. I think there were three of them, or supervisors, people he worked with, some legal documents including answers to interrogatories, some materials maybe in answers to interrogatories or letters from family members about him, a letter or report from Dr. Seidman that came in after, some additional records from A-1 Mutual, performance reviews and kind of personnel records. I think that's pretty much it. It's all here. I know you had a chance to look at them. And maybe I've forgotten something that you're aware of, but that's basically what I can recall off the top of my head.[31]

Q. So from what you can recall, those matters which—Strike that—those documents which you reviewed in forming your opinion of December 17, 2002 are the 17 items listed in that report?

A. Mm-hmm.[32]

Q. Yes?

A. Yes.

Q. And subsequent to that, you've described some additional materials which you have reviewed, at least to your best memory today?

A. Correct.

Q. Now, have you reviewed any other additional depositions besides what may be listed in Exhibit No. 3 and what you've just recently recalled by way of testimony today?

A. I don't believe I have.[33]

Q. With respect to the documents that you reviewed subsequent to writing your December 17, 2002 report, have any of those documents in any way changed your opinion or opinions as expressed in your December 17, 2002 report?

A. No, they have not.

Trying to lock down the expert's opinions

Q. With respect to your opinions in the Lytle matter, are those opinions all contained in Exhibit No. 3, your December 17, 2002 report?

---

[29] In many instances, an expert is allowed to rely upon the work of other experts in reaching his conclusion.

[30] Again, trying to lock down the expert without wasting time. If materials reviewed were in the report, there is no real reason to ask him this at the deposition.

[31] Note how the expert leaves himself some room to maneuver by qualifying his response.

[32] Grunts do not look good on a transcript and should be avoided.

[33] The expert's carefully worded response leaves him some wiggle room.

A. I believe they are. I'm not consciously withholding any opinion that I—I'm not hiding any opinion that I—And I think that, you know, the report reflected my opinion at the time I wrote it, and nothing has, you know, basically changed from the new material.[34]

Q. And as you sit here today, then, the—is the extent of the opinion that you anticipate giving at trial contained within Exhibit No. 3, your report of December 17, 2002?

A. Yes, I believe it is.[35]

Specific clinical experience and knowledge

Q. With respect to the private patients that you see, and of course protecting their privacy, do you treat currently any patients who have a traumatic brain injury?

A. I have over the years. I'm not recalling that I have anyone in active treatment in my private practice who's got a traumatic brain injury.

Q. Are you able to estimate for me either the number of patients that you've treated who have traumatic brain injuries or the percentage of your private practice devoted to patients with traumatic brain injuries?[36]

A. The bulk of the people with brain injury that I've seen have been at the Youngstown Hospital in the nature of my practice there, psychiatrist in a medical hospital that doesn't have psychiatric beds. In terms of patients over the years with traumatic brain injury that I've treated here or in my private offices, five to ten in 30 plus years of practice in terms of coming for—The nature of my practice here is—tends to be intensive, long-term psychotherapy oriented. Some patients are on medication, but it's more longer term therapy on a frequent basis.

Q. Doctor, you're familiar, are you not, with the term "concussion"?

A. Yes.

Q. What is a concussion?

A. It's subject to a lot of definitions, but it is a term probably best reserved for people who sustain trauma to the head and develop symptoms because of the trauma to the head.

Q. Is loss of consciousness necessary for a person to sustain a concussion?

A. No.

Q. Are you familiar with the term "diffuse axonal injury"?[37]

A. Yes.

---

[34] The expert leaves himself some wiggle room.

[35] Counsel does not ask follow-up questions because the expert is, in effect, locked into his report.

[36] Trying to establish a lack of clinical experience with the type of patient at issue in this case. This is an area of inquiry because it is information that does not appear in the expert's CV or report.

[37] Testing the expert's knowledge.

Controversial medical issue

Q. What's a diffuse axonal injury?

A. It's a theory about the mechanism of degeneration of symptoms after head trauma.

Q. Well, when you say "theory," isn't there a scientific research behind that theory with respect to diffuse axonal injury?

A. In my view, that research is controversial. There are certain circumstances in which it seems—It's a controversial area. I personally and in my own profession in looking into this question am not convinced of the firm scientific basis for it.

Q. Is your opinion that there is no scientific basis for a diffuse axonal injury?

A. Probably it is as—it's a generalization. Has it ever happened to individuals? Yes. I don't have any doubt that it does in certain types of trauma.

Q. For the record, are you able to define what a diffuse axonal injury is?

A. It is the theory that when an individual suffers head trauma, that the axons, the filaments of the nerves are injured by the forces applied to the skull. And it's diffuse, namely it's thought to be all over the brain.

Q. Would you agree, Doctor, that if enough force is imparted on the skull and brain that a person can sustain injury to the axons?

A. Yes.[38]

Q. Would you agree also that those injuries to the axons would not show up on a CAT scan and MRI?[39]

A. Yes.

Q. Would you agree also that a normal—

A. Might not. Might not.

Q. Are you aware that an injury to an axon would show up on a—could show up on an MRI or CAT scan?

A. Not an axon.

Q. Would you agree that a normal CAT scan, x-ray, MRI of the brain doesn't necessarily rule out that the person sustained a brain injury?

A. Correct.

Q. Why is that? Why do you agree with that statement?

A. Because not all brain injuries would show up on MRIs or CAT scans or even more sophisticated testings.

Q. Why is that? Why would they not show up?[40]

A. Because the machinery is not sophisticated enough to indicate the injury.

Q. Also, would you agree that if a person did not lose consciousness, that doesn't necessarily rule out that they had a brain injury?

A. Correct.

---

[38] The expert correctly makes a ready concession. The wise expert does not dispute the obvious.

[39] Note how counsel knows much about the area of medicine in question.

[40] Plaintiff's counsel is using the defense expert to help blunt one of the defense's anticipated arguments.

More concessions obtained from the doctor

Q. Would you agree, Doctor, that a concussion is a form of brain injury?[41]

A. In the broad sense of the term, yes.[42]

Q. And what do you mean in the broad sense of the term?

A. That if one accepts that there is a concussion and the person has certain symptoms, then the origin of those symptoms has to be the brain, and in that sense the brain is injured.

Q. And what certain symptoms are you referring to?

A. It can be various symptoms, nausea, headache, mood problems, difficulty concentrating, emotional liability, things of that sort.

Q. Are you familiar with the term "contrecoup injury"?

A. Yes.

Q. What is that?

A. It's a term used to describe certain kinds of injuries to the brain in which basically force is applied to one side or one part of the brain but the damage is more pronounced on the opposite side from the place the force was applied.

Q. Are you familiar with the term "traumatic brain injury"?

A. Yes.[43]

Q. Are you familiar with how a traumatic brain injury occurs in an acceleration/deceleration accident?

A. I'm not sure I understand the question.

Q. Are you aware of a traumatic brain injury occurring when the skull and brain goes through an acceleration/deceleration force or forces?

A. I'm aware of that, yes.

Q. And—

A. I'm aware of that concept, yes.

Witness again disagrees with controversial area

Q. Do you agree with that as a scientific basis?

A. It's my same problem with diffuse axonal injury. Okay? I don't really feel it has—It's more a theoretical explanation of why symptoms develop, but in terms of clear proof in a typically accepted scientific way, it's—I'm not convinced that that's been established to that degree of scientific certainty.

Q. Would you be convinced if there were research on persons who had sustained supposedly a traumatic brain injury and on autopsy microscopic analysis of their brain confirmed that their axons were sheared or torn?[44]

---

[41] "Would you agree" questions are a red flag that counsel is looking for a concession.

[42] The expert answers more narrowly than a simple "yes."

[43] Note how the expert narrowly answers the specific question asked and does not leap into a dissertation of his thoughts on traumatic brain injury.

[44] Possibly setting up the expert to confront him with research as is described in this question.

A. Yes.[45]

Q. And if there were such scientific research, that would take it outside of the realm of theory or hypothesis, correct?

A. Well, I'd need to know more about the case. Okay? Did they die from the head injury and hence there is an autopsy? You'd need to know more about the individual case.[46]

Q. Doctor, are you familiar with what you call the theory of acceleration/deceleration forces causing a traumatic brain injury?

A. I'm familiar with that.

Q. And what is the theory that you're familiar with?

A. That in the process of acceleration/deceleration, such as automobile accidents, or in some people's minds fighters who get repeatedly hit in the head and that the brain accelerates and then decelerates inside the skull, that that causes, among other things, quote, diffuse axonal injury and traumatic brain injury.

Q. Do you not agree with that, as you characterized it, that theory?

A. I understand it as a theory. I am not—I have not yet been convinced of its solid scientific basis.

Q. Now, with respect to boxers, do you not accept that from repeated punching and forces imparted on the skull, do you agree or not agree with the characterization of a theory that that acceleration/deceleration can cause axonal damage to the boxer's brain?

A. Again, I am not convinced of the scientific validity of acceleration/deceleration causing diffuse axonal injury or axonal shearing as the cause of the punch drunk fighter.[47]

Q. Now, are you aware of any scientific basis which supports your belief with respect—or your lack of belief, I guess it is, with respect to the theory about acceleration/deceleration causing or not causing brain injury? In other words, can you refer me to some authorities that support your non-belief in that theory?

MR. ONG: Object to the form of the question. [48]

A. From time to time I've looked into the literature on axonal shearing, diffuse axonal injury, done literature searches, and I've never been particularly convinced about the scientific basis of it, so—But I don't have any proof that it doesn't happen either. Okay?[49]

---

[45] Perhaps the expert should have hedged his answer: "Maybe. I'd have to see the research in question."

[46] Now the doctor hedges his concession.

[47] Note that it was the expert who opened up the line of questioning about boxers by his response to a previous question.

[48] Compound question objected to. Notice how few objections there have been. Under the rules and stipulations, grounds for objections at depositions are very narrow.

[49] The expert seems to be getting fatigued. It would be preferable not to have the last "Okay?"

Trying to establish bias

Q. Do you know whether your non-belief of this acceleration/deceleration injury having a scientific basis, whether your belief about that affects your forensic opinion involving brain injury cases?

A. I don't believe that it does.

Q. Why is that?

A. Because I don't believe it does.

Trying to get expert to admit to authorities on subject in question

Q. Do you refer to any authorities in the area of traumatic brain injury—Let me rephrase the question. Do you consider anyone an authority in the area of traumatic brain injury?[50]

A. Whose word must be accepted by everyone? Probably not. I mean I—There are a number of very good neurologists, very good psychiatrists, very good neuropsychiatrists and neuropsychologists, physiatrists that are very competent in head injury.[51]

Q. My question is a little bit different. My question is is there anyone you consider an authority in the field of traumatic brain injury?

A. No one person.

Q. Any group of people that you consider authorities in the field of traumatic brain injury?

A. No.

Q. Is there any particular treatise, publication, book that you consider authoritative in the field of traumatic brain injury?

A. Well, I read journals and respect various texts. I think there may be brain trauma and rehabilitation, but, you know, it's—There are very good refereed publications and excellent books, but none that's the last word. It's an evolving medical area, and so there's no kind of this is the one book that I go to, it's the Bible. It's not that kind of situation.

Q. Just so the record is clear, there's no particular publication, book, journal that you consider an authority on traumatic brain injury; is that right?

A. Correct.

Trying to use the expert's own office against him

Q. You mentioned you had here in your office some publication or publications with respect to brain injury?

A. I know it may have not survived the reorganization of this, but there was a journal that we had for a while on brain injury, trauma and rehabilitation or some such thing.

Q. If I suggest the name of "Journal of Head Trauma Rehabilitation," was that the publication?

---

[50] Another set-up question.

[51] Nice, carefully worded answer.

A. Possibly, yes.

Q. If I suggest to you it's a red covered journal published by Aspen, does that in any way refresh you as to the publication?

A. No.

Trying to set up the witness

Q. Did you ever hear of Dr. Jane Nupp?

A. I'm not recalling that.

Q. Have you ever heard of Dr. Scott Salber?

A. It's ringing a distant bell and I think it has to do with axonal injury, but I may be wrong with that.

Q. Are you familiar with the works of either of those physicians?

A. Not off the top of my head, no.

Q. Are you familiar with the work of Dr. Kevin Osazee?

A. I'm not recalling that. I mean I'm not—I don't—My brain doesn't work by tracking names, so—I may have read material by him, but I'm not recognizing the name as you mention it.

More medical questions

Q. Doctor, are you familiar with symptoms of a seizure?

A. Yes.

Q. And what symptoms are diagnostic of a seizure?

A. Well, there are different kinds of seizures.

Q. What symptoms are diagnostic of a partial complex seizure?

A. There can be varying symptoms, but it often refers to states in which a person suddenly is non-responsive to their environment. They are detached, non-responsive. They're sitting or—sitting there usually, but they are absent. Okay?

Q. Staring off into space, for example?

A. Yes.

Q. When a person sustains a partial complex seizure, are they able to recall the time they spent during that seizure?

A. Usually not.

Q. Are you familiar with the term "postictal stage"?

A. State, usually.[52]

Q. State.

A. Yes.

Q. And what is the postictal state?

A. It's—The ictal refers to seizure, post after the seizure in which a person is coming out of the seizure.

Q. Are individuals able to recall what was going on during the postictal state?

---

[52] The expert corrects counsel's misstatement and thus helps counsel. A better answer might have been "no."

A. Sometimes, but often not.

Q. If a person sustains—

A. It's sort of like—Postictal state is not an instant. It is a period of time and it's like clearing after a seizure, so that's...

Q. Is there a range of time that a postictal state lasts?

A. Yes, there is a range.

Q. What's the range?

A. Usually after—again, you have to—after a grand mal seizure, after a partial complex seizure, after—but it basically lasts minutes to a couple of hours typically. Closer to minutes than hours, generally.

Trying to gain admissions

Q. If a person sustains a partial complex seizure, are they at increased risk for sustaining a seizure in the future?[53]

A. I think it's probably true that if you've had one seizure, you're more likely to—in an untreated individual likely to have seizures in the future. To say it another way, there's nothing protective to having a seizure out of the way or immunizing you against seizures in the future.

Q. Do you know what the percentage of increased risk is for an individual who has sustained one partial complex seizure to sustain another one?

A. I don't know the statistics on that.

Q. With respect to traumatic brain injury, if an individual has sustained a serious traumatic brain injury, are they at increased risk to sustain another one?[54]

A. Only in the sense that if they suffer another head trauma, it is likely to—it is—they are at increased risk of having disproportionate response to the second trauma.

Q. Is that because the effects of a traumatic brain injury are cumulative in that if someone sustains a serious or severe brain injury and sustains a later brain injury, they are at increased risk for having disproportionate symptoms as a result of that second one?

A. I have a problem with the word "cumulative" in the early part of that, but...[55]

Q. Maybe, then, let me rephrase the question for you. I want you to assume that an individual sustains a severe brain injury. Are you familiar with that term, "severe brain injury"?

A. Yes.

Q. And what's your understanding of that term?

A. Well, the traumatic brain injuries are sometimes graded mild, moderate and severe. Severe is usually a very serious injury, usually obvious signs of it on imaging

---

[53] Notice how these questions were set up with previous questions.

[54] Using the expert to build counsel's case.

[55] The expert uses his active listening skills and responds appropriately.

and loss of consciousness and coma lasting hours, days, obvious neurological signs and objective signs of injury, and sequela of it going forward usually.

Q. Well, Doctor, isn't it true that the continuum of traumatic brain injury from mild, moderate to severe is defined by the duration of loss of consciousness or coma?

A. I'm not aware of the definitional aspects of it. Mild, moderate or severe in my mind has to do with clearly the extent of the trauma and the extent of the loss of consciousness but also neurological signs, but also has a concept of their degree of symptoms going forward at least in the short term.

Q. So, Doctor, is there scientific research out there which says that the definition of mild, moderate and severe traumatic brain injury is defined by the duration, if any, of loss of consciousness to coma and not the extent of consequences of that brain injury? You don't agree with that, do you?[56]

MR. ONG: Objection to the form of the question.[57]

A. I'm not sure I understand the question.

Q. Let me try it again. If there is scientific research accepted in the medical community which defines mild, moderate and severe traumatic brain injury as referring to the duration of loss of consciousness, if any, through and including coma, and not the consequences of the brain injury, in other words it just refers to the length and duration, if any, of unconsciousness, you don't agree with that definition?

A. My problem with your question is that coma is a consequence. That's a symptom, if you will. And the duration of coma is related and I agree with that it has to do with the severity of brain injury. But after the person comes out of the coma, do they come out quickly and completely oriented or does it take a while? Those in the short term in the acute phase are relevant to me in my approaching an understanding of what constitutes severe brain injury.

Now, there may be definitions out there that are narrower than that or—but I don't—I don't—I'm not familiar with them and would not—I mean I have my own understanding of it and I think it's pretty much the consensus of people who deal with acute brain injury.

Q. So if the American Academy of Neurology defines mild, moderate and severe brain injury as related to the duration of unconsciousness only and not the consequences, you don't agree with that definition, do you?[58]

A. Well, I'd have to see the definition. If the American Academy of Neurology said mild is no unconsciousness and severe is more than X minutes, I probably don't have a problem with that.

---

[56] Setting up the expert. Note how counsel appears to know more about the topic than this very highly qualified expert. Counsel prepares very hard for depositions. Experts need to prepare as hard or harder.

[57] Another compound question.

[58] Counsel shows his hand.

The expert's notes

Q. One of the things that you provided to me was Exhibit No. 4. And, for the record, could you just tell me what it is?

A. This is a dictation I did after the initial records were sent to me back in the fall of 2002.[59]

Q. In part, did Exhibit No. 4 form the basis of your December 17, 2002 report?

A. Not as a primary document. I mean I looked at the records again. That was a dictation. I sent some records. I reviewed them. I wanted to kind of summarize them in case I went back and I would have a quick reference rather than have to read them all again, so—But it's not a primary source for me because it goes back to the records that I reviewed that are referenced there.

Q. With respect to Mr. Lytle, did you review the records prior to examining him?

A. Yes.

Q. Let me show you a handwritten document dated September 25, 2002. Could you identify that, please?

A. Yes. This is probably some notes I took either after or while I was talking to Attorney Ong on September 25, 2002.

MR. GLENN: Let's mark it as the next exhibit.

(Exhibit 10 marked for identification.)

Q. Now, directing your attention to Exhibit No. 28.

A. Which one is that?

Q. That's what's placed in front of you, your notes of September 25, 2002, telephone conference with defense counsel. In the middle of the page it's written, "In 1998, slow rear-end"—Can you read what it says after that?

A. "To his pickup."

Q. "To his pickup." What's that in reference to? In other words, where did you get that information?

A. It would have been from Mr. Ong.

Q. That's what you were told?

A. Yes.

Digging into the expert's factual assumptions

Q. With respect to this accident that Mr. Lytle was involved in, was it a slow rear-end accident?

A. The accident—The ambulance report said slow to moderate.[60]

Q. What did you understand to be the speed of the defendant's vehicle when it struck Mr. Lytle's vehicle?

---

[59] The expert wisely did not discard or try to hide his notes.

[60] A prepared expert knows the facts, in this case, the ambulance report.

A. I didn't assume any particular number. I mean it was—The folks on the scene called it slow to moderate, so I didn't have any reason to translate that into 37.5 miles an hour or anything. Slow to moderate was sufficient for my purposes.

Q. Well, wouldn't the amount of speed of the defendant's vehicle and the amount of force that was imparted onto his vehicle and onto his body affect your opinion as to whether Mr. Lytle sustained a traumatic brain injury in the automobile accident?

MR. ONG: Objection.

A. In a general sense probably it's relevant.

Q. In what general sense is it relevant?

A. That the faster the car ran—or truck, whatever, ran into him, the greater the impact was going to be on his vehicle and on his body.

Q. And do you know what amount of force is necessary for someone to sustain a traumatic brain injury in an acceleration/deceleration situation?

A. Well, again, we're back into the acceleration/deceleration theories about things. I think I recall some experiments done a while back that one thousand Gs, you know, kind of 1,000 times gravity kind of thing, but that's only one of the variables, and, again, with my caution about—or my concerns about the scientific basis for it.

More admissions

Q. Do you agree that the axons in a person's brain can be torn?

A. Yes.

Q. Do you agree that axons in a person's brain can be sheared?

A. I don't know how that differs from torn in your…

Q. Do you agree that if an axon is torn that—in some cases that axon is permanently torn?

A. Yes.

Q. You would agree, would you not, that an axonal injury can be permanent?

A. Yes.

Q. You would agree, would you not, that an axonal injury that is permanent would not show up on a CAT scan, MRI or x-ray of the skull and brain, correct?

A. An axon, correct.

Questioned on notes

Q. Directing your attention to Exhibit No. 10, in the middle in parentheses is written, "Seems recovered."

A. Yes.

Q. Do you see that? Is that information you obtained in your telephone conversation from Attorney Ong?

A. Yes.

Q. And there, then, is an arrow with "spells" in quotes and "seizure." Were you told by Mr. Ong that Mr. Lytle had spells and a seizure?

A. I presume so.

Q. Well, that's what you wrote there.
A. Yes. Well, I had no other source of information on September 25, so I presume that most of what's there came from him—all of what's there. I mean I had no other source.
Q. So just so the record is clear, Mr. Ong told you that the plaintiff had spells and a seizure?
A. Correct. It says SZ.
Q. Correct. And that's the medical symbol for seizure, is it not?
A. Yes.
Q. And the next line with an arrow—a down arrow, FX, which stands for function at work; is that correct?
A. Yes.
Q. And—
A. It's not the next line. I mean the next line is, "Seizure, meds. and Prozac."
Q. Correct. But down below, you've written would you agree that means decreased function at work, right?
A. Yes.
Q. And that's what Mr. Ong told you about Mr. Lytle?
A. Correct.
MR. ONG: Objection.
Q. What's written below that?
A. "NP evals."
Q. What does that stand for?
A. Neuropsychological evaluations.
Q. Lower right is a trial in quotes of October 18. And then it says pending what?
A. Evals. That was October 22, 2002.
(Exhibit 11 marked for identification.)

Documents received from retaining counsel
Q. The next exhibit, No. 11, is a provider index. Do you know what that's in reference to?
A. This is the index that came with the records.
Q. And those are the records from Mr. Ong's office?
A. Correct.
Q. Thank you. Now, Exhibit No. 7 and Exhibit No. 8, those are copies, are they not, of the scoring sheet from the MMPI?
A. Yes, they are.

Testing administered by the expert
Q. Now, did Mr. Lytle take the MMPI during your examination of him?
A. He took it while he was here. I mean he went into one of the offices and sat down with the booklet and number 2 pencil and worked on his own in private.

Q. What instruction did you give him before having him take the MMPI?

A. That it was a standard psychological test. It was true or false. There were many questions, that he should endeavor to answer them if they were true or mostly true for him, false or mostly false, that he should try to answer all the questions because that helps the validity, that I or anyone in the office could not interpret the question, what does I have a good appetite mean. He would have to do his best to understand the questions. They were very straightforward. There were no trick questions. And that he could work at it at his own pace, take a break if he wanted. His other attorney was here with him at that time. He was free to take a break, go to the men's room, get a soda, what have you. But those were the general instructions.

Q. But his attorney was not present in the room when he was taking the MMPI?

A. Correct.

Q. And you weren't present?

A. Correct. I started him off and I checked on him on a couple of occasions. I believe I did. It's my typical procedure to go in and sort of say, you know, How are you doing, you know, just to check on an individual.

Q. Do you remember actually doing that with Mr. Lytle?

A. I don't—It's over a year ago. I assume I did, but I don't have any memory that I certainly did or that I absolutely did not.

Q. During the time that he took the exam, though, you didn't sit in the room and observe him while he was taking the exam, did you?

A. No.

Opinion

Q. Now, in rendering your opinion, did you form a diagnosis regarding Mr. Lytle?

A. My diagnosis had to do with whether or not I thought to a reasonable medical certainty that he had cognitive or other neuropsychiatric symptoms causally related to the January '98 accident, so that's where I focused my opinion, if you will, rather than an affirmative diagnosis, if you will.

Q. Did you use the MMPI to see whether or not he had cognitive deficits?

A. That's not a test of cognitive deficits.[61]

Q. Did you use the MMPI to see whether or not he had any neurological consequences as a result of his January 1998 motor vehicle accident?

A. Not specifically, no.

Q. So you don't remember, do you, making any observations of Mr. Lytle while he was taking the MMPI, do you?

A. Correct.

Q. You don't know whether or not he followed your instructions, do you?

A. I assume he did because the test has kind of internal validity constructs, and if someone is behaving unusually, the test often can spot that.

---

[61] A less misleading answer than a simple "no."

Q. Was this a valid test? The results of his test, were they valid?

A. I regard them as valid, yes.

Q. Do you in your opinion question the validity of the test results from Mr. Lytle's MMPI?

A. I don't necessarily agree with everything that was in the written opinion that came back. I agreed with much of it, but there were parts I found, you know, some disagreement with.

Q. My question was different. Did you—

A. I'm sorry. I may not have understood your question.

Q. Let me ask you the question this way: Did you consider that the test results on Mr. Lytle's MMPI were valid?

A. In general, yes.[62]

Q. Are you familiar with the psychological testing term validity?

A. Yes.

Q. And so when you answered that you believe his test results were valid, you're using that definition in your mind, correct?

A. Right.

Q. Now, you didn't interpret the scoring of the MMPI that Mr. Lytle took, correct?

A. I had it scored by NCS in Minnesota, but I am very familiar with the test. I've administered hundreds of them, so I'm quite familiar with them, and the graphs and the scoring and, you know, that kind of thing. So I didn't just read what they had to say. I looked at the graphs. I considered it together with the other information that I had about Mr. Lytle.

Q. You didn't interpret the data, did you?

A. I don't know how I can clarify it any more than my last statement. I don't know what you're meaning by interpret.

Q. You didn't write the interpretive report of Mr. Lytle's MMPI, did you?

A. Correct.

Q. As a matter of fact, that was generated by a software program, was it not?[63]

A. Correct.

Q. And the name Dr. Baker is a person who has something to do with the software program, correct?

A. Yes.

Q. And Dr. Baker never examined Mr. Lytle, did he?

A. Correct.

Q. Dr. Baker never met Mr. Lytle, did he?

A. Correct.

---

[62] Hedged response that leaves some wiggle room.

[63] If an expert relies on a computer program, it's a very good idea to use a reliable computer program.

Ethics questions

Q. Doctor, is it ethical for a psychologist to render a diagnosis regarding an individual without seeing him?

A. I can't speak to the ethics of a psychologist. I'm a psychiatrist. I think it would very much depend on the circumstances, however.[64, 65]

Q. Would it bother you as a physician who relies upon a psychologist that the psychologist violated one of the ethical guidelines of the American Psychological Association in rendering a diagnosis without seeing or examining the plaintiff?[66]

MR. ONG: Objection to the form.

A. There are many circumstances in which a psychiatrist or psychologist might not see a person, and, in my opinion, it is reasonable for them to render a diagnosis. And it would very much depend on the circumstance. Particularly in the area of testing, I don't find there's any ethical problem with Dr. Baker or people working with him to have a service such as they do to interpret MMPIs with sophisticated computer programs.

Q. Would it change your opinion if there were an American Psychological Association ethical guideline which says it is unethical for a psychologist involved in a forensic case to give a diagnosis without examining the person?

A. No, I mean for the reasons I mentioned earlier.[67]

Q. Have you ever testified in court and given a diagnosis of a plaintiff without ever examining that plaintiff?

A. I think I have on occasion, usually because there was legal wrangling and I was not allowed to actually examine the person, and so I had to render my opinion solely on the record. However, it is my general principle when I'm going to go to court about a matter and testify to examine the person if they're available and if there's sort of no legal wrangling about why I can't. So I think that's my usual, but I think there have been circumstances in which I have been involved in cases, and I don't remember them off the top of my head, in which the basic issue was discovery deadline had gone by or something had happened that precluded my actually seeing them. Now, in some instances, if it's a suicide case, the individual is dead, you may not. But I mean if the person is available, I think it is good practice and my practice to examine the individual that I'm rendering an opinion about at court.

Q. So with respect to your own practice and experience in forensic psychiatry, the only occasion or occasions where you've testified in court and given a diagnosis and not seen the plaintiff is where there has been legal wrangling and/or discovery

---

[64] Good answer.

[65] The expert could bring up the example of a radiologist or pathologist commonly issuing reports on patients they have never seen.

[66] Counsel has done his homework and researched these standards. This is a plaintiff's counsel who only gets paid if he wins. He is likely to be very well motivated.

[67] The expert is distinguishing diagnosis from test interpretation.

deadlines, in those situations where you were prohibited from seeing the plaintiff; is that right?

MR. ONG: Objection for the use of the term "plaintiff" repeatedly.

A. I'm not recalling any, but there might have been some. The only—To my best recollection, that's generally been the circumstance.

Reliance on work of other experts

Q. In what manner did the MMPI affect your opinion as expressed in your December 17, 2002 report regarding Mr. Lytle?[68]

A. Well, I think it gave a glimpse into his personality. There are parts of the interpretation of it, the interpretation I agreed with. I think on balance I agreed with most of it. And it was—because it's such a standardized test, it's so valid and respected in the field, it's nice if you get some confirmation of things that you have surmised on clinical grounds from talking with the individual as well as the take on the individual that you might get from various medical and other types of records.

Q. What portions of the MMPI did you disagree with?

A. If you have the report there, let me—Do you have a copy?[69]

Q. I'm handing you Exhibit No. 6.

A. Well, we can start with the validity, the issues that you made. He had an elevated L scale, and the interpretation from NCS and the program was that he was claiming to be, quote, unrealistically virtuous. And then the test goes on to—The remark is this weakens the validity, shows an unwillingness to, et cetera, et cetera. I think that Mr. Lytle is kind of more virtuous than the average individual. Okay? I think that this was a valid assessment of Alfred Lytle who is—He's a kind of straight arrow. Okay? So that was my take on him when I was talking with him, and I found it—I disagreed with he's being unrealistically virtuous.[70] I think it's an accurate reflection of his being a kind of fairly moral, straight—And thus, you know, I would disagree with maybe, "This is a conscience distortion to present himself in a favorable light." So that was one kind of thing. I think with regard to the concepts in here of a neurotic pattern of adjustment, clinical diagnosis of conversion disorder, I thought that that was something that I sensed. And there's a particular pattern in here called a conversion triad with elevations of certain skills, so I thought that that was valid and I was in agreement with that. There are other parts of this that in terms of his socialization—I'm just recalling this off the top of my head. I disagreed that he—he may be passive dependent in relationships, but he's not demanding. That was the kind of comment. There was also quite outgoing and sociable. That's not Alfred Lytle, so I disagreed with that. That was not how he came across. That's not

---

[68] Counsel is trying to establish "garbage in, garbage out."

[69] The expert wisely refers to the record in question instead of answering off the top of his head.

[70] His disagreement actually bolsters the plaintiff. Such an honest concession will bolster the expert's credibility.

reflected in personnel and other records. But, on balance, particularly about the probability that he tends to use physical complaints as a way of discharging emotional issues for him, I think that that's probably correct.

Q. Doctor, do you know whether or not any of his neurological deficits or cognitive deficits caused him to have elevated scales on his MMPI?

A. That presumes he has them. Individuals with neurological problems can have particular patterns on the MMPI that need to be corrected for.[71]

Q. Sort of what they refer to as a neuro correction?

A. It's called various things, but it could be called—yes.

Q. So it is possible that some of the elevated scales that are on his MMPI are due to a neurological—

A. Could be.

Q. —condition, right?

A. Could be, yes.

Q. Now, the interpretation that was done by ACS, who's ACS?

A. American Computer Systems.

Q. So the American Computer Systems that did the interpretive report, they developed what is known as a profile, correct?

A. Yes.

Q. And this is—

A. Well, I mean all MMPIs have profiles, and that's not new to them.

Q. Right. And it's not—It is also a hypothesis, is it not?

A. Yes.

Q. It's a hypothesis about Mr. Lytle?

A. Yes.

Q. Now, with respect to the F scale, did he have an elevated F scale?

A. I don't think so. No.

Q. And there was nothing on his MMPI that suggested in any way that Mr. Lytle was—is faking, correct?

A. Correct.[72]

Q. And there's nothing on his MMPI that suggests in any way that Mr. Lytle is a malingerer, correct?

A. Correct.[73]

---

[71] More active listening.

[72] The expert wisely makes a ready concession.

[73] Another ready concession.

Expert's qualifications

Q. Do you consider yourself a trained, qualified test interpreter?

A. I'm very familiar with certain psychological tests. An expert in interpretation? Probably not. But I mean I use them all the time. I can look at the profiles and pretty much understand them fairly well. I mean it's just—I don't—Well...

Q. Dr. Davis, can you answer me yes or no? Do you consider yourself a trained, qualified test interpreter of the MMPI?

A. I consider myself qualified. The issue of, quote, training is another matter.[74]

Q. So, then, the answer to whether you are a trained and qualified test interpreter of the MMPI is that you are not; is that correct?

A. I have not had extensive specific training in interpreting the MMPI. I have extensive experience and have administered hundreds, maybe creeping on one thousand in my professional life of these tests, and I read the reports and I look at the charts and I'm very familiar with them, and so I feel myself that I am qualified to administer and to look at the scales and come to conclusions, including here, to disagree with Dr. Baker and about the L scale and about whether he's outgoing and sociable. So in that sense I am free to agree or disagree with, you know, other people's interpretations, so I think I'm qualified. The issue of training, do I have extensive training in MMPIs? No. I have some training in them, but I have used them for—looked at them, administered them for years.

Q. Has any medical or psychological organization ever qualified you in interpreting the MMPI?

A. No.

Q. You say you administered the test hundreds of times. Doesn't that mean you give some instructions to the person and have them go into a room by themselves, they answer the questions by filling out the scoring sheet, which is Exhibit 7 or 8, and then you send it off to the American Computer Systems, correct?

A. Yes.

Q. And that's the extent of you administering the MMPI, right?

A. Sometimes I will read the questions to people, you know, but—but that's how MMPIs are administered by me and anybody else.

Q. When you say you have this extensive experience in administering the test, the administering of the test involves explaining what it is, letting the person sit alone in a room, perhaps checking in with them, and then when they fill out the scoring sheet sending it off to NCS, and that's the extent of you administering the test, correct?

A. Yes, at least in recent years.

Q. Did Mr. Lytle have elevated scales of 8 or 9?

A. No.

Q. Did he have elevated scores of 1, 2 and 3?

---

[74] This witness is an excellent active listener and these skills serve him well.

A. Yes.
Q. And you would agree, would you not, that the MMPI should not be used to diagnose organicity?
A. Correct. You can sometimes see organicity in it, but the purpose is not to diagnose organicity.

Examination of plaintiff
Q. Now, I want to direct your attention to the medical examination that you did of Mr. Lytle and the report that you generated as a result of that. The first part of the examination of Mr. Lytle lasted how long?
A. My best recollection is there were two interviews each of them lasting an hour and a half or two, and in between he had a break and he did the MMPI.
MR. GLENN: Let's go off the record.
(Discussion off the record.)
BY MR. GLENN:
Q. With respect to the examination, did you do a mental status examination of Mr. Lytle?
A. Not as such.
Q. Did you—
A. Well, what do you mean metal status examination?[75]
Q. Well, are you familiar with the term "mental status examination"?
A. Yes.
Q. What's your understanding of it?
A. It means many different things. Sometimes it means a formal mini mental status examination, full-steam examination which there are certain questions that you ask and diagrams and scored on 30 points and things of that sort. Other times it's referred to as kind of a codification of a number of formal either observations and/or questions that might be asked of an individual.
Q. Did you do some form of mental status examination?
A. Yes.
Q. During that examination did you take notes of what went on during that examination?
A. No—Well, I—Not during the, quote, examination. There's notes of the interview. It should have been in there. Did you see that?[76]
Q. No.
(Discussion off the record.)
(Exhibit 12 marked for identification.)
Q. Doctor, do you have in front of you what I've had marked as Exhibit No. 12?

---

[75] The expert correctly realizes that he may have given a misleading answer and immediately takes steps to clarify his response.
[76] The doctor is transparent and does not play games with his notes.

A. No, but it's coming. Yes, I do now.

Q. Now, is Exhibit No. 12 the extent of the notes that you took during your mental status examination of Mr. Lytle?

A. Yes. It's the extent of the notes I took period.

Q. I want to direct your attention to family psychiatric history. Could you read what's written on that line there?

A. There is—That is not—What's written on that line is not about family psychiatric history. It's the stuff that's drifting up from below.

Q. Okay.

A. All right?

Q. You need not read it, then. I appreciate that.

A. Tallis College, did not graduate, four years, symbolic logic philosophy and computer science. That was his majors. That's what that stuff is.

Q. On the second page of this exhibit there's a line down at the bottom to A-1 Mutual. And could you read what's under there?

A. "More predictable, larger."

Q. What is that in reference to?

A. His previous job was with Team Management or Marketing Associates, 8 to 45 employees. He was there three, three and a half years. Too many hours, days, too little money, too hectic. A-1 Mutual, quiet, large, an insurance company.

Q. You make some notes in the upper right-hand corner of page 2, "very," and I believe it says "catatonic"—

A. Yes.

Q. —in parentheses? What's that in reference to?

A. It has to do with basically facial—I don't mean literally catatonic. That's why I put it in the brackets. He is a very—His face is very inexpressive. It's like a mask like face. He has very little body movement. He's kind of rigid. If you watch him walk, he doesn't have much of an arm swing.

So he's kind of—He sat extensive—hardly moved at all. That's an overstatement. But he—Compared to me who's waving his hands in the air all the time, he didn't move much, was rigid, and his facial expression was very masklike.

Q. What's the reference "EPS like"?

A. Extrapyramidal syndrome. Okay? Parkinsonian like.

Q. Did he in fact have those?

A. This is my little code to me about capturing what he was like to sit with in terms of extrapyramidal symptoms. EPS refers to a syndrome you get when you're on powerful antipsychotic medications like Haldol and things of that sort, so it was EPS like. That's what I was describing. It's like a person who's got Parkinsonian like symptoms.

Q. Well, did you see moving his extremities similar to that?

A. No.

Q. What's the reference to abulia?
A. Abulia.
Q. What is that?
A. It has to do with the flatness of his affect. He's not very expressive, and it's a term used to describe that kind of flatness in people with frontal lobe problems.
Q. Why did you say that was secondary to his motor vehicle accident—Excuse me— second to old motor vehicle accident?
A. That it was my opinion that it was likely secondary to the old motor vehicle accident.
Q. What was that opinion based on?
A. My sitting with him. By that point I had read the records. I thought it was related to that.
Q. Did he have more flat affect after the second motor vehicle accident as compared to his affect before it?
A. I could not find a convincing connection close in time to the second motor vehicle accident or the change in his affect.
Q. Were you aware of any evidence indicating that his affect after the second accident was either flatter than it was before or he was more withdrawn than prior to the accident, the second one?
A. I think that the evidence that I'm recalling has to do with that well after the second accident, okay, and conceivably after—and probably after the '99 issue of a question of seizure and antidepressant medication and things of that sort. But I could not find—or I'm not recalling any convincing evidence that in the time immediately after the, you know, weeks, months, year after the second accident that that was the case.

Opinions
Q. Do you have an opinion with a reasonable degree of medical certainty as to whether or not in August of 1999 Mr. Lytle sustained a seizure?
A. It's unclear whether he did. He might have.
Q. Well—
A. I think it's unlikely, frankly, but he was treated empirically as if he had a seizure.
Q. Do you have an opinion with a reasonable degree of medical certainty as to whether or not in August of 1999 he likely had a seizure?
A. I think it's unlikely that he did, but it's possible.
Q. And that's your opinion?
A. Yes.
Q. Do you have an opinion with a reasonable degree of medical certainty of whether or not Mr. Lytle sustained a concussion, that is likely sustained a concussion in his January 1998 motor vehicle accident?
A. Well, I think it's possible, but the evidence is better that he didn't, as I think I expressed in my report.

Looking for more admissions

Q. Is it of any medical significance that according to your report Mr. Lytle denied any loss of consciousness?

A. Yes.

Q. Why is that of medical significance to you?

A. Well, it is one of the measures of the likelihood of concussion and the severity of any head trauma.

Q. Whether or not an individual denies or admits to having had loss of consciousness affects the diagnosis as to whether or not they had a concussion; is that your opinion?

A. In general, yes.

Q. Doctor, would a person who's unconscious know that they're unconscious?

A. While they're unconscious?

Q. Well, first while they're unconscious.

A. No.

Q. After they're unconscious?

A. They may.

Q. They may not, right?

A. Correct.

Q. Why is that?

A. Well, they may not—It requires the function of memory to go back and put together a time line, if you will, of before and after a head injury, so an individual may not remember certain kinds of things around the time, particularly after an injury, but may have been conscious but may say, I woke up in the ambulance on the way to the hospital when in point in fact at the scene they were walking around and talking with people and things of that sort. So the memory can confound the question of whether a person knows if they were unconscious and for how long.

Q. So a person may not be aware because of memory problems as to whether or not they lost consciousness, correct?

A. Correct.

Q. If there are events immediately after an accident which the person can't recall, that would be evidence, would it not, of a possible loss of consciousness?

A. Possible, yes.[77]

Factual assumptions

Q. In your report you write at page 2, "At the scene he was alert, oriented and able to give comprehensive personal information and the details of the accident." Where did you get that information?

A. The ambulance report.

Q. And the ambulance—

---

[77] Another wisely hedged response.

A. And his own account to me when he was here, but it was in the accident report, the ambulance, EMT…

Q. So two general sources you used for that statement, the EMT ambulance report and what he, Mr. Lytle, told you in 2002?

A. And the emergency room records and the fact that he gives an account to Dr. Woodbridge and Dr. Hume and to the orthopedic doctor and things of that sort, so…

Q. And you don't know what sources of information Mr. Lytle used when he gave you his recollection of what happened at the accident, do you?

A. It seemed to be coming from his memory.

Q. Yes. But you don't know whether that's a memory of a conversation he had with someone else about the accident or it's his memory of the events of the accident, do you?

A. I think—He gave me a great deal of detail of things that were not in the records. Okay? So—That he was going to visit this couple and that he, you know—Just various pieces of information that I can conceive of can only come from his memory. I was going to visit this couple in—

I think he was living in Ayerie and was going to Newport or southern Maine and it was late, but it was not unusual for him to visit at that hour. And, no, he had not been drinking. So he gave me a lot of details that led me to conclude that they were coming from his own primary memory rather than his reading his medical records or being told by people that this is what you did or this is what happened.[78]

Q. When he was recalling for you events around the accident, did you ask him whether or not that's his memory of the event or he was told that by someone or he read medical records or he read depositions or he had conversations with other people? Did you ask him that?

A. No. My interview with him was an associative interview. It's not like a deposition did you ask so and so. It's not an interrogation. I encourage people to tell me their situation and circumstances in a narrative style, so I don't have a list of kind of interrogations, and so I wouldn't have asked a question of that sort or in that way.

Q. So, for the record, you didn't ask him—when he described his recollection in 2002 of the accident, you didn't ask him where that memory was coming from, did you?

A. No.

Q. You state in part that his intellectual functions on a clinical estimate appear to be in the well above average range. Did you administer any tests during your interview of him?

A. No.

---

[78] The doctor once again demonstrates an impressive knowledge of the facts. This is a prepared, impressive expert.

Q. And what is the basis of your opinion that his intellectual functions on a clinical estimate appear to be in the well above average range?

A. Psychiatrists are used to doing estimates of individuals' intellectual function based on concept formation, speed of calculation and perception, vocabulary, degree of information, degree of sophistication and things of that sort, so it's a common kind of—common for a psychiatrist to do a rough estimation of an individual's intelligence on the basis of having extended conversation or interview with them.[79]

Q. So you had a conversation or extended interview with him and you got a feel, did you not, for his intellectual functioning?

A. Correct.

Q. And that's all it is, right?

A. Correct.

Q. Now, you also said that he had a good capacity for attention. Did you give him any tests for attention?

A. No, I did not.

Q. Did you give him any tests for concentration?

A. No, I did not.

Q. Did you give him any tests for abstract reasoning?

A. No. I don't believe I did. No, I did not. I can't recall that I did. I think it's unlikely that I did.

Q. What testing did you give him for his memory?

A. I didn't give him any tests for memory.

Q. What tests did you give him for his fund of information?[80]

A. There's no—None.

Q. And so that when you say he had good capacity for attention, concentration, abstract reasoning, memory and fund of information, that's based on your conversation with him and a feel that you got, right?

A. Yes.

Q. Now, you also say that his insight and judgment appeared excellent. Did you give him any test to measure his insight and judgment?

A. No.

Q. Again, your opinion regarding his insight and judgment appearing excellent was based on your conversation with him and a feel that you got, right?

A. Yes.

Q. What did Mr. Lytle tell you with respect to the detailed circumstances of the accident and the moments immediately after?

A. I don't recall all the details, you know, a year plus later. It was where he was going, who he was visiting; that he was driving his pickup truck; he was hit from the

---

[79] A well-reasoned, powerful response.
[80] Trying to establish that the expert's examination was cursory.

rear; his head was turned, I believe, to the left so that he had a laceration on his left ear; that he was wearing a seat belt; that he got out. I think the fire department was very nearby or something to that effect, so they were quickly on the scene. Those kinds of things.

Q. Well, when you say those kinds of things, your report says that he gave you detailed circumstances of the accident.[81] And this is during this interview. And leaving aside what you may have learned from other sources, what other details did Mr. Lytle give you during your conversation with him back in 2002?

A. Well, things like he was stopped at a light and he was rear-ended, and I believe the other driver might have been intoxicated or charged with that. I'm not recalling the details of it. It was, I was stopped at a light, this was my pickup truck, it had a— you know, and I was rear-ended and things of that sort, and my ear was cut and I had a headache and my neck and shoulders were sore and things of that sort.

Q. Did you make any notes at the time he was talking to you about the details, the detailed circumstances of the accident?

A. No.

Delay in writing report?

Q. By the way, how long after your interview with him did you write or dictate your report?

A. I usually do it fairly quickly, at least for the portion that's going to be the interview. The history piece I can always kind of go back and put together from the records and from the—I likely—I saw him when, probably just before Thanksgiving? I probably did it right away, and it went through a couple of drafts[82] and proofs in the next couple of weeks.

Q. When—

A. But I have no record of when I did it specifically, but it's my custom to do it right after seeing someone while the interview is fresh in my mind.

Q. Well, would it be fair to—You did it sometime by December 17, 2002?

A. Certainly then, because the report went out by then.

Q. Some almost four weeks later?[83]

A. Yes—Well, whatever. The 22nd—The 21st to the 17th, sure.

Q. Now, you also write in part, "His present description of his postaccident symptoms were more numerous than recorded by the doctors treating him close in time to the accident." What symptoms did he report that were more numerous?

A. I think it had to do with balance, particularly the issue of bicycling and some fears associated with that. He described being a pretty active cyclist. But I'm not at this point remembering sort of specific things except to—I likely looked at the records;

---

[81] Notice how well counsel knows the expert's report.
[82] Volunteered information.
[83] Counsel is trying to establish a timeline to use against the expert.

that at this point now four plus years, almost five years out that he was having—mentioning more symptoms about the period.

And he thought he was out of work for a longer period than he was. He thought he was out for two, maybe three months, but in fact he had gone back by the 22nd of February although probably part time and going for medical appointments.

Q. Mr. Lytle's present description of his postaccident symptoms that were more numerous than recorded by the doctors, the ones you recall is that he no longer bicycled; is that right?

A. Well, he—I don't know that he said he didn't bicycle, but he felt he was unsure. And there was a physical component to it as well as kind of a fear and balance component to it.

Other notes

Q. Now, Doctor, you've made it clear that with the exception of Exhibit No. 12 you didn't take any other notes of your conversation with Mr. Lytle that day, correct?

A. Correct.

No recording of examination

Q. And you didn't allow a recording of that conversation of Mr. Lytle, did you?

A. Was one—I'm not recalling whether it was raised. I generally feel that recording interferes with the psychiatric exam, and I always object to it.

Q. You didn't ask Mr. Lytle's attorney to sit in while you did the interviewing conversation of Mr. Lytle, correct?

A. No, I did not.

Q. So when you wrote your report, whenever you wrote the report and made statements about his intellectual functioning, his attention concentration, his recording of the detailed circumstances of the accident, there's no recording of what Mr. Lytle told you, right?

A. Correct.

Q. There's no other witness to what went on in that room, correct?

A. Correct.[84]

Q. And you made no other notes in particular about what he reported the symptoms to be, right?

A. Mm-hmm.[85]

Q. Yes?

A. Correct.

Q. And you made no notes of the basis of your opinion about his intellectual capacity, his attention concentration, his abstract reasoning, his memory, his fund of

---

[84] The expert does not get angry at the implication of this question, but wisely just answers the question.
[85] Avoid non-verbal responses like this.

information, all of which you found to be sometimes excellent and well above average, right?

A. Yes.

More opinions

Q. Do you have an opinion with a reasonable degree of medical certainty as to whether or not this accident likely affected Mr. Lytle's vocational capacity?

A. Yes.

Q. What's your opinion?

A. That it did not affect his vocational capacity.

Q. What's the basis of your opinion?

A. I don't think that he has any cognitive problems causally connected to the accident, hence no cognitive problems that would interfere with his being able to function at work.[86]

Q. In the records that you reviewed, was there any evidence of Mr. Lytle having cognitive deficits after this accident?

A. He had neuropsychological testing with Dr. Seidman that was done after the accident, and, in my opinion, they show some cognitive problems which in my opinion are related to the first accident, but the testing was after the second. Okay? But in terms of cognitive problems other than that, and his own self report and family members' reports, I'm not aware of it—I'm not thinking of any at this moment.

Contrary opinion of treating doctor

Q. Did Dr. Seidman write the opinion that some of the cognitive deficits that he found on neurological testing were likely caused in the January 1998 motor vehicle accident?

A. I think that that's Dr. Seidman's opinion.

Q. Do you agree with that opinion?

A. No, I do not.

Q. What's the basis of your disagreement with Dr. Seidman's opinion that Mr. Lytle likely sustained cognitive deficits as a result of the January 1998 motor vehicle accident?

A. Well, it's contained in my report. Basically, in my opinion, the nature of the trauma was unlikely to produce brain injury of a temporary or permanent sort; that the—there's no objective evidence of brain injury in terms of the imaging studies and EEGs that have been done; that his work performance does not reveal an association with that accident; that all the neurological examinations that have been done have been negative, and his—medical records don't support it.[87]

---

[86] The expert is prepared to answer this key question.

[87] The expert correctly disagrees with the opinion of another professional by stating objective reasons why he disagrees as opposed to trashing the other professional.

Q. Doctor, what is it about the nature of the trauma that you say in your opinion did not likely cause Mr. Lytle to have a traumatic brain injury?

A. It was not significant enough, it was not powerful enough, it was not serious enough to likely lead to permanent brain injury.[88]

Q. When you say it was not powerful enough, serious enough, what do you mean?

A. That the nature of the injury to his head was not likely serious enough to cause permanent brain damage.

Q. Are you saying that because he sustained only a laceration to his ear?

A. In part, yes.

Q. What else?

A. No loss of consciousness. His excellent memory before and after the accident, at the time and subsequently.

Would new fact change opinion?

Q. Now, Doctor, if there was evidence that he was struck, that is his vehicle was struck by a motor vehicle going approximately 25 miles an hour causing Mr. Lytle's head to snap and strike and break the rear window in his truck, would that affect your opinion as to whether or not he had traumatic brain injury?

A. I assumed all of that. I am aware of all that, and I still don't feel that he has traumatic brain injury.[89]

Q. Now, one of the things you said in forming your opinion that he doesn't have a traumatic brain injury is that he didn't have a loss of consciousness, correct?

A. Correct.

Q. You would agree, would you not, however, that loss of consciousness is not necessary for there to be a traumatic brain injury?

A. Correct.

Q. Now, you also said in part your opinion is he didn't have a traumatic brain injury because there's no objective evidence. You're referring to diagnostic studies such as x-ray, CAT scan and MRI?

A. And EEG, yes.

Q. And EEG. And even those tests being normal or negative, they don't rule out that he had a traumatic brain injury, do they?

A. Not absolutely.

Q. I'm sorry?

A. Not absolutely.

Q. And you indicated that Mr. Lytle had a—had neurological examinations which were negative or normal. And that in part forms your opinion that he didn't have a traumatic brain injury, correct?

A. Correct.

---

[88] An explanation that a lay jury would likely understand.

[89] "New" fact that is not new.

Q. Now, having a normal neurological examination, that does not rule out that Mr. Lytle had a traumatic brain injury, does it?
A. Not absolutely, correct.[90]

More factual basis questions
Q. Doctor, did Mr. Lytle's job requirements change after this accident as compared to his job requirements before the accident?
A. I believe they did.
Q. Do you know whether or not that was a demotion?
A. At one point he was taken from a more complicated type of computer activity and put on a less complicated one, but that was like several years after the accident.
Q. How many years after?
A. I believe it was three.
Q. And the change in his job requirements was to a position that was less cognitively demanding; isn't that so?
A. I think in a general sense, yes, that's...
Q. And his job performances after the accident when he had his job requirements changed, those job performances reflected that job change, didn't they?
A. I'm not sure I understand the question.[91]
Q. You compared, did you not, the 1997 job performance evaluations with the 1998?
A. Yes.
Q. And in part you said that the performance evaluations before the accident were in some areas not as good as the evaluations after the accident; is that fair?
A. Yes, it's a fair summary.
Q. And wasn't that due to the fact that Mr. Lytle had his job requirements changed, that they were less cognitively demanding and he was able to perform on a less demanding job?
MR. ONG: Objection. Factually incorrect. Your factual assumptions for the question are incorrect.
A. That's not my understanding.[92]

Qualifications
Q. Do you have any training, experience or education in the field of vocational rehabilitation?
A. Not—It's not a major interest of mine. I am concerned about it in various kinds of ways and circumstances, but it's not something that I'm substantially—I'm not— As a field, no. I'll just cut to the chase here.
Q. You're not an expert on vocational assessment, are you?
A. Correct.

---

[90] Note the qualified response.
[91] The proper answer to an unintelligible question.
[92] The expert may have been listening to the objection before he responded.

Q. And you're not going to testify or render an opinion about Mr. Lytle's vocational capacity, are you?

A. Only to the degree that in my opinion he has no change in cognitive capacity as a result of the accident, and to the degree that that bears on his work function, I would comment on it, but other than that area of neuropsychiatry, if you will, and brain injury, cognitive, no.[93]

Report

Q. Part of your report says "as yet," meaning as of December 17, 2002?

A. Where are we?[94]

Q. "No expert opinion has been provided by Mr. Lytle concerning psychiatric and neuropsychiatric damages causally related to the motor vehicle accident of January 17, 1998." But subsequent to writing this report, there has been expert opinion about that, correct?

A. You're referring to Dr. Seidman?

Q. Well, let me ask you, has there been psychiatric and neuropsychiatric expert opinion that there are psychiatric and neuropsychiatric damages causally related to his accident?

A. I have subsequently been provided with the comments of Dr. Stuart Seidman and Dr. Hume in various legal documents. They are both treaters, but if they are considered—And this is a legal technical thing that you'll have to tell me about. If they are the experts, then I have gotten their information, their views, yes.

Q. Did you have their opinions, their views, their records prior to writing the December 17, 2002 report?

A. I had their treatment records, yes.

Q. You say in your report, "From the general medical records provided, it appears that the claim might well be postconcussive syndrome, traumatic brain injury with transient or permanent cognitive damages." What medical records are you referring to?

A. Dr. Woodbridge, Dr. Hume, Dr.—it begins with L, the orthopedic doctor that he saw. He saw an orthopedist.

Q. At Shelton?

A. Maybe. Dr. Lason? Shelton Orthopedic. Yes, Dr. Lason. And then Dr. Seidman, Dr. Rorke, Rorke, R-O-R-K-E. Those were the records basically that I was referring to.

---

[93] Another carefully worded response that gives the expert some room to later comment on the subject in question.

[94] The expert correctly refuses to answer the question until he knows specifically where counsel is referring to and has a chance to review the language in question and the context in which it was written.

Q. And you disagree with their medical diagnosis, correct?

A. To the degree that he claims he has traumatic brain injury with cognitive problems, yes.

Opinions

Q. Do you agree that he had a concussion?

A. I've said in my record—my report I think it's more likely than not that he didn't, but he might have.

Q. Do you have an opinion that he likely had postconcussive syndrome?

A. More likely than not he did not have it, but he could have.

Throwing more facts at the expert

Q. If Mr. Lytle was given a head injury warning sheet by the emergency room at Valley Hospital, would that affect your opinion as to whether or not he had sustained a brain injury?

A. It would be—It was one of the things I considered because he was—it was not circled in the postdischarge kind of thing, and that coupled with the fact that they didn't make the diagnosis were things that I read. If they had given him a head injury sheet, and, frankly, in the current medical legal climate I would expect that you give a person all the sheets with any, any, any question to protect themselves, they might have given a head injury sheet even if I would not think it was warranted on the medical records.[95]

Q. Would it affect your opinion if they had given him a head injury warning sheet?

A. I don't think so.

Q. Why not?

A. How much time?

More questions on the expert's report

Q. Let me withdraw the question. At the end of your page on Dr. Stuart Seidman, a neuropsychologist, you go on to say, "He does not attribute those mild weaknesses to the January 1998 accident and, in my view, cannot." Would it affect your opinion if Dr. Seidman had attributed some of the cognitive deficits to the January 1998 accident?

A. It wouldn't affect my opinion, and it is my understanding that he clearly has subsequent to my writing of the report.[96]

Q. When you say in your report, "There are no significant pattern deteriorations shown in his work records," that is Mr. Lytle's work records, did you find any deterioration in his work performance evaluations after his 1999—1998 motor vehicle accident?

A. I didn't pick up that pattern, no.

---

[95] A plausible explanation.

[96] The expert is not intimidated by the fact that other professionals may have a different opinion.

Q. At the end of your report you say, "In summary, though it is arguable that Mr. Lytle suffered a concussion in the January 1998 accident," and you go on to say more. What do you mean it's arguable that he had a concussion?
A. Well, that I think people could look at these records and in good faith say, yes, there was a concussion, and, no, there was not. I believe that the evidence is more likely that he did not, but it would not be irresponsible or without any merit to say, no, given this, that he might well have had a concussion.[97]
MR. GLENN: Thank you.

(Whereupon the deposition was concluded at 6:35 P.M.)

---

[97] Counsel ends with this admission. The expert has made a significant concession, but, more importantly, he has demonstrated intellectual honesty. This will boost the expert's credibility.

CERTIFICATE

I, GREG S. DAVIS, M.D., do hereby certify that I have read the foregoing transcript of my testimony, and further certify that said transcript is a true and accurate record of said testimony with the exception of the following corrections listed below:

Signed under the pains and penalties of perjury
this _____ day of _____, 2003.

_____
GREG S. DAVIS, M.D.

COMMONWEALTH OF MASSACHUSETTS
SUFFOLK, SS.
I, Robert A. Tiressta, Registered Professional Reporter and Notary Public in and for the Commonwealth of Massachusetts, do hereby certify that GREG S. DAVIS, M.D., the witness whose deposition is hereinbefore set forth, was duly sworn by me and that such deposition is a true record of the testimony given by the witness. I further certify that I am neither related to nor employed by any of the parties in or counsel to this action, nor am I financially interested in the outcome of this action. In witness whereof, I have hereunto set my hand and seal this 24th day of January, 2004.

Notary Public
My commission expires
March 18, 2005

12.3 Sample Annotated Technical Expert Transcript
This case involved an auto accident on a highway that was being repaved. The expert witness was an engineer who was retained by the attorney for the engineers for the project. The expert was very experienced and the deposition was conducted in a professional, polite manner. The case was interesting in that the accident scene was unavailable to the expert because the construction had been completed shortly after the accident. Of crucial importance to the case was the condition of the road at the time of the accident and how the expert could piece this together based (out of necessity) on second-hand information.

   This expert demonstrated a great command of his field and was prepared to answer the key questions in the case. Importantly, the expert prudently stayed within his field and resisted the temptation to opine on accident reconstruction issues. The expert also readily made required concessions, did not try to hide information, was not combative, and immediately corrected the record when he realized that he had made a mistake. Finally, the expert employed excellent active listening skills and used these to prevent counsel from mischaracterizing his testimony.

There were several areas where the expert could have done a better job. Numerous times the expert responded to statements by counsel that were not questions. Experts are better served by waiting for a question and just answering the question. The expert also often responded to questions by volunteering far more information than was asked for in the question. This is almost always a mistake. The expert used slang, which does not reflect well on a witness. The same is true of the expert's gratuitous characterization of himself as being "lazy." Finally, the expert's command of some of the less central facts of the case were not as strong as they could have been.

Tom Pederson, PE/PSM having been produced and first duly sworn as a witness on behalf of Plaintiffs, testified as follows:

DIRECT EXAMINATION
BY MR. SCHWARTZ:

Complete file?
Q. Mr. Pederson, before we get started with the deposition itself, I had asked you to bring a complete copy of your file and some other documents. Do you have that?
A. Yes, I do, sir. Let me first indicate this is—This is a list of everything I've reviewed. And I purposely did not carry all the depositions back with me, but that's everything that I've reviewed. The depositions are listed on the first page. And these that have been—by ink, I looked at today. The paving crew people. And then the material that I've reviewed is on the second page.

Past testimony
Q. All right. And I'd asked you to bring, as I said, a complete copy of your file. What else do you have there?
A. I have a list of—I had it faxed this morning—cases that I've been retained in since—the last four years. The bold print who I was hired by, whether it be plaintiff or defendant, and the asterisk indicates whether a deposition was given or trial testimony.
Q. Asterisk means what, now?
A. Asterisk means there was either a deposition given or trial testimony.
Q. All right. What percentage of your work is done for plaintiffs and what percentage for defendants?
A. I've been saying 50/50. This one works out at about 40 percent plaintiff and 60 percent defendant.[98]

---

[98] The expert is neither defensive nor evasive.

Q. How long have you been giving opinions as a forensic expert?
A. I began—the first case I probably ever did was in 1974.

Percentage of income

Q. What percentage of your income is from forensic testimony?
A. At the present time probably less than 50 percent.
Q. Now, when you say less than 50 percent, that narrows it down some. Can you narrow it down a little bit more than that? Are you talking about close to 50 percent, or—
A. No. it's probably closer to, at the present time, 30 percent.[99]

Questions about information in CV

Q. And if you could, tell me a little bit more about some of the things on your CV. I see that you initially started out working with the state road department with DOT as an engineer?
A. Yes.[100] 1960, when I graduated from the University of Arizona, I went to work for then the Arizona State Road Department. I actually worked in Tucson. The first two years was in the training program. When I completed that I was assigned to Scottsdale construction, at which time I took over the construction of I-75 through Maricopa and Gila County.
Q. I don't know much about road construction at all,[101] so as you go along through your different experiences, tell me in a little bit more detail what your job duties were.
A. Fine. Beginning in 1963, when I—after having completed the—'62, when I completed the training program, I went to work as the project resident engineer for the construction of I-75. In those days, the Department of Transportation—well, the State Road Department basically did all the inspection in-house. With the exception of some major expressway jobs, everything was done by state employees.

The governor just, of course, constructed—Jonathan Rice had just finished constructing the Arizona Turnpike from Yuma to Flagstaff, and they were starving because of no revenue, so I-75 became a top priority and trying to get it extended all the way to Flagstaff.

So about the same time, even though the Gila County line was a divide between the second district, which was in Tucson, and the fifth district in Prescott, they had moved all the people from the fifth district to Kingman, because Kingman was very hot in those days. So I took over and basically had 50 miles. I had ten projects on Interstate 75.

---

[99] Again, the expert is not evasive and has nothing to hide. He answers the question and forces counsel to move on.
[100] The expert probably should have stopped here and not volunteered the additional information. If counsel wants additional details beyond the specific question asked, he can ask.
[101] The attorney here is trying to "play dumb" and get the expert to open up.

My job was to see that the contractors built the job in sequential compliance with the plans and specifications. I had probably about two or three inspectors on each job. Some were 24-hour-a-day jobs, seven-day-a-week jobs. So that was basically constructing I-75. So I acted as both the project and the resident engineer on those jobs.

So we did all the testing; we did all the monitoring of construction activities; we prepared the daily reports, weekly reports, the monthly pay estimates; and when the jobs were completed, we did what was referred to as final estimate for final payment.[102]

Q. Then after that I see that in '64/'65 you had a little different job.[103]

A. Yeah.[104] In 1964 when I completed that work, I was promoted to the district office in Tucson, and I acted as the assistant to the district—assistant to the district engineer of construction. Tucson in those days had 16 counties, and most of the work was actually here in Wickenberg. At that time we thought the world's biggest bond program was under way, which was $25 million.

So I spent a great deal of my time here basically troubleshooting. When they had a problem with a contractor or there was a claim or a lawsuit or some problem with construction details, my job from Tucson was to go meet with the resident project engineer and the contractor, try and resolve the issues and handle problems.

Q. Okay.[105]

A. A year later I got promoted to Chandler as first the assistant, and then later the state construction engineer. My role was the same—almost the same, except now it was statewide. It basically was to travel around whenever there was a major problem or minor problem. If there was a conflict on reading specifications or a conflict between the contractor and state road department employees, my job was to intercede and resolve those issues.

We were also at that time building I-10 from Chandler to Nogales, so a great deal of my time was spent in the Sonoran Desert.

In 1968, I was promoted then to the district engineer, which is—now they refer to them as district secretaries for the Department of Transportation. And that was District 4, which was in those days the nine southern counties. The district office in Tucson—I mean, in Casa Grande—handled Mohave County, Coconino County,

---

[102] The expert might have been better served by providing a more concise answer to counsel's broad and vague question. If counsel wants specific information, he can ask.

[103] This is not a question.

[104] "Yes," would be a more professional sounding response. Also, the expert should have stopped his answer and forced counsel to ask follow-up questions instead of just volunteering more and more information that might be used against him.

[105] This is not a question. A sophisticated expert would not respond to an "Okay." He would wait for a question to be propounded and then answer the specific question asked.

Navajo County, Apache, Yavapai, La Paz, Pinal, Graham County and Cochise County.

Q. And, briefly, what were the duties of the district engineer?

A. I had roughly—I had 1700 employees at that time. Our job was to see that the roads got designed, all the necessary approvals were obtained, that the right-of-way was acquired. And then the job was let to contract. We would administer the construction project, and then I had maintenance people.

In 1970 it changed and became the Arizona Department of Transportation. At the time the turnpike also then came under my jurisdiction as well as aviation-type expenditures. So my job was the CEO, if you will, to adhere to making sure jobs were designed, constructed and then maintained.

Q. And then in '73 you left the state?

A. I had a choice of either going back to Chandler or staying in south Arizona. And at that point I elected to leave the Department of Transportation and I went to work for a private land development company, Adobe Land Development.

At that time my role in that company was to—I did all the engineering. They were large developers. They had anywhere from 5,000 to 10,000 acre parcels, one in Wickenberg, one there in Cottonwood, one in Pima County, and one outside of the Payson area.

My role was to see that—I obtained all the necessary approvals through the governmental entities, all the zoning approvals, all the site plan approvals, did all the engineering. We had our own companies do the road construction, water and sewer, highway-type design. We would then sell home sites or parcels of land to builders.

Except with the exception of the Payson area. The company did not do any construction itself for the buildings. We either sold large commercial properties and/or parcels that could be subdivided. But my role was to see that the water, sewer, grading, paving, drainage and the road system was in.[106]

Q. And then in '77—[107]

A. In 1978, I left Adobe Land. The original owners had died. There was a change in ownership. I elected to leave and go back into engineering.

I went to work for a company called Cave Creek Engineering, a small little company in Casa Grande that was doing some DOT work, some county work.

I later left that company after we closed it and actually went with Pilsch & Ross doing basically civil engineering. The company did surveying, did highway design, bridge design. I did testing. I did environmental studies. I did construction supervision, CEI-type work.

Q. By "construction supervision", you're talking about on roads?

---

[106] A better answer to the specific question propounded would have been a simple "yes."

[107] The expert interrupts the question. This is a mistake because the expert may end up answering a question he was never going to be asked and thus volunteer information. An expert interrupting the question at deposition is a sign of an expert who is overeager to give information.

A. Roads, as well as land-development-type projects. Shopping centers, land-development-type—housing projects and all that. But the bulk of the work was governmental.

And during that time I continued to do—I actually started the forensic work when I left the Department of Transportation in 1973. And all these firms I continued to do as part of the company basically what I call forensic engineering.[108]

Q. And you said now that perhaps 30 percent of your business was forensic engineering. What has the percentage been, generally speaking, throughout the years? I'm sure it's probably varied.[109]

A. Probably a lot less than that, because it was a small portion of the work. I've enjoyed doing it. It was just one part. The company basically, from a building standpoint, did a lot more work in other areas, which—and I've always been involved in traffic engineering, supervision of construction, as well as designing highways.

Q. And so you left—you were with that company for about 18 years?

A. Yes.[110] I—my oldest son was the controller in that company. He died from cancer.[111] And at that time I decided it was time to retire. My other partner had no interest in sharing the ownership, so we were creating a lot of new engineering companies with a lot of good young engineers, so I sold my stock two and a half years ago to five of the key employees and retired from the firm.

Q. So you were one of the owners of the company?

A. Yes,[112] in 1983 when I joined the firm—1981—I was—basically there were three partners. We bought out the original founding partner several years ago, and then it was just two of us. We each owned 45 percent and—actually 49 percent, and we had minority owners at 2 percent, and he didn't want to expand that.

Q. So you retired in 2001—

A. Yes, sir.

Q. From that company?

A. Yes, sir.

Q. And are you doing anything now other than forensic?

---

[108] The second part of his answer volunteers information. The witness was asked about "construction supervision," not when he started forensic work.

[109] Note how the expert's volunteering of the forensic information leads to a new question. This question may not have ever been asked had the expert not volunteered information and answered beyond what was asked for in the question propounded to him.

[110] This would have been a good place to stop his answer.

[111] Here's a good example of where volunteering can come back to haunt an expert. Let's say the expert had not volunteered this information about his son and was asked at trial something to the effect that he has been retired for a number of years and is out of the game. The expert could have stopped counsel cold at trial by truthfully describing the tragic circumstances that led to his decision to retire early. Since the witness has volunteered this information at the deposition, competent counsel will not give the witness a chance to do this at trial.

[112] Every word after the "yes" is an unnecessary volunteering of information.

A. Yes.[113] I'm still acting—well, I'm still working actually helping that company on some projects that I had under way. I'm still acting as traffic engineer for a couple of major cities. I also do a lot of permitting work. I get involved in trying to resolve issues for people trying to get permits from the Department of Transportation, both land developers as well as governmental entities.

Forensic income questions

Q. I don't mean to pry, but I just want to be sure I'm clear.[114] When you said forensics was about 30 percent of your income, did that include any retirement income you might have?

A. No. Well, there is retirement income. That's why—it changes this year. After this year, forensics will probably be about 60 percent of my income.

Q. So the 30 percent of your income that forensics provides now, is 100 percent of that income including retirement?

A. No. No. What I'm trying to say, at the current time—as part of a buy-out, they kept me on the payroll for three years, and it ends this year. So when someone asks about income, the income is 30 percent from the forensic work.

Q. Right. Roughly.

A. Roughly. Once the—at the end of this year, when the retirement pay is completed, then the forensic, the kind of work we're talking about doing today here, is about 60 percent. 40 percent is the permitting, the approval and acting as a traffic consultant.

Past work for retaining counsel

Q. And I can probably go through the list and determine, but can you tell me whether or not you've been retained by Mr. Cole's firm or Mr. Horowitz's firm before?[115]

A. Not with Mr. Horowitz's firm. Mr. Cole's, as you go through here you'll find basically three jobs.

Q. Which ones are they?

MR. PORTER: Actually there's only one on the paper.

THE WITNESS: And Matthews. And White was listed.

MR. PORTER: It is on the list?

THE WITNESS: Yes, we found it. So there are three.

BY MR. SCHWARTZ:

Q. And have you been involved in any other cases other than those three with Mr. Porter's firm?

---

[113] More volunteering. The expert would have been better served to answer with a simple "yes," and then see if counsel wants to ask "What else besides forensic work are you doing now?"

[114] Classic attorney tactic of appearing to be nice. The whole point of a deposition is to pry and gather information that can be used against the expert. Attorneys know that the best way to get the expert to talk and keep talking is to act politely, especially when there is an eager and cooperative witness as in this example.

[115] Trying to establish bias.

A. Years ago, on a case in Scottsdale, Arizona, dealing—for the developer that owned a Bruce shopping center.

Q. So you'd been hired by Mr. Porter's firm three times before he hired you on the Franco case?

A. That's correct, sir.

Relationship to party in case

Q. Now, what contact over the years, if any, have you had with the Herrington General or Spielman & Wilkins companies?

A. Spielman & Wilkins, I—as a matter of fact, I met Jordan Wilkins before he became part of Spielman & Wilkins, while he was with the Department of Transportation. He actually moved to Chandler while I was still in Chandler, then moved to Tucson, then he moved elsewhere.

So I've known Tom from time to time. I haven't seen him in a long time, but that's—from that standpoint, I'd know Mr. Spielman if he walked in this door.

Q. Have you had any business dealings with Tom or Spielman & Wilkins before this?

A. No, sir. Other than they're involved currently in a couple of cases where I'm on the other side.

Q. And do you know offhand what cases those are?

A. There's a case in Apache County that's on I-95, which is Mark Richards versus a number of people.

Q. And—

MR. PORTER: He's working for the plaintiffs in those cases, not – when you say business dealings—

THE WITNESS: I'm working for the plaintiff.

MR. PORTER: Mr. Pederson is a consultant, an expert consultant for the plaintiffs, in that case. I got to him too late.

THE WITNESS: And Herrington General, I'm not—I don't think I ever been on any job with the DOT or the SRD.

BY MR. SCHWARTZ:

Q. And have you had any other dealings or connections with Herrington General at all?

A. Not that I can remember.

Fishing around for information

Q. Now, I forgot to ask you. Tell me a little bit about where you grew up, where you're from and that sort of thing.

A. Okay. I was born and raised in Gilbert, Arizona, grew up in Gilbert, and left in 1955 when I went to the University of Arizona, never did return home. And graduated from the University of Arizona, and then my career started. But basically born and reared in Gilbert.[116]

Reviewed deposition transcript?

Q. Now, on the list of exhibits that you reviewed, I'm a little bit unclear whether or not you reviewed Peter Cruz's deposition.

A. I did. What happened is I couldn't find his name. I knew I had it. And then after I wrote it in, I noticed that it was typed in.

Contents of file

Q. Now, what else do you have in your file? I'd asked you to bring—

A. All right. The only other thing I have is the original letter of engagement from Mr. Porter of April 7th, 2003.[117]

MR. PORTER: Now, he's got other stuff, Bill. I don't know if you want to—I mean, if you want to look through all the stuff he's got—

MR. SCHWARTZ: Well, I don't know. I want to know what he's got.

MR. PORTER: I told him he didn't need to bring everything.

MR. SCHWARTZ: I understand.

MR. PORTER: So he brought some stuff here. And then if you notice at the end of the table I've got every deposition, I've got the plans, I've got the specs, I've got the Spielman & Wilkins contract. He couldn't bring everything up here on the plane.

MR. SCHWARTZ Sure. That's fine.

MR. PORTER: But this is what he's got that he had physically brought with him.

BY MR. SCHWARTZ:

Q. Well, let me just summarize it this way. The documents that have been put on the table, are those documents that are listed here in your—[118]

A. Yes.

Q. "Exhibits Reviewed by Tom Pederson"?

A. Yes, sir, they are.

Communications with retaining counsel

Q. All right. What I'm trying to determine is to make sure that there's been no correspondence or no written opinions or written information between you and your lawyer[119] that I don't have.

A. I have not prepared a report and I have not written any other notes other than those notes I prepared to have these typed up.

And I don't have a copy, but there's currently an invoice that's outstanding for about $3,500.

---

[116] A good, succinct answer.

[117] The expert wisely did not remove or hide the engagement letter because he has nothing to hide.

[118] The witness again interrupts the questioner and thus volunteers information since no question had yet been asked.

[119] Retaining counsel is not the witness's lawyer because the lawyer does not represent the witness.

Q. Is that what you've spent on the case in terms of time up to this point—[120]
A. Through last week.
Q. Roughly?

Fee questions
A. Last week I actually cranked back up and started going through everything again, so there's been another probably 20 hours.
Q. What's your hourly rate?
A. $200 per hour for preparation and $350 an hour for deposition. And I want to commend you. You're one of the first that I sent a letter to that actually came through. Most people don't do it.[121]
Q. Let's see the copy of the bill that you mentioned.
A. I thought I had it here. I do not have it here.
MR. SCHWARTZ: Can we just agree. Mr. Porter, that you'll produce that to Mr. Porter and he'll get that to me?
THE WITNESS: Yes, sir.
MR. PORTER: Yes.
BY MR. SCHWARTZ:

What were you asked to do?
Q. Now, what were you asked to do in this case?
A. I had a telephone conversation with Mr. Porter, at which time he indicated that he was representing Spielman & Wilkins and went through the various parties in there to make sure that I did not have a conflict. So after having gone through the parties, I indicated I did not. You know, none of them were in my database of people that have retained me.

So he explained that there had been an accident where there were two fatalities. And he wanted to ship me a bunch of data and indicated to me, would I go through and see whether I felt at that time that what they had done was in keeping with what a good CEI would do.[122]
Q. Okay.[123]
A. I also later was asked to look at some of the issues, the issues being the drop-off from the lane to lane and the lane to shoulder, and to see whether I felt that themselves and the—"themselves" being Spielman & Wilkins—in doing the CEI-type monitoring had done their job, and also whether Herrington General had been responsive in doing what they were doing.

---

[120] The witness again interrupts.
[121] The lawyer apparently did not fight about paying for the expert's preparation time. This "investment" paid off in a very cooperative, happy, and talkative expert.
[122] A better answer might have been more succinct: "conduct an investigation and issue opinions."
[123] This is not a question and should not have been responded to.

Specific experience with these types of cases

Q. How many times have you performed this kind of evaluation and opinion with regard to whether or not CEIs properly complied with the terms of their contract with the DOT?

A. Probably—both plaintiff and defendant, probably at least 20-30 of these cases, if not more, I've been involved with that. About 50 or 60 of them have been involved with drop-offs. As a matter of fact, the drop-off or the safe recovery area has been an area that I've done a lot of work in.

Publications

Q. When you say done a lot of work, have you ever written any articles or anything like that?

A. No. I've been too lazy, I guess, to write any articles.[124]

Forensic experience

Q. So let me be sure that I'm clear. It's your judgment that you've testified in probably 50-60 drop-off cases?

A. I'm not sure if I've testified, but I've been involved in.[125]

Q. I'm sorry. That you've been involved in.

A. I've been involved in probably at least that many cases since 1974.

Q. And, again, what percentage of—

A. Let me—[126]

Q. I'm sorry.

A. I said drop-off and also safe recovery area, because they both go hand-in-hand.

Counsel follows up on information revealed by witness

Q. Now, what's your understanding when you say "safe recovery area"? What are you talking about?

A. Well, Arizona did something that no other state did, and that was in 1976, based on some legislation passed by the legislature, created some minimum design standards referred to as Arizona's Green Book. And they began to really put emphasis, both with contractors, designers, as well as city and county governments and the private sector utility companies, on maintaining what's referred to as a clear zone or safe zone, a roadway clear zone.

And that's based on studies that indicated that at various speeds the majority of drivers leaving the travel way had an opportunity to recover if there were no obstructions, if they had a firm, solid area to drive in and to recover.

---

[124] This expert just testified under oath that he is lazy. This could come back to haunt him. A better answer to this question about publications would have been a simple and truthful "no."

[125] The expert employs good active listening skills here and correctly differentiates between "involved with" and "testified in."

[126] The expert wisely works to immediately correct any misimpression that may have been left by his previous answer.

Q. So, excuse me. I didn't mean to interrupt.

A. So, based on that, Arizona developed some standards, and those have been very important. Those standards have gone forward.

And the first case in 1974 had to do with that. It had to do with a huge rock that a city government put next to the roadway because somebody was riding over their grass. And of course a young man hit that and became a paraplegic.

Q. So another way of addressing what safe recovery area means is you're talking about the shoulder of the road?

A. Well, the shoulder is part of that. It depends on the speed, the design speed, and in construction the posted speed. But it's from the edge of the travel way—normally that's the way it's defined—in other words, the driving lane, which encompasses the shoulder, the front slope, the back slope, and depending on the distances, depending on the speed. It varies anywhere from—if you have a curb and gutter, it's four to six feet from the face of the curb. If you don't have a curb and gutter, it's 14, 18, 24, 30 feet.

Counsel asks about the case at hand

Q. And what was your understanding of the safe recovery area that would apply in this paving project that we're here about?

A. Well, in this case that would apply—since you're under construction, it's the posted speed versus the design speed. And the posted speed of 55 would have required a clear zone of at least 24 feet. The median was 40 feet so in that area there was ample distance from the travel way, and on both sides.

Opinions on safe recovery area

Q. And basically is that the only opinion you have regarding the safe recovery area, or are there others?

A. There are others. Basically in construction one also then looks at Index 600 to see whether the drop-offs—drop-offs become part of the criteria within a safe recovery area.[127]

Which standards apply

Q. Now, you mentioned some—and we're going to get into all the drop-off stuff in a little while. But you mentioned some standards, and you just mentioned Index 600. What standards, in your opinion, applied to this construction job?

A. The MOT plan that became Herrington General's plan, even though it was prepared by others, is when—you know, at the preconstruction meeting the contractor at that point basically indicates which plan he will follow. And if it's the plan that's in the set of plans that's been provided, that becomes his plan.

Q. Now, let me just interrupt you there and let's talk about that a little bit. When you say "MOT," you mean maintenance of traffic or transportation?

---

[127] The expert is prepared to offer his other opinions in this area.

A. Maintenance of traffic.

Q. Okay.[128]

A. Normally in the plans you'll see it known as the traffic control plan. But it's known as MOT, which is maintenance of traffic.

Q. And that was pages 36-38, I believe, in—

A. Whatever the pages are.[129]

Q. Okay. Let me see if I can find it.

A. I didn't put page numbers on it, but I had it.

Q. Well, we'll get to that I'm sure. Now, you said something I was interested in there about that that plan becomes the contractor's plan at the preconstruction meeting. Is that—[130]

A. That's correct, sir.

Q. And the way I understood from what you said is that the plans, the DOT plans, will have a proposed maintenance of traffic plan or may have more than one. Is that a fair statement?

A. They generally have one.

Q. Okay.[131]

A. The contractor, whoever the successful low bidder is, can then either elect to use that plan or provide his own plan.

Plans

Q. And in this case Herrington General elected to use that plan?

A. That's correct, sir.[132]

Q. And what speed limit did that plan call for?

A. They did not post a speed limit, so it was basically the existing speed limit, which my understanding was 55 miles per hour at that time.

Assumption

Q. All right. So your understanding was the maintenance of traffic did not post a speed limit?

A. Did not change the speed limit that was on the existing roadway. That's correct, sir.[133]

---

[128] This is not a question. The witness should wait for a question before responding.

[129] A poor response. First, the expert interrupted counsel. Second, the expert was "too lazy" to refer to the publication in question and verify the citation.

[130] The expert once again interrupts the question with a premature answer.

[131] This is not a question.

[132] The expert might have been better served by requesting clarification to the word "that" so that he was sure to answer correctly.

[133] Good active listening skills displayed here.

Change in assumptions

Q. Are you aware or are you familiar with the fact that the speed limit was 45 miles an hour during construction, according to that plan?

A. No.

Q. All right. Well, we'll come back to that in a minute then. Do you agree that if that MOT plan did provide for a 45 mile-an-hour speed limit, that the 55 would be in violation of the plan? Is that a fair statement?

MR. PORTER: Note an objection to the form of the question.[134]

THE WITNESS: If the plan has provided for something and there's been no change, yes, then you're violating the plans.

Assumptions

BY MR. SCHWARTZ:

Q. You're not aware of any change to the MOT plans, are you?

A. No, sir, I am not.

Q. I believe it's paragraph 2. I could be wrong about the paragraph.

A. It does say that in paragraph 3, 45 miles per hour. And the contract shall recommend any regulatory speed reduction from that.

Expert refuses to make damaging admission

Q. Yes, sir. So you agree, then, that the 55 mile-an-hour speed limit that Herrington General used in this job violated the maintenance of traffic plan; is that a fair statement?

MR. PORTER: Object to the form of the question.

THE WITNESS: All I can tell you is I'm going by what the highway patrol reported. And the only signs I saw—actually the only photographs I saw were 45 miles per hour. That's one of the questions I raised, were there 55 mile-per-hour signs? Because I did see—in one of the photographs I looked at was a 45 mile-per-hour sign.[135]

BY MR. SCHWARTZ:

Q. So let me make sure that I understand what you're saying. You reviewed some photographs?

A. Yes.

Q. And you're talking about the photographs from the homicide report?

A. No, not the homicide report. I think there were some photographs taken by Spielman & Wilkins and there may have been others by other individuals that indicated—they kept showing a 45 mile-per-hour sign. I don't know where it was located.

Q. So is it a fair statement to say, that you don't know what the actual speed limit was on that project?

---

[134] The question here is compound. Counsel has asked two questions, hence the "form" objection.

[135] The expert backs up his opinion with facts.

Dispute between counsel that expert wisely stays out of
MR. PORTER: Again, object to the form of the question.
THE WITNESS: Only—
MR. SCHWARTZ: Let's slow down a minute. What's the problem with the form of that question? I want to clear it up so that I don't have that problem.
MR. PORTER: I think it's a misstatement of his testimony.
MR. SCHWARTZ: Okay. Well I'll—
MR. PORTER: You keep saying "is it a fair statement" or "would it be correct to say". I don't think that's a proper form question.
MR. SCHWARTZ: Okay. Well, I appreciate you letting me know that. I'll try to avoid doing that.
BY MR. SCHWARTZ:
Q. What do you know regarding what the speed limit was on that project?
A. I reviewed the accident report and the homicide report, which I thought showed the posted speed of 55. I did not ask anyone whether it was 55 or 45.[136]
   Now, that—all the difference between 55 and 45, it reduces the clear zone. But it doesn't make any other changes.
Q. Yes, sir. But part of your job as an expert for Mr. Porter was to review the maintenance of traffic that you have in front of you. Is that correct?
A. That's correct, sir.
Q. And did you review that?

Expert admits serious mistake
A. I did review that and I missed that 45. Absolutely.
Q. All right. And what do you know with regard to whether or not, if the MOT plan, and it apparently does, says 45 and the actual speed was 55—whether or not that would be in violation of the MOT plan?
MR. PORTER: Same objection.
THE WITNESS: Unless there was a change in the speed, yes, it would be in violation—not in violation, but it would be difference from what's set forth there.
BY MR. SCHWARTZ:
Q. Well, if it's different, why wouldn't it be in violation?
A. I'm not sure somebody didn't approve it. But I have not seen that in writing.[137]

Counsel counterpunches to refute the out the witness has left himself
Q. Do you agree that there's no indication that anybody has made changes to the MOT plan?
A. I have not seen any changes, that's correct, sir, to the MOT plan.[138]

---

[136] Here's an example of where the expert's "lazy" comment can come back to haunt him on cross-examination. Counsel may later ask: "Were you too lazy to ask what the posted speed was?"
[137] The expert tries to give himself some hope for recovery.
[138] After getting this dangerous admission, counsel wisely moves on.

Back to standards

Q. All right. Now, what standards—I started out and we kind of got sidetracked, and we'll probably do that a few more times as we go through this deposition. What standards, in your opinion, apply to this project as it relates to the issues you've rendered an opinion about in terms of the shoulder drop-offs and the—[139]

A. Well, my first opinion was on what role Spielman & Wilkins played as the CEI consultants on this job.

Opinions

Q. I guess probably a better way for me to do it is to let you tell me what your opinions are and then come back and ask you what standards apply.

A. My first opinion I had, did Spielman & Wilkins perform their duties in keeping with what is the standard required of a consultant that's hired to do the CEI work. And in my opinion they did. Actually, they document some things that I've seen some others CEIs fail to document, and they did send letters and—so from an engineering standpoint, in my opinion, Spielman & Wilkins did do—not only meet the normal engineering standards but I think[140] exceeded that.

Q. Okay. And I'm going to come back and ask you in a few minutes what you base that on.

A. All right.

Standards supporting opinion

Q. But while you're talking about it, you might as well tell me what standards you feel—if there are any standards that apply to that opinion, or if that's just an opinion based on your experience and review of the documents.

A. It's an opinion based on my background and experience. If you look at—there's minimum standards that a CEI has to meet. And those standards basically deal with the type of experience that each of the individuals that's listed or will be listed on the job is required to have.

Q. That's by the DOT?

A. By the DOT.

Q. So basically, as I understand it, the only standard that a—let me start over. The only written standard that a CEI has to meet is to provide for the minimum limits of experience as required by the DOT?

A. No, sir.

Q. Okay. I'm sorry.

---

[139] The expert yet again interrupts the question. The witness should wait for the entire question and then truthfully answer the specific question asked.

[140] "I think" is not the strongest language. The expert may have been better served by using the words "in my opinion."

A. That's just one of the—one of the criteria is they normally—the DOT will normally list the type of individual, by individual, by title: resident engineer, project engineer, senior inspector and so forth.

Q. And they'll list experience requirements for all those?

A. And they put a list of—they will then list experience. They also require that the individuals have experience in construction, that they have certification. If they're doing asphalt, they've got to have asphalt certification. They've got to have MOT certification. They need to have qualified individuals that can check compaction, both from the asphalt as well as the soils.

Q. There's a bunch of standards. We don't need to go into all of them.[141]

A. Yes. There's a whole list of things that individuals need to be qualified in. There's also a requirement that daily reports be prepared, and then at the end of each week that the reports be compiled into a weekly report.

They require that they have experience in EEO-type opportunities, to review contractor payrolls and compliance with various federal and state regulations. There's a minority goal in the contract, and most of them have one. They've got to have someone that can certify that the contractor is meeting the minority goal.

There is basically also the requirement of the office and the—but the experience factor is probably one of the hardest things to meet. If you haven't had experience in similar-type projects, it's difficult to get on the long list or even the short list or get selected on a project.[142]

Q. Now, those standards, are they put out by the DOT?

A. Yes.[143] The DOT—the DOT basically, when they advertise the job and anybody responds, there's a whole list of things that they then put out as to the prequalification, if you will, the qualifications of anybody responding.

You also have to be preapproved by the department in various categories. And in CEI work there's also levels of approvals; major bridges, major roadways, major interchanges, minor roadways, minor bridges. So there's various levels, and if your firm is not qualified in that area, you waste postage by submitting a letter in response to the invitation.

Q. What are those standards called by the DOT that are put out, or how is it—

A. As I sit here today I don't know if there's a name for the standards. But basically they do have—for the selection of a consultant, there is a competitive negotiation act which they have to follow, which is a state law. And then administratively the department has their own rules in selecting consultants.

Q. So you're familiar with those generally, but you didn't review them in preparing for your testimony here today?

---

[141] Again, this is not a question.

[142] A very long response filled with potentially damaging information has been given and counsel never even asked a question.

[143] The expert should have stopped his response here.

A. No, I did not.

Q. Now, do you know whether or not there are any standards in the DOT standards that relate to the quality of performance of their job; in other words, that require them to perform their job to a certain standard or anything of that nature?

A. Well, there's the CPAM which is basically the construction manual that puts certain criteria and spells out certain things that the consultant will do or their employees. Actually it's written like it's their employees, but the consultant's taking the place of DOT as far as monitoring is concerned.

Q. That's the Construction Project Administration Manual?

A. Yes.

Q. And that applied to this project?

A. Applies to all state projects and certainly this one.

Q. And basically that, though, sets forth the duties of the CEI that they're going to perform and the manner in which they perform them; is that a fair statement?

A. No, it sets out the duty of a DOT employee.

Q. Right.

A. But since the CEI is sort of taking their place, it's written so that that's the duty the CEI would do. But it's not really just primarily for CEIs.

Q. And that CPAM manual is directed toward the specific duties that need to be performed, not the quality of those duties; would you agree with that?

A. That is correct, sir.

Q. And would you agree that there is nothing that sets forth the quality requirements for the performance by the CEI?

A. Well, only to the extent that the department in every job will basically then grade—as the CEI grades contractors, the department also grades consultants.

Q. And would they have graded the consultants on this job?

A. I have not seen that, but I would assume they had.

Q. And you haven't reviewed their report card, so to speak, on this job?[144]

A. No, sir, I have not.

Q. All right. Now, we were talking about the opinion that you rendered that they complied with their duties in administering this contract.

A. Yes.

Back to drop-off opinions

Q. We're going to come back to that and talk about that in detail later. What about your other opinion with regard to the drop-offs?

A. There are basically two drop-offs in issue or discussion, at least early on. One was the drop-off between lane to lane or pavement to pavement, if you will, which is set forth—and that one's set forth actually in the maintenance of traffic plan, both in condition 7 and 25.

---

[144] More evidence of an expert that counsel may try to characterize as lazy.

And then there's the requirement to follow Index 600. 600 is where you go to look at what is required for drop-offs between the pavement and the shoulder.

And in my opinion, first looking at the drop-off between the lane and the shoulder, with the exception of measurements that I saw taken—with the exception of photographs of the measurements taken I guess by Trooper O'Connor, which I think are suspect only because of the way they were taken, the only other measurements that I was able to see was one set of measurements taken by I think it was Mr. Ivy, a consultant for—a safety consultant for Herrington General, and then also reviewing the photographs. And I have not seen any documentation that would, either in photograph or physical evidence, other than that one—those highway patrol photos—that would indicate that the drop-off exceeded three inches.[145]

Factual assumptions

Q. Now, Mr. Ivy, do you know whether or not he measured the drop-off, or did he just measure the lane-to-lane drop-offs?

A. No, he measured—there's a photograph in the exhibits that I looked at today that showed clearly him measuring the way it should be measured a shoulder drop-off, and it showed I think a drop-off in the range of anywhere from two and a quarter to two and a half inches.

Q. Do you have those photographs here?

A. Yes.

Q. We'll get them later. And you might make a note that I want to look at that photograph closely.

I think—I don't mean to trick you, but I think that photograph is going to show that Mr. Ivy was measuring from lane to lane. But you or I, one, is mistaken, and we'll figure it out who it is later on.

A. Yeah, I looked at it today, and very clearly it's from the edge of pavement into the dirt and just not lane to lane.

Q. Well, we'll look at that later on. You may be right.[146]

A. Yes. And it's the first time I've seen it, because I know in his deposition he did indicate that he had measured, but I never saw—and he may have made statements to the—but he only took that one measurement.

Q. Do you know where that one measurement of Mr. Ivy's was located?

A. I think he indicated—he referred to it as within the zone of the accident. So as I sit here today I don't know where that was, other than the zone of the accident.

Opinion

Q. So let me come back and ask you now: What's your opinion with regard to the drop-off question?

---

[145] "I guess," "I think." The expert would have been better served by being more thoroughly prepared and being more familiar with the facts.

[146] This is not a question.

A. The photographs I look at, the—knowing the pavement operation that was under way, I didn't see—with the exception of the photographs taken by the highway patrol, by that one trooper, I didn't see—I don't think there was any area, other than isolated conditions which were not shown in the photographs, where the drop-off was in excess of three inches.

But we're dealing with one good measurement, a couple of suspect measurements, and then photographs.

Asking about "other opinions" to lock down the expert

Q. Have you been asked to render any other opinions?

A. the other—

Q. Other than just stuff relating to this, these two. Any separate major opinions?

A. No, sir. I say that, and I'm not trying to think and I can't—

Q. Well, I'm not trying to trick you.

A. No, I understand.

Q. If it comes out later on, we'll deal with it.

A. Yeah. And then the—

MR. PORTER: There are a lot of sub opinions that relate to those general things.

MR. SCHWARTZ: I understand.

THE WITNESS: The third area was the lane-to-lane drop off.[147]

BY MR. SCHWARTZ:

Q. And what's your opinion about that?

A. Once again, I saw basically two measurements. Now, I think Trooper O'Connor indicates something like two and a half. I did not see photographs or even—a photograph of his measurement or how he measured that.

I did not see measurements taken by Mr. Daniel Birge on the day of the accident, where he took a number of them, and they varied from one and a half to one and five-eighths inches. And then today I did see some measurements taken by Mr.—is it Ruddick?[148]

Q. Roderick.

A. —Roderick which showed some—I think he showed some at one and three-quarters and two inches and then also showed one and a half to one and five-eighths.

Additional opinions

Q. And what were your opinions about that?

A. That given the paving operation that was going in with both the armor coat as well as the super pave, that the lane-to-lane was probably—one and a half to 1.6 was probably about where it should have been, not more than that.

---

[147] The expert corrects the record as soon as he remembers the third opinion he will be providing.

[148] The witness again demonstrates a less than masterful knowledge of the facts. Counsel will note this when sizing up how well the expert will likely do at trial.

Certification

Q. Now, I want to go back and cover a couple of things that I overlooked earlier in my questioning. You were explaining to me some different things that the CEI would have to have in order to get the job, and one of the things you said was MOT certification, as I recall. Is that correct?

A. They normally have to provide—the CEI normally needs to have somebody that is qualified in maintenance of traffic. But they do not provide the maintenance of traffic personnel for the job. That's up to the contractor to provide.

Q. Right. I understand that. And who filled that role in this case for CEI?

A. I don't know.

Q. And what is the role of the person with the CEI that has MOT certification?

A. Normally the project engineer or the resident engineer needs to be aware of what's required in the maintenance of traffic, to make sure that the contractor is building the job in keeping with the maintenance of traffic plan and also meeting the various criteria.

Q. Do you know whether or not Daniel Birge was MOT-certified?

A. I'm not sure if he was MOT-certified. I know he had a great deal of experience, which in my experience would qualify him to review what the contractor was doing.

Q. What is MOT certification?

A. There are two courses. There's one eight-hour course and a 16-hour course in which they go through the handbook and take an exam at the end.

Q. What's the purpose of MOT certification?

A. To certify contractors, because the specifications now require that the contractors has, on these jobs—at least identify who the maintenance of traffic certified technician would be, or certified individual would be.

Q. What's the purpose of that?

A. That's to make sure that someone gives enough attention to the maintenance of traffic to protect both the public as well as the individuals working on the project.

Q. Now, what's your understanding with regard to whether or not an MOT certified person should be present on the construction job at all times that it's being worked on? Do you know?[149]

A. The specifications don't require that. They require that there be a person designated and that that individual be available, if necessary, and that that individual also periodically do holiday looks and nights and other—just not simply an eight-hour day during the day, but basically at various times. And that's by contract.

Basis of first opinion

Q. Now, let me go back to your first opinion that the CEI adequately performed their requirements under the contract and ask you to explain to me in as much detail as you can what documents you relied on and what experience you relied on in reaching that

---

[149] This is a compound question that could have been objected to based on its form.

conclusion. You told me generally, but I'd like for you to be as specific as possible with regard to that opinion.

A. Okay. I looked at—primarily within the period of time leading up to the accident and then some time after that, I looked at the daily reports.

Q. Now, excuse me for interrupting you, but if I don't, I'll forget my question. When you say "daily reports," which daily reports are you referring to?

A. There's only one legitimate daily report and one legal report—"legal" is the wrong term. The CEI or DOT employee, if that happened to be a DOT job, is required to fill out a daily activity report for every activity that's currently under way on the job.

They accumulate those and prepare a weekly report, which copies are given to the contractor and various people. The contractor may keep his own reports, but that's not—but the report that becomes the daily official log on this project, which is sent to—if you ever look at the bottom of the daily report, you see all the various people that get copies.

Q. Right.

A. That is prepared by the CEI. And that report lists—normally will list the equipment, the personnel that was working—by personnel, not name, so much as "two laborers, four technicians"—

Q. Let's look at those to make sure I've got them. I think I have. I can't imagine not having them. But I want to make sure.

A. Here we go. This covers a period of time from February 28th through September 3rd, 2000, and also some from June 26, 2000 to—it says October 1st.

Q. Well, what was it about these reports that caused you to feel like they complied with their requirements?

A. Well, the reports are just part of it.

Q. I understand that.

A. The daily that—I reviewed the daily to see what activities were under way. I also saw letters that basically Daniel Birge wrote to the contractor.

Q. Right. We're going to talk about those.

A. Well, that's part of the explanation as to what they were doing. Most CEIs fail to put—document things. They tend to do a lot of verbal direction, which is fine, except that later it's difficult to document. In this case, you know, Daniel Birge, Spielman & Wilkins, did—as they went through the job and found various deficiencies, took photographs, also advised the contractor of a number of areas that were deficient that needed attention and correction.

And then not only prior to the accident on the 27th, but there was some correspondence that I read from Daniel Birge that continued through the remainder of the job, where he basically initiated the same action of advising the contractor when there was a deficiency or an area that needed to be corrected or a missing sign or other—

Q. And what were those dates, again, of those letters, roughly?
A. Actually there were three that are referenced a number of times here.
Q. Right.
A. And then there was also a package. The ones that everybody keeps marking is the one dated April 27th, May 24th, and June 1st.
MR. PORTER: Plaintiff's Exhibit 13 in prior depos.
MR. SCHWARTZ: Yes, that's true.
THE WITNESS: And then also there were some letters that continued after that—
BY MR. SCHWARTZ:
Q. That's Plaintiff's Exhibit 17 from previous depos.
A. Right. From Daniel Birge in which basically he continued to give punch list items and also a list of areas that needed to be addressed; washouts, some drop-offs and other issues.

Expert locked down regarding basis of opinion
Q. So you considered the weekly and daily reports which you've shown me. You considered the letters that you've just testified about. What else did you rely on to reach a conclusion? Other than your experience, now. I understand that.
A. That's pretty much what I've looked at. Of course, I did read the various depositions of the—
Q. Of the witnesses?
A. —Witnesses that are listed.

Expert locked down on area he will not be opining on
Q. Right. Now you're not offering any opinion, are you, on whether or not Herrington General was proper or careful in the way that they responded to the Spielman & Wilkins supervision?
A. Only to the extent that from what I understand most of the responses were done within 24 hours to 48 hours. And in my opinion—
Q. That's adequate?
A. That's adequate and certainly in keeping with the industry standards.

Basis for second opinion
Q. Okay. And the same question with regard to your second major opinion, and that's the one regarding the drop-offs. You've already testified you reviewed photographs. What else did you rely on, other than your experience and the depositions or documents that we've gone through?
A. I reviewed photographs. I read depositions, particularly of the people doing the paving. I also then saw that one measurement taken by Mr. Ivy. I looked at the measurements taken by Trooper O'Connor.
    And with some interpretation I did not see anything that I felt, at least by photograph or by anything else, that—with one literally small area, and I think there's

337

an answer for that—that would show a drop-off that exceeded three inches, which is in keeping with the standards.

Q. Now, tell me again what was important to you in the depositions that you reviewed regarding your conclusion that there was only one area that you needed to interpret.

A. Well, there are several areas to interpret. I said there's one area where it may be a little bit in excess of three inches. And there may have been areas throughout the job.

But based on the reviews of the photographs, reviewing the depositions, and knowing the process that was used for the paving, one would expect normally the differential in paving between layers to be in the vicinity of about 1.6 inches or an inch and a half, a little bit more than an inch and a half, given the armor coat and the super pave, the process.

And that was—I think there was a Clinton Williams[150] whose deposition was just recently taken, and he probably did the clearest job of basically indicating the probe that he used and the fact that when he took the probe, his probe went down all the way through—as a matter of fact, into the rubberized membrane, and roughly it was an inch and a half.

So knowing that and also knowing that basically one of the first things that was done on this job after the paving started was to basically put a leveling coat down, if you will, leveling layer down, that was to be 25 millimeters, which is still—I have trouble with millimeters into the English system,[151] but was probably a little bit less than an inch.

So given those two measurements, the inch and the inch and a half, and that's verified by the measurements that Mr. Roderick too, I think one could look at those photographs and see that anywhere from two and a half to three inches or less than three inches is what shows in most areas, with the exception of the way that Highway Patrolmen O'Connor laid his tape. You just never lay a tape that way, because it's always going to show a greater distance. But that's not a drop-off.

Q. So basically your opinion is that the drop-off between the lanes was an inch and a half to and inch and six-tenths? In other words, you're reaching an opinion regarding a factual issue.

A. That and also looking at the measurements taken by Daniel Birge the day of the accident, in which his measurements indicate that.

Now, today Mr. Roderick's measurements indicated that next to the paved median, the crossover, whose were about an inch and a half to and inch and five-eighths. He showed measurements in the center at one location—I'm not sure

---

[150] The expert would have been better served by knowing the witness's name. If he needed to, he could refer to a document to refresh his recollection.

[151] Now this expert engineer volunteers that he has difficulty with the metric system. Such a pointless admission does not inspire confidence in his technical skills.

where—where I think he had a measurements of an inch and three-quarters to two inches.

Q. So basically, as I understand it, your only opinion regarding the lane-to-lane drop-off is that the drop-off should be an inch and a half to and inch and six-tenths?

A. That's according to the 40 millimeters which is required by the maintenance of traffic plan.

Q. Yes, sir. So basically you're rendering an opinion about a fact; is that correct?

MR. PORTER: Object to form.

THE WITNESS: I'm rendering an opinion as to what the standards require. And looking at the standards, then I looked at the only measurements that were legitimate measurements taken, which coincide with what paving operation indicated, which is consistent with what I would expect.

BY MR. SCHWARTZ:

Q. Now, it's clear that the standards require no more than a 40-millimeter drop-off between lanes under this situation; is that a fair statement?

MR. PORTER: Note an objection to form.

THE WITNESS: No. It's a statement that—that's what it says if you're not to provide any wedge or lane closures or other devices that are permitted to be done.

BY MR. SCHWARTZ:

Q. Well, that's what I said. I said under the circumstances of this case, which there was no wedge or anything provided. Is that correct?

A. That's correct. On lane-to-lane, that's correct.

Q. So it's clear that the requirement on this project was that the lane-to-lane drop-off be no more than 40 millimeters. Is that a fair statement?

A. That's a fair statement.

Q. And why do you need to be an expert to tell me that?

MR. PORTER: Object to form.

MR. HOROWITZ: Object to form.

THE WITNESS: Well, because it seems to me that in some of the depositions I've read, they were stacking the three-quarter inch stone on top of the inch and a half, and they were up in some areas to almost two inches or two and a half inches of paving, which—and the trooper basically shows not a measurement, but he indicated that the lane-to-lane was two and two and a half inches.[152]

BY MR. SCHWARTZ:

Contradictory deposition transcript reviewed

Q. Yes, sir. You've indicated in your list of items you reviewed that you reviewed the deposition of Mr. Murray, Robert Murray.

A. Yes, sir.

Q. Are you aware of his testimony on that issue?

---

[152] The expert was prepared with a good explanation.

A. Yes. And he was totally wrong when he began to stack. If he'd been out in the field, he would have known that was not the case.

Q. Are you aware that after this claim was made, Mr. Murray had to fill out a report, and his report in writing said that it was 1.98 inches or 1.96?

A. No. I think in his deposition he indicated what he did in the report was to basically take the various measurements of the various things, the 10 millimeters of membrane, the three-quarter inch of stone, the inch and a half or 1.6 inch of paving, and add them together.[153]

Q. Yes, sir. And I didn't do a good job of asking the question. Let me ask it again. You reviewed his deposition, and that's what he seemed to be saying in his deposition. You reviewed some other documents, these exhibits that I've attached to my other depositions, 17 and 13—there's about 18 of them. You reviewed those, didn't you, all of them?

A. Yes, sir.

Q. All right. Well, now, are you aware—and we're going to get into the specific exhibit in just a moment. But are you aware that Mr. Murray, after a claim was made in this case, wrote a letter indicating again in writing that he felt that the difference between lanes was either 1.96 or 1.98—

A. I think he was up to 1.97—

MR. PORTER: One second, Joe. Let him finish the question and them give me a chance to object.[154]

THE WITNESS: Sorry.

MR. SCHWARTZ: Well, let me start over.

THE WITNESS: Okay.

BY MR. SCHWARTZ:

Contradictory written report

Q. Are you aware that Mr. Murray, after a claim was made in this case, made a written report to someone? Did you know that?

A. I know. I saw the report. I'm not sure if it was done after the claim was filed or at some point. But I did see a report that he prepared.

Q. Okay. And that's separate from the documents that you saw in his deposition?

A. I've not seen that. I've seen the documents in the deposition, which I thought included such a statement.

Q. Well, let's just go ahead and look at the exhibit, 15—I believe that's the correct number—and ask if you've had an opportunity to review that. No, not his deposition.

A. I know. But I'm reading the memorandum here.

---

[153] The expert was prepared on this critical issue.

[154] Counsel steps in to protect the witness and allow opposing counsel to finish his question and thus not leave a deceptive deposition transcript.

Q. Yeah. Well that's the one that's attached as Exhibit 15. And that memorandum date is May 17, 2001?

A. That's correct, sir.

Q. All right. Now, read the part to me where he talks about the height of the distance between lanes.

A. No. 5: "The roadway was under construction the day of the accident. All four lanes were paved with approximately .79 inches of overbuild paving. The two inside lanes were paved with .39 inches of armor rubberized membrane inner layer and 1.57 inches of structure."

Q. All right. Now, is he wrong about that or not?

A. Each of those is probably in themselves correct. But you don't do a cumulative-type thing, other than—the .79 of overbuilding is the leveling course that's there, and that was on both lanes. So you don't take the .39 and add it to the 1.57.

You can do that if you want to mathematically, but in the real world, when you have a rubberized membrane with three-quarter inch stone and you put in the super pave and inch and a half over the top of it, it's going to basically push down into that and overall you will probably have about an inch and a half to an inch and six-tenths.[155]

Counsel tries to have the expert educate him

Q. Well, I want to make sure that I understand that. I'm still having a little trouble understanding it. And, remember, I don't know anything about construction, particularly road construction.[156] So I want to go back through it step by step.

He says all four lanes were paved with .79 inches of overbuild paving. And I'm referring to his memorandum.

A. Yes, sir.

Q. Tell me briefly what that is.

A. That's the leveling course.

Q. Okay. The leveling course was already on all four lanes before this wreck occurred?

A. That's correct, sir.

Q. And then the two inside lanes were paved with .39 inches of armor inner layer?

A. The armor coat was placed there, yes, sir.

Q. And 1.57 inches of structure?

A. That's the inch and a half, inch and six-tenths of the super pave structure.

Q. So basically what you're telling me is that the armor layer adds no thickness to speak of to the structure layer. Is that what you are saying?

A. That's what I'm saying.

---

[155] The expert is prepared with a plausible explanation on this key point.

[156] Counsel plays dumb.

Q. Now, Mr. Murray in some other documents indicated that your armor layer again was about four-tenths of an inch.

A. Four tenths?

MR. PORTER: Note an objection to form.

BY MR. SCHWARTZ:

Q. .39 inches.

A. Okay.

Questioning about key facts

Q. That's about four-tenths of an inch. We'll use .39 inches so there's no objection. He says the armor layer was .39 inches. Was it?

A. The layer when probably first placed may have been, because you basically—you spray the rubberized asphalt , then you put some 57—some three-quarter inch stone on top of it and distribute it. So if you measure it at that point, it's conceivable that you could get a .39 inch measurement.

Q. Now, the actual people that pave the road, you read their depositions?

A. Yes, sir.

Q. What did they say the depth of the armor layer was?

A. I'm telling you what Mr. Clinton Williams, who was in the pack of the screed with a probe checking, and he indicates very clearly that his probe was an inch and half. and when he reached down there, he went through the rock and through the membrane.

Q. Yeah. Well, I know he said that, but that wasn't the question. Let me ask the question again, and listen closely and then—we're talking about apples and oranges.

A. All right.

Q. The people that were out there on that paving crew, I asked every one of them what the depth of the armor layer was. Do you remember reading that?

A. Yes, sir.

Q. And what did they say?

A. Some said the asphalt was probably about ten millimeters, and a three-quarter inch stone.

Q. So some of them said that the armor layer could be as much as three-quarters of an inch?

A. Well, if you've got three-quarter inch stone, it would be. Because with the exception of what stone gets crushed, you do have some three-quarter inch stone, yes, sir.

Q. Now, are you familiar with the fact that all of them said that the armor layer had at least .25 inch thickness, the armor layer itself?

MR. PORTER: Again, object to form.

THE WITNESS: No.

MR. SCHWARTZ: What's the reason for the objection?

MR. PORTER: I think it misstates the witness's testimony, these other—

MR. SCHWARTZ: Well, what I was talking about—

THE WITNESS: I didn't—I don't think I read anything where they talked about .25.[157]

BY MR. SCHWARTZ:

Q. Did you read anything in those depositions that you claim you read where those witnesses that paved the road told me what their estimate was of how thick the armor layer was?

A. Let me first correct a thing. I did read every one of those depositions, and I reread them again in the last three days.

Q. Okay.

A. And to a person, they basically—and I'm not disagreeing with you that you don't have three-quarter in stone. And they talked about the rubberized membrane. They were talking about—one of them talked about the—as a matter of fact, I think he said about the size of a paper. Others said 10 millimeters.

But basically they talked about three-quarters. I'm not sure if anybody said what the overall—other than Robert Murray, on what the thickness of that was.

Q. So it's clear in the record, do you remember what any of the employees that were actually on the paving crew said they thought the thickness of the armor layer was?

A. Yes, three-quarter inch.

Q. Other than three-quarter inch?

A. That's what I remember primarily indicating, which is about what would happen. Because when you put down rubberized asphalt, I don't care how thick it is, whether it be 10 millimeters or the size of a paper, when that stone gets in there and gets pushed down, that asphalt comes around part of the stone so that stone is up against the overbuild, if you will, the leveling course. And at that time what you have sticking up is three-quarter inch in most places, maybe a little less, because as they toll and brush it back and forth, some of that stone does crush.[158]

More questioning on expert's understanding of the facts

Q. Now, do you know what volume of stone, three-quarter-inch stone they put out when they put the armor layer in?

A. No, other than they basically had a spread rate. And I didn't go in and check the spread rate other than—normally on armor coat, at least from what I read in the depo, they pretty well distributed it evenly so they didn't have the stone built up. They were basically an open grade of three-quarter-inch stone.

Q. So let me just kind of paraphrase what you're claiming here today. When you put that three-quarter-inch stone from the armor later on the overbuild paving, it squishes down into the overbuild paving? Is that what you're telling me?

---

[157] The expert listens carefully to the basis of counsel's objection.

[158] The expert again cogently explains the key reason for his belief.

A. No. That's not what I said. What I said is if you—you have the overbuild paving. That's the leveling course. Then you come through and you spray the hot rubberized asphalt membrane. And while it's hot, then you spread the stone on with a spreader.

That stone basically then sets itself into the membrane. It doesn't sit on top of the membrane; it goes into the membrane. And then you basically brush it and prepare it so that it's distributed evenly in one layer. And that layer historically is normally about three-quarter-inch open grade mix.[159]

Q. What does that mean?

A. What that means is you don't have stone on top of stone. You've got to go to a second and third layer of surface treatment. So when you do the 57 stone, the three-quarter-inch stone, and you spread it, you have one stone, another stone next to it, and they basically form what's referred to as open grade.

Q. And how thick is that armor layer?

A. That armor layer is three-quarter-inch at the time it's put down after the stone is distributed.

Q. And then how does it get less than three-quarter-inch?

A. Then you come through with a hot asphalt mix.

Q. And that's the structure?

A. That's the structure, which in this case was super pave.

When you put that down—and they're checking the screed, because they're trying to put down an inch and a half. That inch and a half is also rolled, so it compresses.

Actually if you put down an inch and a half of asphalt, eliminate the armor coat—let's say we're just doing a typical resurfacing job where you have a leveling course and you come back with asphalt and you put down an inch and a half. When the rollers get through, you lose about three-quarters of an inch or more.

What happens when you put down an inch and a half of super build, or the structure course, and it's paved over the top of the armor coat, it basically vibrates in, because it's a vibrator going out the back of the asphalt spreader. It goes into the voids. And then it's rolled.

And no one said it any clearer than Mr. Johnson when he indicated that when he puts his probe down, he did not—others have said it, but they weren't as clear. Mr. Newman said it, too.

But Mr. Clinton Williams made a very clear statement that when he stuck the probe in the there, he went down through the rock, past the rock, into the membrane, through the membrane, down to the overbuild, if you will, or leveling course, and he measured historically about an inch and a half.[160]

---

[159] The expert again gives a good explanation for a key opinion.

[160] Notice how comfortable this eminently qualified expert is when talking about road paving. Experts who stay within their true area of expertise are difficult to challenge.

Q. Well, let me just tell you what's bothering me and let you address it. What's bothering me is I don't understand how you can have a structure course of 1.57 inches and then put an armor layer on it of .39 inches and come out with a layer of 1.5 to 1.6 inches. From an engineering standpoint, how can that be?

MR. PORTER: Again, object to form. Go ahead.

THE WITNESS: All right. Let me explain it, because you've got it turned around. You don't put down the structure course and then put the armor course. If you did that, then yes, you would have a build up of three-quarter-inch higher.

You do the reverse. You put down on the base that you're working with, which in this case they call it overbuild, but basically it's a leveling course—you spray the asphalt, rubberized asphalt. You then spread the stone, and that stone is seated.

Now, all the stone is doing is basically trying to get you off the rubberized membrane. Because rubberized membrane is made to try and seal all the cracks—

BY MR. SCHWARTZ:

Q. Beneath it.

A. Beneath it, and also in the future there's a reflection—

Q. To give?

A. And it doesn't allow that crack to reflect through the pavement. That's why you use a rubberized thing. If you could pave right over the rubberized thing, then normally you probably wouldn't use a 57 stone. But they put the stone so that the paver then has the ability to go over the top without getting bogged down in the rubberized asphalt.

And when you get an open grade mix and you put asphalt over the top of it with the kind of equipment that vibrates and compacts it, and you have someone checking that they're putting down about an inch and a half, and then you get the rollers coming behind it, you're not going to have an inch and a half or, as they said, 1.57 inches and .39 inches on top. It will not measure that.

You may have a few spots, if the subgrade or the overbuild area had a low dip or something, for some reason it wasn't leveled correctly; you may get a little deviation. But you're not going to get much deviation.[161]

MR. PORTER: I need a break.

MR. SCHWARTZ: That's fine.

(Short recess)

BY MR. SCHWARTZ:

Q. I think I understand what you're staying. I'm not sure I agree with you. But you're saying basically when you put the last layer on, it squishes down so that you don't have any buildup in depth.

---

[161] Another good explanation from a very well qualified expert.

A. Very little, if any, and only if you have an area that already was low to start with. But you basically will have—if you took corings later, you will find anywhere from an inch and a half to 1.6 inches.

Data unavailable

Q. Now, corings have not been taken in this case, have they?

A. Not that I know of.

Q. How many cases have you worked on in a construction case like this where corings have not been taken?

A. Most of them.

Q. Is that right?

A. Where they were paves by the ton. If they're paved by the square yard or the square meter, then corings are taken to determine the pavement. But that's not the case here.

Q. Would corings be helpful here?

A. It certainly would tell us what the various layers would be.

Q. So the corings would be more accurate, in your opinion?

MR. HOROWITZ: Object to form.

MR. PORTER: Objection to form.

THE WITNESS: Well, my opinion is based on photographs—not photographs. It's based on some measurements that were taken by what I think are very competent individuals.

BY MR. SCHWARTZ:

Q. What do you know regarding whether or not a core sample in this case could determine the depth of the various layers that we've been discussing here?

A. I think your coring—I think a core could give you within a fairly close engineering probability—

Q. The actual depth?

A. The actual depth of each of the layers.

Q. Now, how did Mr. Murray miss it? You read his deposition. Can you explain that to me?

MR. PORTER: Object to form.

THE WITNESS: I'm not sure how. I read that part, and I just couldn't understand what he was doing, other than he was talking—he was building—you did a great job of asking the question and he followed you right along through that thing, including the talk about a 40 millimeter drop-off in the shoulder, which is not the standard.

BY MR. SCHWARTZ:

Q. But it was—and I'm asking: It was the agreement as far as this contract, wasn't it?

MR. PORTER: Object to form

THE WITNESS: Not on the shoulder, no, sir.

BY MR. SCHWARTZ:

Questioning regarding a document

Q. What does paragraph 25 say about that?

A. Paragraph 25—

Q. Of the MOT.

A. Paragraph 25: "The contractor shall ensure at the end of each day all pavement drop-off"—pavement drop-off. If you ever deal with drop-off, they're talking about shoulder drop-offs—"pavement drop-offs shall not exceed 40 millimeters unless barricaded by a suitable warning device as described in Index 600."

That 40 millimeters is referring to lane-to-lane. As a matter of fact, I talked to Mr. Patrick Morisette, Jr., who prepared this, to verify. He said, "Absolutely." He said, "If not, I would have just said—if we had no pavement, I would have said see Index 600." Because when you go to Index 600, they talk about shoulder drop-offs. This is talking about pavement drop-off or lane-to-lane drop-offs.[162]

Q. Well, where does the MOT talk about the shoulder drop-off?

A. They basically say that—Paragraph No. 1, Note No. 1, says you use the 600 series.[163]

Q. Okay.

A. And you go to 600 series and this starts talking about shoulder drop-offs.

Information provided in answer leads to new line of questioning

Q. Now, I asked you about all the materials you reviewed, and you told me the depositions that you reviewed and you listed them out. You didn't list that fellow on the materials reviewed, so let me go back and ask the question in a different way. Have you talked to any witnesses in this case?

A. No. And I apologize. I should have put him down. That's the only gentleman I've talked to here.

Q. That's not a problem.

A. No. I did talk to him because I was concerned of the repetitious—what I thought was a repetitious note.

First opinion

Q. Now, I want to shift back to some other questions, other areas, regarding your first opinion that Spielman & Wilkins properly administered the contract.

You mentioned that part of your opinion was based on the letters that Daniel Birge wrote to Peter Cruz with Herrington General. Is that correct?

A. That's correct, sir.

Q. And explain to me, in your opinion, again, or in your own words, why that was important to you, what that showed, and so forth?

---

[162] The witness yet again volunteers information that was not asked for.
[163] The expert knows the key document very well.

A. In reviewing both the photographs that he took showing signs down and other comments that he wrote in those memos and other memos that followed, he was putting something in writing.

Most CEI consultants, and even DOT employees, for that matter, tend to do a lot of verbal direction and there's no documentation. Then later the contractor says, "Gee, I forgot you told me that." At least these were in writing. So I think it's what should be.

CPAM even talks about trying to get the response back, after they get it corrected, in writing. That was not the case, but Mr. Birge indicated that he would check after he made those—if he advised Mr. White at some period of time that there were some—within 24 to 48 hours, there was generally a response.

Q. CPAM appears to require that the response be in writing, doesn't it?

A. They do. But basically it's something that's—very seldom is even the direction to the contractor of deficiencies put in writing.

Q. Yes. Well, I understand that that's your position, that very seldom it is. But the way CPAM says or talks, it requires the contractor to respond in writing to those written letters from Spielman & Wilkins?

A. Yeah.[164] And that would be a nice thing to have, but it's more important, based on construction, that if there is a deficiency that the deficiency be addressed. And if you're there to see it addressed, then there's no need to get a response that "By the way, the sign that was down now is up." It's been verified.

Q. But my question is—first I want to establish that CPAM requires the contractor to respond to the Spielman & Wilkins letters that you've talked about in writing.

A. That's correct.

Q. And second, what is the purpose of requiring that response be in writing?

A. So that later when someone says, "Did they do everything," there's a response by the contractor that he did. That's a burden put on the contractor, not the CEI.

Q. And in this case the contractor did not comply with that CPAM requirement?

A. No. He did the work, but he did not put it in writing.[165]

Q. Well, isn't part of the requirement that it be in writing so that the contractor will do the work? Isn't that the real reason for the requirement in writing?

A. No. I think more important is—basically it's to build a paper trail. I think it's more important to the traveling public and the employees that are working on the job that if there is a deficiency, if there's a sign down or there's a drop-off or washout or something's missing, that that's brought to the contractor's attention.

And there were probably a lot of things that Mr. Birge indicated that were done verbally that never got in writing. But if they were serious enough to put in writing

---

[164] Experts should avoid slang.
[165] The expert shrewdly gives a carefully worded response.

and someone goes out there the next day and sees it's corrected, that's served its purpose.

Now, the contractor should have probably put it in writing. But that doesn't protect the public, if that issue gets done correctly.

Q. And we're assuming that the contractor, from the information you have, corrected the problem within 24 to 48 hours.

A. That's the deposition—or that's the testimony of Mr. Birge and others that—Mr. Perry, I guess, that also indicated that.

Q. Now, is it common in your experience to have the CEI of a construction project have this many problems with the shoulder drop-offs in a project such as this?

MR. HOROWITZ: Object to form.

BY MR. SCHWARTZ:

Q. That's fine. You can [go] ahead and answer.

A. Not at all. As a matter of fact, drop-offs is probably the one single-most problem that one experiences in construction, for a lot of reasons, particularly in a building and resurfacing project, in that you normally have either shoulders that have been built up over a long time that need to be cut down or you have low shoulders or you have erosion problems.

Particularly as you begin to widen roads or do better paving, there's always the problem of washouts. If you're in the rainy period, if you've got a lot of truck traffic—you show me a road that is under construction or a road that's been finished that has a lot of truck traffic and I'm going to show you some drop-offs.

It's a problem. As a matter of fact, it's addressed by making it something that the contractors have to look at. But is it unusual? No, sir. If the job didn't have any drop-offs, I'd be concerned.[166]

Regulations

Q. Now, do you agree that the purpose of Index 600 is to protect the traveling public?

A. No, it's to serve two purposes. It protects the traveling public as well as the employees that are doing the work.[167]

Q. Do you agree that one of the primary purposes of Index 600 is to protect the traveling public?

A. Not solely. If you read Index 600—and I was part of the authorship of that thing originally,[168] when it first came about—was to protect—matter of fact, same thing

---

[166] The expert again demonstrates his vast experience in this field and the comfort he has in his area of expertise.

[167] Good answer.

[168] A powerful fact, but something that should not have been volunteered at deposition. Had the expert not volunteered this at deposition, he would have been able to bring this out at trial when counsel did not expect it and possibly derail a line of inquiry and break counsel's momentum.

with the clear zone. They talk about protecting not only the public that also the workmen that may be building the job or be involved in construction.

Q. Well, I understand it's not the only purpose, to protect the public, but let me ask the question and listen closely. Do you agree that one of the primary purposes of Index 600 is to protect the general public?

A. That is one of those—of many, yes, sir.

Trying to get a concession

Q. And do you agree that, with regard to the shoulder drop-off, that a shoulder drop-off greater than three inches is dangerous to the general motoring public?

MR. PORTER: Object to form.

THE WITNESS: Studies have been done that indicate that when you start getting in excess of three inches, three and a half or four—as a matter of fact, some of the early discussions was to have the drop-off at four inches. Three inches was chosen.

But yes, shoulder drop-offs as they begin to build up begin to be a major problem, particularly after the job is completed. That's where you see a lot of the accidents happen, because of overcorrection.

BY MR. SCHWARTZ:

Q. Just like what we claim happened in this case?

MR. PORTER: Let me object—

THE WITNESS: You claim. I have not seen any physical evidence in what I've reviewed. Even I think the experts on both sides are not sure whether he ever dropped off or not. There's no doubt that he did lose control and it was a tragic accident.[169]

BY MR. SCHWARTZ:

Q. Now, if you get drop-offs created by erosion, you get drop-offs created by trucks, if drop-offs of over three inches can be dangerous, why is it that you have so many problems with contractors on construction projects, getting them to keep the shoulder safed up?

MR. HOROWITZ: Object to form.

THE WITNESS: The typical problem—there's no excuse for it. They typical problem normally is the contractor is trying to basically complete the project and to meet schedules and to get pay quantities out. And therefore the less maintenance they do, the better it is.

But I didn't see anything in the photographs that would indicate that this—that there was a major problem that would have created a problem there that showed the contractor not doing a reasonable job.

BY MR. SCHWARTZ:

---

[169] The expert is prepared. The concession only goes so far.

More factual assumptions

Q. The contractor was behind schedule on this job, wasn't he, got behind schedule?

A. I have not seen that. You've asked that question of I think everyone, and I've not seen any contractor or any individual indicate that they were. So I don't know.[170, 171]

Q. Now, you're aware that in the letters that Mr. Birge wrote to Peter Cruz, Exhibit 13, that in one of those letters Mr. Birge complained about shoulder drop-offs that violated the rule throughout the project; is that a fair statement? You can take your time, and if there's one—

A. That was the—as a matter of fact, the May 30th letter I think he indicated—

Q. Right. Just take your time.

(Examines instruments.)[172]

A. "Edge of pavement at shoulder drop-off throughout project," parentheses, "unsafe condition."

Q. Now, did that surprise you, since he'd already notified him of shoulder drop-off problems in two earlier letters there shown in Exhibit 13 that there were no shoulder drop-offs throughout the project?

A. No. From Spielman & Wilkins's standpoint, they continued to monitor and tell the contractor. They were just simply—in the other letters they have specific locations that they talked about.

Q. Right.

A. Here they're telling him that he needs to look at the overall job and correct the drop-offs that may occur.

Factual questions

Q. Why would there be overall drop-off problems that time of year? Do you have any idea, from reviewing the materials, the depositions, the information you have?

A. Once again, I don't know why. I know that in the review of the photographs I looked at and saw the video—there was video taken by Southwest Traffic. I'm not sure if it was taken the day before or the day after the accident. But they videotaped the whole job.

And from what I saw on that video was that the shoulders were in reasonably good shape. There were some basic low areas, but I don't think anything was excessive.

Q. Do you agree that Daniel Birge had an obligation to make sure that those shoulder drop-offs did not exceed three inches?

MR. PORTER: Object to form.

---

[170] This experienced expert is correctly not afraid to answer "I don't know" when he doesn't in fact know the answer.

[171] The expert also wisely resists the temptation to take a cheap shot at a co-defendant.

[172] The expert wisely takes time to carefully review the document prior to responding.

THE WITNESS: Yes. And I think he did so in putting the contractor on notice. And I'm not sure what checking—I didn't see much measurement, but if something—once you know how much asphalt you're putting down, it's not difficult for someone to look through—or drive through and look at it and see that you're probably in the two-and-a-half inch range or three-inch range.[173]

BY MR. SCHWARTZ:

Challenging a witness's version of the facts

Q. Do you know whether or not Daniel Birge ever physically measured the shoulder drop-offs on that project before this wreck occurred?

A. I did not see anyplace in his deposition that he said he did, other than knowing how much asphalt was going down and about what it appeared to be.

Q Yes, sir. Do you remember in his deposition that he said the way he checked the drop-offs was by driving through the project? Do you remember reading that?

A. I think I just finished saying that, that he knew how much asphalt they were doing and by visually going through there he was able to pretty well tell that it was two and a half to three inches or in that range.

Q. Do you remember him saying that he drove down the project on the lane that wasn't being paved, where the traveling public normally rode?

A. Yes, sir.

Q. And do you agree that if he's driving down the road that the traveling public travels on—and that's the outside lane, we agree, in both the northbound and southbound lanes—is that correct?—at the time of the wreck?

A. That's correct.

Q. And leading up to the wreck? And the paving was on the inside lane. Is that a fair statement?

A. That's a correct statement.

Q. Going north and south?

A. That's correct.

Q. And so what you're telling me is that in your experience—are you saying that it's your opinion that it was proper for him to ride down the road where the traveling public was and fulfill his responsibility of checking that three-inch shoulder drop-off on the median without getting out of his truck? Is that—

A. I was waiting to see—I don't think you are characterizing his statement correctly. He indicated that most of the time, if he had a choice, he drove on that, but he did check—from time to time, he did go back. And there's no doubt in my mind that during the course of the job that one time or the other he probably did go on the inside lanes to look.

Q. He never—you agree, though, that he never said he did in his deposition, did he?

---

[173] The expert does not dispute that the engineers had a responsibility for safety (which would not have been credible), but he firmly states that that obligation was met.

MR PORTER: Object to form.

THE WITNESS: Well, I think he indicated that he checked the bump, if you will, to see that. So if you do that, then you are in the inside lane. How often he did that, I don't know.

BY MR. SCHWARTZ:

Q. Let me make sure I understand. In his deposition he admitted that most of the time he rode down the outside lane where the traveling public was; isn't that right?

A. Well, yeah.

Q. Most of the time?

A. That's correct.

Q. And that he checked the drop-off visually while riding along. He said that, didn't he?

MR. PORTER: Object to form.

THE WITNESS: I don't know if he said it for that lane. So what I'm saying is that even though he did indicate—I think we're putting two things together that don't belong together.

I think he did indicate that he—if he had the choice, I think he liked traveling on the outside lane, not the inside lane, which was probably a slower lane and one that was easier to drive in, even though it was rougher, based on the testimony. But I think he also indicated he did some visual tests.

I've done both, and I tend to drive on the outside lanes most of the time.

Expert's personal practices questioned

BY MR. SCHWARTZ:

Q. So you do it like he does?

A. I do. But I can tell you that when I look at the job, even though—if you asked me where I drove, I would say the outside lane. But I can tell you that I know enough that I've driven on both lanes to check drop-offs.

Q. Did you see anywhere Daniel Birge's deposition where he said he checked the shoulder drop-off from the inside lane?

A. I didn't see that he said that, but I did not see where he said he checked the shoulder drop-off from the outside lane, either.

And I did look at the photographs and know how much asphalt went down and feel that at least the photographs I looked at, the majority—not the majority—all of them—

Q. Well, what's your understanding of how Mr. Birge said he checked the—

A. Visually.

Q. Driving in the outside lane?

A. I don't know what lane he was in.

Q. Okay. That's fair enough. So you're telling me that from a consulting engineer's standpoint it's adequate for Mr. Birge to visually check the drop-off of the shoulders on the inside lane without getting out and looking at it; is that a fair statement?

MR. PORTER: Object to form.

THE WITNESS: Given the conditions of what I saw in the video and also the photographs, there was no reason to think otherwise on this job. If you had a job— I'm doing one currently where I have some 10 to 12 inch drop offs. I can tell you that I get out and measure those, because it's hard to believe that you have that kind of a drop-off. Those are very visible.

BY MR. SCHWARTZ:

Q. So what you're saying is because he knew about how much asphalt they were putting out, he could just check those shoulder drop-offs visually and didn't have a responsibility to go check them and measure them; is that correct or not?

MR. PORTER: Object to form.

THE WITNESS: I don't think you characterize it correctly when you say he didn't have a duty to. Certainly I think an inspector or someone doing a reasonably good job can look at something visually—as a matter of fact, there are photographs taken during the course of that job where the buildup was such that they actually had to trim back the shoulder—so basically the shoulder is two and a half to three inches down low.

I think overall from what I saw would indicate that there was no need in this job to get out and check it. I wish he had done so. He took some great measurements on the lane-to-lane. I wish he'd taken those same measurements as Mr. Ivy did.[174]

Counsel seeks more admissions

BY MR. SCHWARTZ:

Q. You agree it would be better practice for him to get out and at least spot-check the shoulder drop-offs to make sure they're not over three inches, don't you?

MR. PORTER: Object to form.

THE WITNESS: If there was a problem, yes, sir. And I wish he'd have done it at this location, because I think we would have seen that it was three inches or less.

BY MR. SCHWARTZ:

Q. Now, I'm a little bit unclear. Mr. Birge knew that he'd been having shoulder drop-off problems throughout the project before this wreck occurred, didn't he?

A. There had been a lot of washouts. There had been mitered end—drop-offs in the mitered end—drop offs in a lot of the mitered ends. There had been some isolated locations. I don't see—even in that letter of June 1st, where he said basically look at the drop-off, unsafe conditions, I think he's just telling the contractor that you do have low shoulders that you need to be addressing.

Q. You'd agree that Mr. Birge was aware that washouts and other types of shoulder drop-off problems had occurred basically throughout the length of that project; is that correct?

---

[174] The expert gives as good of an explanation as possible to a key problem area in his factual assumptions.

MR. HOROWITZ: Object to the form.

THE WITNESS: In isolated conditions, yes, sir.

BY MR. SCHWARTZ:

Q. And you'd agree that he had an obligation to continue to check that even as this last pavement was occurring in the few days leading up to this wreck?

MR. PORTER: Again, object to form.

THE WITNESS: In my opinion he did do the check by doing visual.

BY MR. SCHWARTZ:

Q. I understand that.

A. Now, if the contractor said—

Q. I didn't ask you if he did it or not. I asked you if he had a duty to.

A. Certainly that's one of the things he ought to be looking at.

Q. All right. He's actually required to inspect the drop-off daily, isn't he?

MR. PORTER: Object to form.

THE WITNESS: I'm not sure daily. Certainly anytime you're on the job that becomes an important issue so you ought to look at it.[175]

BY MR. SCHWARTZ:

Q. You reviewed those exhibits I attached to the other depositions. We've talked about 13 and 17. Let's look at Exhibit 2, which is the CPAM.

MR. PORTER: Exhibit 2 to whose depo? Do you remember?

MR. SCHWARTZ: Well, I've just numbered these—they're the same in all of them. I've got it handy, it you don't have it.

THE WITNESS: Yeah, it is here. It's No. 2 here.

BY MR. SCHWARTZ:

Questioned on applicable regulation

Q. What I'm asking you is whether or not Exhibit 2, which is the CPAM book, requires Spielman & Wilkins or the DOT to inspect the drop-offs daily.

A. Let me read this one more time,[176] because I'm not sure if it says daily. It says drop-off and clear zone criteria are one of the things that need to be considered, but it reads "department personnel," which in this case would be Spielman & Wilkins, "shall make both day MOT inspections and weekly night inspections."

What they're telling you is just don't inspect it on the day each time; you've got to do daytimes and nighttimes. It doesn't say daily.

Q. But you agree that Spielman & Wilkins was under the impression they had to inspect it daily, aren't you?

A. I'm not sure if they had to do it daily, but I would certainly think that as a responsible—but if you read this, it says "any deficiency noted shall be notified in

---

[175] The expert again demonstrates active listening skills.

[176] The expert correctly takes his time to carefully review the document before responding.

writing and notation made in the contract daily diary," which was not done in the diary but it was done by letter.

Q. So you agree that Spielman & Wilkins did not comply with the introductory portion of the CPAM manual that's listed in Exhibit 2 in that they failed to document deficiencies in their project daily diary; isn't that correct?

MR. PORTER: Object to form.

THE WITNESS: I don't agree with that. I think the letters suffice. They certainly did it in writing when they felt they had to. And if it was serious enough, then the notation—you probably should have done it in the daily diary if you're trying to take some action.

BY MR. SCHWARTZ:

Q. They never documented any shoulder drop-off problem in the project daily diary, did they?

A. No. They did it by basically writing letters and sending copies to all the appropriate parties.

Q. Do you agree that they violated a portion of this CPAM requirement where it says a notation regarding the deficiency shall be documented in the project daily diary?

A. That's what it says. But in my opinion, if you're out in the field and you're actually documenting, which they were doing and most CEIs don't do it, they did a more than adequate job.

Q. Well, you'd agree, though, they didn't follow that requirement?

MR. PORTER: Object to form.

THE WITNESS: That's correct, sir.[177]

BY MR. SCHWARTZ:

More admissions

Q. All right. Thank you. Do you agree—and I'm just trying to establish parameters— that if there is a drop-off of more than three inches on the shoulder, that drop-off should be corrected before the road is opened to the motoring public?

MR. PORTER: Object to form.

THE WITNESS: If you have a drop-off in excess of three inches, then that needs to be corrected. It could be corrected one of several ways; either a wedge, rework the shoulders, or barricade that lane.

BY MR. SCHWARTZ:

Q. And that needs to be done before it's opened to the traveling public?

A. If there's over three inches, yes, sir.[178]

---

[177] An important admission, but with the caveat that the engineers followed the spirit of the regulation with their other documentation.

[178] The expert wisely makes this concession without forcing counsel to drag it out of him.

Opinion expert will not be giving
Q. Thank you. And it is my understanding that you have not been asked to render any opinion about whether or not the speed limit on this job was appropriate? Is that a fair statement?
MR. PORTER: Object to form.
THE WITNESS: Only to the extent that I know I read some statements by other expert witnesses in this job where they talked about it should have been a no-passing lane and all that, and reduced speed. I think that would have been impractical and not certainly in keeping with good Arizona standards.
So whether the speed needed to be changed, I don't know. Whether you would need to have this as a no-passing zone, I think that would have been impractical.
BY MR. SCHWARTZ:
Q. But it would be proper to have it as a no-passing zone if the drop-off between the lanes was greater than 1.6 inches?
A. If that's what it was and you were going to maintain that, yes. But that's probably the least desireable [sic], because you create other problems when you begin no-passing lanes. Because people tend to pass, and if you've got a condition like that, you ought to correct the condition.

Normal construction procedure
Q. Okay. Now, I want to ask you some questions about construction procedure in terms of the shoulders and so forth and how they're handled normally during a paving project such as this.
We agree that there's some drop-off created when you pave the shoulder of the road or pave the lane of travel as was done in this case?
A. In this location, yes, sir.
Q. And what is the normal procedure, in your experience, that contractors should use or do use to correct or eliminate that drop-off that's created?
A. Within some reasonable time, and that reasonable time varies, you normally would come back. In this case, since there was basically some more asphalt to come before that second lift was to start, by that time 'the shoulder should have been corrected. If not, you would have a drop-off that would exceed three inches. So as long as the drop-off—you want to try to eliminate drop-off at any time you can.
Q. Right.
A. Any kind of drop-off.
Q. Why is that?
A. Because basically drop-offs tend to have—most drivers tend to overreact. Even though I'm not a re-constructionist, I've seen that happen.
But a three inch drop-off, and particularly a drop-off where you've got a beveled—or an edge on the asphalt as this job had is not a difficult drop-off to handle.
So at some period of time, whether it be a week or two weeks or sometime later, it's not unreasonable—I read someplace, and I don't know whether that's being done

357

on this job, that they would pave through Thursday and then begin to do some work later. I know that after the accident they did rework the shoulders. Whether that was the normal schedule or done because of the accident, I'm not sure.

But I don't find any criticism in the fact that the shoulders had not been reworked even thought they'd been paved for some time.

Other witness's deposition

Q. Well, do you remember reading Mr. Bishop's deposition? He was the man that operated the road grader that safed up the shoulders?

A. Yes, sir.

Q. Do you remember him testifying that that was their normal schedule and that it wasn't—the safing up of the shoulders was not done in response to the wreck?

A. That's what he said, yes, sir.

Q. So do you have some evidence to indicate that the safing up of the shoulders was not done in response to the wreck but was done in the ordinary course of their plan?

A. Yeah. If they normally paved through Thursday and stopped and then came back.

Q. But you admitted earlier that it's better to eliminate all drop-offs when you can; is that a fair statement?

A. If you can avoid all drop-offs, you're better off. But there's been enough studies to indicate that as long as the drop-off doesn't exceed three inches, that's one that's not going to create a major problem.

Q. In this case you've read the depositions of the workers, all of the workers of Herrington General that worked on building that road; is that correct?

A. If they're listed there, yes, sir.

Q. Well, you've read all the ones that are listed on your exhibit?

A. Yes, sir.

Fishing around for information and opinions to be used against a co-defendant

Q. And from reading that, do you agree that they had access to the proper equipment needed to safe up those shoulders after they finished paving it and before it was open to the general public?

A. I would not expect in a resurfacing job such as this that before you open that lane at the end of the paving night—that you'd open that lane before safing up the shoulders. You may do that on the interstate, but certainly not on this kind of a facility, particularly if your drop-off is in the two and a half to three inch range.

Q. Well, I understand that, but that really wasn't my question. Listen to me closely. We're talking about apples and oranges again. My question was: Do you agree that Herrington General has access to the equipment they needed to safe up the shoulders of that road before they opened it back up to the general public after they paved?[179]

---

[179] Note that when the witness does not answer the question asked, counsel simply repeats the question until it is answered.

A. I didn't see anyplace that they did not have—I'm not sure, but I think there was some discussion one time about whether the motor grader was there or not. But the answer is yes, that equipment was there and could have—was there, yes.

Q. And what equipment do they need to safe up those shoulders?

A. Normally a disc. Maybe—if you've got material—normally a grader.

Q. And they can safe up the shoulders at night, I believe too; is that correct?

A. They can do a lot of things, if necessary. In my opinion it was not necessary here.

Q. Well, I understand that you saw it wasn't necessary. We aren't talking about whether it was necessary; we're talking about whether or not they could do it. And what I want to do is establish clearly on the record that they had the ability to disc and grade those shoulders and safe them up so they were level with the road before they opened it to the traveling public. Is that true?

A. I would assume so. I don't know what their schedule was. Yes.

Q. And there was some discussion about the fact that the road grader was somewhere else while they were doing the paving of the inside lanes. Is that correct?

A. There was some discussion of that, but I think later in the dailies it showed up it was there. But I think in one the depositions that I read—I'm not sure if it was Daniel Birge or something—but there was some discussion that it might have been moved to another job or moved someplace for a while.

Counsel seeks more admissions

Q. Now, you said you looked at the photographs of the trooper and that you found some photographs that did show one isolated spot, or maybe two, where the drop-off was more than three inches?

A. No. I indicated there's one area, one isolated location, that it's conceivable that that one spot could have been more than three inches.[180]

Q. I want to show you what we've all marked as photographs 1, 2 and 3 exhibits 1, 2 and 3 to the trooper's deposition, and ask you to examine those photographs. Is that the isolated spot you're talking about?

A. No, sir. I think in those, by the way, when you lay out this thing and you know what asphalt went on here, you're dealing with about two and a half inches.

Q. You're talking about in exhibits 1, 2, and 3?

A. Yes, 1, 2, and 3. That shows—you know, basically it shows the overbuild and then the inch and a half, which you're dealing with an inch and a half with a well established shoulder. And I can tell you that I can duplicate that and then take a core right there and find out that you—

Q. Exhibits 4, 5, and 6 are the next group I'd like for you to examine.

A. This is the one that I had there, where you basically are talking—

Q. Excuse me. For the record, we're looking at—

---

[180] The expert answers carefully and does not permit counsel to mischaracterize his prior testimony.

A. Right now I'm looking at exhibit no. 6. and where the—you basically have—this is the overbuild that was shown to be .79 inches. I said less than an inch. Here's the inch and a half. As a matter of fact, it was measured by Mr. Roderick in this area, that showed this between these two levels being about an inch and a half to an inch and five-eighths. This is one inch.

Q. Well, let me make sure it's clear for the record. On photograph number 6 you're saying that Mr. Roderick measured the difference between the travel lane and the crossover—

A. And the crossover.

Q. And that is was one and a half to one and five-eighths?

A. I think that's the two measurements he had. He had some at one and a half and some at one and five-eighths in this general area.

Q. And this general area—

A. This general area being the area between the asphalt pavement, the pavement that was in place at the time of the accident, and the pavement on the crossover which was lower.

Q. And how much of a drop-off was measured between the crossover and the grassy shoulder?

A. I didn't see any measurements there, other than this is an overbuild—

Q. Why do you say that?

A. It's a leveling course that was put on the total roadway, and that leveling course, based on that, was supposed to be—and I see no reason why it would not be—the .79 to one inch. Actually, a little less than one inch.

Now, in this area the trooper not only bends this thing and follows the wedge but actually has to put a rock over this thing. I'm not saying in this small area—and I'm talking about when we look at exhibit no. 6 and we look at this rock in this general area—that that might be—and I say "might be" because, once again, you're looking at this, this being the pavement of the crossover and the ground. That doesn't appear to be that much different. And then we know what the super pave was.

So in this area is the only one I say that that one spot may well be more than three inches, but I doubt it. And I know we can't go further because—

Q. Now, exhibits 4 and 5, let me represent to you, have been reported to be of the same location as photograph 6 by the trooper. Okay?

Questioning about key measurement made by another witness

A. Okay. I see that now. He's back at the pavement and there's the rock, where he's having to bend the tape measure around the rock to hold it. So I don't know if that inch is up in the air or basically—because if you notice he didn't take any pictures that showed this.

Q. Showed what?

A. That first reading may well be on the ground or it may well be up in the air. It looks like it's the area—we see some stone right here.

Q. I'm confused about what you're saying right now. I'm sorry.

A. All right. He took a tape measure, and to hold it there he put a rock on it and bent it up. And you see a 1 showing.

Q. Yes, sir, in photograph no. 5.

A. 5 and 6.

Q. And 4. They're all the same.

A. So what I'm saying, part of that measurement that he's showing here is occupied by the rock itself.

Q. Well, excuse me for interrupting, but let me ask you: What about photograph no. 5 makes you believe that his tape measure is bent?

A. Let's go to no. 6. There's the ground. There's the one inch. That's probably the ground. So what I'm saying is I don't know if he was using this rock to hold down— if you notice in your other photographs—

Q. You're looking at?

A. Now I'm looking at number 2. There is no rock where he bent over. As a matter of fact, you can see it even clearer here. If he is, he's got—

Q. No. 3?

A. On number 3. But here to hold it down for some reason he ended up using a rock. He can explain that better than anybody else.

Q. Right. Now, do you know if he used that rock to hold it down or just to put up against it?

A. I don't know. I don't know. But I can tell you that looking at that—here's a 1. Here's a 1 right here, which still shows some of the natural ground.

It's also a fairly long wedge. I think if you did the mathematics in this area, I think you're going to find it's going to be close to three inches.

Q. Now, you haven't done the mathematics in that area, have you?

A. No. I intend to blow that up and do that, even though, as I said earlier, this one hole, this one area where the rock is, conceivably could be less.

Q. Well, let me ask you some more questions about photographs 4, 5, and 6. We agree in photograph 5 that the end of the tape measure where the rock is, that you can clearly see the one inch mark on it. Is that accurate?

A. That's a fair statement, yes, sir.

Q. All right. And how many inches does the trooper show there are from the top of the paved area down to the ground in that photograph?

A. I'm not sure if he put what number was here. I know he indicated five inches, five to eight inches. This is probably the eight inch area, because there's number 8 there, which you can see better on this wedge here.

Q. So, now, tell me again how you're going to turn that eight inches that we just agreed to into slightly more than three inches.

MR. PORTER: Again, object to form. Go ahead.

THE WITNESS: I think you just take this information right here alone and come up with a good full interpretation, or basically go in and take a core here when you get to the overbuild, because we know this overbuild right here is either close to or no less than three-quarters of an inch above the natural ground right here, and that this is one and a half inches. And if you add one inch to that, then you're at two and a half inches.

BY MR. SCHWARTZ:

Q. So what you did basically is ignored the fact that he measured but eight inches—that he measured eight inches and decided it was two and a half, based on the overbuild being an inch and the pavement that was put on top of the overbuild being an inch and a half?

MR. PORTER: Object to form.

THE WITNESS: No, I didn't ignore it. I said that if it was important enough to take measurements and this picture, then it would have been important enough, since he had a second trooper in that area that could have assisted him, to put a level here and measured down.

If he had done that, I would have accepted his measurement, but—just like I don't accept the two and a half inches on the pavement-to-pavement drop-offs.[181]

BY MR. SCHWARTZ:

Q. Now, do you have any idea on exhibit 6 what the angle is that's shown in that photograph from the edge of the pavement down to the bottom of the tape measure where the rock—

A. Appears to be about a 45-degree, but I—

Q. Is there any way to measure that?

A. No. You could probably do some photo interpretation. You couldn't do it here. That's probably—if you were going to try that at all, it would be on No. 6, it would appear to be about a 45.

Q. Now, are you aware that the trooper in his deposition said Mr. Franco dropped off the shoulder of the road and then came back onto the road?

A. About 36 feet back from this location, yes, sir.

Q. Yes, sir. And are you aware that the trooper said that he came back on the road where he took these photographs, 4, 5, and 6?

MR. PORTER: Object to form.

THE WITNESS: That's where the trooper said. You know, in looking at the photographs before the shoulder was reworked, I did not see any evidence in these photographs—there were the photographs taken I think the day after the accident or the same day. And I didn't see any indication, so I couldn't tell you, and I would just—I would rely on someone else that's doing the reconstruction to find out

---

[181] The expert is prepared to give a plausible reason why the trooper's measurement was unreliable.

whether—because I know eyewitnesses, and particularly Mr. Rogers, clearly has him not going off the pavement.

The expert wisely refuses to stray beyond his own area of expertise
BY MR. SCHWARTZ:

Q. But you aren't rendering any opinion with regard to whether or not he went off the pavement; you're just regarding the shoulder drop-off?
A. That's right. I'm leaving that to other people, yes, sir.
Q. And you're aware that the trooper testified that in photographs 1, 2, and 3, that was where he dropped off the road initially the first time?
A. That's where he indicates, yes, sir.
Q. All right. Now, you've said that photographs 4, 5, and 6 might be a little bit over three inches, the drop-off?
A. I said if you had any spot at all in this area right where the rock is, that that one location might be. However, the minute you start looking here, it may not be. Photographs are very deceptive when taken this way. If he had put a level and measured down and taken that—I wish he had done that, because I would rather rely on a measurement. Similar to what Mr. Ivy did on this, even though it was just one.[182]

Counsel seeks more admissions
Q. Now, do you agree that if it turns out this one spot at 4, 5, and 6 has a drop-off of more than three inches, that that would violate Index 600?
A. No.
Q. Why?
A. There isn't any way in the real world to go in and start looking at one spot here and saying, "Oh, my gosh, there's a violation right there."

I don't know if it does or not, but if this spot were determined to be more that three inches—and I don't think it's going to be much more, but if it were to be that, you've got one isolated area next to a paved crossover.

So what happens at that point with a drop-off, if you happen to go off, not coming back on, but at that one location if that's where your wheel happened to go off, less than six inches later you're back into a paved median or crossover and then back into the pavement?

So if you're going to have a drop-off, a small isolated area, that's probably where you want to have it, even though it's best not to have one. So it doesn't constitute a violation, because there isn't a job that I couldn't go and find an area that—a truck yesterday might have gouged out an area.[183]
Q. But any drop-off of over three inch violates Index 600, doesn't it?
MR. PORTER: Object to form.

---

[182] The witness once again refused to let counsel mischaracterize his prior testimony.
[183] The witness plausibly explains his opinion as best as he can.

THE WITNESS: It doesn't violate the standards. It says if you've got drop-offs more than three inches they need to be addressed, and addressing them by basically either barricading them or redoing them.[184]

BY MR. SCHWARTZ:

Q. Are you telling me that—and I just want to be sure that I understand what you're saying. Are you telling me that if you've got a drop-off of over three inches, that's not a violation of 600?

MR. PORTER: Again, object to form.

THE WITNESS: You're using some great words. Let me try and say it in my own simple way. Yes, Index 600 says that if you have a drop-off in excess of three inches, then you've got other things you can do. No, you don't go and tell a contractor, "By the way, you've just violated"—if a large truck today came down this road and dropped a tire and spun off and ended up in that one area, yes, that has to be fixed, because it's different from what the standards call for. But when you use the word "violation," it's like giving somebody a ticket because you found an area that's there. I think the most important thing is to make sure that the drop-offs consistently in this area were not in excess of three inches.

BY MR. SCHWARTZ:

Key factual assumptions again questioned

Q. Now, is it your judgment that the drop-offs shown in photographs 1, 2, and 3 were less than three inches?

A. Absolutely. I think in this area, given the turf and given the way—I don't know where he put that bottom on this thing. I can see bottoms around here, and yet he's almost at two inches when he's right near the bottom of this thing. So I don't know where the bend starts.

Q. Where is this? At 6?

A. This at 6 looks like where it's starting to bend up on the wedge on this thing here.

Q. How deep did he measure, in your judgment, the drop-off?

A. I think he said—this is probably the one he said five inches. I know he used the five to eight inches, so it would probably be in this area.

Q. What does the ruler show the drop-offs to be, just looking at it the way it is in photograph 2?

A. I don't know if it's five inches or six inches. Certainly at—let me see if there's a better—all right. At this point here he's starting to make the bend. So it would look to be that he's showing six inches there.

Q. Okay. Now, let's get Mr. Ivy's pictures out and look at them. I talked to you and said we were going to do that earlier.

A. Let me see. I think they're here in the—

---

[184] The expert is very familiar with the applicable regulation.

Q. And we've got the photographs out, and again, I wanted to—I don't know—we haven't marked them, but I don't think we need to. Let's just—for the record, let me report that we're talking to the witness about photographs that are an exhibit contained in a letter dated April 11th, 2003, to me from Mr. Horowitz, where he reports that these were photographs that were taken on or about July 28th. And we later learned Mr. Ivy took those. And you were showing me the drop-off that he measured from, and you were saying that it was two and a half inches, I believe?

A. I said two and a quarter to two and a half.[185] Let me first say you indicated you weren't sure this photograph in the earlier testimony that I gave—whether that was pavement-to-pavement or pavement-to-drop-off. And that's the shoulder. That's—this area is not drop-off—I mean, this is the shoulder drop-off. It's not a pavement-to-pavement. And what it's showing here is—I'd say two and a half. I think his testimony was two and a half. I think his testimony was two and a quarter to two and a half.

Q. Now, I'm still not convinced that he's talking about a shoulder.

A. The other photographs of the roadway are here.

MR. PORTER: Let's try to keep this in a question and answer format. I don't think there's any pending question. So if you want to ask a question, go ahead.[186]

THE WITNESS: I reread the deposition today, and it just talked about that he found an area within the work zone of shoulder drop-off, but I can't—it's not this area where you have grass. It's not this area.

MR. PORTER: I think he said within the zone of the accident.

THE WITNESS: The zone of the accident. The reason I'm saying that is he's looking at—this fresh asphalt. You know, at one time I thought it might be here, but you would have—this is overbuild, versus what was there before. So it would have to be on this side. If it was near the median, I don't know. I think he called it the—in his deposition he said the zone of the accident. So—and I can tell you it's not—let me go back.

BY MR. SCHWARTZ:

Q. I think we'd better—

A. Let me show you something a minute, if I can, in exhibit number 6. If this measurement were taken here, you would—if he had taken this kind of a measurement here, then you would be looking at pavement. That's not what you see here. There's basically some rocks and other things there. I just wish I knew where that was, because it would be great to see whether it was in this general area or forward of that site.[187]

---

[185] Excellent. The expert does not let counsel misstate his testimony. This requires a high level of concentration.

[186] Retaining counsel correctly points out to the witness to simply answer questions propounded, not to respond to statements of opposing counsel.

[187] This expert seems to have an irresistible urge to volunteer information.

Q. Are there any photographs that you looked at of the trooper that show any area at the time of the wreck that did not have grassy shoulders?

A. Yes.

Q. Where?

A. Oh, that did not have grassy shoulders? I'm sorry.

Q. Right.

A. Yes, I saw some that had grassy shoulder.

Q. Did you see any photographs of the trooper that did not demonstrate grassy shoulders?

MR. PORTER: Are you talking about at the time of the accident?

Q. At the time of the accident.

A. No, sir.

Q. But you agree that these photographs that you say are the measurement between the freshly paved road and what you say is the shoulder shows a shoulder that does not have a grassy shoulder?

A. Well, first let me say if you're trying to find an isolated area, there were some areas—as a matter of fact, I can point you to some here—that did not have—here's a good example. Here's one that doesn't have grass right there at that spot.

Now, did he measure that spot? That's just forward of the crossover. So I don't know where he measured, other than the accident zone. I get the impression he measured between the crossover and where Mr. Franco left the pavement, but I couldn't tell you.

Q. In forming your opinion that the drop-off of the shoulder is less than three inches, would it matter to you if Mr. Ivy had taken a measurement of the northbound lane as opposed to the southbound lane?

A. Well, certainly to the extent that I wish somebody had measured other than the way the trooper did it, because it would eliminate a lot of the things. I wish Mr. Birge, as he measured the lane-to-lane drop-off, would have also measured this. I would have been great to have.

So, yes. If he'd measured the northbound—the northbound is not as important as the southbound, because the southbound—the issue is did the drop off and therefore—

Q. On the southbound?

A. On the southbound—and cause an erratic motion.

Q. So not saying it is, but if Mr. Ivy was measuring the northbound, then you really wouldn't rely on that measurement of the shoulder drop-off?

MR. PORTER: Object to form.

A. Only to the extent that he indicated that he looked at what was typical in the area and he took a measurement. I wish he'd taken more than one measurement.

But I can tell you that looking at these photographs—and these photographs were taken—as a matter of fact, the shoulders have not yet been reworked. There's the mark of the thing.

And you can see in this general area the fact that the shoulder drop-off—that basically you don't have the case there so one could look at the kind of pavement that went into the overbuild and the armor coat and the super pave here and pretty well get an idea that you're looking at shoulders.

And you indicate, by the way—I don't know where Mr. Birge looked from, but there's a car. I can tell you if I was in that car looking here, I could pretty well tell you whether you had shoulders that were in the three-inch range or less. But I would rather be in the other lane.

Q. You agree it would be better to measure instead of guess at it by looking at it from the opposite lane, don't you?

MR. PORTER: Object to form.

A. Certainly a measurement would eliminate all the discussion today.

Q. A measurement would be better, wouldn't it?

A. Would be better, but is it practical? Is it done? No, sir.

MR. PORTER: Object to form.

Q. It's practical?

A. It's practical. But is it done normally in the standard industry practice? No it's not.

Q. Now, let me ask you this question: In these photographs of Mr. Ivy where he took the measurement, this material you say is on the shoulder of the road, are you saying that's totally inconsistent with the kind of material that you would see on a paved road that people would drive on or not?

A. I don't know if that's a driveway or what it is, in all honesty. As I look at it, I—I just know that he took measurements, he said, in the shoulder drop-off. So I don't know if he was taking a shoulder drop-off to a stabilized subgrade or driveway. I couldn't tell you.

Q. Can you tell me if the area where he was taking the measurements, the area you say was not the paved area, obviously—could that have been a paved lane of that highway where that overstructure had been, just from looking at it? I know you don't think it was, and I know you said he didn't—he said it wasn't. But—

A. No way. Not when you look at the aggregate and the dirt and the other things in here. That's not to say that may not be an old asphalt driveway, but it's certainly not pavement.

Q. Now, you mentioned something earlier that I wanted to come back and ask you. You said something about a bevel, and some of these photographs show that it isn't— the shoulder drop-off isn't straight down.

A. Yeah. I think even, as a matter of fact—let's go with this.

Q. Photograph number 3?

A. Number 3. Basically—you have drop-offs, and the drop-offs that create all the problems are the drop-offs that are very sharp, where there is basically the tendency for tires to begin to rub. And when you start getting lower than three or four inches, then the tire has difficulty.

But when you have a rounded or—as a matter of fact, here's a good example, where they've basically asphalted—and I'm looking at, one again, photograph number 3. You can also tell in this photograph that basically—

Q. Photograph 6?

A. Number 6. In the photographs I looked at, in all of them, including the photographs that we looked at taken before and after the accident, that edge had been rounded off or basically wedged. It's probably more rounded, tends to be more—it wasn't a wedge, necessarily.

But if you're going to have a drop-off—if you're going to have an edge with any kind of a drop-off, even if it's less than three inches, that's the preferable way to do it, because your tire will ride up on that thing.

The only time you have problems with a drop-off such as this is when the tire has difficulty of gaining traction, unless it all of a sudden bounces up, and then you lose control. But anytime you have a rounded edge or a wedge or a beveled edge, you're better off.

And that's—these photographs and all the photographs I saw through here all indicate that beyond the pavement, beyond the lane line, there was a roll-down or a wedge.

Opinion expert will not be giving

Q. But in terms of your opinions, you haven't been asked to reconstruct the wreck and give an opinion about how this car would have behaved when it left the road and came back on the road and all of that, have you?

A. I am not a reconstructionist, even though I've given opinions similar to that. But, no, I am not a reconstructionist and do not intend to.

Q. And in terms of the bevel or the angle of that drop-off, you aren't planning to render any opinions about that, are you?

MR. PORTER: Object to the form.

A. Other than to the extent that if you're going to have even a drop-off within the three inches or less, it's a better way to do it.

Q. Right. I understand that. But in terms of specific opinion other than that, you haven't been asked to render any and don't plan to?

MR. PORTER: Object to form.

A. I am not a reconstructionist. So if it had to do with reconstruction, I would not be talking about it.

Q. All right.

MR. PORTER: I want to make sure there's no misunderstanding. As far as this construction and construction practices—

MR. SCHWARTZ: No, I understand.

MR. PORTER: As to whether or not this particular pavement in this particular shoulder was an appropriate construction method or application, he is going to testify about that.

MR. SCHWARTZ: I understand that, and I appreciate your clarifying that. There is no lack of clarity here.

MR. PORTER: Okay.

More focus on key measurements made by others

BY MR. SCHWARTZ:

Q. Now, do you know, in terms of measuring, whether or not there's any margin of error in measuring with the tape measure?

A. Versus.

Q. Well, versus a roller wheel?

A. I've used them both, so I don't—certainly a tape that you can look at physically is probably more accurate, but how close I'm not sure. I've done both and feel comfortable having, from a traffic engineering standpoint, used a roller tape and felt very close that what I was doing was significantly accurate enough.

MR. PORTER: I hate to slow things down, but I need a break.[188]

MR. SCHWARTZ: This is a good time.

(short recess)

Follow-up questions following break

BY MR. SCHWARTZ:

Q. I want to go back and clear up a couple of things. You had a conversation with someone that wrote to the MOT?[189]

A. Yes. That was—the MOT had been subcontracted out from the original designer with a firm—and I'm going to spell it out, because I mispronounce their names all the time. But the name of the firm was Perciante, p-e-r-c-i-a-n-t-e, Dias, d-i-a-s, Morisette, m-o-r-r-i-s-e-t-t-e, Myers, m-y-e-r-s, and Knopf, k-n-o-p-f, P.A. Patrick Morisette, Jr., is the gentleman that basically supervised, is the one whose name is on here?

Q. And that's who you talked to?

A. And that's who I talked to. And basically—

Q. Excuse me. When did you talk to him?

A. I talked to him three weeks ago.

Q. And did you know him before that date?

A. I knew of the firm, and I had one of my old employees that went to work for him, so I'm very familiar with the firm. But other than talking by telephone, no, sir.

---

[188] Retaining counsel asks for the break. This will give the expert time to refresh and recharge before the deposition continues.

[189] Counsel most likely used the break to review his notes and identify follow-up lines of inquiry.

Q. All right. And what conversation did you have with him?

A. The conversation I had with him, I told him about the job and there were some questions. He did what a good engineer should do. He said, "Give me the job. Let me get all the things from my files. Let me review it and then ask me a question."

So a day later he called me back. He said, "Okay. I've got all the information. Tell me your question." So my questions was: "Note 7 is very clear. Why did you have Note 25, and did that 40 millimeters refers to the shoulder drop-off or lane-to-lane?"

He said, "No, no. The shoulder drop-off is handled by Index 600, which we specify in Note number 1." That was just reemphasizing again that if you for whatever reason—you shouldn't do it, but if you were going to leave it more than 50 millimeters, then you needed to do one of the other things, such as barricade, close the lane, or do other things.

Q. Did he say why he reemphasized it?

A. No.

Q. Did you have any other conversation with him?

A. That was the only conversation I had with him and the only issue I asked.

Standard of care questions

Q. Now, I want to go back to the consultant and their role in the construction process. We've established that they are to ensure that the contractor complies with the terms of the contract. Is that correct?

MR. PORTER: Object to form.

A. Their job is to monitor and do the inspection and testing to make sure the job is being built in substantial conformance to plans and specifications.

Q. And as I understand it from what you're telling me, the kind of first step in dealing with the contractor is to verbally talk to him and the second step is to write him a letter, like they did?

A. Well, the CPAM basically talks about writing a letter. Most CEI consultants will tend to basically give the superintendent or whoever the main person is on the job— verbally tell them when they see something wrong that needs to be corrected. Some document it in the dailies, and you see it in the dailies. In this case they wrote letters.

Q. Yes, sir.

A. But normally—and I think Mr. Birge's deposition indicated that a lot of the conversation he had with the contractor was verbal and not necessarily in letter form.

Q. What's the next step after the letters, if the contractor doesn't do what he's requested to do?

A. Probably—you know what? The best example in this job is the incident that happened and there's a letter by a Mr. Silko from the DOT. I think it's Silko.[190]

Q. It is. And we can pull it if you need it. But just tell me generally what—

---

[190] This answer demonstrates the expert's mastery of key facts in the file. Such a mastery is essential and can only be obtained through diligent preparation.

A. That's where he had come through the job, had observed them doing some work on the shoulder, some activity on the shoulder that was within two feet of the edge of the pavement.

At this point he stopped and indicated to one of the Spielman & Wilkins employees that they were in violation of the standard, Mr. Perry, and that they needed to stop the work or get them to do something else.

Mr. Perry had some discussion with him, said he'd just gone to traffic control school and he didn't read where they had to do that, and the fellow said, "Well, you have to."

So he went back, at which time he got a call from somebody that wasn't part of the job at Spielman & Wilkins, sort of saying, "You shouldn't be talking to the employees. You ought to talk to us."

Right after that—and this is a process that I think works well—Mr. Birge called to apologize and said, "I'm glad you brought that to our attention. We'll see that it gets done."

He did inform verbally—because there's nothing in writing other than the discussion—he did inform the contractor of the issue. He then called Mr. Silko to say, "The contractor says he doesn't have to do that, because that's not the way—he's been in the business 20, 25 years and he didn't have to do it."

Mr. Silko at that point basically then called the contractor and had discussion with him and went so far as to indicate that he would probably take steps to shut the job down. They then complied.

Q. So, in summarizing, you agree that the next step after writing letters by the CEI can be to notify the DOT and request that the job be shut down?

MR. PORTER: Note an objection to form.

A. If the contractor is doing something that's contrary to the specifications, either in his method of building or violating some criteria, and he's instructed, whether it's verbal or in writing, and he elects to continue and then you go back and you work with him thought the chain of command and if nothing happens, then the process is to go through your program manager of the DOT eventually which will get to the district construction engineer, who can then basically decide whether he wants to shut the job down or not. That's the only authority basically where the job can be stopped.

Clarifying opinions

Q. Let's be real clear about one thing. You agree that Daniel Birge felt that Herrington General was violating the specifications of the contract each time he wrote them the letters telling them about the shoulder drop-off problems?

A. I think he talked to—I don't know, because he didn't put any measurements there. So, yes, he indicated there was a need to address shoulder drop-offs, some washouts and other areas.

You used the word "violate" the standards. I think it's just—it may have been that they were three inches, but he felt they needed to be safed up or corrected.

So he certainly was bringing it to their attention. In some cases they were missing signs; some signs were down; washouts, drop-offs. So, yes, he was—and he called in unsafe conditions. Inlets missing from inlet tops.

Q. Mr. Birge in his deposition acknowledged that the shoulder drop-off problems all were drop-off problems that were more than three inches that he notified them about in writing, didn't he?

A. I don't remember as I sit here today whether he said that, but he certainly did call them unsafe, so I would assume they were three inches or more.

Counsel tries to use the expert to help case against co-defendant

Q. So it's clear, Herrington General had been notified before this wreck occurred, in writing on three different occasions, that unsafe conditions regarding the shoulder existed on that project; is that correct?

MR. HOROWITZ: Object to form.

Q. Go ahead.

A. Let me answer it this way, which may not be the way you want me to answer it, but—I guess I shouldn't say that.

Yes, they were—but it wasn't the same issue. Other issues were brought to their attention and corrected. So the way you phrase the question sounds like they were told three times to fix something and never did and then there was a wreck.

Q. They were told three times to fix three different problems with the shoulders.

A. They were told to fix drop-offs that occurred in different locations. They did respond and fix the drop-offs. The last letter was actually June 1st, before the July 27th accident. There's not drop-off letters that—there are some that follow after that, so there's no reason to believe that the shoulders were not at that point in a safe condition.

Q. You agree that there were unsafe shoulders after the last letter and before this wreck, though, don't you?

A. Give me the dates again.

Q. The last letter I believe was on May 31st, and the wreck was July 27th of 2000.

A. I think that's what I said, that the last letter was dated June 1st, 2000—

Q. Right.

A. Where he said unsafe shoulders there.

Q. Yes.

A. It was addressed, and then there were no other letters until sometime after the July 27th accident, when there were other letters written in other places.

So that would lead me to believe that with the kind of job that Mr. Birge was doing, that there were no existing drop-offs that were in excess of three inches.

Q. Between the time that the last letter and the date of the wreck?

A. Between the time that the last letter had been addressed and corrected to the wreck.

Q. And that would have been a day or two after the last letter was written?

A. No, a month and a half.
Q. No, I understand that. We're talking apples and oranges.
A. I'm sorry.
Q. Let me rephrase my question. Mr. Birge wrote him on June 1st and told Herrington General there were problems throughout the job with shoulder drop-offs.
A. Correct.
Q. And according to Mr. Birge, those problems were always corrected within 24 to 48 hours after he notified Herrington General.
A. That's correct.
Q. So assume, then, that those problems documented in that letter of June 1st would have been corrected by June 3rd or thereabouts. Can we agree with that?
A. Yes.
Q. After June 3rd, are you aware of any shoulder drop-off problems that existed before the wreck of July 27th?
A. I'm not aware of any letters or notations or any statement by Mr. Birge that he did find any shoulders, after having been corrected, not to have met the standards.
Q. But you're aware that Mr. Birge did have a problem with conditions on that project after June 3rd and before July 27th, aren't you?
MR. PORTER: Object to form.
A. No, I'm not aware of that.
Q. Did you review the photographs that Mr. Birge took dated June 15th, 2000?
A. Yes.
Q. Didn't those photographs document problems, what he felt like were problems with that project, after June 3rd and before the wreck?
A. Such as the missing signs, the signs down and other things?
Q. There were some shoulder problems documented in those photographs as well, weren't there?
A. I don't think so.
Q. Well, let me just ask you: Do you remember whether or not there were any shoulder problems documented in those photographs of June 15th of 2000?
A. No, other than the area where there was some widening taking place where some barrels were down, or had been knocked down and all that, which is typical. But nothing—if it had been severe enough, I think a letter would have been forthcoming. So I didn't see anything concerning unsafe shoulder conditions on the drop-off between the new pavement and the shoulder.
Q. In the photographs?
A. In the photographs.
Q. Are you aware of any letters back and forth between Spielman & Wilkins and Daniel Birge and Herrington General from June 1st until this wreck occurred? In other words, there's a gap; is that correct?
A. Yes, sir. Just so that we don't—

Q. And you—

A. I was just going to say, just so we don't—there was a gap between April 27th and May 24th and then a gap between—of course May 24th and June 1st are closer together.

Asks for another concession

Q. Now, do you agree that if the testimony of Justin O'Connor is correct when he said there was a five-to-eight-inch drop-off where Mr. Franco dropped off, that that would be an unsafe condition?[191]

MR. PORTER: Note an objection to form.

A. If the drop-offs were five to eight inches, it would be an unsafe condition. I question his testimony only because of the way I saw the measurements made and the alleged two-and-a-half inch drop-off lane to lane, which no one's come up with.[192]

Q. Well, assume for the purposes of my next series of questions that the testimony of Justin O'Connor is accurate.

A. I—go ahead and ask your questions. I—

MR. PORTER: You need to let him finish his question and you've got to give me time to object. Okay? And I think I might. But let him finish his question.[193]

A. Go ahead, sir.

Q. Assume for the purpose of my next series of questions that Justin O'Connor's testimony is accurate. Do you have an opinion with regard to whether or not those conditions would have violated Index 600?

MR. PORTER: I object to the form of the question. It's an inadequate and incomplete and inaccurate hypothetical, assumes facts not in evidence.[194]

A. If proper measurements were taken that show it to be five to eight inches, yes, the drop-off would be in violation of Index 600.

Q. And that would be an unsafe condition?

A. That would be an unsafe condition. If he based his five to eight inches on the measurements that I saw by the photographs that he took, then I would be suspect of any measurements that he took.[195]

Q. And it is an unsafe condition that would need to be corrected before the traveling public was allowed to travel on the road?

A. It's hard to say, because that condition could have existed—the pavement could have—we know that it was paved some time before that. That may have been an area that basically got tore up.

---

[191] Counsel is asking the witness to change assumptions to those that the other side is making.

[192] The expert prudently gives a plausible reason why he disagrees with the testimony/assumption in question.

[193] Retaining counsel is beginning to show exasperation at the witness's habit of responding before a question is completed or before a question is even started.

[194] The witness listens carefully to counsel's objections.

[195] The expert is truthful and does not deny the obvious.

We know it's not—because certainly if somebody did the paving and said that we've got—and saw that they had five to eight inch drop-offs, then the drop-offs should have been corrected before traffic came on that road.

Counsel follows up on information that was volunteered by the expert
Q. Now, you said something earlier I want to go back and question you about a little more. You said that when Index 600 first got established, you had some connection with that or worked on it or something of that nature.
A. Index 600, if you look at the dates—
MR. PORTER: Do you want the Index?
A. I've got it here in one of my exhibits. Here it is. Index 600 was originally developed in 1987. There was one before that, and it was actually an Index 700 that since has been done away with and combined. And prior to that, there was an index that was developed back in 1973.

It basically began—Arizona in 1970 began to actually—1968 and 1969, Arizona began to be concerned with drivers leaving the edge of the pavement. There was a whole series of federal publications concerning the forgiving highway. So designers began to try and be more concerned with breakaway signs, drop-offs and other issues.

So in the late '60s early '70s, some of Index 600 began to emerge. And for a long time 600 was separate from Index 700, which really dealt with a contractor undertaking to do certain roles during construction. So it's evolved over a period of time.

And I was there at the conference in 1968 when we began to develop the first standards.
Q. Did you have any role in developing those standards, and if so, what was the role?
A. The role was that in 1968 the department convened a—as a matter of fact, in Mesa, Arizona, convened a design charade, if you will, with the key DOT people, State Road Department people in those days, to begin to try and develop standards for a more forgiving highway and how to better address telling the contractor how to maintain traffic through work zones.
Q. So tell me what your involvement in that was other than—how long was the conference?
A. It was about a week long. From there standards began to develop. They were sent to me as the district secretary in those days, district engineer. I reviewed it with out people. We imputed some changes. I continue to do that today, even, as an outside consultant to the department.
Q. How often do you serve as an outside consultant or how much have you served as an outside consultant to the DOT?
A. I currently have probably about four engagements with the DOT. And many of them involve acquiring right-of-way; some involve accidents, their own standards.

And, by the way, I'm on both sides, because I've got about five or six cases where the department is a defendant where I'm working for the plaintiff. But in those areas I continue to give input to the department. So they've accepted. Over a period of time, changes do get made.

Testifying history

Q. Do you have an estimate of the number of times that you've been hired by the DOT as a forensic expert since you left their employment?

A. Since 1973?

Q. Yes, sir.

A. Actually, I left, yes in '73. Probably in the last ten years more so, about 20 or 30 times in the area of accidents. And I'm currently under contract with about 25 cases, but that involves right of way acquisition, which is different than forensic.

Q. Right, I understand that. What's your estimate of the number of times that you've testified as a forensic expert against the DOT since 1973?

A. Probably the same number of times.

Q. And tell me a little bit more about your involvement with the DOT with regard to right of way acquisition. What are you doing for—

A. I act as their court engineer, because they have more difficulty sending their own designers to court to try and show necessity and why certain things are being done. So I'm under contract as a matter of fact with two districts right now, three different contracts, where I go to court on their behalf and act as their engineer. They actually passed a resolution empowering me to commit the department to whatever I say in court.

Q. And how long have you been doing that?

A. I've been doing that for about 10 years.

Q. And how many times have you done that in ten years?

A. Well, let's see. I probably have completed—State Road 76 in Yavapai County, US-1 in Yavapai County—

Q. Just a rough estimate.

A. Probably about ten cases, and I'm currently doing three others right now, two in District 4 and one in Paradise Valley.

MR. SCHWARTZ: I don't believe I have any other questions.

Appendix A FRCP Rule 26. General Provisions Governing Discovery; Duty of Disclosure

Rule 26. General Provisions Governing Discovery; Duty of Disclosure
(a) Required Disclosures; Methods to Discover Additional Matter.
(1) Initial Disclosures.
Except in categories of proceedings specified in Rule 26(a)(1)(E), or to the extent otherwise stipulated or directed by order, a party must, without awaiting a discovery request, provide to other parties:

(a) the name and, if known, the address and telephone number of each individual likely to have discoverable information that the disclosing party may use to support its claims or defenses, unless solely for impeachment, identifying the subjects of the information;

(b) a copy of, or a description by category and location of, all documents, data compilations, and tangible things that are in the possession, custody, or control of the party and that the disclosing party may use to support its claims or defenses, unless solely for impeachment;

(c) a computation of any category of damages claimed by the disclosing party, making available for inspection and copying as under Rule 34 the documents or other evidentiary material, not privileged or protected from disclosure, on which such computation is based, including materials bearing on the nature and extent of injuries suffered; and

(d) for inspection and copying as under Rule 34 any insurance agreement under which any person carrying on an insurance business may be liable to satisfy part or all of a judgment which may be entered in the action or to indemnify or reimburse for payments made to satisfy the judgment.

(e) The following categories of proceedings are exempt from initial disclosure under Rule 26(a)(1):

    (i) an action for review on an administrative record;
    (ii) a petition for habeas corpus or other proceeding to challenge a criminal conviction or sentence;
    (iii) an action brought without counsel by a person in custody of the United States, a state, or a state subdivision;
    (iv) an action to enforce or quash an administrative summons or subpoena;
    (v) an action by the United States to recover benefit payments;
    (vi) an action by the United States to collect on a student loan guaranteed by the United States;
    (vii) a proceeding ancillary to proceedings in other courts; and
    (viii) an action to enforce an arbitration award.

These disclosures must be made at or within 14 days after the Rule 26(f) conference unless a different time is set by stipulation or court order, or unless a party objects during the conference that initial disclosures are not appropriate in the circumstances of the action and states the objection in the Rule 26(f) discovery plan. In ruling on the objection, the court must determine what disclosures—if any—are to be made, and set the time for disclosure. Any party first served or otherwise joined after the Rule 26(f) conference must make these disclosures within 30 days after being served or joined unless a different time is set by stipulation or court order. A party must make its initial disclosures based on the information then reasonably available to it and is not excused from making its disclosures because it has not fully completed its investigation of the case or because it challenges the sufficiency of another party's disclosures or because another party has not made its disclosures.

(2) Disclosure of Expert Testimony.

(a) In addition to the disclosures required by paragraph (1), a party shall disclose to other parties the identity of any person who may be used at trial to present evidence under Rules 702, 703, or 705 of the Federal Rules of Evidence.

(b) Except as otherwise stipulated or directed by the court, this disclosure shall, with respect to a witness who is retained or specially employed to provide expert testimony in the case or whose duties as an employee of the party regularly involve giving expert testimony, be accompanied by a written report prepared and signed by the witness. The report shall contain a complete statement of all opinions to be expressed and the basis and reasons therefor; the data or other information considered by the witness in forming the opinions; any exhibits to be used as a summary of or support for the opinions; the qualifications of the witness, including a list of all publications authored by the witness within the preceding ten years; the compensation to be paid for the study and testimony; and a listing of any other cases in which the witness has testified as an expert at trial or by deposition within the preceding four years.

(c) These disclosures shall be made at the times and in the sequence directed by the court. In the absence of other directions from the court or stipulation by the parties, the disclosures shall be made at least 90 days before the trial date or the date the case is to be ready for trial or, if the evidence is intended solely to contradict or rebut evidence on the same subject matter identified by another party under paragraph (2)(B), within 30 days after the disclosure made by the other party. The parties shall supplement these disclosures when required under subdivision (e)(1).

(3) Pretrial Disclosures.

In addition to the disclosures required by Rule 26(a)(1) and (2), a party must provide to other parties and promptly file with the court the following information regarding the evidence that it may present at trial other than solely for impeachment:

(a) the name and, if not previously provided, the address and telephone number of each witness, separately identifying those whom the party expects to present and those whom the party may call if the need arises;

(b) the designation of those witnesses whose testimony is expected to be presented by means of a deposition and, if not taken stenographically, a transcript of the pertinent portions of the deposition testimony; and

(c) an appropriate identification of each document or other exhibit, including summaries of other evidence, separately identifying those which the party expects to offer and those which the party may offer if the need arises.

Unless otherwise directed by the court, these disclosures must be made at least 30 days before trial. Within 14 days thereafter, unless a different time is specified by the court, a party may serve and promptly file a list disclosing (i) any objections to the use under Rule 32(a) of a deposition designated by another party under Rule 26(a)(3)(B), and (ii) any objection, together with the grounds therefor, that may be made to the admissibility of materials identified under Rule 26(a)(3)(C). Objections not so disclosed, other than objections under Rules 402 and 403 of the Federal Rules of Evidence, are waived unless excused by the court for good cause.

(4) Form of Disclosures; Filing.

Unless the court orders otherwise, all disclosures under Rules 26(a)(1) through (3) must be made in writing, signed, and served.

(5) Methods to Discover Additional Matter.

Parties may obtain discovery by one or more of the following methods: depositions upon oral examination or written questions; written interrogatories; production of documents or things or permission to enter upon land or other property under Rule 34 or 45(a)(1)(C), for inspection and other purposes; physical and mental examinations; and requests for admission.

(b) Discovery Scope and Limits.

Unless otherwise limited by order of the court in accordance with these rules, the scope of discovery is as follows:

(1) In General.

Parties may obtain discovery regarding any matter, not privileged, that is relevant to the claim or defense of any party, including the existence, description, nature, custody, condition, and location of any books, documents, or other tangible things and the identity and location of persons having knowledge of any discoverable matter. For good cause, the court may order discovery of any matter relevant to the subject matter involved in the action. Relevant information need not be admissible at the trial if the discovery appears reasonably calculated to lead to the discovery of admissible evidence. All discovery is subject to the limitations imposed by Rule 26(b)(2)(i), (ii), and (iii).

(2) Limitations.

By order, the court may alter the limits in these rules on the number of depositions and interrogatories or the length of depositions under Rule 30. By order or local rule, the court may also limit the number of requests under Rule 36. The frequency or extent of use of the discovery methods otherwise permitted under these rules and by any local rule shall be limited by the court if it determines that: (i) the discovery sought is unreasonably cumulative or duplicative, or is obtainable from some other source that is more convenient, less burdensome, or less expensive; (ii) the party seeking discovery has had ample opportunity by discovery in the action to obtain the information sought; or (iii) the burden or expense of the proposed discovery outweighs its likely benefit, taking into account the needs of the case, the amount in controversy, the parties' resources, the importance of the issues at stake in the litigation, and the importance of the proposed discovery in resolving the issues. The court may act upon its own initiative after reasonable notice or pursuant to a motion under Rule 26(c).

(3) Trial Preparation: Materials.

Subject to the provisions of subdivision (b)(4) of this rule, a party may obtain discovery of documents and tangible things otherwise discoverable under subdivision (b)(1) of this rule and prepared in anticipation of litigation or for trial by or for another party or by or for that other party's representative (including the other party's attorney, consultant, surety, indemnitor, insurer, or agent) only upon a showing that the party seeking discovery has substantial need of the materials in the preparation of the party's case and that the party is unable without undue hardship to obtain the substantial equivalent of the materials by other means. In ordering discovery of such materials when the required showing has been made, the court shall protect against disclosure of the mental impressions, conclusions, opinions, or legal theories of an attorney or other representative of a party concerning the litigation.

A party may obtain without the required showing a statement concerning the action or its subject matter previously made by that party. Upon request, a person not a party may obtain without the required showing a statement concerning the action or its subject matter previously made by that person. If the request is refused, the person may move for a court order. The provisions of Rule 37(a)(4) apply to the award of expenses incurred in relation to the motion. For purposes of this paragraph, a statement previously made is (A) a written statement signed or otherwise adopted or approved by the person making it, or (B) a stenographic, mechanical, electrical, or other recording, or a transcription thereof, which is a substantially verbatim recital of an oral statement by the person making it and contemporaneously recorded.

(4) Trial Preparation: Experts.

(a) A party may depose any person who has been identified as an expert whose opinions may be presented at trial. If a report from the expert is required under subdivision (a)(2)(B), the deposition shall not be conducted until after the report is provided.

(b) A party may, through interrogatories or by deposition, discover facts known or opinions held by an expert who has been retained or specially employed by another party in anticipation of litigation or preparation for trial and who is not expected to be called as a witness at trial, only as provided in Rule 35(b) or upon a showing of exceptional circumstances under which it is impracticable for the party seeking discovery to obtain facts or opinions on the same subject by other means.

(c) Unless manifest injustice would result, (i) the court shall require that the party seeking discovery pay the expert a reasonable fee for time spent in responding to discovery under this subdivision; and (ii) with respect to discovery obtained under subdivision (b)(4)(B) of this rule the court shall require the party seeking discovery to pay the other party a fair portion of the fees and expenses reasonably incurred by the latter party in obtaining facts and opinions from the expert.

(5) Claims of Privilege or Protection of Trial Preparation Materials.
When a party withholds information otherwise discoverable under these rules by claiming that it is privileged or subject to protection as trial preparation material, the party shall make the claim expressly and shall describe the nature of the documents, communications, or things not produced or disclosed in a manner that, without revealing information itself privileged or protected, will enable other parties to assess the applicability of the privilege or protection.

(c) Protective Orders.
Upon motion by a party or by the person from whom discovery is sought, accompanied by a certification that the movant has in good faith conferred or attempted to confer with other affected parties in an effort to resolve the dispute without court action, and for good cause shown, the court in which the action is pending or alternatively, on matters relating to a deposition, the court in the district where the deposition is to be taken may make any order which justice requires to protect a party or person from annoyance, embarrassment, oppression, or undue burden or expense, including one or more of the following:

    (1) that the disclosure or discovery not be had;

    (2) that the disclosure or discovery may be had only on specified terms and conditions, including a designation of the time or place;

    (3) that the discovery may be had only by a method of discovery other than that selected by the party seeking discovery;

    (4) that certain matters not be inquired into, or that the scope of the disclosure or discovery be limited to certain matters;

    (5) that discovery be conducted with no one present except persons designated by the court;

    (6) that a deposition, after being sealed, be opened only by order of the court;

(7) that a trade secret or other confidential research, development, or commercial information not be revealed or be revealed only in a designated way; and

(8) that the parties simultaneously file specified documents or information enclosed in sealed envelopes to be opened as directed by the court.

If the motion for a protective order is denied in whole or in part, the court may, on such terms and conditions as are just, order that any party or other person provide or permit discovery. The provisions of Rule 37(a)(4) apply to the award of expenses incurred in relation to the motion.

(d) Timing and Sequence of Discovery.
Except in categories of proceedings exempted from initial disclosure under Rule 26(a)(1)(E), or when authorized under these rules or by order or agreement of the parties, a party may not seek discovery from any source before the parties have conferred as required by Rule 26(f). Unless the court upon motion, for the convenience of parties and witnesses and in the interests of justice, orders otherwise, methods of discovery may be used in any sequence, and the fact that a party is conducting discovery, whether by deposition or otherwise, does not operate to delay any other party's discovery.

(e) Supplementation of Disclosures and Responses.
A party who has made a disclosure under subdivision (a) or responded to a request for discovery with a disclosure or response is under a duty to supplement or correct the disclosure or response to include information thereafter acquired if ordered by the court or in the following circumstances:

(1) A party is under a duty to supplement at appropriate intervals its disclosures under subdivision (a) if the party learns that in some material respect the information disclosed is incomplete or incorrect and if the additional or corrective information has not otherwise been made known to the other parties during the discovery process or in writing. With respect to testimony of an expert from whom a report is required under subdivision (a)(2)(B) the duty extends both to information contained in the report and to information provided through a deposition of the expert, and any additions or other changes to this information shall be disclosed by the time the party's disclosures under Rule 26(a)(3) are due.

(2) A party is under a duty seasonably to amend a prior response to an interrogatory, request for production, or request for admission if the party learns that the response is in some material respect incomplete or incorrect and if the additional or corrective information has not otherwise been made known to the other parties during the discovery process or in writing.

(f) Meeting of Parties; Planning for Discovery.
Except in categories of proceedings exempted from initial disclosure under Rule 26(a)(1)(E) or when otherwise ordered, the parties must, as soon as practicable and in

any event at least 21 days before a scheduling conference is held or a scheduling order is due under Rule 16(b), confer to consider the nature and basis of their claims and defenses and the possibilities for a prompt settlement or resolution of the case, to make or arrange for the disclosures required by Rule 26(a)(1), and to develop a proposed discovery plan that indicates the parties' views and proposals concerning:
(1) what changes should be made in the timing, form, or requirement for disclosures under Rule 26(a), including a statement as to when disclosures under Rule 26(a)(1) were made or will be made;
(2) the subjects on which discovery may be needed, when discovery should be completed, and whether discovery should be conducted in phases or be limited to or focused upon particular issues;
(3) what changes should be made in the limitations on discovery imposed under these rules or by local rule, and what other limitations should be imposed; and
(4) any other orders that should be entered by the court under Rule 26(c) or under Rule 16(b) and (c).

The attorneys of record and all unrepresented parties that have appeared in the case are jointly responsible for arranging the conference, for attempting in good faith to agree on the proposed discovery plan, and for submitting to the court within 14 days after the conference a written report outlining the plan. A court may order that the parties or attorneys attend the conference in person. If necessary to comply with its expedited schedule for Rule 16(b) conferences, a court may by local rule (i) require that the conference between the parties occur fewer than 21 days before the scheduling conference is held or a scheduling order is due under Rule 16(b), and (ii) require that the written report outlining the discovery plan be filed fewer than 14 days after the conference between the parties, or excuse the parties from submitting a written report and permit them to report orally on their discovery plan at the Rule 16(b) conference.

(g) Signing of Disclosures, Discovery Requests, Responses, and Objections.
(1) Every disclosure made pursuant to subdivision (a)(1) or subdivision (a)(3) shall be signed by at least one attorney of record in the attorney's individual name, whose address shall be stated. An unrepresented party shall sign the disclosure and state the party's address. The signature of the attorney or party constitutes a certification that to the best of the signer's knowledge, information, and belief, formed after a reasonable inquiry, the disclosure is complete and correct as of the time it is made.
(2) Every discovery request, response, or objection made by a party represented by an attorney shall be signed by at least one attorney of record in the attorney's individual name, whose address shall be stated. An unrepresented party shall sign the request, response, or objection and state the party's address. The signature of the attorney or party constitutes a certification that to the best of the signer's knowledge, information, and belief, formed after a reasonable inquiry, the request, response, or objection is:

(a) consistent with these rules and warranted by existing law or a good faith argument for the extension, modification, or reversal of existing law;

(b) not interposed for any improper purpose, such as to harass or to cause unnecessary delay or needless increase in the cost of litigation; and

(c) not unreasonable or unduly burdensome or expensive, given the needs of the case, the discovery already had in the case, the amount in controversy, and the importance of the issues at stake in the litigation.

If a request, response, or objection is not signed, it shall be stricken unless it is signed promptly after the omission is called to the attention of the party making the request, response, or objection, and a party shall not be obligated to take any action with respect to it until it is signed.

(3) If without substantial justification a certification is made in violation of the rule, the court, upon motion or upon its own initiative, shall impose upon the person who made the certification, the party on whose behalf the disclosure, request, response, or objection is made, or both, an appropriate sanction, which may include an order to pay the amount of the reasonable expenses incurred because of the violation, including a reasonable attorney's fee.

Appendix B FRCP Rule 30. Deposition upon Oral Examination

Rule 30. Deposition upon Oral Examination
(a) When Depositions May Be Taken; When Leave Required.
(1) A party may take the testimony of any person, including a party, by deposition upon oral examination without leave of court except as provided in paragraph (2). The attendance of witnesses may be compelled by subpoena as provided in Rule 45.
(2) A party must obtain leave of court, which shall be granted to the extent consistent with the principles stated in Rule 26(b)(2), if the person to be examined is confined in prison or if, without the written stipulation of the parties.
(a) a proposed deposition would result in more than ten depositions being taken under this rule or Rule 31 by the plaintiffs, or by the defendants, or by third-party defendants;
(b) the person to be examined already has been deposed in the case; or
(c) a party seeks to take a deposition before the time specified in Rule 26(d) unless the notice contains a certification, with supporting facts, that the person to be examined is expected to leave the United States and be unavailable for examination in this country unless deposed before that time.

(b) Notice of Examination: General Requirements; Method of Recording; Production of Documents and Things; Deposition of Organization; Deposition by Telephone.
(1) A party desiring to take the deposition of any person upon oral examination shall give reasonable notice in writing to every other party to the action. The notice shall state the time and place for taking the deposition and the name and address of each person to be examined, if known, and, if the name is not known, a general description sufficient to identify the person or the particular class or group to which the person belongs. If a subpoena duces tecum is to be served on the person to be examined, the designation of the materials to be produced as set forth in the subpoena shall be attached to, or included in, the notice.
(2) The party taking the deposition shall state in the notice the method by which the testimony shall be recorded. Unless the court orders otherwise, it may be recorded by sound, sound-and-visual, or stenographic means, and the party taking the deposition shall bear the cost of the recording. Any party may arrange for a transcription to be made from the recording of a deposition taken by nonstenographic means.
(3) With prior notice to the deponent and other parties, any party may designate another method to record the deponent's testimony in addition to the method specified by the person taking the deposition. The additional record or transcript shall be made at that party's expense unless the court otherwise orders.

(4) Unless otherwise agreed by the parties, a deposition shall be conducted before an officer appointed or designated under Rule 28 and shall begin with a statement on the record by the officer that includes (A) the officer's name and business address; (B) the date, time and place of the deposition; (C) the name of the deponent; (D) the administration of the oath or affirmation to the deponent; and (E) an identification of all persons present. If the deposition is recorded other than stenographically, the officer shall repeat items (A) through (C) at the beginning of each unit of recorded tape or other recording medium. The appearance or demeanor of deponents or attorneys shall not be distorted through camera or sound-recording techniques. At the end of the deposition, the officer shall state on the record that the deposition is complete and shall set forth any stipulations made by counsel concerning the custody of the transcript or recording and the exhibits, or concerning other pertinent matters.
(5) The notice to a party deponent may be accompanied by a request made in compliance with Rule 34 for the production of documents and tangible things at the taking of the deposition. The procedure of Rule 34 shall apply to the request.
(6) A party may in the party's notice and in a subpoena name as the deponent a public or private corporation or a partnership or association or governmental agency and describe with reasonable particularity the matters on which examination is requested. In that event, the organization so named shall designate one or more officers, directors, or managing agents, or other persons who consent to testify on its behalf, and may set forth, for each person designated, the matters on which the person will testify. A subpoena shall advise a non-party organization of its duty to make such a designation. The persons so designated shall testify as to matters known or reasonably available to the organization. This subdivision (b)(6) does not preclude taking a deposition by any other procedure authorized in these rules.
(7) The parties may stipulate in writing or the court may upon motion order that a deposition be taken by telephone or other remote electronic means. For the purposes of this rule and Rules 28(a), 37(a)(1), and 37(b)(1), a deposition taken by such means is taken in the district and at the place where the deponent is to answer questions.
(c) Examination and Cross-Examination; Record of Examination; Oath; Objections
Examination and cross-examination of witnesses may proceed as permitted at the trial under the provisions of the Federal Rules of Evidence except Rules 103 and 615. The officer before whom the deposition is to be taken shall put the witness on oath or affirmation and shall personally, or by someone acting under the officer's direction and in the officer's presence, record the testimony of the witness. The testimony shall be taken stenographically or recorded by any other method authorized by subdivision (b)(2) of this rule. All objections made at the time of the examination to the qualifications of the officer taking the deposition, to the manner of taking it, to the evidence presented, to the conduct of any party, or to any other aspect of the proceedings shall be noted by the officer upon the record of the deposition; but the

examination shall proceed, with the testimony being taken subject to the objections. In lieu of participating in the oral examination, parties may serve written questions in a sealed envelope on the party taking the deposition and the party taking the deposition shall transmit them to the officer, who shall propound them to the witness and record the answers verbatim.

(d) Schedule and Duration; Motion to Terminate or Limit Examination.
(1) Any objection during a deposition must be stated concisely and in a non-argumentative and non-suggestive manner. A person may instruct a deponent not to answer only when necessary to preserve a privilege, to enforce a limitation directed by the court, or to present a motion under Rule 30(d)(4).
(2) Unless otherwise authorized by the court or stipulated by the parties, a deposition is limited to one day of seven hours. The court must allow additional time consistent with Rule 26(b)(2) if needed for a fair examination of the deponent or if the deponent or another person, or other circumstance, impedes or delays the examination.
(3) If the court finds that any impediment, delay, or other conduct has frustrated the fair examination of the deponent, it may impose upon the persons responsible an appropriate sanction, including the reasonable costs and attorney's fees incurred by any parties as a result thereof.
(4) At any time during a deposition, on motion of a party or of the deponent and upon a showing that the examination is being conducted in bad faith or in such manner as unreasonably to annoy, embarrass, or oppress the deponent or party, the court in which the action is pending or the court in the district where the deposition is being taken may order the officer conducting the examination to cease forthwith from taking the deposition, or may limit the scope and manner of the taking of the deposition as provided in Rule 26(c). If the order made terminates the examination, it may be resumed thereafter only upon the order of the court in which the action is pending. Upon demand of the objecting party or deponent, the taking of the deposition must be suspended for the time necessary to make a motion for an order. The provisions of Rule 37(a)(4) apply to the award of expenses incurred in relation to the motion.

(e) Review by Witness; Changes; Signing.
If requested by the deponent or a party before completion of the deposition, the deponent shall have 30 days after being notified by the officer that the transcript or recording is available in which to review the transcript or recording and, if there are changes in form or substance, to sign a statement reciting such changes and the reasons given by the deponent for making them. The officer shall indicate in the certificate prescribed by subdivision (f)(1) whether any review was requested and, if so, shall append any changes made by the deponent during the period allowed.

(f) Certification and Filing by Officer; Exhibits; Copies; Notices of Filing.
(1) The officer must certify that the witness was duly sworn by the officer and that the deposition is a true record of the testimony given by the witness. This certificate

must be in writing and accompany the record of the deposition. Unless otherwise ordered by the court, the officer must securely seal the deposition in an envelope or package indorsed with the title of the action and marked "Deposition of [here insert name of witness]" and must promptly send it to the attorney who arranged for the transcript or recording, who must store it under conditions that will protect it against loss, destruction, tampering, or deterioration. Documents and things produced for inspection during the examination of the witness must, upon the request of a party, be marked for identification and annexed to the deposition and may be inspected and copied by any party, except that if the person producing the materials desires to retain them the person may (A) offer copies to be marked for identification and annexed to the deposition and to serve thereafter as originals if the person affords to all parties fair opportunity to verify the copies by comparison with the originals, or (B) offer the originals to be marked for identification, after giving to each party an opportunity to inspect and copy them, in which event the materials may then be used in the same manner as if annexed to the deposition. Any party may move for an order that the original be annexed to and returned with the deposition to the court, pending final disposition of the case.

(2) Unless otherwise ordered by the court or agreed by the parties, the officer shall retain stenographic notes of any deposition taken stenographically or a copy of the recording of any deposition taken by another method. Upon payment of reasonable charges therefor, the officer shall furnish a copy of the transcript or other recording of the deposition to any party or to the deponent.

(3) The party taking the deposition shall give prompt notice of its filing to all other parties.

(g) Failure to Attend or to Serve Subpoena; Expenses.
(1) If the party giving the notice of the taking of a deposition fails to attend and proceed therewith and another party attends in person or by attorney pursuant to the notice, the court may order the party giving the notice to pay to such other party the reasonable expenses incurred by that party and that party's attorney in attending, including reasonable attorney's fees.

(2) If the party giving the notice of the taking of a deposition of a witness fails to serve a subpoena upon the witness and the witness because of such failure does not attend, and if another party attends in person or by attorney because that party expects the deposition of that witness to be taken, the court may order the party giving the notice to pay to such other party the reasonable expenses incurred by that party and that party's attorney in attending, including reasonable attorney's fees.

Appendix C An Example of Abusive Behavior Sanctioned by the Court

192 F.R.D. 187, 46 Fed.R.Serv.3d 783
United States District Court, D. Maryland.

Laretha DAVIS, Plaintiff,
v.
Jeffrey A. BIGLER, *et al.*, Defendant.

No. CIV. A. Y-98-958.

MEMORANDUM AND ORDER
GARNER, United States Magistrate Judge.
Defendants Weiss Associates Inc. ("Weiss") and Smith, Neff & Hollett ("S, N & H") (collectively "Defendants") have filed a motion, (Paper No. 55), to preclude one of the plaintiff's expert witnesses, Holly O'Leary, M.D., from testifying at trial, because, they contend, she failed to comply with this Court's order of October 15, 1999, allowing the Defendants additional time to depose Dr. O'Leary. [FN1] In this order, (Paper No. 46), the Court found that when originally deposed by the Defendants, Dr. O'Leary's answers often were evasive, incomplete, and non-responsive. Accordingly, Defendants were given additional time to depose Dr. O'Leary, and Plaintiff's counsel was warned that if she failed to give proper answers the Court would consider additional sanctions, including ordering that she not be permitted to testify at trial, as allowed by Fed.R.Civ.P. 37(b)(2)(B). Defendants contend that when Dr. O'Leary was redeposed on January 18 and 19, 2000, she violated this Court's order, and, as a sanction, she should not be permitted to testify at trial. Plaintiff has filed an opposition, (Paper No. 57), and Defendants filed a reply, (Paper No. 58). I have considered these filings, and determined that no hearing is necessary. Local Rule 105.6. For the reasons stated below, Defendants' motion is denied, and sanctions will be entered against Defendants' attorney, Mr. Keith A. Pledge, for his unprofessional conduct during the resumption of the O'Leary deposition.

FN1. Previously, on August 31, 1999, I granted Defendants an additional 5 hours of deposition time for Dr. O'Leary, because Plaintiff's Rule 26(a)(2)(B) disclosures for this witness were incomplete. Paper No. 38. The effect of the August 31 and October 15 orders was to give the Defendants two days, seven hours each, of additional deposition time for Dr. O'Leary.

[1] Local Rule 606 provides "[t]he Court expects all of its judges and all counsel to conduct themselves in a professional and courteous manner in connection with all matters pending before the Court." Discovery Guideline 1.c. of this Court provides

"[a]ttorneys are expected to behave professionally and with courtesy towards all involved in the discovery process, including but not limited to opposing counsel, parties and non-parties." The cited local rule and guideline apply to the conduct of an attorney taking a deposition, and an attorney who is abusive to counsel and/or a witness during a deposition violates them.

During the seven hours of the first day of Dr. O'Leary's renewed deposition, January 18, 2000, Defendants' counsel repeatedly and flagrantly was insulting to Plaintiff's counsel and Dr. O'Leary [FN2] (taunting Plaintiff's counsel about his case, accusing the deponent of "playing games," demeaning the professional competence of the deponent, suggesting that the deponent had cognitive difficulties, referring to the deponent as "a piece of work," and implying that the deponent was dishonest, to name a few examples). Additionally, Defendants' counsel made antagonistic and hostile comments throughout the first day of the deposition [FN3] (baiting the deponent by saying she was going to "get three strikes" and be "out," taunting the deponent about the fact that the plaintiff was paying his fee as a sanction for her past deposition responses, accusing the deponent of having a hearing problem, peremptorily telling the deponent and Plaintiff's counsel that "I'm running this deposition," and "I'm asking the questions," and accusing the deponent of playing "semantic games").

FN2. See Attachment A to this order, which is incorporated herein, which provides specific examples of Defense Counsel's insulting comments.

FN3. See Attachment B, incorporated in this order by reference, for specific examples.

Defendants' counsel also was sarcastic throughout the deposition [FN4] (baiting the deponent about making "legal objections" to questions, and asking if she was going to instruct herself not to answer questions during the deposition, mocking the Plaintiff's counsel by mimicking him, and remarking "Yeah, yeah, yeah" when he made an objection, making light of the fact that the plaintiff was to bear the expense of the deposition pursuant to the Court's earlier order, and making derisive comments about the deponent's professional qualifications). Finally, Defendants' counsel frequently made threatening comments to the deponent and Plaintiff's counsel during the deposition [FN5] (repeatedly threatening to terminate the deposition and "slap" another motion to dismiss the case on plaintiff's counsel).

FN4. See Attachment C, incorporated in this order by reference, for specific examples.

FN5. See Attachment D, incorporated by reference in this order, for specific examples.

Viewed as a whole, the conduct of Defendants' counsel during the first day of the deposition was appallingly unprofessional and discourteous, suggesting that he took the Court's orders allowing him additional time to depose Dr. O'Leary, and ordering her to be responsive, as license to do whatever he wanted during the deposition. No one expects the deposition of a key witness in a hotly contested case to be a non-stop exchange of pleasantries. However, it must not be allowed to become an excuse for counsel to engage in acts of rhetorical road rage against a deponent and opposing counsel, using an order of the court as the vehicle for the abuse. While isolated acts of discourtesy or loss of temper can be expected, even from the best of counsel, and excused by the court, systematic and deliberate abuses such as displayed by Defendants' counsel during Dr. O'Leary's deposition cannot go unsanctioned as they are destructive of the very fabric which holds together the process of pretrial discovery—cooperative exchange of information without the need for constant court intervention. [FN6]

FN6. When an attorney for one of the parties misbehaves badly during pretrial discovery, there is a very real danger that others will do the same, fighting fire with fire. In this case, though, Plaintiff's attorney resisted the impulse to do so, and displayed commendable, indeed remarkable, self-control during the deposition of Dr. O'Leary. Throughout the deposition he intervened to calm the waters between Dr. O'Leary and Defendants' counsel, trying to keep the examination focused, and the deponent's answers responsive, despite the conduct of Defendants' counsel.

There also is a more pragmatic reason why counsel should not engage in the type of behavior that Defendants' counsel displayed during the first day of the deposition. It is counterproductive. At the beginning of the second day of the deposition, January 19, 2000, Dr. O'Leary brought in a video photographer to record the deposition. Although Defendants' counsel objected, and threatened to call the Court for a ruling as to whether the video recording could be made, he did not do so, acquiescing in the recording. While being videotaped during the second day of the deposition, the conduct of Defendants' counsel markedly improved, as did the responsiveness of Dr. O'Leary's answers to his questions. This suggests that Defendants' counsel realized the impropriety of his conduct during the first day. The Court cannot help but wonder whether Dr. O'Leary's testimony during the first day of the deposition would not have been more complete and responsive had Defendants' counsel behaved professionally. In such circumstances, it would be improper to order that Dr. O'Leary not be permitted to testify at trial because to do so would punish the Plaintiff for the misconduct of Defendants' attorney. However, the Plaintiff and Dr. O'Leary should take note that if, at trial, her testimony in response to properly framed questions is evasive, or non-responsive, it will be stricken.

[2] For the reasons stated above, the Defendants' motion to exclude Dr. O'Leary's testimony at trial is DENIED. Furthermore, it is ORDERED that, as a sanction for his unprofessional behavior, and to help insure that it is not repeated in the future, Defendants' counsel, Mr. Keith A. Pledge, will, within 10 days of this order write a letter of apology to Dr. O'Leary and Mr. Erikson, Plaintiff's counsel, for his unprofessional conduct. Further, any payment made by the Plaintiff of Mr. Pledge's fees in connection with the taking of the deposition of Dr. O'Leary on January 18 and 19 will be returned to the Plaintiff or her counsel within 30 days of this order. If no such payment has been made to date, the obligation to do so is rescinded. And, finally, Mr. Pledge will be required to take a professionalism course approved by the Court. Within 30 days of this order he will provide the Court with information regarding such a course that he proposes to take. Upon review and approval of the proposed course, he will be required to attend it, and provide proof of satisfactory completion to the Court. If the course suggested is unacceptable, the Court will designate the course he will attend.

Attachment A: Examples of Insulting Comments by Defense Counsel During 1/18/00 Deposition

Page   Comment

670   [to Plaintiff's counsel] "You're about as bad as she is."

672   [to Plaintiff's counsel, after he objected to one of defense counsel's questions] "You don't like the compound part of it, is that the problem, Mr. Erikson, too difficult for you?"

675   [to Plaintiff's counsel] "Yes, you are nervous, Mr. Erikson, because this case is rapidly diminishing."

682   [to witness] "So say it. Don't play your typical games."

695   [to Plaintiff's counsel] "And you've been right now how often in this litigation. How often have you been right in this litigation in your viewpoints?"

698   Witness: "I've never been subjected to such hostility from any defense lawyer."
        Defense counsel: "I've never been treated like this by any witness, touché. Can you finish your answer?"

724   [to witness] "What don't you understand about the question, Dr. O'Leary? Is this the feigned ignorance part that has been the subject of a previous motion?"

737   [to witness] "Maybe you have MCS [multiple chemical sensitivity, a condition which Plaintiff asserts causes cognitive impairment] then..."

767   [to witness] "You are a piece of work, Dr. O'Leary."

775   Witness: "I've never had such difficulty with a defense lawyer, Mr. —."
        Defense counsel: "Oh, Dr. O'Leary, the feeling is mutual."

777   Witness: "I'm trying to be scientific."
        Defense counsel: "And evasive, which you get an A plus in."

807   [referring to witness and Plaintiff's counsel] "Both you two, it's like Jekyll and Hyde in here, its unbelievable. It's like a tag team that I've never seen before. It's called hide the ball, lay the record—muddle up the issues—."

843   [to witness] "Answer the question. You know, I don't need...a sideshow."

882   Witness [referring to Plaintiff's alleged cognitive difficulties] "Yes, and she's having difficulty remembering her lines [in theater class]..." Defense counsel: "Just as you're having difficulty today remembering your previous legal cases in which you were excluded from testifying in, correct?"

882-83 [to witness] "And your inability to recall the prior cases in which you've been excluded from testifying in, do you find that hinders your ability to function normally in today's society?"

888   [responding to witness's offer to make him a more legible copy of an exhibit] "For some reason I just cannot take your word for it."

Attachment B: Examples of Antagonistic and Hostile Comments by Defense Counsel During 1/18/00 Deposition

Page   Comment

635   [to witness] "You're going to get three strikes and you're out today....No games today."

636   [to witness] "Well, your time is out in this case."

667   [to witness] "I'm not being hostile....you're reverting to your old self."

716   [to Plaintiff's counsel] "Don't lecture me....Don't even think about it....Don't even dream about it."

772   [to witness] "You're not going to obstruct this deposition any more than you have..."
        Defense counsel: "Say no then."
        Plaintiff's counsel: "She did."
        Defense counsel: "She said the long-winded version, which she loves to do, and which got her into trouble before."

787   [to witness] "And incidentally, who's paying your bills today, or are you eating the costs? Are you getting paid today for your testimony? Witness: "Yes, are you?"
        Defense counsel: [referring to plaintiffs' counsel] "He's paying me, thanks to you. See how it works?"

798   [asked not to raise his voice by Plaintiff's counsel] "I'm not raising my voice. I think she has a problem hearing now....This is the hearing tactic I didn't mention before....I didn't think your ears were that bad."

834   Witness: "I would like to read the question [on questionnaire, an exhibit] into the record. If you—"
        Defense counsel: "No, you're not. I'm running this deposition."

853   [to witness] "Just answer the question. Let's start anew for once. I'm tired of your old answers which don't answer the questions."

857   [to witness] "I'm not going to play semantic games with you, as you constantly are trying to do here."

884   [responding to witness's offer to get him some test data] "Get it to me by tomorrow. Stop wasting my time now."

Attachment C: Examples of Sarcastic Comments by Defense Counsel During 1/18/00 Deposition

Page   Comment

695   Plaintiff's counsel: "Mr. Pledge, not necessary. She's answered your question."
       Defense counsel: "Which comes first the chicken or the egg, Mr. Erikson?"

741   [responding to the witness' answer] "Yeah, right."

744   "She [referring to witness] always has to hedge, doesn't she? You always have to cover yourself; nothing's ever a straight answer."

749   [to witness] "I appreciate the legal objection, Dr. O'Leary, it seems like you know more than you've pretended to know all along about your legal knowledge....I'm curious, are you going to instruct yourself not to answer certain questions today?"

776   Witness: "They're all related to reactive airway disease and how it's produced."
       Defense counsel: "Sure, they are."
       Plaintiffs' counsel "We don't need sarcastic comments."
       Defense counsel: "I'm not being sarcastic. I'm totally believing everything your witness says, and I'm taking everything she says on face value, unchallenged. You know, I'm the naive attorney you've always dreamed of."

790   Defense counsel: "Can you please read the question again. I don't think she answered it, as usual."
       Plaintiff's counsel: "Objection. Save the speeches"
       Defense counsel: "Objection."
       Plaintiff's counsel: "Save the sarcasm."
       Defense counsel: "Yeah, yeah, yeah."

805   [after suggestion by Defense counsel that witness was not telling the truth, the witness insisted she was. Defense counsel replied]: "Gee, you know, I'm convinced."

814   [responding to witness saying she does not understand the question] "Should I be surprised?"

821   [Defense counsel, to witness] "...you're paying me for my time."

Witness: "A disabled patient is paying you for your time."
Defense counsel: "Should I feel sorry?"

824   [to witness, who sought clarification of a question] "What do you think? Are you playing that game again?"

847   [to Plaintiff's counsel] "It certainly makes it easier, doesn't it...when she answers the question appropriately the first time. This is a first."

870   [to witness following an answer to a question] "Back to game playing, huh?"

883   [responding to witness's reference to her credentials in her CV] "Am I supposed to be impressed?"

893   [In response to witness's request to clarify a question asked] "What do you think I mean? Do you think I'm talking about foods she ate ten years ago as a kid?"

Attachment D: Examples of Threatening Comments by Defense Counsel During 1/18/00 Deposition

Page   Comment

635   "There will be a motion forthcoming to exclude her testimony in this case...."

667   "Well, we're going to end this deposition...."

667   "It's not my case that's on the line here. You're on treading some thin ice."

683   "And I tell you, this case is really close to being dismissed."

711   [asked by Plaintiff's counsel not to yell at the witness and to keep his report to himself] "I'm not doing either...And if you want to continue with your antics, then you will see another motion.

805   [to witness] "I'll check up on you, Dr. O'Leary, see if you're telling the truth. That is the point of this exercise."

854   [to Plaintiff's counsel] "Laugh all you want. The last laugh is always with me....You think this is really funny. I'm taking this very seriously. I'm outraged at the way this has proceeded. And, as you know, I'm continuously debating in my mind whether to stop at any given moment and slap one more motion to end this case on you."

Appendix D   An Example of Obstructive Behavior by Retaining Counsel Sanctioned by the Court

88 S.W.3d 343
Court of Appeals of Texas, San Antonio.

Briefs and Other Related Documents
In re ALAMO LIVING COMMUNITIES OF SAN ANTONIO, INC., d/b/a ALAMO COMMUNITIES OF ADKINS.

No. 04-02-00410-CV.
July 31, 2002.

Opinion by GEORGE MARMON, Chief Justice.
Alamo Living of San Antonio, Inc. d/b/a Alamo Living of Adkins ("Alamo") seeks mandamus relief from an order striking its expert Dr. Arnold Vitanza from testifying. [FN1] We do not condone the behavior of Alamo's counsel, Tom Bitzer. We also agree with the trial court that Bitzer's actions are sanctionable, but we conditionally grant the writ because striking Dr. Vitanza's testimony was a death penalty sanction, and the trial court made no effort to remedy the situation with a lesser sanction.
FN1. The order also strikes Dr. Connor Zwart as an expert witness; however, Alamo does not seek relief from that portion of the trial court's order in its petition.

BACKGROUND
Harold Trent is mentally retarded and is a patient at Alamo. The Trents sued Alamo in 1999, claiming that Alamo was negligent in connection with its care of Harold when he suffered a ruptured appendix. The lawsuit was stayed due to Alamo's bankruptcy proceedings. After the stay was lifted, a scheduling order was entered in December of 2001. Alamo timely designated two medical experts—Dr. Zwart and Dr. Vitanza.

Alamo's attorneys failed to respond to a request by the Trents' attorneys for deposition dates. On April 23, 2002, the Trents sent a letter to Alamo's attorney noting that in his letter, Alamo's attorney stated that Dr. Zwart would not be available until 1:00 p.m. on May 9. The Trents' attorneys stated that Dr. Zwart's deposition would be taken at 1:00 p.m. on May 9, and Dr. Vitanza's deposition would be taken on May 10 at 10:00 a.m. On April 16, the Trents' attorneys sent deposition notices to Alamo's attorney, stating "We have contacted your office on numerous occasions asking for dates for these depositions but have been unsuccessful. Therefore, we are proceeding with noticing these depositions."

On the morning of May 9, as the Trents' attorneys were traveling to Kirby for Dr. Zwart's deposition, they were notified that Dr. Vitanza would not be available on May 10 due to a conflict. There is some confusion in the record about Dr. Vitanza's problem, but Dr. Vitanza states in an affidavit that he was obligated to attend an emergency meeting as Department Chairman and Surgery Section Chief concerning a physician on May 10 at 1:00 p.m., and he might not have time to finish the deposition.

When counsel arrived for Dr. Zwart's deposition, Bitzer confirmed that Dr. Vitanza would not be available for his deposition the following day. Bitzer offered an alternative schedule and offered to pay for any expenses incurred by the Trents' attorneys due to the rescheduling. Bitzer denies that his production of Dr. Vitanza was conditioned on the production of plaintiff's experts, and the reporter's record from Dr. Zwart's deposition reflects that in response to whether Bitzer was conditioning the tender of Dr. Vitanza, Bitzer stated, "No. You know, you can get him deposed, and if there's any expense because it's undue [sic] to you, we'll see that you get compensated for it."

During the deposition of Dr. Zwart, counsel became involved in a heated exchange. After the exchange, the deposition was prematurely terminated.

The discovery deadline was May 17, 2002. A motion for continuance was denied. On May 17, the trial court conducted a hearing on the Trents' motion to strike Dr. Zwart and Dr. Vitanza as a sanction for discovery abuse. The trial court granted the motion. Alamo filed a motion to reconsider with regard to Dr. Vitanza. The motion to reconsider was denied. Alamo seeks mandamus relief only as to the portion of the trial court's order striking Dr. Vitanza.

DISCUSSION

[1][2] Rule 215 of the Texas Rules of Civil Procedure provides for the imposition of sanctions in the event of an abuse of discovery. Tex.R. Civ. P. 215. The rule leaves the choice of sanctions to the sound discretion of the trial court, subject only to the sanctions being "just." TransAmerican Natural Gas Corp. v. Powell, 811 S.W.2d 913, 917 (Tex.1991). Whether sanctions are just is determined by a two-part test. Id. First, there must be a direct relationship between the offensive conduct and the sanction imposed, which requires a trial court to at least attempt to determine whether the offensive conduct is attributable to counsel only, or to the party only, or to both. Id. Second, the sanction must not be excessive. Id.

The trial court found that the conduct of Alamo's attorney, Tom Bitzer, in the deposition of Alamo's expert, Dr. Zwart, was "egregious and merit[ed] the imposition of sanctions." There is evidence in our record to support the trial court's finding.

[3] Trents' counsel, who was taking the deposition, was repeatedly interrupted by long, argumentative objections by Bitzer, some of which lasted several pages. These objections were in violation of Rule 199.5(e) which limits objections to questions during the oral deposition to "Objection, leading" and "Objection, form." See Tex.R. Civ. P. 199.5(e). The purpose of the Rule was to prevent the kind of obstructive behavior that was exhibited here and to save substantive complaints for a later hearing before the trial court. Reminders by Trents' counsel to Bitzer regarding the applicable Rules of Civil Procedure and efforts to ensure that Bitzer complied with the rules were given short shrift. In a typical exchange during the deposition, Trents' counsel complained of Bitzer's speech-making and reminded Bitzer, "You're entitled to make the objection as to form—and then you are to stop." Counsel's reminder was a fair restatement of Rule 199.5(e), but Bitzer's response was: "You're not going to tell me a thing. You just keep your mouth shut. We're through." Shortly thereafter, the deposition terminated when Bitzer said, "…seek your sanctions. It's over."

Bitzer was also not shy to put on the record what he thought about the ability of Trents' counsel to ask questions. Bitzer characterized the questions as "incredible," "nonsense," "an incredible waste of time," "preposterous," and "absurd." Before prematurely terminating Dr. Zwart's deposition, Bitzer gave his parting opinion, stating that Trents' counsel had asked, "…the most preposterous questions I've seen in nearly—in 39 years of practicing law, I've never seen anybody like you." Such comments clearly are not in keeping with a lawyer's responsibilities under the Texas Disciplinary Rules of Professional Conduct which requires a lawyer to demonstrate respect for the legal system and for those who serve it, including other lawyers. TEX. DISCIPLINARY R. PROF'L CONDUCT preamble ¶ 4, reprinted in TEX. GOV'T CODE ANN., tit. 2, subtit. G app. A (Vernon 1998).

The termination of the deposition by Bitzer came at a difficult time. The Discovery Control Plan that governed the case provided for the conclusion of discovery on May 17, only eight days after the abrupt termination of Dr. Zwart's deposition. The Trents did not do any better with their efforts to depose Alamo's other expert, Dr. Vitanza. That deposition had been scheduled the morning after Dr. Zwart's deposition and was documented by a formal notice and a confirming phone call. Nevertheless, the Trents' attorneys were informed on their drive to Kirby from San Antonio to take Dr. Zwart's deposition that Dr. Vitanza's deposition was going to be unexpectedly cancelled because of a meeting the doctor needed to attend. The trial court found that the Trents "repeatedly requested the depositions of the Defendant's two designated experts" and the "Defendants had never provided dates for the deposition." The record supports this finding. Ultimately, eight days before discovery ended, the Trents had only been able to take one partial deposition of the two experts designated by Alamo.

Alamo offered to reschedule the deposition of Dr. Vitanza, but after having been so roughly treated during Dr. Zwart's deposition, counsel for the Trents elected to return to San Antonio and seek the sanctions that they had been invited to seek by Bitzer.

[4] In its motion requesting the trial court to reconsider the sanctions, Alamo did not challenge the striking of Dr. Zwart. Alamo takes the position that by limiting its motion to reconsider to the striking of Dr. Vitanza, the discovery abuse that occurred with respect to and during Dr. Zwart's deposition no longer has any relevance. The history of Dr. Zwart's deposition, however, could be considered by the trial court in its overall consideration of the appropriate sanction and can be considered by this court in our review of that sanction. Witnesses are designated and dedesignated for many reasons. The selection of witnesses is, indeed, as Alamo conceded, "a tactical decision." Perhaps the concession with regard to Dr. Zwart was self-penance for Bitzer's behavior in Dr. Zwart's deposition, but perhaps Alamo's attorneys simply believed that Dr. Zwart would not be an effective witness. The trial judge has the authority to look at the entire course of discovery, and not simply what the parties wish to present in isolation for inspection.

[5] The trial court was well within his discretion to assess sanctions in this case, including harsh sanctions. Such attorney misbehavior demeans the entire profession, and should be punished. This does not end the discussion though because the sanctions must be just and the punishment must fit the crime. TransAmerican, 811 S.W.2d at 917.

TransAmerican teaches us that the concept of "just," among other things means "whether the offensive conduct is attributable to counsel only, or to the party only, or to both," and that "just sanctions must not be excessive" 811 S.W.2d at 917. Striking all of the expert witnesses in a medical malpractice case is a serious matter.

The Trents contend that the trial court's order striking Dr. Vitanza is not a death penalty sanction because Alamo had designated 12 other possible experts. Alamo's second supplemental designation of experts does list 12 additional "treating physicians and health care providers who can be expected to give expert testimony at trial" and the designation does state that Alamo "anticipates that expert testimony may be elicited from some of these treating health care providers regarding standard of care issues, causation issues, and damages issues to the extent the individual provider is qualified to render same." However, these treating physicians and health care providers are not experts retained by Alamo to provide an opinion as indicated by the fact that Alamo lists its "independently retained experts" in a separate section of its designation.

We agree with Alamo that there is a difference between a retained expert and an expert who is a fact witness. As defense counsel explained, "They are non-retained experts, which means they will not do a history, they will not be in position to study the records and give a picture to anyone what the chronology was in the events that take place so that they can give an opinion, much more than what they just did. [The] [o]nly thing they are going to testify about is what they saw and did." Unlike these fact witnesses, Dr. Vitanza was retained to review the entirety of the medical records and was "expected to testify regarding the medical probability that the Decedent's appendix ruptured after he was no longer under the Defendant's care." At the time Dr. Vitanza's testimony was stricken, Alamo had no other expert that it could rely on to controvert the causation element of the Trents' claim.

[6][7] "[A] party should not be punished for counsel's conduct in which it is not implicated apart from having entrusted to counsel its legal representation." TransAmerican, 811 S.W.2d at 917. Except under the most extreme circumstances, a party should not be denied its Constitutional right to a trial by jury simply because its attorney misbehaved and ignored the Rules of Civil Procedure. Lesser sanctions were possible in this case, and we appreciate the candor evidenced by the Trents' attorney in oral argument in agreeing that the record does not reflect that the trial court considered a lesser sanction.

[8][9] A great deal of information was relayed to the panel during oral argument that is outside the record that was before the trial court at the time the trial court made its ruling, including depositions that the parties agreed to take after the trial court's ruling and testimony by the witnesses in those depositions. However, a judgment cannot rest upon what may or may not occur after its rendition. Taylor v. Hicks, 691 S.W.2d 839, 841 (Tex.App.-Fort Worth 1985, no writ); Beavers v. Beavers, 675 S.W.2d 296, 300 (Tex.App.-Dallas 1984, no writ). A judgment must take its validity from the action of the court at the time it is rendered and not from what persons may or may not do after the court has rendered the judgment. Taylor, 691 S.W.2d at 841. We believe a similar rule must be applied in considering whether the trial court's order was an abuse of discretion in this case. We can only consider the record that was before the trial court at the time of the hearing in determining whether the trial court's ruling was in accordance with the guiding rules and principles set forth in TransAmerican. Based on that record, we conclude that the trial court's order striking Dr. Vitanza's testimony was an improper death penalty sanction because the trial court failed to consider lesser sanctions.

[10] Our holding should not be read as condoning Bitzer's antics. The discovery abuse in this case deserves sanctions; however, we simply hold that before a death penalty sanction can be levied, the trial court must "consider the availability of less stringent sanctions and whether such lesser sanctions would fully promote compliance." TransAmerican, 811 S.W.2d at 917. We also note that our holding is necessarily limited to the record presented to the trial court at the sanctions hearing.

On remand to the trial court, the trial court is not similarly constrained and will be able to consider an appropriate sanction based on the entirety of the record, including the events that unfolded since the last sanctions hearing.

CONCLUSION

Because the trial court failed to consider lesser sanctions before imposing a death penalty sanction, we conditionally grant the writ of mandamus. The writ will only issue if Judge Michael fails to withdraw his order striking Dr. Vitanza as an expert within ten days from the date of our opinion and order. After withdrawing his order, Judge Michael may reconsider an appropriate sanction for the discovery abuse that occurred based on the entirety of the record presented to him at the subsequent hearing.

Tex.App.-San Antonio, 2002.

Appendix E Sample Schedule from Subpoena Duces Tecum

SCHEDULE A.

You are requested to bring with you any and all materials of the following descriptions which (a) you referred to in preparing your report of November 28, 2007; and/or (b) to which you may refer in giving testimony at trial.

1.   Notes prepared by you in the course of your inspection of the 480DM screener and/or in the course of your research (excluding notes which memorialize communications with counsel or which may otherwise be privileged).

2.   Diagrams, blueprints, plans, drawings and sketches.

3.   Graphs and/or charts.

4.   Records and reports from other persons or entities.

5.   Photographs, films and/or videotapes.

6.   Deposition excerpts to which you referred in preparing your report.

7.   Governmental regulations, including OSHA.

8.   Published standards of any industrial or professional associations, including ANSI and ASME.

9.   Non-published written standards from any industrial or professional source.

10.   Product brochures and/or manuals.

11.   Written or transcribed statements of any person.

12.   Treatises and/or publications.

13.   Test results and survey reports.

14.   Physical objects, to include without limitation any exemplar wrenches used by you in performing any test or experiment on the 480DM screener and any instruments used by you in performing any such test or experiment.

Appendix F Sample Notice of Deposition

IN THE COURT OF COMMON PLEAS
WILLIAMS COUNTY, WISCONSIN

CASE NO.: **12CV345678**

LEWIS PAGET,	)	
Plaintiff.	)	
	)	JUDGE: BERKELEY
	)	
v.	)	
	)	
	)	
ACME MOTOR COMPANY,	)	
et al.,	)	
Defendants	)	

NOTICE OF DEPOSITION

Please take notice that on Wednesday, January 13, 2007 at 4:00 pm, plaintiff in the above entitled action will take the deposition pursuant to the Rules of Civil Procedure, upon oral examination to preserve testimony for trial of:

Peter Selfe, Ph.D.

Said deposition will be taken at the offices of Stark, Floding, and Associates, 114 Main St., Lakeland, WI 00550 before a court reporter duly authorized to take and transcribe depositions and may be recorded upon videotape pursuant to said rules.

Respectfully submitted,

Meghan L. Stark

STARK, FLODING, & Assoc., Co., L.P.A.
114 Main St.
Lakeland, WI 00550
(111) 555-0000

Appendix G Example of Deposition Errata Sheet

PAGE	LINE	CHANGE
11	2	Chiasmal Glioma not Chiasmaglioma
14	3	$1,100.00 = $11,000.00 (correct)
22	15	Milloy = Meloy Klien = Klein
22	20	S-P-A-S-M-U-S N-U-T-A-N-S
22	20	chiasmal gliomas
22	22	Milloy = Meloy (correct)
22	23	A Guide to Visual & Perceptual Learning Disabilities
24	10	6 then 7 hours
27	1	Alice Gee
37	3	trauma and esotropia
49	2	incidents = incidences
61	20	conduit = conduct
68	14	and = on

ACKNOWLEDGEMENT OF DEPONENT

I, Kumar White, do hereby certify that I have read the foregoing pages, 1-78, and that the same is a correct transcription of the answers given by me to the questions therein propounded, except for the corrections or changes in form or substance, if any, noted in the attached Errata Sheet.

WITNESS NAME:
DATE   01-23-06

Appendix H Expert Deposition Preparation Checklist

OPINIONS
A. The opinions you will and will not be testifying to
B. The facts and assumptions upon which the opinions are based
C. The methodology employed in deriving the opinion
D. When the opinion was first formed
E. The documents you used in forming the opinion
F. The degree of flexibility in the opinion
G. How the proposed opinion compares to answers previously given during discovery

TYPE OF DEPOSITION
A. Preservation of evidence
B. Discovery

SUBPOENAS
A. Have you received a subpoena duces tecum?
B. Have you complied with the subpoena?

HOUSEKEEPING DETAILS
A. Manner of dress
B. Where and when to report
C. Parking availability
D. Estimated time of deposition
E. Who will be present for deposition

CURRICULUM VITAE
A. Make sure it is accurate and up-to-date
B. Bring extra copies to deposition
C. Any exaggerations?

INCONSISTENT PRIOR STATEMENTS
A. Interrogatories
B. Prior written statements and reports
C. Prior cases

COMPENSATION
A. Obtain fee in advance
B. Charge for preparation, travel, and out-of-pocket expenses
C. Charge for last-minute cancellations

ORGANIZATIONS
A. What professional organizations and societies are you a member of?
B. What is your status in these organization(s)?
C. Have you ever paid a fee to obtain additional credentials?

INVOLVEMENT IN CASE
A. When were you first contacted concerning this case?
B. By whom were you contacted?
C. How were you contacted: Phone, letter, e-mail, other?
D. When did you accept the case?

STIPULATIONS
A. Decide whether to agree to waive reading and signing

FORENSIC INCOME
A. Percentage of income from forensic work
B. Percentage of time testifying for plaintiffs
C. Percentage of time testifying for defendants

YOUR PREPARATION
A. Locate all records and tests you have reviewed
B. Organize your file for easy reference
C. Review your opinion and case weaknesses/strengths
D. Discuss case with client attorney
E. Try to get opposing counsel's style, techniques, and theory of the case
F. Think about the difficult questions and issues
G. Know the timeline in the case
H. Touch every piece of paper in your file.

RELATIONSHIP WITH COUNSEL
A. What is your personal/financial relationship with counsel who has retained you in this case?

PUBLICATIONS
A. State all of the articles, chapters, books, reviews, abstracts, and other writings that you have had published
B. When and where were these published?
C. Specify if any of your writings have not been accepted for publication

WORK YOU HAVE DONE IN THIS CASE
A. Records and documents reviewed: Which ones and when?
B. Examination: What was done and when was it done?
C. Testing: What was done, when was it done, and what were the results?

D. Is all of this work reflected on your bills and invoices?
E. What additional work do you anticipate doing prior to the trial?

PREPARATION WITH COUNSEL
A. Types of questions opposing counsel will ask
B. Questions retaining counsel will ask
C. Review legal standards and "magic words"
D. Look at contents of your file
E. Discuss what to bring to deposition
F. Update on status of litigation
G. Review of opinions

DATES
Make sure you know the key dates:
A. When you were first contacted by counsel
B. When you were retained as an expert
C. When you received the records
D. From whom they were received
E. When you formed your opinion(s) in the case
F. The date of the event in question
G. The date(s) key tests were performed

EDUCATIONAL BACKGROUND
A. What schools have you attended?
B. What were your major areas of study?
C. What degrees did you obtain?
D. What are the dates for your attendance and degrees?
E. What additional training courses have you attended?
F. What continuing education courses have you attended in the past ten years?
G. Have you been the subject of any disciplinary actions?
H. Have your licenses ever been suspended or revoked?
I. What were your grades?
J. What did you do between any gaps in your education?

IN DISCOVERY DEPOSITION, COUNSEL'S GOALS ARE TO
A. Learn opinions
B. Explore qualifications
C. Lock down the expert
D. Evaluate credibility
E. Probe for bias
F. Learn factual assumptions
G. Gather as much information as possible

H. Use the expert to bolster counsel's case
I. Intimidate the expert
J. Learn as much as possible about the case

FEES
A. Hourly rate
B. Rate for deposition and trial testimony
C. Amount billed/paid to date
D. Future billing
E. Percentage of total income from forensic work

ANSWERING DEPOSITION QUESTIONS
A. Tell the truth
B. Answer only what you are asked and do not volunteer information
C. Pause before answering
D. Actively listen to the entire question and do not interrupt
E. "I don't know" may be an appropriate response
F. Don't exaggerate, speculate, or guess
G. Keep your cool
H. Do not argue with counsel or get involved in the lawyers' arguments
I. Don't fall for the "silence" gambit
J. Avoid jokes, sarcasm, and inappropriate remarks
K. Don't ramble
L. Avoid absolute words
M. Be flexible and be prepared to concede some points
N. Avoid slang
O. Don't fall for the "bumble and fumble" gambit
P. Do not act like a jerk
Q. If confused, ask for the question to be repeated
R. Ask to see documents, reports, and statements before answering questions about them
S. Take adequate time to review any "new" documents, reports, etc.
T. Prepare thoroughly

GENERAL ADVICE
A. Tell the truth
B. Act naturally
C. Don't be arrogant
D. Avoid slang
E. Be careful of what you highlight or write down
F. Don't argue with counsel
G. Don't elaborate

H. Don't estimate
I. Don't exaggerate
J. Don't guess
K. Don't interrupt the question
L. Don't lose your temper
M. Don't speculate
N. Leave yourself an out
O. Listen carefully to the questions
P. Make sure you know your role in the case
Q. Don't joke
R. Pause before answering
S. Read the documents before you testify about them
T. Say you don't know if you don't know
U. Say you don't remember if you don't remember
V. Stay within your area of expertise
W. Take breaks when needed
X. Avoid absolute and hedge words

WHAT MATERIALS OR RECORDS WERE YOU PROVIDED? BY WHOM? WHEN WERE THEY PROVIDED?

A. Correspondence
B. Reports
C. Messages
D. Notes
E. Computer disks/e-mails/files
F. Police reports
G. Investigative reports
H. Medical and hospital records
I. Literature
J. Tables
K. Standards
L. Contracts
M. Photographs
N. Videotapes
O. Research
P. Test results
Q. Other materials

VIDEOTAPED DEPOSITIONS

A. Prepare with counsel and practice before a videotape camera
B. Dress conservatively
C. Look directly at the camera when testifying

D. Avoid long pauses that may make you look evasive or uninformed
E. When handling exhibits, make sure you hold them so that they can be appreciated by the viewers
F. Avoid eating, smoking, drinking, chewing gum, or chewing on pens or pencils
G. Turn off pagers, cell phones, and beepers
H. Avoid making unnecessary and distracting noise by rustling papers, touching the microphone, or moving furniture
I. Avoid being goaded into flashes of anger, arrogance, and combativeness
J. Watch out for your nonverbal behavior and body language
K. Don't let counsel lead your eyes away from the camera

PLEADINGS
A. Complaint
B. Answer
C. Interrogatories
D. Depositions
E. Motions
F. Motions to compel
G. Others

DAUBERT ISSUES
A. Has the theory or technique used been tested?
B. Has the theory or technique been subjected to peer review and publication?
C. What is the known or potential rate of error of the method used?
D. What is the degree of the method's acceptance within the relevant scientific community?

BREAKS
A. Ask for breaks when needed
B. Don't consult with retaining counsel during breaks
C. Ask retaining counsel to get an agreement on breaks in advance and enforce this for you

INDEX